Fodor's EXPLORING ISRAEL

FODOR'S TRAVEL PUBLICATIONS
NEW YORK • TORONTO • LONDON • SYDNEY • AUCKLAND

WWW.FODORS.COM

Important Note
Time inevitably brings changes, so always confirm prices, travel facts, and other perishable information when it matters. Although Fodor's cannot accept responsibility for errors, you can use this guide in the confidence that we have taken every care to ensure its accuracy.

 Distributed by Random House, Inc., New York.

Published in the United States by Fodor's Travel Publications
Published in the United Kingdom by AA Publishing.

ISBN 0-679-00683-4
ISSN 1520-7757
Third Edition

Fodor's Exploring Israel

Author: **Andrew Sanger**
Revision verifier: **Andrew Sanger**
Additional writing by Deborah Wald and Geraldine Dunham
Series Adviser: **Christopher Catling**
Copy Editor: **Janet Tabinski**
Original Photography: **Jon Arnold** and **Pat Athie**
Cartography: **The Automobile Association**
Cover Design: **Tigist Getachew, Fabrizio La Rocca**
Cover Photograph: **Hugh Sitton/Stone**
Cover Silhouette: **Owen Franken**

Special Sales
Fodor's Travel Publications are available at special discounts for bulk purchases for sales promotions or premiums. Special editions, including personalized covers, excerpts of existing guides, and corporate imprints, can be created in large quantities for special needs. For more information, contact your local bookseller or write to Special Markets, Fodor's Travel Publications, 280 Park Avenue, New York, NY 10017. Inquiries from Canada should be directed to your local Canadian bookseller or sent to Random House of Canada, Ltd., Marketing Department, 2775 Matheson Blvd. East, Mississauga, Ontario L4W 4P7.

Printed and bound in Italy by Printer Trento srl
10 9 8 7 6 5 4 3 2 1

How to use this book

ORGANIZATION

Israel Is, Israel Was
Discusses aspects of life and culture in contemporary Israel and explores significant periods in its history.

A–Z
Breaks down the country into regional chapters, and covers places to visit, including walks and drives. Within this section fall the Focus On articles, which consider a variety of subjects in greater detail.

Travel Facts
Contains the strictly practical information vital for a successful trip.

Accommodations and Restaurants
Lists recommended establishments throughout Israel, giving a brief summary of their attractions. Entries are graded budget, moderate or expensive.

ADMISSION CHARGES
An indication of an establishment's admission charge is given by categorizing the standard, adult rate as: Expensive (over 20 NIS), Moderate (10–20 NIS), or Inexpensive (under 10 NIS).

OPENING TIMES
Services and attractions in Israel close during Shabbat—Jewish Sabbath—which lasts from sunset on Friday to sunset on Saturday (see page 58).

ABOUT THE RATINGS
Most places described in this book have been given a separate rating. These are as follow:

▶▶▶ **Do not miss**

▶▶ **Highly recommended**

▶ **Worth seeing**

MAP REFERENCES
To make the location of a particular place easier to find, every main entry in this book has a map reference. This includes a number, followed by a letter, followed by another number, such as176B3. The first number (176) refers to the page on which the map can be found. The letter (B) and the second number (3) pinpoint the square in which the place is located. The maps on the inside front cover and inside back cover are referred to as IFC and IBC, respectively.

Contents

A–Z

Jaffa
Jaffa
Jaffa

ART & JU

Andrew Sanger is an award-winning travel writer who has contributed to many British newspapers and magazines. He is the editor of French Railway's holiday magazine Top Rail, and the author of a dozen guidebooks to France, Ireland and other European countries. Despite long familiarity with the country, this is his first book about Israel.

My Israel

Scratch the present and you'll find the past. Look at the past and you'll see the future. There's something about this place that thrills me. Places, like people, are all unique. But Israel is different. It just *isn't* like *anywhere* else.

Of course, certain comparisons are tempting, and inevitable. For example, I often see how Israel and Israelis fit into the warm, lively, noisy, out-of-doors Eastern Mediterranean culture that runs from, say, Italy to the Levant. And in its efforts to restore itself after years of Ottoman domination, there's an obvious similarity to Greece.

But in Israel there's something else going on. There's a dizzying, exciting sensation, like being at the vortex of human experience, living in a vibrant, emphatic here-and-now that yet looks with passion to both the past and the future.

The land itself mirrors this. Everything converges here. Not only all human life, not only the old and the new are fused, but the climate and the topography—from sweet Galilee to searing Negev—are fantastically varied, and the flora and fauna of Europe, Asia, and Africa combine at this spot.

Once upon a time, we are told, this was a land of forests and fields, rich with milk and honey, or at least olives and grapes. Now as its people return and clear the dust from their heritage, they plant, irrigate, and rebuild. Every day in Israel, traveling from ancient site to beach resort, to hardworking town or kibbutz, I am astonished, impressed, and delighted by what is happening here.

This little patch of Mediterranean landscape, which already has taught so much to the rest of humanity, now offers another inspiration. Exploring the strange, tiny, kaleidoscopic country that is modern Israel is not just tourism or research: Here I catch a glimpse of the potential of human beings, if they are willing to cling to their dreams, to overcome even the most extraordinary obstacles, and make dreams come true at last.

Andrew Sanger

Israel

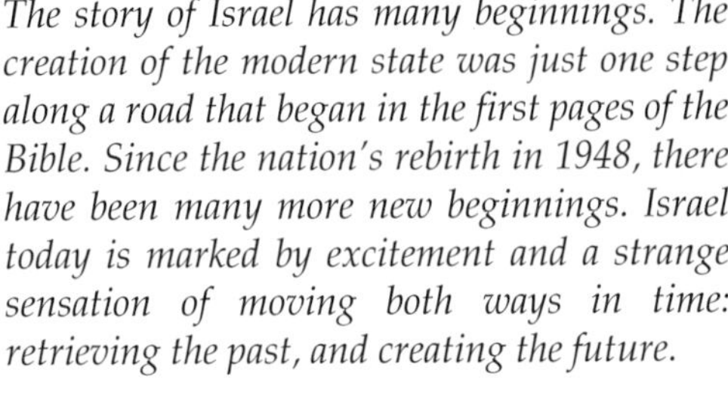

The story of Israel has many beginnings. The creation of the modern state was just one step along a road that began in the first pages of the Bible. Since the nation's rebirth in 1948, there have been many more new beginnings. Israel today is marked by excitement and a strange sensation of moving both ways in time: retrieving the past, and creating the future.

UNDER THE SPOTLIGHT The gaze of the world often focuses on Israel. It is a place that exists deep in the psyche of the Western world but that, for many, is more myth than reality. For anyone with Sunday school notions about "the Holy Land," the dynamic, restless, abrasively energetic modern nation of Israel will come as a big surprise. Many Israelis just wish theirs could be a "normal" country. But normal countries do not encourage waves of large-scale immigration when they already have an unemployment problem. In normal countries, vibrant capitalism would not thrive within a monolithic socialist infrastructure where the state owns nearly all the land. But then, normal countries do not have Israel's problems. And somehow, the world does not expect Israel to find normal solutions.

MATTERS OF OPINION People hold strong views about Israel. It is hard to grasp that a place only the size of Wales or Massachusetts can be so crucial to world politics and world religion. The problems have an old-new look about them too. Those ancient Assyrians, Egyptians, and Babylonians who vied for control over the land of the Hebrews have modern inheritors. Those Canaanite tribes who made life difficult for conquering Israelites might almost have been the prototype for today's West Bank militants.

As always, different people lay claim to the same patch of earth. Can such deep and intractable conflicts ever be resolved? The world's press certainly has plenty of easy answers, as do governments around the globe. Politicians and pundits, concerned more about their own national interest, are all too ready to instruct Israel in the error of its ways. Visitors often come up with quick solutions. Israelis know it is not so simple, and that their whole survival is at stake. They, more than anyone, want to be free to enjoy life in peace. Would it be better to hand over the whole West

❑ The official emblem of the State of Israel is the Golden Menorah, the seven-branched ritual candelabrum once used in the Temple in Jerusalem. ❑

Above right: Roman-era menorah
Below: timeless architecture—Jerusalem's Islamic Museum

Bank to the P.L.O.? Some of it? What if Hamas or Islamic Jihad took over? The P.L.O. itself contains elements at odds with Arafat—what if they win control when Arafat dies? Parts of the West Bank are almost in the Tel Aviv suburbs. Would it have been better to hang on to it forever? Was it a mistake to do a deal with Arafat? But then, Arab nations have made peace because of that. The country is alive with debate, a kaleidoscope of opinions, ideas, choice, diversity.

THE LAND That diversity of opinions is just one other facet of Israel's extraordinary spectrum of peoples and landscapes. For sheer physical variety, the country is phenomenal, with four climate zones and four types of terrain, ranging from handsome and verdant Mediterranean hills in the north to parched desert in the south; from majestic snow-capped Mount Hermon to the salty Dead Sea, the lowest point on the earth. Journeying between the two, you will pass vineyards and olive groves mentioned in the Bible, apple orchards, fields of corn and banana plantations, tomatoes and strawberries—truly a bewildering range of crops. Today, after just a century of labor and reclamation, Israel looks again like a land of milk and honey. This is the ancient-modern "Eretz Israel"—literally, Land of Israel. Some call it the Promised Land, some the Holy Land, some the Zionist Entity. Most Israelis call it simply HaAretz: the Land.

HISTORY AND HERITAGE Past, present, and future seem to converge here. Uninspired apartment complexes in well-ordered planned towns give an impression of modernity, but builders digging the foundations usually have to call in the archeologists. Every walk or drive involves an encounter with Israel's long and dramatic history. Almost every Israeli family has its own story of events that span the globe—but that started here.

Unchanging desert landscapes, which the Children of Israel crossed thousands of years ago

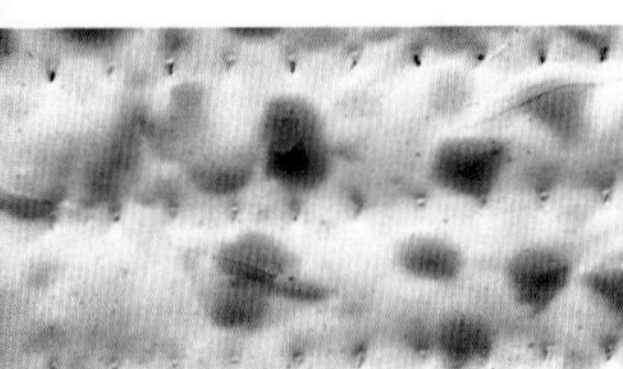

Israel's population has been growing fast—most recently by around 12 percent every year—and is reaching the 6 million mark. The bulk of the growth comes from immigration. From all over the world, Jews are still arriving to make a home in the Land of Israel.

Many migrants are motivated by religious or cultural zeal, many by the simple promise of food, a roof, and a regular job, and many by the longing to escape persecution. The service that Jewish families read together over the annual Passover meal, celebrating the Exodus from Egypt, concludes "Next year in Jerusalem." Daily, that wish is made a reality.

NO ORDINARY HOMELAND The cornerstone of Israel's existence is the Zionist dream of gathering in all the Jews who have been exiled across the globe and bringing them back to their true home. The idea was even set down in the Book of Genesis. Yet any country that willingly promotes a policy of mass immigration must seem at best foolishly philanthropic, at worst, suicidal. The economic logistics alone appear formidable. To an Israeli, however, the case looks different. Israel is a nation born of new immigrants: They are its life force.

Since 1948 more than 2 million have "made *aliyah*"—literally, gone up—to Israel. These *olim* (new arrivals) not only must they adjust to a new language and culture, but also to the fact that their new country is itself at risk. Despite the pressure new immigrants sometimes impose on the employment sector, their decision to make a life in Israel is greeted by Israelis as evidence that the creation of a Jewish homeland really is working as its founders had planned.

Top: Matzoh, unleavened bread eaten during Passover
Below: a Hasidic Jew wearing traditional dress

WHO CAN COME? In 1950, the Israeli parliament passed the Law of Return. This enshrined as a right what had, until then, been an unwritten tenet: namely, that any person who could claim Jewish descent would be welcomed to the country. Even as Orthodox authorities restricted the definition of Jewishness, immigrants have arrived in waves from Eastern Europe, North Africa, the Gulf states, the former Soviet Union, and Ethiopia.

MAKING IT HAPPEN Often these "exiles" were in such difficult circumstances that they could not afford to make their own way to Israel. Some were not even in a position to let anyone know of their plight.

So the job of finding and retrieving the exiles goes on. The task of bringing to Israel any Jew who wishes to come is planned, if need be, with military precision—often capturing the attention of the world in the process. One such operation was its daring airlift to safety of 30,000 Ethiopian Jews, rescued in two phases in the mid-1980s and early 1990s, called Operation Moses. Contrast this with the arrival of a

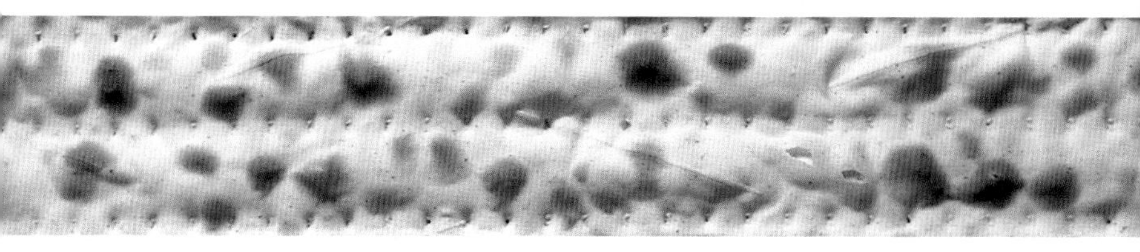

Refugees from the former Soviet Union in Tel Aviv

well-to-do family of South Americans who simply want to be closer to their heritage. Either way, each new arrival is channeled through a welter of absorption processes: language school, location and housing choices, educational options, career guidance, health service registration. Those who arrive with few possessions, such as refugees from the former Soviet Union, receive welfare benefits to help ease the first months. All immigrants receive start-up assistance, such as tax rebates on the essentials of a new home.

The induction process takes six months, but full integration may take longer. It may not be until the next generation that people feel thoroughly Israeli. Among the immigrant generation, some groups, like the

❑ All new immigrants attend *ulpan*, an intensive Hebrew language school with daily lessons for every standard, from total beginners to advanced. Since an *ulpan* may comprise as many as 45 different nationalities, all lessons are in Hebrew. By the end of the five-month course, most immigrants can read, write and converse in the language of the Bible. ❑

Yemenites, see no reason to abandon all their old ways. Some, like the Ethiopians, find it almost too hard to adapt to the Israeli lifestyle. Others, like the new Russians, are criticized for their lack of Jewishness and their perceived unwillingness to pull their weight for the country. Yet, as Jews, all are entitled to make their escape to Israel, and the belief is that all will eventually play their part in Israel's destiny.

A jeweler in the Jewish Quarter, Jerusalem

Israel came into being through the efforts of idealists. Not for nothing is its national anthem called The Hope (HaTikvah). *The greatest hope is still the old one: to be accepted as a country like any other, yet without losing its biblical imperative to be "a Light unto the Nations." Underlying that is a simpler hope: that the Jewish homeland will survive.*

ALL FOR ONE If you listen to Israelis discussing the most innocent topic, it is easy to get the impression that divisions burn deep. Everyone has individual goals, but all that is forgotten when the country is under threat. War has been Israel's jailer since 1948, and you would not need to be religious to say a morning prayer for peace sometimes. What Israelis crave more than anything is the ordinariness of daily life enjoyed by other nations, and an end to the loss of life. Yet the demanding and tense pattern of daily life in Israel—begun by early settlers who fought adversity with undaunted optimism—has created a unique national character. In Israelis, you will find a rare pride and a sense of achievement that relishes the differences, feeds off stresses, and outshines any disagreement.

Top: pioneers
Below: Jews from Ethiopia

REDEMPTION OF THE LAND No matter what their politics or attitude to religion, Israelis all have a bond with the earth of Israel—the land of their origin, of their identity, faith, and history. Since the Jews fled the Romans in AD 70, religious belief has fueled the hope of all Jews that they will be able to return to their homeland. In the 19th century, when Diaspora Jews (those living outside Palestine) were the target of persecution, that ambition took on a political dimension and became known as Zionism. In Israel, Jews of whatever affiliation believe that reclaiming the land is a fundamental responsibility, metaphorically and literally. It is their dream to see the Promised Land bloom with the life of returned Jews and, for the secular, to see it flourish again with the fruits of their labors.

THE KIBBUTZ One of Israel's least exportable triumphs is simple, communal living in hardworking

❑ *HaTikvah* (*The Hope*), Israel's poignant national anthem, was composed by Naftali Herz Imber more than 60 years before the founding of the state. It includes the words: "As long as...the soul of a Jew yearns, our hope is not yet lost, the hope of two thousand years, to be a free people in our land, the land of Zion and Jerusalem." ❑

rural settlements. Here, members possess nothing of their own, share equally the burden of work, and put back all the profits. Kibbutzim may not have taken off around the world, and may be declining in Israel itself, but they were in the vanguard of the creation of the state. They took on much of the responsibility for immigrants, defense, and agriculture and most importantly advocated an ethos of community care. The legacy of the kibbutz movement to the country can hardly be overestimated. One of the most potent forces in Israel is still the commitment to a dream, the sharing of burdens and of rewards, which has its seeds in these early socialist communities.

Sentiment motivates many Israelis to achieve near-impossible dreams

THE PRICE OF PEACE Becoming 18 in most parts of the world means entering adulthood, with unrestricted access to all its risks and rewards. In Israel, however, it is also the time when girls and boys hold a gun for the first time, and begin their compulsory army service.

Israel's greatest dream is to live in peace, and it looks as if that dream may come true one day soon. Paradoxically, were peace ever fully to envelop the Middle East and end the necessity to have a fit, young army on standby all the time, Israel might well lose a vital part of its character.

One nation, a hundred nationalities—people from all over the world have poured their influence into this tiny state. Then there are the country's non-Jews, a significant minority. Israel manages to accommodate—and celebrate—all their diversity under a single unifying flag.

THE TYPICAL ISRAELI The average Israeli is hard to define. He or she may be dark-eyed and olive-skinned. Then again, you can find pale-skinned blondes, brunettes, and redheads, and black skin too. The Jewish majority may (or may not) share a common faith, but each person is colored by his or her background, and maintains traditions from the "old country," be it in food, music, or family structure.

Israelis of Eastern European origin are called Ashkenazim. Those from the Mediterranean, many of whose ancestors were expelled from Spain in 1492, are Sephardim. Jews from the other Islamic states are Oriental, or Mizrahim.

Israel's non-Jews, totaling more than one in six of the population, are found mainly in Jerusalem, Akko, Haifa, and the smaller northern towns. They are Muslim and Christian Arabs and east Mediterraneans, Druze, and other religious groups, as well as Bedouin in the south, and a plethora of other cultures that have set up home here.

Israeli legislation aspires to full equality of all citizens regardless of race or creed, and each group has had a distinctive cultural impact on Israel. As these backgrounds mix and matchmake (about a quarter of Jewish marriages are between Ashkenazim and Sephardim), exciting combinations emerge. With each new wave of immigration, the picture of the typical Israeli is constantly being reinvented.

❑ About half of the population of Israel are Sabras—Israeli-born Jews. It is interesting that they do have, already, a distinct character. Like the fruit from which they take their name (also known as prickly pear), Sabras are said to be spiky on the outside, but sweet inside. Israelis do sometimes appear rude, unpolished, and peremptory. The direct, forthright speech and abrasive manner really come from a dislike of pretence, combined perhaps with the effects of living a knife-edge existence. After all, Sabras are also noted for their astonishing informality, irreverence, spontaneous warmth, and unexpected generosity. ❑

Top: native Israelis are called Sabras (prickly pears): spiky on the outside but sweet within
Below: every generation contributes to the Israeli identity

POWER PLAY Chaim Weizmann, David Gruen (better known as David Ben-Gurion), Isaac Shimshelevitz (Moshe Sharett), Zakam Rubashov (Zalman Shazar), Levi Shkolnik (Levi

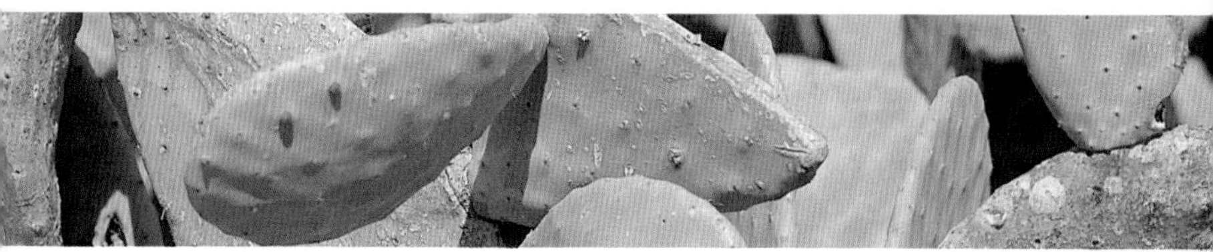

Sephardi Jews came to Israel from Mediterranean countries

Eshkol), Golda Meir—the names of the first prime ministers and presidents of Israel reveal that they were all of East European origin. For decades, this sector of society, for whom Hebrew was a second language, dominated all important areas of life, from commerce and politics to education and defense. The Sephardic and Oriental communities, which now constitute over 40 percent of society, came from lands where democracy was unheard of and education optional. Only recently have they made strides into the power zones of life in Israel, taking government positions, wielding industrial clout, and spicing up public debate. Eventually, Israelis say, every group and community will be equally involved.

LANGUAGE AND CULTURE If speaking Hebrew and English does not work with your interlocutor, try French, Arabic, Portuguese, Romanian, Russian, or a mix of tongues. Not only did most older Israelis master Hebrew only after settling here, many already spoke more than one language when they arrived. Every facet of Israeli culture—music, theater, literature, politics—has become textured with the threads of other lands. Ethnic variations mean diverse cuisines, and there are restaurants to reflect each one: Moroccan, Indian, Italian, American, Argentinian, French, Russian, and native Israeli, to name a few. Most towns have a "Chinese" restaurant—often in fact Vietnamese, since Israel gave haven to a number of boat people.

THE DIVERSE LANDSCAPE Israel also packs a great deal into its borders. A short drive can begin in a mountain range and end at lush, fertile plains. It's a quick trip from the urban metropolis to the stillness of the desert. Tel Aviv is humid, but Jerusalem, an hour away, is dry. You can ski in the north, then fly south for an hour to scuba dive in the tropics.

Israeli soldiers in training. All single women undergo two years of service

Religion

Israel teems with the passion of its believers. In few other places is devotion so concentrated as in the country that gave monotheism to the world. For Jews, Christians, Muslims, and their many offshoots, the land is filled with holy sites—a great source of inspiration for living faiths.

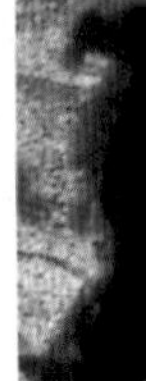

THREE PARALLEL ROADS Israel's population of nearly 6 million is roughly 80 percent Jewish and 15 percent Sunni Muslim Arabs. There are about 100,000 Christians too—Maronite, Greek Orthodox, Roman and Greek Catholic. The land has been the spiritual home of Jews since the time of Joshua (12th century BC). King David founded Jerusalem as the Jewish capital in 1004 BC. The "Common Era" (as Israelis call it) starts with Christianity's presence in the Holy Land. Since Byzantine times (the 4th century AD), Bethlehem and Nazareth have ranked close behind Rome as spiritual centers for Christians. Though Mecca is holiest for Islam, with Medina a runner-up, the legend was born in the 8th century AD that Muhammad ascended to heaven from the rock now enclosed within Jerusalem's Dome of the Rock. Thus, Israel brings together three monotheistic religions, all with unbreakable links: yet those who practice these faiths live remarkably separate and antagonistic lives.

Jerusalem's Muslim Dome of the Rock

CITY CENTER OF FAITH The skyline of Jerusalem's Old City reveals the hold it has on the hearts of millions. At sunset, the rosy light throws into relief the cross atop the Church of the Holy Sepulcher and the golden Dome of the Rock glistens as muezzins call the Muslim quarter to prayer. Below stand the immense, immutable stones of the Western Wall—remains of the Jews' Second Temple. In the noisy, confused maze of Old City streets that divide it into four sectors—Jewish, Muslim, Christian, and Armenian—nuns, priests, rabbis, and imams hurry past each other to fulfill God's work.

Each faith has jurisdiction over its own religious sites, and at festival time Jerusalem swells with millions more devoted pilgrims. But this "eternal city" bears the scars of such divisions and heightened atmosphere. Though Judaism and Islam meet in Jerusalem, Jew and Arab do not easily converse. It is often said that the meaning of the word Jerusalem is "City of Peace." If so, the name is an expression of hope, rather than of any kind of reality.

SECTS AND SECRECY The biblical Good Samaritan has descendants. Six hundred altogether, they live in Holon, south of Tel Aviv, and in

Nablus, in Samaria, and treat the Torah (the first five books of the Old Testament) and the Book of Joshua as their scripture. Their first language is Arabic. The Karaites, a separate group that believes in the Torah but rejects all later writings, number 15,000. Up in the Galilee are 3,000 Sunni Muslim Circassians. Neither Arab nor Islamic in origin, they maintain an independent identity, even speaking the Circassian language. Elsewhere, over 70,000 Druze populate 22 villages in the north. Little is known about their religion except that they have a small caste of learned initiates, though the concept of loyalty to the ruling power is one precept. Israel is also the world center of the Baha'i faith, an independent religion promoting universal love and equality, whose base is in Haifa.

Christian pilgrims pray at Solomon's Pools, near Bethlehem

NON-JEWS Many non-Jews see Israel as a place of divinity, and seek to live there. One group is known as the Black Hebrews, African-Americans with a communal creed, who regard themselves as Jewish. They came to Israel during the 1970s, but since they are not descended from Jewish families and do not practice Judaism their status as Jews is not recognized by the State. Many other groups around the world say they are Jews—but are not always accepted by the Israeli authorities. Ethiopia's Falash Mura, who claim to have been converted from Judaism; Bene Israel, an ancient Indian community; and the descendents of all non-Orthodox converts, are examples. The Israeli media periodically reports the finding of communities who claim a religious or cultural connection to the Holy Land.

THE MANY FORMS OF JUDAISM
Judaism comes in many forms, with differences based on attitudes to the Jewish books of law (the Torah), subsequent prophetic writings, the codified oral law, and the Talmud (rabbinic commentary). The Orthodox purport to believe that the scriptures were all physically handed down by the Divine, already written. Hasids (with side locks, long black coats, and wide black hats) are the most observant of the Orthodox. Conservative (or Masorti) Jews believe that the scriptures are divinely inspired, but written by human beings. Reform and Liberal Jews prefer to emphasize Judaism's ethical tenets, seeing the scriptures as inspired, but not binding. Some secular Jews adopt a humanist version of Judaism that rejects the authority of the scriptures completely.

Israel works hard and plays hard. The country nearly bursts with joie de vivre, the very picture of an energetic, upbeat nation hurtling toward success. Eager for income and rewards, Israelis put in long hours and struggle for promotion. But the real point of life is not money but what it can buy: leisure, pleasure, fun, and freedom.

WANTING IT ALL Almost anything you care to name is available in Israel. A combination of enterprise and acquisitiveness has made it the consumer country par excellence. Since the early days, the price of imported goods has been sky-high, so Israelis are used to supporting their lifestyle by working ferociously hard. With salaries roughly one-third lower than in most Western countries, and with the constant tension of war, the population has learned to extract the maximum intensity from every experience. Israelis will not miss an opportunity to enjoy themselves, yet they still manage to be up and at it early next morning.

The working day starts at 7 or 8 AM and can last till 8 PM or later. All the while, the bars and restaurants quench the Israeli thirst for social interaction, virtually 24 hours a day. Many Israelis work a six-day week, as set down in biblical law, resting only on the Sabbath (Saturday). Sunday is a regular weekday in Israel, though working on Friday, when the Sabbath starts, is increasingly on the way to becoming optional.

WORKERS' RIGHTS Despite the long hours many Israelis put in, almost all workers are members of Histadrut, which is powerful and active—indeed, it is part of the bedrock of Israeli society. Histadrut takes a cradle-to-grave approach to its role, running a vast health-insurance plan, with its own hospitals, as well as offering social and welfare services to its members.

Some question Histadrut's position, and many workers feel obliged to

Israelis are great readers of newspapers—in several languages

stay within its health plan when they might prefer an alternative. This monolithic organization, in an apparent possible clash of interests, is also the nation's largest nongovernmental employer. Yet Histadrut has been the strongest ally of both Jewish and Arabic workers since it was established in the 1920s, with formidable leverage. Strikes are not uncommon in Israel, but Histadrut has, on the whole, been a positive force in ensuring that wages and conditions reach a consistently high standard.

LOVE OF LIFE With their free time, Israelis head for the beach, the streets, sports grounds, pools, national parks, and picnic places in the country, or open-air cafés in the cities. On the beaches, they swim and

play interminable games of beachball and *matkot*—a simple bat-and-ball game. Israel has a vibrant cultural life, in which opera, theater, and classical concerts are not viewed as elitist or remote, but are tremendously popular. Tel Aviv and Haifa are the main cultural centers. Tel Aviv is also the focal point for late-night entertainment, discos, and nightclubs. But even people who are not going out anywhere special will spend the evening hours strolling in the open air, meeting and talking.

SPEAK UP! Conversation is easy to strike up in Israel: all you need is split-second eye contact and you're connected. People are friendly and outgoing, even though sometimes desperately short on politeness and pleasantries. The ease with which people get together is a lesson in human relations. Explanations for this, perhaps, lie in the crowded apartment complexes, the group ethos of schools and institutions, and the universal army experience—a great leveler as well as a dumping ground for prejudices and vanities. The downside is that it is hard to find privacy or peace and quiet.

Surprisingly, Israel is a country of erotic encounters, too. Though immodest behavior is frowned on for people above a certain age, youngsters—who seem to radiate health and energy—have an unashamed physical confidence. Coyness is certainly not an Israeli characteristic.

WHY STAY INDOORS? The sun is usually shining somewhere in Israel. Even in the brief winter, the temperature in the southern city of Eilat is likely to be around 70°F. And when the sun is out in Israel, so are the people. At the end of the day, in the balmy sweet-scented evenings, the balconies of the ubiquitous Israeli apartment houses are used as informal dining rooms and lounges. Entertainment of every kind is available under the Mediterranean sky—from spontaneous beach parties to classical concerts at ancient amphitheaters, from craft markets to weddings. In this respect, Israelis enjoy a superb quality of life.

The varied climate even allows for winter sports

Having an opinion is not optional for Israelis—it is inevitable. Passions run high on every issue. To say that Israel is the only democracy in the Middle East understates the case. While the rest of the region consists largely of one-party dictatorships, Israel is bursting with debate. Thanks to proportional representation, almost every viewpoint finds expression.

THE SYSTEM The Knesset (literally "Meeting" or "Assembly"), the Israeli parliament, takes its name from an ancient Jewish assembly that functioned in Jerusalem in the 5th century BC. Now, as then, there are 120 seats. Proportional representation ensures that any party with at least 1.3 percent of the vote gains a seat. The result is a bewildering number of political parties. The advantage of the system is that it accurately reflects the diversity of viewpoints in Israeli society. The clear disadvantage is that the need to build coalitions gives undue power to small parties. Elections are held every four years both for a government and (in a separate vote) for a prime minister. Israel also has a president, elected by Knesset members, whose term lasts five years.

PARTY PLAYERS Nothing is quite as it seems in Israeli politics. Foreign journalists generally brand the Labor party as left wing and Likud as right. In fact, both are broadly in favor of free enterprise, and both wish to protect the country's socialist and egalitarian infrastructure. Labor—or "One Israel," as Premier Ehud Barak renamed it—arose from the mainstream, dominant, collectivist forces in the pre-State Zionist movement. Likud was born of the hard-line Zionists of the Revisionist breakaway, which considered the mainstream too soft toward the Arabs and the British (see page 44).

Historically, Labor is the party of the affluent. Its "constituency" is the intellectual East European section of society. Likud garners support from the poorer people, especially of North African and Gulf states communities. Smaller parties cover every religious and philosophical hue—from Communist to far right. No Israeli government has ever won a full majority. Therefore, a succession of coalition

Begin, Carter and Sadat at the Camp David peace summit, September 1978

❑ The 1999 Knesset elections typified Israel's vibrant democracy. Thirty-one parties put up candidates, some representing special interests such as Romanians, Russian-speakers, Israeli Arabs, West Bank settlers, pensioners, and fathers. Winning party One Israel (or Labor) gained only 20 percent (26 seats). Likud garnered 14 percent (19 seats), with the Orthodox religious party Shas coming third with 13 percent (17 seats). Ten seats were won by Russian immigrant parties. Eleven members of Knesset are Muslims, and two are Druze. ❑

❑ Almost all political parties in Israel, including the far left and the peace lobby, are Zionist (that is, they believe Israel should be maintained as a homeland for the Jews). There are also non-Zionist parties and organizations in Israel, some Arab, some religious. They oppose Israel's existence as a Jewish state. ❑

deals and mergers has had to be struck between the most unlikely of bedfellows.

POLITICS AND PEACE Since the birth of modern Israel in 1948, politics has been dominated by the Arab/Israeli conflict. Enormous amounts of energy, and vast sums of money, have been spent on defense, slimming down the budget for everything else. Now, the peace process has freed some of that budget for investment in health, education, and industry.

It was so-called "right-wing" Menachem Begin and Likud who shook hands with President Sadat of Egypt in 1979 and made the first lasting peace treaty. In 1994 Prime Minister Rabin and Labor achieved the same with Jordan and instituted limited self-rule for the Palestinians. The bloody fatigue of war has made peace more desirable than ever, and trading land for that vision seems to offer a tentative way forward. No one in Israel expects such cordial arrangements with their Arab neighbors as exist between some European countries. But even if peace simply means no war, it would be priceless to almost all Israelis—whatever their political views.

A UNIQUE POSITION As the only democracy in an undemocratic and anti-Western region, Israel has long been seen by the United States as its "ally in the desert" (the U.K. and Europe have tended to see their best interests being served through support for the Arab states). America's "special relationship" has provided Israel with billions of dollars as a buffer against biting economic sanctions in the form of trade boycotts, arms embargos, and diplomatic cold shoulders. The stumbling block to Israel's acceptance has been the Palestinian question. But since the start of Palestinian self-rule, and mutual interests expressed between the West and the Arab Gulf War allies, the possibilities for international entente now look more promising.

Israeli coalition governments involve unlikely alliances

It was a tough battle to bring the nation of Israel into being, and it is a tough battle to prevent it from being destroyed. That is why security is tight at all entry points into the country, and soldiers, both men and women, are a distinct part of everyday life. Of course, soldiers are inseparable from the very existence of this constantly threatened country.

ON PERMANENT STANDBY On and off duty, conscripts or professionals, members of the armed forces—the Israel Defense Forces (IDF)—carry their weapons at all times. This can be startling for unsuspecting tourists who have never seen anything like it before. Out of uniform, most of the conscripts wear jeans, T-shirts, and sneakers, with an Uzi submachine gun hanging from one shoulder. In uniform, it has been normal for gun-carrying soldiers to travel the country by hitchhiking (now, though, they enjoy free bus travel).

Israeli armed forces maintain a watchful but unobtrusive role

Soldiers are treated with enormous respect and affection by the public. For one thing, and unlike the situation in many other countries, Israelis feel that the army is on their side. In fact, Israel is in one sense just one big army. All boys and all girls join the IDF at the age of 18, complete their term (three years for men, two for women), and in effect remain in the army as reservists until the age of 51 (men) or 24 (women). Reservists have to serve around 30 days a year minimum. Certain occupations are entitled to exemption, and women do not serve if they have children.

The IDF is one of the most highly trained and battle-experienced armies in the world, having endured five wars since 1948. As a spinoff, Israel has become a major weapons manufacturer, a process started when the U.S. arms embargo on Israel took effect. As a result, Israel started its own arms manufacture—now it even sells weapons to the United States.

THE TERROR THREAT High standards of vigilance have kept terrorist incidents down to levels lower than many other nations, despite the well-publicized intention of certain Arab states (notably Iran and Iraq), guerrilla groups (Islamic Jihad and Hamas), and militias (Hezbullah) to destroy the Israeli state. Another terror threat that Israel has to guard

against is that posed by some of its own citizens, bent on retaliation: the probable consequences of an attack by tough-minded settlers on West Bank Arabs could be disastrous. The assassination of Prime Minister Rabin, in November 1995, by Yigal Amir, a student opposed to peace with the Palestinians, exposed the threat posed by right-wing religious Jews.

Security is tight throughout the country. The ubiquitous groups of schoolchildren are always accompanied by an armed guard, usually an army reservist, and generally a parent of a child in the group. In the past, children were a favorite target for Arab terrorists, but since the armed guards were introduced in the 1970s, there has been only one attack on a school group.

A JEWISH ARMY Israeli soldiers are sworn in at Masada (see page 35), where they vow that "Masada shall not fall again." Back in 1973, Golda Meir was asked by a reporter whether Israelis did not have some sort of Masada complex. "Yes," she said, "we do. And a pogrom complex, and a Hitler complex." The point was that Israelis see themselves as having a duty to protect the Jewish people and ensure their survival. The name Israel Defense Force is intended to be taken literally. The military grew out of brigades that stood guard at agricultural settlements, and continues to see itself in that defensive light. Memories of the Holocaust, of the powerlessness of Jews before the creation of the state of Israel, add extra force to the idea of Jews being armed and capable of self-defense. Even so, there remains, for Israelis and other Jews, something remarkable about the idea of an army of Jews. Despite the ferocity of the biblical Israelites, Jews came to be regarded, and to regard themselves, as vulnerable to attack. Israel, by changing that, has had a profound effect on Jewish psychology.

Jerusalem's Damascus Gate, the main entrance to the Old City

Israel has always held an uneasy place in the world community. Many countries were slow to recognize the state and quick to condemn its handling of the Intifada. But since the collapse of the Soviet Union, which had bolstered many anti-Israeli states, peace has been made with old enemies and Israel is on the way to acceptance.

THE WEST BANK In the 1980s and early 1990s, Israel was routinely portrayed on news programs as harrassing, hounding, and harming the Palestinians. World media perceptions of Israel using violence against Arab civilians were based on a reality: since 1987, Israeli security forces sought to contain armed and organized resistance to their presence in the West Bank. They also tried to police a chaotic and menacing state of unrest where activists—often hooded teenagers and rock-throwing children—frequently attacked and killed fellow Palestinians.

Serious attacks, including murders, remain commonplace in the West Bank. News stories covering the disturbances tend to dwell on the police or army response, depicting rioters as victims, and shy away from the complex background to these events. On the other hand, it is not just outsiders who find the situation disturbing—most Israelis do too. The latest, risky, approach is to strengthen Fatah, the most moderate power-seeking faction within the P.L.O.—and let it deal with the unrest, whose root cause is not the occupation of the West Bank, but, as Palestinians put it, "the occupation of Akko, Haifa, and Jaffa."

ISRAEL AND THE ARABS Israel came into being in a region that did not want it. Palestine's Arabs fought tooth and nail to prevent the state of Israel being established. The surrounding Arab regimes pledged to destroy the "Zionist entity," which they have seen as an outpost of Western imperialism. From its inception in 1948 right up to 1994, when treaties were signed with former adversaries, the Jewish state was officially "at war" with most of the other nations in the Middle East.

Israel was not only threatened with military action, but faced economic war too. The Arab Boycott office in Damascus spent decades coordinating a worldwide campaign to pressure all companies into ceasing trade with any other company that dealt with Israel. Such boycotts nevertheless failed to prevent Israel from becoming the most economically active country in the Middle East. That fact, plus the loss

War relics—abandoned Egyptian tanks in the Negev desert

The famous handshake: Israeli Prime Minister Rabin and P.L.O. Chairman Arafat make peace in 1993, watched by President Clinton

of their Soviet support, has tempted Arab states away from their traditional party line, to look instead at ways of making peace with their new, unstoppable neighbor.

ISRAEL AND THE WEST In the United States, there is a certain amount of warmth toward Israel, and the United States has greatly assisted Israel in holding its ground for furious tactical reasons— among them Israel's presence as a pro-Western state in a hostile region and the importance of the Jewish vote in national elections. Without American support, Israel might well have been destroyed by now.

The European Union has over the years shown favor to the Arab cause—both Britain and France have long-standing links in the Arab world, which they think it is in their interest to preserve. The treaty with the P.L.O., and growing Israeli economic strength, have given the E.U. countries an excuse to look for ways to make closer ties with Israel, which already does a huge proportion of its trade with Europe.

ISRAEL AND THE THIRD WORLD
Not all Third World and nonaligned states joined the anti-Israel bloc. Latin America has long had friendly relations with Israel. With the changing political scene, dozens more countries have struck up ties with the Jewish state. For some, there is a chance of tangible benefits. The states in the Organization of African Unity maintained amicable relations and close contacts with Israel, while openly admitting that Russian and Arab pressure had forced them to cut off diplomatic relations. As a result, Israel has given a lot of commercial, cultural and technical assistance to these countries, including aid in the form of freshwater wells, hospitals, and medical staff.

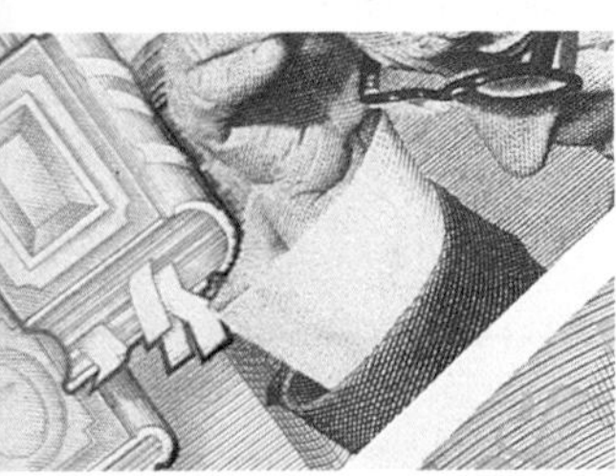

Israel seems to be on the verge of another new beginning. With peace accords in place, the hostilities of past decades might at last be swept aside. Freed from preoccupation with defense, Israel has boundless plans and potential that could make it an influence for good in the world out of all proportion to its size.

WHAT WILL PEACE BE LIKE? A hundred years of Zionism from the 1890s to the 1990s, have created a Jewish nation state on the verge of international acceptance. The next step is normalization. After peace treaties, perhaps trade treaties could come. But peace raises more questions. Army service played an essential part in forging the national identity. Can anything else fulfill that role? And without external enemies, Israel faces two explosive internal divides: between Sephardim and Ashkenazim, and between Orthodox and secular. Three other groups—Ethiopian *olim*, Israeli Arabs, and non-Orthodox religious Jews—all urgently demand equality as citizens of Israel.

THE AGE OF ECONOMIC MIRACLES Peace brings tangible benefits. Israel's economy is one of the fastest-growing in the world. Even taking into account the 10 percent unemployment rate (the labor force grows by 3 percent per year) and even after the late-1990s slowdown, growth is around 3–4 percent and still rising. In high-tech industries, medical and scientific research, fashion design, diamonds and jewelry making, Israel ranks among world leaders. The country's stock market is becoming a focal point for the Middle East sector, and foreign investment is pouring into the country. Each treaty-signing brings about a jump in share prices. And as centers of entertainment and leisure, the tourist resort of Eilat and the city of Tel Aviv are fast becoming world-class travel destinations.

GOOD NEIGHBORS Peace and cooperation have the power to bring ambitious regional projects to fruition. Problems such as water shortages can be tackled together. Israel's medical expertise now helps previously hostile states. Israelis believe that their neighbors will abandon their opposition and join with them in a better future when they see the benefits Israel can bring to the region.

Eilat and Tel Aviv are developing into major leisure resorts

Israel Was

The world's best-selling book is essentially the history, cosmology, and ethics of the land and people of Israel. Whether you think God, Adam and Eve, Abraham, Moses, and Jesus are real, symbolic, or imaginary, the Bible's basic story line is broadly accurate. Archeologists are constantly digging up new supporting evidence.

The countryside of this tiny nation is sprinkled with the scenes and sites of great events that have made their mark on humanity. And as you travel from place to place, the Bible deserves to be ranked as one of Israel's best guidebooks.

IN THE BEGINNING The Torah (the Jewish name for the Pentateuch, or the first five books of the Bible) tells the story of the world from Creation up to the Israelite conquest of Canaan. It roughly spans the 20th to the 12th centuries BC. Each part of the narrative is full of information about the peoples of this country, then called Canaan, their beliefs, customs, conflicts, and ambitions. As a record of early habitation in the Middle East, it is an incomparably valuable document, the like of which hardly any other nation possesses. The pre-Israelite tribes that lived here in the late Stone Age and Bronze Age—before and during Abraham's time—are named, and their territories delineated.

The lifestyle and relationships, world view and codes of behavior of nomadic herdsmen of this period, as well as the origins of urbanization, are described in detail. The places where Abraham and the patriarchs and their families pitched their tents are named (and still called by the same names today). The places where they built shrines to the unseen God that Abraham believed in, and the cave that he purchased to bury his wife, are named, their locations described, and their significance known ever since.

Pharaoh's army drowns chasing the Israelites through the Red Sea

THE PROMISED LAND Around 1700 BC, many of the Israelites (more correctly called Hebrews in this pre-Judaic era) made their way to Egypt. The Sinai and Negev are thoroughly described, and their landmarks identified, in the biblical account of the Exodus, the return from Egypt that took place in about 1250 BC. That adventure is celebrated in the festival of Pesach (Passover). On the way, the Israelites paused at Mount Sinai, where Jewish Law was born,

Top: the Israelites advancing with the Ark of the Covenant. Above: Moses descending from Mount Sinai with the Ten Commandments

an event remembered at the festival of Shavuot.

In 1200 BC, Joshua led the Israelites across the Jordan to defeat one local king after another. In places, the Israelites failed to secure a victory, but by and large the land of Canaan was won. These Children of Israel had only a weak grasp of their forefathers' religion, and frequently took up the local cults of Ba'al and Astarte, which required human sacrifice. Much of the Torah deals with the consolidation of power among the Israelite tribes, and the growing hold of the Jewish ethical code.

DEFENDING THE LAND In the time of the Book of Judges (the 10th and 11th centuries BC), the Israelites were often at war, notably with the Philistines, who established "the five cities" on the Israelite shore (later six). These subsequently became known as Philistia: Gaza, Ashkelon, Ashdod, Ekron, Gath, and Jaffa. From here, they extended their territory across Judah and Galilee, the Israelites unable to defeat them until the era of the Book of Kings (from 1025 BC).

In the reign of King Saul, the shepherd boy, David of Bethlehem, considerably weakened the Philistines by killing their "giant," Goliath. In 1006 BC, King Saul was killed fighting the Philistines. He had already chosen David to be his successor.

THE FIRST TEMPLE David's outstanding achievement was to complete the Israelite conquest and bind together the Jewish people. Under him, the Land of Israel stretched from Damascus to the Red Sea. Conquering Jerusalem, the city of the Jebusites, he built a shrine there for the Ark of the Covenant. The ark was a gold-encrusted wooden chest containing Moses' tablets of stone, inscribed with the Law, which the Israelites had been carrying with them for several centuries. Deeming himself, or being deemed by God, unfit for the task of constructing the Holy Temple as a permanent sanctuary for the Ark, he left this to his son Solomon. In 953 BC, King Solomon built the awesome, magnificent Temple on what was to be called Temple Mount. Much subsequent political and religious history was to emanate from here.

A new era started under Solomon. The Temple became the focal point of the nation, and Jerusalem extended its political authority throughout the country. But it was a land caught between empires, crossed by trade routes and coveted by others. Its strength, in forming the wealth and character of the nation, was its weakness too, as one regional power after another laid claim to the Land of Israel.

FIGHTING FOR SURVIVAL Solomon's unified nation did not survive long after his death in 928 BC. A split resulted in two Jewish kingdoms: Israel in the north, and Judah in the south. Jerusalem remained the spiritual center for both until, in the 8th century BC, the northern kingdom came more and more under the influence of Phoenicians, Assyrians, and others. The 7th century BC saw a similar trend in Judah, but, in 727 BC, King Hezekiah purified the Temple and vigorously revived Jewish practice. Despite today's Orthodox belief that the Torah (the first five books of the Bible) was given to Moses at Sinai, the text makes plain that it was written in Jerusalem at this time.

Meanwhile, Assyrians conquered the northern kingdom; the mixing of the local Jews (many of whom were taken into slavery) with their colonists created the Samaritan people. Assyria moved on to re-create Philistia, virtually surrounding Judah. However, the Babylonians were also at war with the Assyrians. When they crushed the Assyrians in 630 BC, King Josiah of Judah quickly retook the north. He closed down all places of worship, except for the Temple at Jerusalem, which he purified.

A NEW TEMPLE The whole of Israel was then conquered by the Babylonians under Nebuchadnezzar II. In 597 BC, the Jews rebelled against Babylonian rule, but soon lost ground. The Jewish élite and priesthood were exiled to Babylon and, in 587 BC, the Temple was demolished. However, though significant in religious terms, the Babylonian Exile only lasted 46 years. In 539 BC, the Persians conquered the Babylonian Empire and permitted the exiles to return to Jerusalem. They marched back in two stages, one of them under Ezra, who revitalized Judaism and inspired the building of the Second Temple, dedicated in 519 BC. It is likely that the last part of the Torah was written at this time.

Jerusalem then enjoyed a renaissance and was enclosed by new ramparts. However, a new influence was being felt throughout the land: Greek culture.

HELLENIZATION During the 5th and 4th centuries BC, Hellenistic Greek culture, ideas, gastronomy, religion, architecture, and art swept through the Mediterranean and the Middle East. In 333 BC, Alexander the Great, the King of Macedonia (northern Greece), set out to conquer the world. He began by defeating the Persians and setting up the Seleucid dynasty, in Damascus, to rule the whole region. The Seleucids often had to go to war to defend their territory, and from 312 BC to 198 BC, much of Judaea, including Jerusalem, fell to the rival Egyptian Ptolomaic dynasty.

As soon as the Seleucids had regained their losses in 198 BC, they started to come under pressure from the growing might of a new rival empire—that of Rome. In 175 BC the new Seleucid king, Antiochus IV, set out to replace Temple Judaism with worship of the Greek gods. He sold off the Temple treasures to pay the debts of his army. An altar to the

Top: Babylon conquers Israel
Above: Mattathias slays the priest

wine god Dionysus (also known as Bacchus) was erected in the Temple in their place.

THE MACCABEES This was too much of a sacrilege for the Hasmoneans, one family of the priestly line, to bear. In 166 BC, the father (Mattathias) and his five sons (including Judah, known as the Maccabee, probably meaning "the Hammer") killed a Seleucid official and a pagan priest. The killing sparked a war between the Jews and the Seleucids. Mattathias was killed, but Judah continued with the rebellion, which resulted in complete independence for Judaea under Hasmonean rule. The Maccabees purified and rededicated the Temple (an act commemorated by the festival of Hanukka). Judah's brother Jonathan became high priest, later replaced by his brother Simeon. Yet the power-hungry Hasmonean dynasty proved a disaster for Israel. From 103 to 63 BC, religious traditionalists and their hellenized neighbors were in open conflict with their Hasmonean rulers. Taking advantage of the chaos, the Romans simply moved in and conquered Judaea.

Five centuries of Roman rule brought dramatic, disastrous changes. It was a messianic age, marked by turmoil, violence, and despair. The Jews were in conflict with their imperial masters, whose repression proved inadequate to break the will of this proud people. Among the several messiahs who attracted a following, the influence of one was to stand far above the rest: Jesus of Nazareth. By the end, Israel was no longer a Jewish land.

HEROD In 37 BC, an ambitious, tough-minded half-Jewish friend of Rome, the notorious governor of Galilee, took control of the country. This was Herod, who arrived in Jerusalem heading a Roman force sent to execute the Hasmonean king, Antigonus. Accepting no opposition to his egomaniacal rule, he murdered anyone who might stand in his way, including his wife, two of his younger sons, his brother-in-law (Aristobulus III, the last Hasmonean high priest), and, finally, his faithful oldest son, Antipater.

Herod's grandiose building schemes took in palaces and forts, such as Masada and Herodion. It also included entire towns, such as Caesarea, and the reconstruction of the Temple along more Hellenistic lines. There was widespread discontent, murmurings of political rebellion and mass longing for the coming of a "messiah" (the Jewish name for a great liberator or leader). Toward the end of his reign (perhaps in 5 BC, though the exact year is not known), Jesus was born.

Top: Romans at war
Below: Roman Jerusalem's main street, the Cardo

JESUS Herod's death, in 4 BC, brought the disintegration of his kingdom, which was divided among his three remaining sons: Herod Antipas, Archelaus, and Philip. All faced a popular mood of seething insurrection. According to Matthew's gospel, the family of Jesus fled to Egypt to escape the unrest, later settling in relatively safe Galilee. A messianic teacher, John the Baptist, attracted a big following. Herod Antipas had him executed. Jesus emerged as another possible messiah, urging Jews to remain faithful to Jewish law. Also, Jesus stressed its ethical content and new egalitarian ideas. After three years, he too was executed, but his following continued. Meanwhile the Zealots, an underground rebel movement whose members combined religious

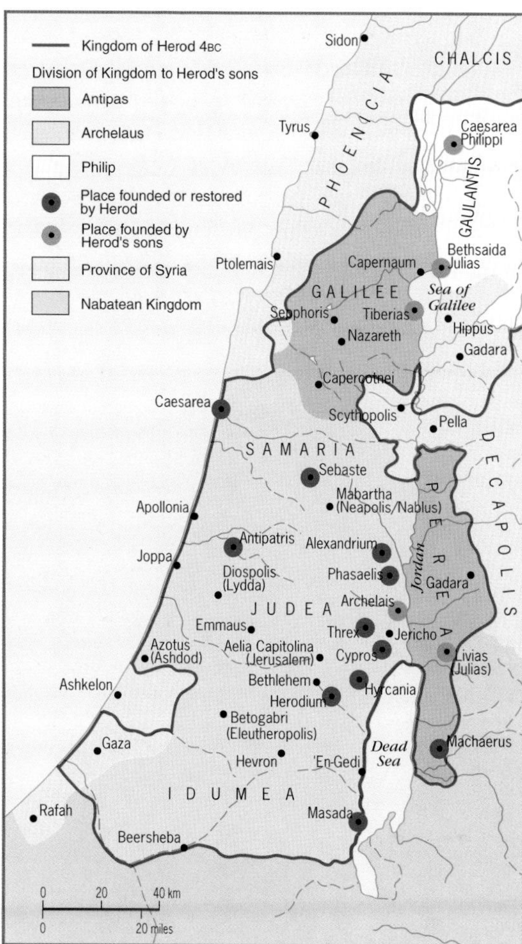

with political fervor, were preparing for all-out war.

THE FIRST REVOLT From AD 44, a succession of brutal Roman procurators were sent to administer the troublesome province, which they named Palaestina, or Palestine. In AD 66, the Zealots made their first attack on a Roman garrison: the soldiers surrendered, but were killed anyway.

This was the trigger for a nation-wide uprising. In one incident, Roman reinforcements numbering 6,000 soldiers, trapped by Jewish insurgents at Beit Horon, were slaughtered. A number of cities came into the hands of the rebels. Eventually, Rome began to master the situation. Town after town was destroyed, including major centers such as Gamla and Jericho. Eventually, in AD 70, Roman troops retook Jerusalem and destroyed the Temple itself. Only the Western Wall survived. Diehard Zealots gathered at Masada, but, facing defeat, they committed mass suicide in AD 73.

THE SECOND REVOLT Roman troops were poured into Palestine, with large new military colonies created on the sites of destroyed towns such as Nablus, Caesaria, and Jerusalem. Yet Jewish life and law continued, even thrived, away from Jerusalem, with Galilee the principal center. Christianity too was on the rise. St. Paul's new universal vision of Christ's message gained ever more converts among the Gentiles, including the Romans.

Hadrian became emperor in 117. He prohibited Torah study, circumcision, and other Jewish practices. In 132, the Second Revolt erupted. Its leader, known as Bar Kochba (Son of the Star), was acclaimed as a messiah and scored "miraculous" victories.
The Roman response was ferocious. Almost a thousand Jewish towns and villages were wiped out. The revolt was smashed by 135. Jerusalem was totally reconstructed, and a statue of Hadrian placed on Temple Mount. Entry to the city was forbidden to Jews, except on just one day a year. The Diaspora began—and would not end until the 20th century.

The decline of Jewish Israel was soon offset by the rise of Christian Israel. The new religion grew beyond its Jewish roots and spread fast through the Roman Empire, its ideas and credo evolving in the Near East. After Emperor Constantine granted tolerance to Christianity, huge numbers embraced the faith. The land of Jesus became the Holy Land. The Byzantine period brought three centuries of piety and pilgrimage, church-building and colonization.

FROM ROME TO BYZANTIUM Following the two revolts, the Romans allowed the decimated Jews freedom to practice their religion and live by their own laws. However, they were only allowed to enter Jerusalem on one day a year—Tisha b'Av, the supposed anniversary of the Temple's destruction. The Jews marked this day by chanting mournful lamentations at the Western Wall (hence the name Wailing Wall). Palestine became increasingly Romanized and Christianized, and when Emperor Constantine decreed official tolerance for Christianity in AD 313, tens of thousands joined the new creed. In 323, Constantine became sole ruler of the Eastern and Western Empires and made Christianity, in effect, the state religion. Later, the Roman Empire split again into eastern and western spheres. In 379, Byzantium, or Constantinopolis (today's Istanbul), became the capital from which Palestine was ruled.

TO BE A PILGRIM Constantine's own mother, Empress Helena, came to the Holy Land in 326 to search out relics of Jesus. She found them, with surprising ease. As soon as she arrived in the Holy City, the Bishop of Jerusalem showed her the exact spot where, he claimed, Jesus had been crucified. The burial tomb was immediately at hand. Nearby were some old crucifixes, one of which she clearly identified as the True Cross. Over the site, Helena ordered the vast, splendid Church of the Holy Sepulcher to be built, still the focal point of Christian devotion in the city. On the Mount of Olives, she made more discoveries, such as the Garden of Gethsemane and the place

Top: Constantine carries the Cross in battle. Above: his baptism

from which Jesus had ascended into heaven. Here, another fine church was erected.

Moving on to Bethlehem, Helena at once identified the place where Jesus had been born, and enclosed it within the Church of the Nativity. Traveling through the Holy Land, she located scores of other sites that she believed were associated with Jesus. Most were of doubtful authenticity, but this did not deter her from ordering churches to be built, or stop Christians from flocking to see them. Relics of saints' bodies were eagerly sought out, and found everywhere. Numerous nonbiblical legends date from this time: Mary drew water from this well, for example, or the Archangel Gabriel appeared in that cave.

Constantine made Christianity the Roman state religion

THE BEGINNINGS OF SCHISM In this early stage, churches became a feature of the land. Christian communities flourished around holy places. Jerusalem again grew to be as large as in Herodian times. By the year 450, most people in Palestine were Christian. But the division of the empire into east and west mirrored a cultural gulf. Arguments about doctrine and practice shattered the unity of the church.

In 451, the Roman and Eastern churches agreed to differ, and the Patriarchate of Jerusalem became part of the Eastern, or Orthodox, Church. In 456, the Monophysite doctrine, that Jesus had a single nature, part human, part divine, was condemned as heresy. The Orthodox view was that Christ had two natures. But large numbers of Christians in Palestine were Monophysite. This rather academic matter threatened the unity of the Byzantine Empire. The Copts and other Eastern churches remained Monophysite.

THE END OF THE DREAM Along with growing discord in the Church, there was sporadic unrest among the Jewish population from 484 onward. When the Persians invaded Palestine in 614, they were aided and advised by disaffected Jews, whose complaints had been ignored by the Byzantines. The empire proved too weak to defend Palestine's holy places, and even the True Cross was carried off as booty. Fourteen years later, the Byzantines took on the Persians, this time defeating them and restoring the Cross to the Church of the Holy Sepulcher. But already the end was in sight for the Byzantine Christians. Islam was on the march from Arabia.

Islam rose like a whirlwind from the Arabian desert, taking the whole of the Middle East by storm. Islam (literally meaning "submission") prescribed forcible conversion of pagans. To the Christians and the Jews—"Peoples of the Book"—Muhammad promised mercy, while replacing their spent, outdated religions with the teachings of the Koran.

MUHAMMAD'S VISION Muhammad, born in Mecca in AD 570, married a wealthy widow and became an influential figure. He took other wives, one of them Jewish, and became interested in religion and ethics. The defeat of the Jews was seen as a lesson. He felt the time was right for a creed that could not be conquered. In 610 he had the first of the "revelations" that were to be recorded in the Koran. He argued that Arabs, like Jews, were descendants of Abraham. He went on to claim that his new religion had been revealed to supersede both Judaism and Christianity. Arming his supporters, he compelled the inhabitants of Mecca to adopt his faith in 630. When Muhammad died in 632, his followers set about fulfilling his dreams.

ISLAM'S TRIUMPH Islamic forces reached Palestine just two years after the Prophet's death, and they defeated the Byzantines in 638.

Top: exquisite tilework, Dome of the Rock
Below: remains of Nimrod, a 12th-century Crusader castle

The region was then ruled from Damascus by the Omayyad dynasty, whose leaders bore the title Caliph (literally, successor—i.e. successor to Muhammad). In Jerusalem (which the Arabs called Aelia, the Roman name) Caliph Omar went to Temple Mount to pray at the rock where tradition has it that Abraham placed his son for sacrifice. He toured the Holy Land, his followers claiming for Islam each place where he prayed. He refused to pray at the Church of the Holy Sepulcher, so that it would remain a Christian shrine. The next caliph, Abd el-Malik, wanted to establish a place of pilgrimage within his own domain. He declared Temple Mount was "the far distant place of worship" to which Muhammad flew in a dream, according to the Koran. He built the Dome of the Rock on top of the Mount about AD 700. Aelia was then renamed Beit al-Makds (from Beit HaMikdash, the Hebrew name of the Temple), later abbreviated to Al-Kds. Abd el-Malik's son, Al-Walid, converted another church on the Temple Mount site into the Al Aqsa (El-Aksa) mosque.

VIOLENCE AND CHAOS In 750 the Abbasids succeeded the Omayyads and gradually lost control of Palestine, which they had ruled from distant Baghdad. For a century, Turkish warlords vied for mastery of the region. Christians were attacked, and the Holy Sepulcher set on fire, but later repaired. Around AD 977, the brutal Fatimid dynasty, based in Egypt, took over. Between 1004 and 1021, their caliph Al-Hakim (the Mad) destroyed almost all Palestine's churches. In 1055, the Fatimids were overrun by the equally savage Seljuk Turks. Christian pilgrims were often murdered when visiting holy sites.

THE CRUSADES Full of naïve zeal, thousands of Christian soldiers (mainly young noblemen) set off in waves from Western Europe to "save" Palestine's holy places. The First Crusade of 20,000 men entered Jerusalem on July 15, 1099, and massacred the entire population. On Christmas Day, 1100, Baldwin I was crowned King of Jerusalem. Meeting no resistance, they conquered more of Palestine, built fortified churches and castles, and discovered countless dubious saintly relics and holy places. Military monastic orders came into being, notably the Knights Hospitallers and the Templars.

The Second Crusade arrived in 1147. Now a powerful Muslim opponent emerged: Salah ed-Din (Saladin), the Egyptian sultan. In 1187, at the Horns of Hittim, he and his army encountered a vast force of Crusaders and slaughtered them. Almost at once, the Crusader kingdom collapsed, though Soldiers of the Cross continued to arrive. With the Third Crusade of 1189, the Fourth of 1202, the Fifth of 1228, and the Sixth of 1248, the Crusaders established a new "capital" at Akko, or Acre. In 1261, the Mamelukes, under Sultan Baibars, rode in. These terrifying master horsemen and swordsmen, bloodthirsty former slaves, were to rule for two centuries. They made brisk work of the Europeans. In 1270, the final Crusade arrived and was massacred.

Christian captives suffer the vengeance of the mighty sultan Salah ed-Din

The Mamelukes ruled Palestine for two centuries, and the Ottomans ruled for four. The Mamelukes were noted for anarchy and turbulence; the Ottomans imposed a regime of suffocating stability. Progress in science and mathematics languished. An obscure Ottoman province, Palestine went into steady decline.

MAMELUKES The Mamelukes were freed slaves of the Egyptians, mostly of Circassian origin. They failed to establish any cohesive government in Palestine. Nevertheless, they constructed fine buildings, some of which still stand to this day. At the end of their period of rule, an Islamic defeat on the other side of the Mediterranean began to send out ripples that would last for centuries: tens of thousands of Jews, expelled from Spain by the Christian conquerors in 1492, began making their way back to Palestine.

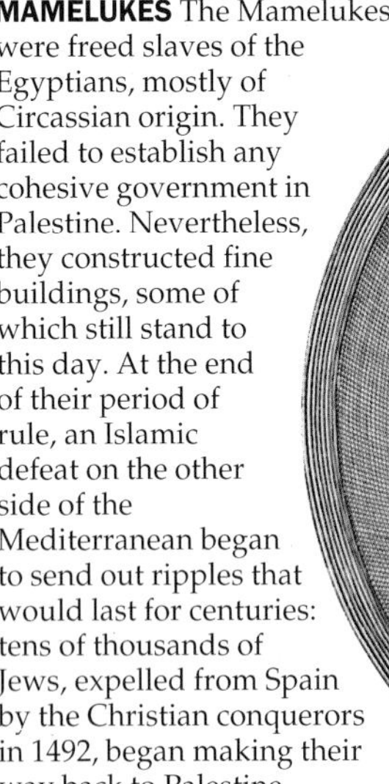

Top: Akko, the once mighty fortress town revived under Ottoman rule
Above: Suleiman the Magnificent

TURKISH RULE The Crusader period was a disaster for the Holy Land, and for Christendom. The Crusader attack on Constantinople so weakened it that Sultan Osman would soon be able to add this remnant of the Byzantine Empire to his own massive Ottoman (i.e. Turkish) Empire. The Ottoman Sultan Selim next defeated the Mamelukes in 1517 to gain the Holy Land. So Palestine was once again ruled from Constantinople (now called Istanbul). The famous flowering of the Ottoman period took place at the start under Selim's son, Suleiman (the Magnificent). He did much to improve Jerusalem, in particular repairing and restoring its ramparts. The majestic city walls that stand today are principally his work.

Thereafter, Ottoman rule was characterized by neglect. The population divided into small local clans and fiefdoms, often involved in insoluble feuds. Exceptions to the general decline were the rebuilding of Galilean towns (notably Akko) by the Druze Emir ed-Din in the mid-17th century. In the late 18th century came the rise to power in Galilee of Ahmed el-Jazzar (known as the Butcher), and the brief early 19th-century takeover of Palestine by Egyptian pashas. Then, in the 1870s, to the surprise of all, large numbers of East European Jews began arriving.

In the 1880s, the destiny of Palestine was being decided by events in Poland and Russia. Czar Alexander III (1881–1894) and his son Czar Nicholas II (1894–1917) oversaw repressive anti-Jewish legislation and vicious pogroms. These added fuel to the new Zionist movement, which was calling for a return to the Jewish homeland.

THE FIRST ALIYAH Aliyah means "ascent," and that is how Jews speak of going to live in Israel. From 1850 to 1880, some 20,000 came to live in Palestine. This was followed, in 1882 to 1903, by the first organized mass immigration driven by religious and political ideals. It brought 25,000 settlers, almost all fleeing Russian pogroms. The settlers' enthusiastic desire to farm and "redeem" the land often petered out as they ran into serious difficulties, many reaching starvation point or dying of disease. Several settlements were bailed out by well-to-do Western Jews, who also contributed large sums for the purchase of land.

THE SECOND ALIYAH In Europe, Theodor Herzl's influential book *The Jewish State* was published in 1896, and the First Zionist Conference, held the following year, announced plans to create a Jewish home in Palestine. The Jewish National Fund was founded to buy land for settlements.

A new type of immigrant also began to appear. Many Russian Jews had been involved in the attempted revolution of 1905; with its failure, and the subsequent pogroms, these tough socialists embraced the dream of creating a Jewish nation in the ancient homeland. From 1904 to 1914, some 40,000 of them settled in Palestine, founding farm collectives and small towns. Arab opposition numbered among the problems they faced, but these Halutzim (pioneers), as they are still known, seemed undeterred by any obstacle. To rousing songs in Hebrew, they took on the Hula swamp, Judaean desert, and coastal dunes. They founded the city of Tel Aviv and set up a network of armed groups for self-protection.

Above and below: Zionist pioneers

As the Second Aliyah ended, the Turks were drawn into World War I—on the losing side. It was to cost them Palestine. The arrival of thousands of Jewish refugees seemed, perhaps, the least important of anyone's concerns. From the end of World War I to the end of World War II, Palestine was in the hands of the British. They were to discover that the Jewish return to Israel was unstoppable.

DIPLOMACY AND DECEPTION In 1914, the Turks joined the war on Germany's side. It was a decision that was later to give the Allies, in victory, an opportunity to exert greater influence in the Near East. Britain was eager for a role in the Arab world. Behind the scenes, a leading Zionist, Chaim Weizmann, a persuasive diplomat as well as a distinguished scientist, was visiting people of influence in the Western world to win international support for a Jewish homeland in Palestine. Due to his efforts, the British Foreign Secretary, A. J. Balfour, wrote a letter, the famous Balfour Declaration of 1917. It guaranteed British support—against the wishes of many other British politicians. In the same year, British forces moved into Palestine, seizing it with ease from the Turks. A dignified and emotional General Allenby entered the Old City of Jerusalem on foot and announced the start of British rule.

General Allenby, head of the British forces

ZIONISM ON THE MARCH 1920 was a busy year. In the aftermath of the war, Palestine (on both sides of the Jordan) came under British Mandate on behalf of the League of Nations. At the same moment, the Third Aliyah (1919–1923) began, bringing 40,000 youthful Zionist activists from Eastern Europe. This Aliyah, the first to be given advance training, had a dramatic effect on farming. Within weeks, the Hashomer defense volunteers regrouped to form Haganah, an underground army whose aim was to protect the Jews of Palestine. In the same year, the first collectives of the new kibbutz and *moshav* movements (see page 174) were established, and the

Arab opposition

labor union, Histadrut, was founded. It remains part of the bedrock of Israeli society. Hebrew was declared the official language of the Yishuv (Jews living in Palestine). Suddenly, the area's 700,000 resident Arabs realized the possible consequences of Zionism.

ATTACK AND DEFENSE 1920 was also the year of the first big anti-Jewish riots by Arabs in several towns. Worse followed in 1921, in two outbreaks that left 79 Jews and 48 Arabs dead. In 1924 came the Fourth Aliyah (1924–1926), and another 80,000 Jews arrived, mainly Polish artisans and small businessmen, accelerating urban development. The ports grew, Tel Aviv expanded, Haifa's Technion research institute opened in 1924, and the Hebrew University at Jerusalem in 1925. Arab fury erupted again in 1929 and left 133 Jews dead, with the destruction of the ancient Jewish community in the city of Hebron.

The decade of the Fifth Aliyah (1931–1940)—the flight from Nazism—brought 180,000 newcomers. The 1929 massacres had led to a split in Haganah, which had failed in its aim of protecting the Jews. The more hard-line Irgun was born, with guerrilla warfare, attacks on hostile strongholds and retaliation its tactics. The year 1936 saw a change in the Arab side too, with the start of the Arab Revolt against both the Jews and the British. Within two years, 415 Jews had been murdered. To appease the Arabs, who were leaning toward the Nazis, the British agreed to curtail Jewish immigration. At the same time, they were attempting to appease Hitler. Both proved to be blind alleys.

Top : Yad Vashem Holocaust memorial
Below: British law enforcement

HOLOCAUST The Fifth Aliyah ended with two years of "restricted immigration" (1939–1940). As many as 15,000 arrived clandestinely, aided by the secret Aliyah Bet group. In Europe, the Nazi conquest had begun, and the Jewish extermination plan was ready to start. Some Jews could see what was coming. The Sixth Aliyah (1941–1947) brought those frantic to escape the Holocaust, and the few who survived.

Throughout the war, the British held the doors of Palestine firmly closed to "unauthorized immigrants." They came anyway and 20,000 were detained as soon as they set foot in Palestine. Most were returned to Europe, via detention centers. In a notorious incident in 1947, the ship *Exodus*, with 4,554 camp survivors crammed on board, reached the coast of Israel. British ships took them all back to Europe, forcibly disembarking them at Hamburg. This was the last year of British rule in Palestine.

Zionist emotion ran high before World War II, due to the trauma of Nazism. The movement split on whether or not to help the British war effort against the Germans. Both viewpoints had their day. When World War II was won, the Zionists reunited for a last push against the British, who finally left Palestine in 1948. After 50 years of determination, Israel was reborn.

FRIENDS AND ENEMIES Palestine's Jews were incensed by the British White Paper of May 1939, proposing that the Balfour Declaration be ditched and Jewish immigration halted. The Irgun decided to use guerrilla tactics against the British. But the outbreak of war with Germany changed all that. The Arabs supported the Nazis. David Ben-Gurion spoke for both Haganah and Irgun when he said: "We shall fight the War as if there were no White Paper , and we shall fight the White Paper as if there were no War." Not all agreed, however. The Irgun breakaway group Lehi (the Stern Gang) vowed to fight the British even during the war.

FIGHTING THE BRITISH With Germany's defeat in 1945, Irgun rejoined Lehi in its battle. The British headquarters, at the King David Hotel, was blown up. Irgun prisoners were daringly freed from Akko's fortress prison. The British took the Jewish homeland issue to the United Nations, and on November 29, 1947, the U.N. voted to partition Palestine (west of the Jordan) into Jewish and Arab areas. Jews would have small, unconnected zones in Galilee, on the coast, and in the Negev. It looked unworkable even on paper, but the Zionists agreed. The Arabs rejected it.

PROCLAIMING A STATE The day after the U.N. vote, the Arabs began a rampage of violence, which flared into full-scale civil war. By April 1948, Haganah held territory that included the coast, western Jerusalem, the Negev, and Galilee. On May 14, 1948, at Tel Aviv, David Ben-Gurion, Israel's first Prime Minister, proclaimed the founding of the State of Israel with the words: "In the Land of Israel the Jewish people came into being." Behind him hung Herzl's portrait. Chaim Weizmann became president. Triumphant yet fearful, Israel awaited the Arab's response.

WAR AND PEACE The very next day, the massed military might of Jordan, Egypt, Iraq, Syria, and Lebanon rolled to crush the newborn "Zionist entity." Israel emerged the victor, as it did in 1956 when Egypt closed the Red Sea to Israeli ships. In 1967, Israel also repulsed an attack by Syria, Jordan, and Egypt. Israel gained Sinai, Judaea, Somalia, Golan, Gaza, and East Jerusalem in six days. In 1973, Syria and Egypt attacked Israel (unsuccessfully) on Yom Kippur, the nation's principal day of prayer and fasting.

In 1977, Egypt's president Anwar Sadat decided to make peace. He and Israel's Prime Minister Menachem Begin signed the Camp David Agreement in 1978 and were jointly presented with the Nobel Peace Prize. Harder to deal with was terrorism.

David Ben-Gurion declares the founding of Israel

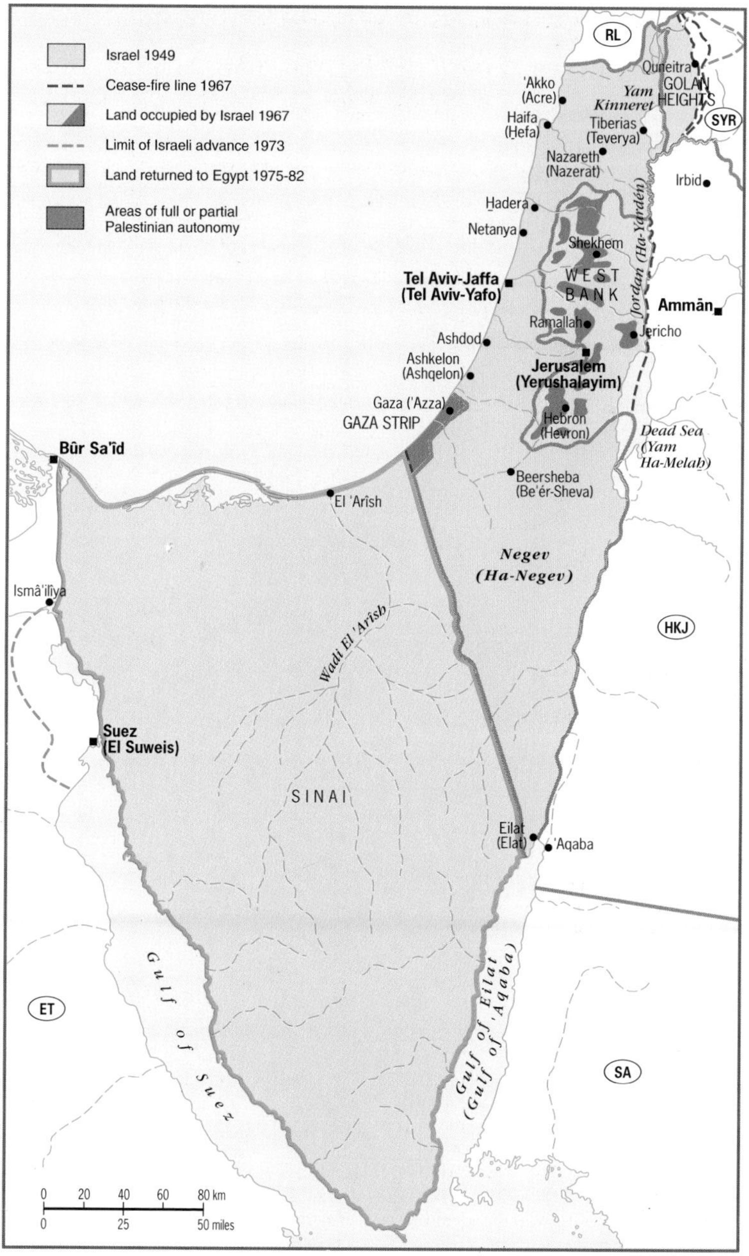

Israel 1949
Cease-fire line 1967
Land occupied by Israel 1967
Limit of Israeli advance 1973
Land returned to Egypt 1975-82
Areas of full or partial Palestinian autonomy

RL
SYR
HKJ
ET
SA
'Akko (Acre)
Haifa (Hefa)
Quneitra
GOLAN HEIGHTS
Yam Kinneret
Tiberias (Teverya)
Nazareth (Nazerat)
Irbid
Hadera
Netanya
Shekhem
WEST BANK
Jordan (Ha-Yarden)
Tel Aviv-Jaffa (Tel Aviv-Yafo)
Ammān
Ramallah
Jericho
Ashdod
Ashkelon (Ashqelon)
Jerusalem (Yerushalayim)
Gaza ('Azza)
GAZA STRIP
Hebron (Hevron)
Dead Sea (Yam Ha-Melah)
Bûr Sa'îd
Beersheba (Be'ér-Sheva)
El 'Arîsh
Negev (Ha-Negev)
Ismâ'ilîya
Wadi El 'Arîsh
Suez (El Suweis)
SINAI
Eilat (Elat)
'Aqaba
Gulf of Suez
Gulf of Eilat (Gulf of 'Aqaba)
0 20 40 60 80 km
0 25 50 miles

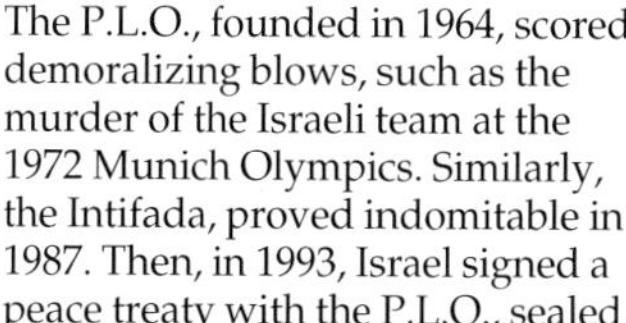

The P.L.O., founded in 1964, scored demoralizing blows, such as the murder of the Israeli team at the 1972 Munich Olympics. Similarly, the Intifada, proved indomitable in 1987. Then, in 1993, Israel signed a peace treaty with the P.L.O., sealed with Rabin and Arafat's famous handshake on the White House lawn. In 1994, Jordan also made peace with Israel. Other former enemies of Israel signaled that they too would like to sign away the bitter past, a cautious peace process that continues today.

KEREM AVRAHAM
Ammunition Hill
SHEMU'EL
ROMEMA
Central Bus Station
SARE YISRA'EL
MEQOR BARUKH
MALKHE YISRA'EL
YEHEZQ'EL
GE'ULLA
BET YISRA'EL
YAFO
NORDAU
4
SEDEROT ZALMAN SHAZAR
YAFO
NATHAN STRAUSS
ME'A SHE'ARIM
ME'A SHE'ARIM
YAFO
MAHANE YEHUDA
Mahane Yehuda Market
KIKKAR HA-HERUT
HA-NEVI'IM
Israel Center
Ethiopian Church
AGRIPPAS
YISRA'EL
HA-NEVI'IM
Clal Building
YAFO
Ticho House
Kook Museum
SHIVTE YISRA'EL
ZIKHRON YOSEF
AGRIPPAS
Agricultural Museum
Pargod Theater
KING GEORGE V
KIKKAR ZIYYON (ZION SQUARE)
Police Headquarters
Russian Cathedral
BEZALEL
RUSSIAN COMPOUND
3
YEHUDA
YAFO
Hall of Heroism Museum
Supreme Court
Sacher Park
SEDEROT HA-NASI BEN ZVI
Gerard Behar Center
Bezalel Academy of Art
BEN
Italian Synagogue (Museum of Italian Jewish Art)
KIKKAR BAR KOKHEVA
Law Courts
Talitha Kumi
HILLEL
SHELOMZION HA-MALKA
Central Post Office
KIKKAR ZAHAL
Wohl Rose Garden
Artists' House
BEN SIRA
MENAHEM USSISHKIN
Tzavta Theater
HA-MELEKH GEORGE V
SH HA-MELEKH
NAHALAT AHIM
QIRYAT BEN-GURION
Independence Park
Mamillah Pool
HA'EMEQ
SHA'ARE HESED
Yeshurun Synagogue
AGRON
Taxation Museum
Hebrew University (Giv'at Ram), Bloomfield Science Museum
Jewish Agency & JNF
Sisters of the Rosary Convent
GERSHON
Hebrew Union College
MERKAZ MISHARI
QIRYAT WOLFSON
US Consulate
Great Synagogue
Papal Bible Museum
Knesset
RUPPIN
Wolfson Museum
KIKKAR ZAREFAT
DAVID HA-MELEKH
2
American Cultural Center
King David Hotel
RAMBAN
RAMBAN
Terra Sancta
Bible Lands Museum
RUPPIN
YMCA
Prime Minister's House
KEREN HA-YESSOD
Shrine of the Book
Schocken Library
Rubin Music Academy & Musical Instruments Museum
YEMIN MOSHE
Valley of the Cross
SEDEROT HAYYIM HAZAZ
BALFOUR
Monastery of the Cross
Montefiore's Windmill
Israel Museum
DEREKH AZZA
KIKKAR PLUMER
Jerusalem Music Center
KIKKAR WINGATE
ZE'EV JABOTINSKY
Art Garden
Van Leer Foundation
Liberty
ZE'EV JABOTINSKY
REHAVYA
QOMEMIYYUT
DAVID REMEZ
Billy Rose Art Pavilion
President's House
MARCUS
Bell Garden
NEWE GRANOT
1
HA-NASI
Islamic Art Museum
CHOPIN
Talbiyeh Rose Garden
Mount Herzl (Har Herzl) Herzl Museum Yad VaShem
HA-RAV HERZOG
CHERNICHOVSKY
QIRYAT SHEMU'EL
Jerusalem Center for the Performing Arts
Leper Hospital (Bet Hansen)
HA-PALMAH
Natural History Museum
EMEQ REFA'IM
DEREKH BET-LEHEM
ZALMAN SHNEUR
Hadassah Medical Center, Holyland Hotel Model of Jerusalem at the time of Christ, Tisch Gardens, Biblical Zoo
A
B
'EMEQ REFA'IM
International Cultural Center for Youth
C
Railway Station

Jerusalem

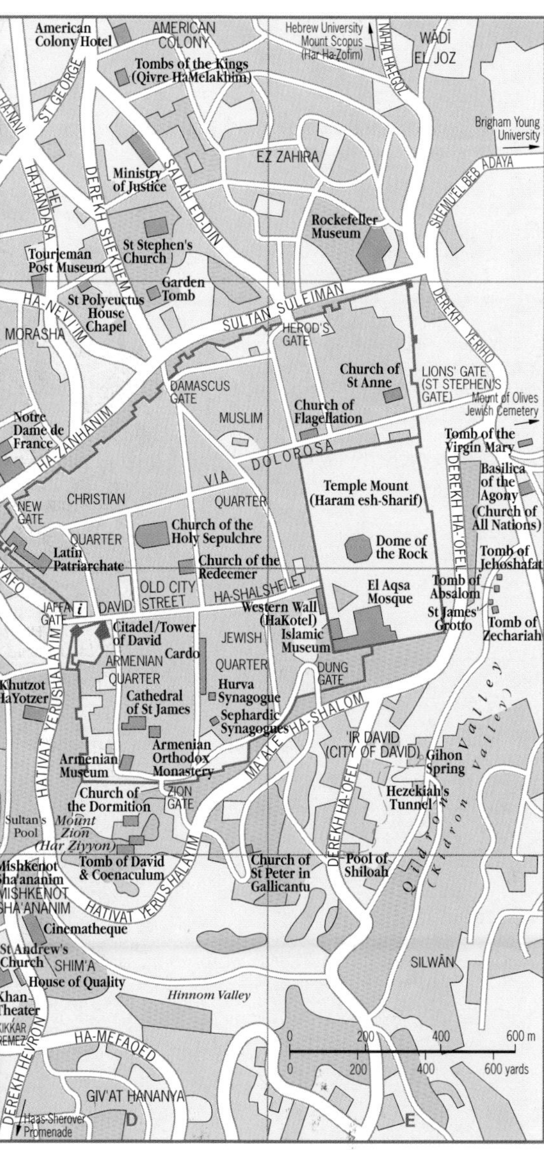

JERUSALEM (Hebrew: Yerushalayim; Arabic: Al-Quds) Highway 1 climbs gradually into the hills of Judaea and up to the city of Jerusalem. This is the way that most people arrive, in a taxi or a rented car. When, at last, the city entrance sign is reached, it makes the town look just like any other. No brilliant light radiates from the earth at this point. The sign is not encrusted with gold or jewels. Yet there is, without doubt, something magical about the name of Jerusalem. The fact that so many people, through the centuries, have yearned for this city—the fact that it became a metaphor for heaven, for the kingdom of God on earth, for a return to the Promised Land—cannot fail to affect anyone who arrives here today.

▶▶▶ CITY HIGHLIGHTS

Previous page: David's Tower, Jerusalem

CULTURE COLLISION In Jerusalem, Israel meets Arabia and West meets East. Behind the scenes, battles rage on diplomatic, economic, and political fronts for full legal title to the city. However, the conflict of interests is barely apparent to outsiders, and visitors are warmly welcomed nearly everywhere. The intensely Arab character of parts of the city creates an exotic air, one that adds another dimension to Israel's otherwise overwhelmingly Jewish capital. In the Muslim and Christian quarters of the walled Old City, and in East Jerusalem just outside the walls, Arab culture powerfully predominates. To wander through the souks (markets) assailed by spicy aromas and numerous invitations to buy—or at least to look at the merchandise—is to plunge straight into the midst of the Orient. It's a reminder, perhaps, that Abraham himself was father of both the Jews and the Arabs, and arrived here from the East.

ANCIENT CAPITAL Archeology and the Bible concur in saying that Jerusalem, as capital of the Jews, was built by King David about 1004 BC. His original city covered a ridge of land encircled to the south by the valleys of the Kidron and Hinnom rivers. The area is now outside the city walls. This was not virgin land, however, and a Jebusite city-state already existed here, on a site that had been inhabited since 3500 BC. Egyptian texts of 1900 BC call

The Old City from the Mount of Olives

it Urushamem. In the Book of Genesis, Chapter 14, it is called Salem, the place where, in about 1800 BC, Abraham visited Melchizedek. Centuries later, the Jews returned to the city, led by David (II Samuel 5). David purchased a threshing floor (II Samuel 24), the site on which his son, King Solomon, was to erect the Temple.

A TIME OF WAR Although the Israelites were to become divided, Jerusalem, with its Temple, was to remain their capital ever afterward. Over the millennia, the city walls were built, knocked down, and then rebuilt, sometimes along a different course. The city suffered conquest, destruction, and oppression (with episodes of Jewish independence in between) at the hands of half a dozen imperial powers. This period of history stretched from the Babylonians to the British (see side panel). Most of these conquering civilizations have waxed and waned; their day is over. Despite their efforts to take and hold Jerusalem, despite competing claims upon the city's holy sites, despite being divided in two (from 1948 to 1967), the city's identity as an "Eternal City" and capital of the people of Israel has survived.

CITY OF FAITH Yet Jerusalem is a city of other peoples too. The city witnessed events that lie near the heart of millions of believers worldwide—Jewish, Christian, and Muslim. The finest landmark in the Old City is an Islamic shrine, the glorious Dome of the Rock. The Dome covers the Holy Rock, which in turn marks the site of the Jewish Temple's Holy of Holies. The latter sanctuary contained the Ark of the Covenant. It is from here, some Muslims believe, that Muhammad flew to meet God on a winged horse. The spires and domes of scores of churches pierce the skyline, chief among them being the Holy Sepulcher. This sepulcher, atop Golgotha, or Calvary, enshrines the place where, Christians believe, Jesus died on the cross and then rose again.

NEW AND OLD There is more to Jerusalem than the Old City at its center. The East and West Jerusalem neighborhoods have, for the most part, sprung up in the last 100 years. West Jerusalem is dynamic and teeming with energy. For most residents, and for many visitors, this is the "real" Jerusalem, the Jerusalem of today. The Old City, within its magnificent cordon of ramparts, serves as an evocative reminder of the city's origins in the unfathomable past.

ORIENTATION The walled Old City, focal point for most visitors, lies close to Jerusalem's eastern edge. The Old City is informally divided into four quarters—Muslim, Christian, Armenian, and Jewish. To the east rises the Mount of Olives. Just north of the Old City walls lies the mainly Arab neighborhood known as East Jerusalem. Farther north are extensive Jewish residential areas, which technically are also part of the eastern section. The majority of the city, extending westward, is known as West Jerusalem or New Jerusalem. Consisting of dozens of more or less modern neighborhoods, this part is almost entirely Jewish. Jerusalem's "downtown" area is around Zion Square, a short distance west of the Old City.

OCCUPIED TERRITORY
Though the people of Israel have regarded Jerusalem as their capital since 1004 BC, the city has been under foreign occupation for much of history. Despite the ferocious attacks made upon it, the city has shown remarkable powers of survival.
The foreign conquerors of Jerusalem were the Babylonians (587 BC), the Egyptians (320–198 BC), the Seleucids (198–167 BC), the Romans and Byzantines (37 BC–AD 638), the Arabs (638–1099), the Crusaders (1099–1187), the Mamelukes (1260–1517), the Ottoman Turks (1517–1917), the British (1917–1948), and the Jordanians (1948–1967).

LITTERED HIGHWAY
Alongside Highway 1, on both sides of the road, are the burned-out wrecks of cars and trucks that once plied between Tel Aviv and Jerusalem, keeping the route open and bringing supplies to the besieged Jews of Jerusalem during the 1948 War of Independence. To reach the city, they had to cross Arab-held territory, and were bombarded all the way. Vehicles that didn't make it were never cleared away—just pushed to the side of the road as a memorial.

Jerusalem's walls are the legacy of Suleiman the Magnificent

Walk

On the City Walls

Turreted ramparts of golden stone enclose the Old City. Built by Suleiman the Magnificent in the 16th century, they stand on top of 2,000-year-old ruins. Part of the walkway, from the Damascus Gate to the Dung Gate (the Muslim quarter), is presently closed for security reasons. The rest is reached in two sections, both starting at the Jaffa Gate (*Open* daily 9–5. *Admission charge*). *Allow 3 hours.*

Jaffa Gate to Damascus Gate A wide stone walkway, skirting the Christian quarter, at first passes by the battlements that peep onto busy West Jerusalem. It then turns a series of corners into the Arab side of town. Below, on the city side, gardens, a school, and the dome of a mosque are passed. The tall spire of the **Franciscan Church of St. Savior** stays in view. Steps take the path up

The towers of the Citadel dominate the west of the city

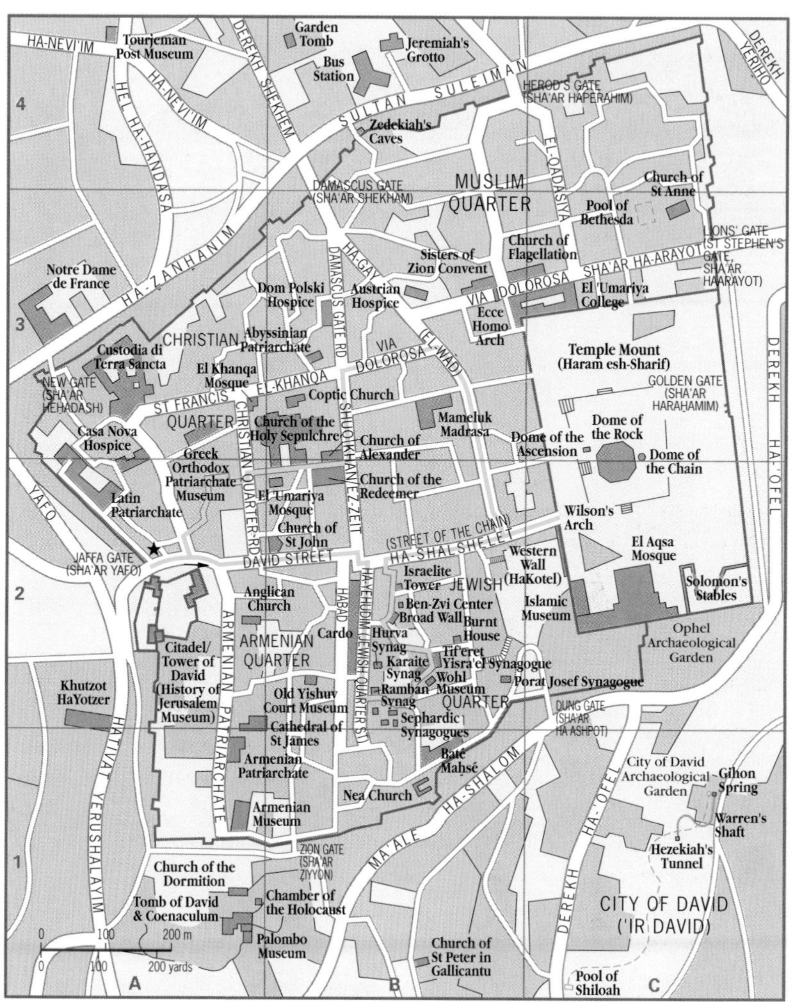

and down, and over the 19th-century **New Gate** (possible exit here). The path then narrows. Suddenly, ahead, the golden **Dome of the Rock** (see page 72) rises spectacularly above the gray roofs. The path then enters the chambers over the fortified **Damascus Gate**, built in the 16th century. Below, the streets throng with Arab crowds, and a wonderful view sweeps over the Old City. Take the same route back.

Jaffa Gate to Dung Gate The footway, reached by metal steps beside the Citadel, goes between high walls. There are views into the **Armenian quarter**, where no housing abuts the wall. At the **southwest tower**, the view extends over stony Judaean hills to the south. Turning here, the wall passes a few dwellings and lush gardens belonging to the Armenian Patriarchate. The Dome of the Rock comes into view. The walk now crosses the splendid 16th-century **Zion Gate** and reaches the **Jewish quarter**. Narrow steps go down to a wider path looking onto a little Old City **archeological park**. Here, the ramparts run along the side of a hill looking over a poor Arab district to barren hills beyond. There is a good view of Temple Mount and the Mount of Olives. The path now descends to the road.

The gateways that enter the Old City tell as much of Jerusalem's story as the walls themselves. From the simple New Gate to the imposing fortifications of Zion Gate, from the sealed and silent Golden Gate to the thronging Jaffa or Damascus Gate, the city's complex character is reflected in its handsome, historic entrances.

HOLE IN THE WALL
The hole that was knocked through the fortifications beside the Jaffa Gate was made by the Ottomans in 1898 to allow Kaiser Wilhelm II to drive through without having to leave his carriage. Contrast the Kaiser with the more respectful General Allenby, who, when taking the city for the British, dismounted from his horse and came through on foot, pausing at the gate to say, "We return to you."

Jaffa Gate Forming the main entrance to the Old City from West Jerusalem, this magnificently fortified gateway (built in 1588) is the best known to visitors, and the most used by residents. Unfortunately, the Ottomans knocked a road through the fortifications beside the gate (see side panel). The original pedestrian entrance turns a couple of sharp corners within the gateway to deter attackers. Jaffa is one of the oldest of the city gates, protected by the might of Herod's Citadel (or David's Tower), rising beside it. The gate opens directly onto David Street, which leads to the Street of the Chain—the Old City's colorful main thoroughfare—marking the boundary between the Armenian and Christian quarters.

Zion Gate This superb fortification of 1540 marks the line between the Armenian and Jewish quarters. The road passing through it forms the main access to West Jerusalem on the south side of the city walls, and is much used by residents of the Jewish quarter. It was through this gate that the quarter's residents were driven out of the city by the Jordanians in 1948. The gateway was then sealed, and remained so until 1967, when the Jews returned.

Dung Gate This historic gateway, built in 1540 on the site of an older gateway mentioned in the Bible, is the closest to the Western Wall. It originally gave access to the Temple. It stands between the Jewish quarter and an Arab district outside the walls, and is therefore subject to security measures, though it is much used by buses, whose terminal is just inside the gate.

Golden Gate Blocked up by the Muslims in 1530 to protect their holy sites, this gateway gives access to the Temple Mount from the Mount of Olives and the Kidron Valley. Christians say that this is the gateway through which Jesus rode on a donkey on Palm Sunday. Some Jews assert that a messiah will one day enter the city through this gate, or that it will be reopened on Judgment Day. Both groups attach much significance to an enigmatic passage in Ezekiel, Chapter 44, which says that the gate will be shut because God has passed through it, and will, in the future, only be used by the prince.

The Jaffa Gate, most splendid of the entrances into the Old City

Lions', or **St. Stephen's, Gate** The only gateway on the eastern wall (apart from the Golden Gate), this guards the main route from the Old City to the Mount of Olives and forms the principal connection between the Muslim quarter, and the Arab neighborhoods to the east and southeast. The gate was built in 1538 on the site of a Roman gateway, and various Christian legends attach to it. One of these says that St. Stephen was led through this gate to be stoned to death; however, this story, and the name St. Stephen's Gate, were originally attached to the Damascus Gate. Another story claims that the Virgin Mary was both born and buried beside it. The charming stone lions on the walls to either side of the entrance have given the gate its other name.

DIVINE WRITING
Pious Orthodox Jews claim to believe that a *mezuzah* (doorpost scroll) hidden within the Jaffa Gate masonry was written by God himself.

Herod's Gate, or **Gate of Flowers** Having nothing at all to do with either Herod or flowers, this 16th-century gate opens from the Muslim quarter into the heart of East Jerusalem.

Damascus, or **Shechem, Gate** Superbly fortified, this turreted main entrance to the Old City, from East Jerusalem, is exotic and fascinating. On the plaza in front, vendors hawk their wares to a bustling Arab crowd. Constructed by Suleiman the Magnificent in 1538, the gateway separates the Muslim and Christian quarters. The Crusader-period and Roman remains upon which it stands are still visible. There is also a Roman courtyard just inside the gateway.

New Gate Correctly named, this simple opening into the Christian quarter at the northwestern corner of the ramparts was constructed in 1887, closed during the Jordanian occupation, and reopened in 1967.

Herod's Gate

The Lions' Gate

The 260-acre plot of land that makes up the Old City of Jerusalem is packed with 20,000 residents of varied faiths and backgrounds. As is normal in the Middle and Near East, different communities live in different areas. Although there are no physical barriers between the Old City's four quarters (and at times their borders do change), in atmosphere and culture the dividing lines between them could hardly be plainer.

ARMENIAN MEMORIES
The Armenian Museum, on Armenian Patriarchate Street (*Open* Mon–Sat, 10–5. *Admission: inexpensive*) contains displays of Armenian art and artifacts, and documents relating to the destruction of the Armenian people. April 24 is the Armenians' Remembrance Day, in honor of the 1.5 million Armenians killed by the Turks during their campaign of genocide, which was carried out between 1894 and 1920.

The Christian quarter The calm, quiet streets and lanes of the northwestern sector are home to thousands of Arab and European Christians. The area contains many hospices and the large, grandiose buildings of the offices, churches, and patriarchates of several sects, clustered around the Holy Sepulcher.

The Armenian quarter Although Armenians are Christians, they have their own separate quarter in the southwestern corner of the Old City. The atmosphere is extremely tranquil, with an almost secretive air, the area's institutions and dwellings concealed behind high walls. Although the place seems virtually uninhabited, thousands of Armenians live here, over 1,000 of them in a single, converted hostel. Apart from the Zion Gate, which it shares with the Jewish quarter, the Armenian district has no city gate of its own. On the city walls as they pass around the Armenian quarter, maps and notices recall massacres of the Armenians at the hands of the Turks in the 25 years leading up to 1920, giving details of locations, dates, and the number of dead. Armenians feel bitter that the world has taken little interest in these events.

The Jewish quarter The Jewish quarter, lying south of the Street of the Chain, is the smallest and most attractive of the city's districts, and it has a distinctively sedate atmosphere. There are even signs requesting visitors not to

An intimate moment in the Jewish quarter

make too much noise. It is clean and new-looking, partly because the entire district had to be rebuilt from scratch after 1967. During their occupation of the Old City (1948–1967), the Jordanians destroyed this neighborhood and attempted to erase all traces of Jewishness. Most of the quarter's ancient buildings were reduced to rubble, though often the ground floors escaped. Some of the ruins have since been beautifully restored. Behavior in these streets is decorous and peaceful. Although densely populated, the narrow winding lanes often seem deserted. The quarter's center is the pleasant Hurva Square plaza.

The Muslim quarter By far the largest and the most colorful district of the Old City, the Muslim area embraces the north and center of the walled city. It is a confusing and densely populated warren of squalid lanes and bustling souks (markets), where Westerners encounter a vibrant culture very different from their own. Arab crowds, in flowing traditional dress, throng the narrow streets, and Oriental music fills the air.

WHAT'S IN A NAME?
The name Jerusalem comes from the Hebrew biblical name of the city, Yerushalayim. It is often said that the name means City of Peace (*shalayim* resembling *shalom*, peace). It is more likely to derive from Salem, the name of the Jebusite settlement that was here before the Israelites arrived. David called his fortress Zion, and this became an alternative poetic name for the city. The Romans called it Aelia Capitolina. Islamic conquerors turned this into Ilya. Muslim Jerusalem became Al-Quds or El Kuds (the Holy). Yet Jews continued to call the city Yerushalayim (the name is used in the Old Testament over 700 times), and this again became the official name of the city in 1948.

Left: Muslim-quarter souk (market). Below: quiet lanes thread the Jewish quarter

Walk

Within the walls, Jerusalem assails the mind with a dizzying blend of sights, sounds, and historic sites. Along busy lanes, stores hawk anything from souvenirs to spices, sandals to silver. East and West mingle freely, natives and tourists together, imams, rabbis, and priests, until you are no longer sure which is which. *Allow a full day.*

Start at the **Jaffa Gate►►►** (see page 52), the superb fortified entrance to the Old City (tourist office here). Beside it is Herod's vast Citadel, or the **Tower of David►►►** (see page 66). Go straight ahead on David Street, a narrow hectic Arab and Jewish souk (market). At the junction, turn right (Jewish Quarter Street) for the **Cardo►►** (see page 58), the Byzantine city's main street. At the end, turn left (Beit El Street) to enter the Jewish quarter's quiet lanes. Pass the **Four Sephardic Synagogues►►** (see page 63) and come to **Hurva Square►►** (see page 68). Around it are many things worth seeing—the **Ramban►** (see page 69), **Hurva►►** (see page 68), and **Karaite►** synagogues, and the **Wohl Archaeological Museum►►** (see page 80).

Across the square, take Tifret Yisrael Street and Plugat HaKotel Street, following the city limits of 2,000 years ago. Pass the **Broad Wall►** (see page 57), remnant of former ramparts. Turn right along the hectic, covered Street of the Chain. At the end, walk to the entrance of **Temple Mount►►►** (see page 72). If it is before 3 PM, go in and visit the **Dome of the Rock►►►** and **Al Aqsa Mosque►►►** (for both see page 72). A few paces back along the Street of the Chain, steps on the left twist down to the tunnel, which leads to the **Western Wall►►►** (see page 78).

Return via the tunnel to El-Wad Street. At a turning on the left, join the **Via Dolorosa►►►** (see page 76), which climbs in steps back into the souk district, passing the Stations of the Cross emblazoned on the walls in Roman numerals. These lead to the **Holy Sepulcher►►►** (see page 60). From here, continue up Souk ed-Dabbagha, cross into St. George Street, and return to the Jaffa Gate.

The Old City

(for map see page 51)

Through the Jaffa Gate, the main entrance to the Old City

Strolling in the souk (market)

The Old City

▶ Batei Mahaseh (Shelter Houses) Square 51B1

Entered through a gate, this attractive little plaza was a main square of the Jewish quarter in the 19th century. It is enclosed on one side by the Rothschilds' almshouse-like dwellings, known as Batei Mahaseh, which provided shelter and temporary accommodations for newly arrived Jews from Europe. A memorial reminds visitors that it was in this square that the Jews of Jerusalem were gathered with their possessions in 1948, when the Jordanians captured the city. The square was largely destroyed. Beside the Rothschild building, steps lead down, through a door, to the ruined subterranean apse of the Nea Church, built in AD 543. Once this was one of the most splendid and best-known churches in Christendom.

▶ Broad Wall 51B2

Plugat HaKotel Street

Just off the Cardo, this is a length of massive, ancient stonework exposed to view. It was constructed in about 800 BC to protect Jerusalem from a Syrian attack, as referred to in Isaiah 22:10–11, Nehemiah 3:8, and 12:38, thus becoming part of the city walls of the period. In total the Broad Wall was 215 feet long (150 feet are now visible) and a full 23 feet thick. The biblical account describes dwellings having to be demolished to make way for the wall, which does run across the ruins of ancient houses.

▶ Burnt House 51B2

Misgave Ladach Street

Admission: inexpensive

This is the basement of a grand private dwelling of the 1st century AD, burned down during the Roman destruction of Jerusalem. Inscriptions inside suggest it was the home of Kathros, a high priest mentioned in the Talmud. An audiovisual on the house and its historical background is shown in the midst of the excavations every 30 minutes.

EXILE'S LAMENT

"By the waters of Babylon
we sat down and wept
When we remembered
thee, O Zion...
If I forget thee,
O Jerusalem, let my right
hand forget her cunning!
If I do not remember thee,
let my tongue cleave to the
roof of my mouth;
yea if I prefer not
Jerusalem in my mouth."
—from "The Babylonian
Exile" (Psalm 137)

Discover Roman Jerusalem in the Burnt House

Souvenirs galore in the Cardo district

OPENING TIMES
Israel shuts down for Shabbat—the Jewish Sabbath, which lasts from Friday sunset to Saturday sunset. Most of the city's sights, museums, shops and attractions are open at the following times:
Sunday to Thursday: 8:30 or 9 AM to 5:30 or 6 PM.
Friday: early closing, usually 1 PM.
Saturday: closed all day.
Exceptions are shown in the text for each entry.

JORDANIAN OCCUPATION
On the Cardo, the One Last Day Museum records details of the events and consequences of May 28, 1948, the day when the Jewish quarter fell into the hands of the Jordanians.

►► The Cardo *51B2*

Off the Street of the Chain, and beside Jewish Quarter Street, can be seen one of the most remarkable archeological accomplishments in Jerusalem, the uncovered 650-foot length of the city's Roman and Byzantine main street. Much of it lies about 20 feet below present-day ground level. Steps lead down to the Byzantine paving, and signs give information about the street. Take a look at the 6th-century mosaic **Madaba Map**, taken from a church in Jordan, which shows the street plan of Jerusalem at that time. From it, much can be learned about the Cardo. A fine arcaded avenue lined with 16-foot-high columns (supporting the roof), the original thoroughfare was more than 65 feet wide and handsomely paved. The Crusaders tried to revive the Cardo, restored part of it, and lined it with vaulted **traders' and craftsmen's shops**. Almost as impressive is the modern attempt, partially successful, to revive the Crusader section of the street by turning it into an arty, stylish shopping area.

A new city After the crushing of the First Jewish Revolt in AD 70, most of Jerusalem was destroyed by the Romans, the population driven out, and their houses demolished. With the defeat of the Second Jewish Revolt, in AD 135, old Jerusalem was razed and the Romans began constructing a completely new city on the site—Aelia Capitolina. The street plan of today originates from that new Roman city.

The main street The main street of Aelia Capitolina was Cardo Maximus. It ran due south from today's Damascus Gate, along the course of what is now Souk Khan ez-Zeit, as far as David Street. After Emperor Constantine legalized Christianity in AD 313, churches sprang up and Christians flocked into the town. It was the start of the Byzantine period. The Holy Sepulcher was built and the town grew and flourished. In the 6th century, the Cardo, its lively central promenade, was extended southward along what is now Jewish Quarter Street. It is that section of the Cardo that can be seen today.

► Cathedral of St. James *51A2*

St. James Street
Open: for services only (around 3 PM daily)
Part of a complex of ecclesiastical and theological buildings at the heart of the Armenian quarter, this 12th-century Crusader-era cathedral has an elaborate interior, heavy with ornament. Note especially the carvings and

painted tiles. It honors both the disciple James, stoned to death, whose body is beneath the altar, and the beheaded James the Apostle, whose head is in a side chapel.

▶ Church of the Holy Sepulcher

See pages 60–62.

▶ Church of the Redeemer *51B2*

Muristan Road.
Closed Sun, Mon PM

This handsome Lutheran church, just outside the Church of the Holy Sepulcher, is all in bare pale stone and almost entirely without adornment, inside or out. There is an excellent view from the top of the tall tower. The ground on which it stands was presented as a gift to Charlemagne by Caliph Haroun el-Rashid. It remained in the hands of Western religious orders until 1868, when Crown Prince Frederic Wilhelm of Prussia made an official visit to Jerusalem. The Ottomans, with debatable legality, gave him this land and he ordered the building of this church, which was consecrated in 1898.

▶ Church of St. Anne *51C3*

Via Dolorosa

Near Lions' Gate, inside a courtyard, this Crusader-era church, with its shallow dome and triangular apse, is striking for its stark dignity. It is said to stand on the site of the home of the Virgin Mary's parents, St. Anne and St. Joachim. A chapel beneath purports to be Mary's birthplace. The adjacent **Pool of Bethesda** is described in the Gospels (see side panel).

▶ Church of St. John *51B2*

Muristan Road

An 11th-century Greek Orthodox church standing on 5th-century Byzantine ruins (which now form the crypt), this intriguing old building incorporates some Roman masonry in the facade.

CURING ON THE SABBATH

In Roman times the Pool of Bethesda was believed to have restorative powers. Here, according to the Gospels (John 5:1–18), Jesus healed a man on the Sabbath simply by saying "Take up thy bed and walk." For this, he incurred the wrath of "the Jews," as the Gospel writer puts it (John often uses this term, creating an impression that only the villains of his tale were Jews, yet Jesus and the sick man were also Jews). The Gospel appears to suggest that "the Jews" objected to Jesus healing on the Sabbath. In fact, Jewish law permits medical treatment on the Sabbath. It does not, however, permit carrying, considered a serious breach in those days. The objection was that Jesus had told the man to carry his bed.

Sphinx-shaped handle (above) and palm-shaded cloister (left) in the Church of the Redeemer

DIFFERENCES OF OPINION
The Church of the Holy Sepulcher and its relics are officially recognized by the Catholic and Orthodox churches. The Protestant churches do not all acknowledge the veracity of the sites, some preferring the Garden Tomb, north of the city walls in East Jerusalem. Nonconformist churches take the same view as the early Christians, that revering such sites is a departure from Christ's teaching and tantamount to paganism.

ONE MAN'S VIEW
"When one stands where the Savior was crucified, he finds it all he can do to keep it strictly before his mind that Christ was not crucified in a Catholic Church. He must remind himself that the great event transpired in the open air, and not in a gloomy candle-lighted cell, upstairs, all bejeweled and bespangled with flashy ornamentation, in execrable taste."
—Mark Twain, on the Church of the Holy Sepulcher, in *The Innocents Abroad* (1869)

Right and below: focus of Christian devotion, the Holy Sepulcher Church is believed to contain Christ's tomb

▶▶▶ Church of the Holy Sepulcher 51B3

Souk ed-Dabagha and Christian Quarter Road
Open: summer, daily 5 AM–8 PM; winter, daily 4 AM–7 PM
This striking edifice, an Old City landmark, the larger of its two domes topped by a gilded cross, is physically and spiritually the heart of the Christian quarter. It has been revered and fought over for centuries. The church is approached across a paved courtyard, and entry is through a large arched doorway trimmed by a narrow facade of pale Jerusalem stone. This complex of shrines, tombs, relics, and churches is all contained under a single roof, and there is even an Ethiopian monastery on the roof. According to the mother of Constantine, the 4th-century Empress Helena, Christ was crucified, laid in his tomb, and resurrected here.

Within the building—main sights To follow the last of the Stations of the Cross marking Jesus's route to his Crucifixion (see pages 76–77), you can, immediately upon entering the dark, labyrinthine interior, turn right onto a short staircase. This leads up 16 feet to the top of a rock reputed to be the summit of Golgotha (Calvary). Here you will find the highly ornate chapels, decorated with mosaics, dedicated to the **Nailing to the Cross** (Station X, at the door—*Jesus Stripped;* Station XI, at the altar—*Jesus Nailed to the Cross*) and the **Crucifixion** (Station XII—*The Cross Is Raised and Jesus Dies*). In the latter is a life-size model of Christ and (behind glass) a slab of rock that is claimed to be the very one on which the cross stood. Between the two chapels is a statue of the Virgin Mary (Station XIII—*Jesus Removed from the Cross*).

Descend the stairs from the second chapel to the **Stone of Unction**, a red slab said to mark the spot where Jesus's body was anointed prior to entombment. Behind this stone (under Golgotha) is the atmospheric **Chapel of Adam**. This chapel houses a skull found during 12th-century excavations and, rather unscientifically, immediately declared to be the skull of Adam. Tombs of two Crusader kings that used to lie here were subsequently destroyed by Greek monks.

To the left of the Stone of Unction, you enter the extravagantly ornate **Rotunda**, probably the only part of the present church resembling Empress Helena's original. At the center is the **Holy Sepulcher** (Station XIV—*Jesus Is Entombed and Returns to Life*). Enter the low doorway into the narrow marble-clad burial chamber, along the side of a marble slab, the place where the body of Jesus is claimed to have lain. Also within the Rotunda, the **Jacobite Chapel** has its own bare and unclad rock-cut tomb. This tomb is said to be that of Joseph of Arimathaea. North and east of the Rotunda are chapels dedicated to events—some biblical, others entirely legendary—associated with the death and resurrection of Christ, including the **Prison of Christ**.

BUILDING REPAIRS
The ownership of the Church of the Holy Sepulcher is divided among six Christian denominations, each with responsibility for its own shrines and areas of the building. They are the Roman Catholics, the Greek Orthodox, and the Armenian, Syrian, Coptic, and Abyssinian churches. Over the years disputes between the factions were so fierce that maintenance of the building could not be carried out. After discussions that lasted from 1927 to 1959, the factions finally agreed to have some building work done at the church. This remains incomplete owing to further disagreements.

Pull of emotions Reactions to this astonishing church vary across the entire spectrum of human emotion. Awe and reverence it certainly does inspire in the most pious. You may even see pilgrims entering on their knees or weeping in their fervor. For others, there is disappointment and disbelief, even despair. Some have come with unreasonable expectations. This is, after all, just a building, standing on ordinary ground. Sometimes, though, the expectation that has been dashed is simply that this would be a splendid edifice, worthy of its sanctity, and that the sites within it would at least seem credible. Instead visitors find a chaotic, confusing structure containing a jumble of implausible holy places and relics. People may be shocked by the uncouth, unseemly behavior of the custodian monks, of a variety of sects, permanently in dispute with one another. To some visitors, and to the dismay of others, the church inspires overt ridicule and disrespect. In addition, there are plenty of tourists who wander in aimlessly without respecting its deserved sanctity.

Sacristy lamp, lit as a sign of the presence of the living Christ

History Empress Helena, mother of Emperor Constantine, ordered the building of the original church in AD 326. It was completed in 335, but destroyed by the Persians in 614. When Emperor Heraclius took Jerusalem again for the

Faithful pilgrim

A VISITOR WITH FAITH
"Tradition could not err in the identity of so famous a spot, and the smallest scepticism would deprive it of all its powerful charm." —John Carne, on the Church of the Holy Sepulcher, in *Letters from the East* (1830)

Handsome buildings of golden stone

Byzantines about 15 years later, the church was rebuilt. The Persians returned Christ's Crucifix, which they had removed. However, in 1009, Caliph el-Hakim demolished the whole church and the Crucifix. In 1048, another smaller church was built on the site by the Byzantine emperor, Constantine IX. The Crusaders enlarged the church in 1149. After an earthquake in 1927, discussions began between the part-owners of the church about renovations. These didn't start until 1959, and have continued intermittently ever since.

Authenticity Most of the sites associated with Christ's early years and ministry are legendary and mythical. But the hill on which he was executed was, and remained, visible for all to see. In AD 70, Jerusalem was destroyed, but in AD 135, when Hadrian built Aelia Capitolina upon its ruins the place of the Crucifixion was so well known that the emperor erected a temple to Venus on the site, to discourage Christian worship.

Constantine the Great legalized Christianity in 313, at the instigation of his convert mother, Helena. In 326 she was taken by Jerusalem's Bishop Macarius to Golgotha. Hadrian's shrine to Venus still stood here, outside the city walls and on the site of a former quarry, exactly as described in the Gospels. In the base of the hill were caverns dug out of rock, one of which Helena declared was the sepulcher of Jesus. In fact, we know from the Gospels that the tomb in which Jesus lay was that of Joseph, "a rich man of Arimathaea" (Matthew 27:57) and that it was a new one, set in a garden (John 19:41). As a rich and pious man, Joseph is not likely to have made his tomb beside a place of public execution. The preferred burial places were on the Mount of Olives, or a little north of the city. However, his tomb was also described as "hewn out of the rock" (Matthew 27:60 and Mark 15:46) and "nigh at hand" (John 19:42).

Nearby, Helena was shown some old wooden crucifixes in an abandoned cistern. Having selected one of these as the cross upon which Christ had died, she ordered it erected on the top of Golgotha, and a church built over the whole site. In the construction, much of the hill was removed. Other holy sites in the church, such as the Stone of Unction and the place where Adam's skull is buried, have no biblical or historical foundation.

Four beautiful little synagogues, the city's center of Sephardi worship since the 16th century

►►► Citadel 51A2

See History of Jerusalem Museum, pages 66–67.

►►► Dome of the Rock and Al-Aqsa Mosque 51C3

See Temple Mount, pages 72–73.

►► Four Sephardic Synagogues 51B2

Off Beit El Street
Open: Sun–Mon and Wed–Thu 9:30–4, Tue and Fri 9:30–12:30. Admission: inexpensive

At the end of a little alley in the heart of the Jewish quarter, these four small connecting synagogues are gems. They are delightfully set together within a courtyard enclosed behind a beautifully carved door and decorated archway. With the closing of the Ramban Synagogue in 1588, the Sephardim made their center here for 300 years.

The oldest of the four synagogues is the Kahal Kadosh Talmud Torah, which became the Eliahu HaNavi Synagogue in 1588—supposedly, according to an appealing legend, because Elijah (Eliahu) appeared during a High Holy Days service to make up a *minyan* (10 men, the minimum worshippers required for a service). Ever since, a chair has been reserved for his next appearance, in a room at the back.

The age of the Kahal Kadosh Gadol, or Rabbi Yohanan ben Zakkai Synagogue, is undetermined but it certainly dates to before 1615, and could be much earlier. Indeed, this may be the oldest of the four. The Middle Synagogue, opened about 1750, was previously the site of a women's courtyard attached to the Yohanan ben Zakkai. The Istambuli Synagogue, of 1764, was erected by refugees from Turkey.

During the 1948 War of Independence, 800 Jewish residents of the Old City hid here for 14 days. Taken by the Jordanians, the synagogues were partially destroyed and looted. After the recapture of the area by Israel, they were painstakingly reconstructed, and were rededicated in 1972. Since then, the synagogues have been in regular use by residents of the Old City, though no longer just by Sephardi Jews.

CITY OF SYNAGOGUES
During and after the Jordanian capture of the Jewish quarter in May 1948, a total of 58 synagogues were destroyed or badly damaged—almost the whole number of synagogues in the city at the time. Although many of the ruins have been preserved or partly restored since 1967, few have been as completely reconstructed as the four Sephardic synagogues. However, there are now 450 synagogues in Jerusalem, most of them outside the Old City walls.

The Jews of modern Israel have come from 80 countries. But the population is mainly divided into two major groups: the Ashkenazim, whose background is in Christian Northern Europe, and the Sephardim, whose culture evolved in the Islamic Mediterranean. Other Israelis include the Mizrahim of Eastern origin, the Ethiopians, the Cochin Jews of India, and others.

THE LANGUAGE OF THE JEWS
A century ago almost no one spoke Hebrew. Yiddish, based on medieval German mixed with Hebrew, was the everyday language of Ashkenazi Jews. Hitler's "Final Solution" decimated the Yiddish-speaking world—its culture, its people, and their language. Those who fled to America and the British Commonwealth became fluent in English, which now stands alongside Hebrew as a new language for the Jews. Many Sephardi Jews, especially the elderly, speak Ladino, a mix of old Spanish, Arabic, and Hebrew created in the Middle Ages.

Top: skull caps
Below: Hasidic sidelocks
Right: young Crusaders

The cross and the swastika Modern Israel's Ashkenazim did not all come here from Eastern Europe—though their parents or grandparents probably did. They probably were born in Israel, England, or America. Their culture absorbed violent antisemitism, as well as the Enlightenment, the French Revolution, the rise of secularism and socialism—and Zionism.

Ashkenaz is a biblical place name that came to mean Germany. As far back as Roman times, Jews settled along the Rhine Valley and from there spread across Germany. The Crusades forced them east into Poland and Russia. For centuries, Eastern Europe was the focal point of Jewish culture and religion. In Russia, there were thousands of *shtetls*—Jewish towns and villages—within the Pale of Settlement (the permitted area of Jewish settlement under the czars). Millions of people lived in the Jewish ghettos of the larger cities. Russian pogroms in the 1880s caused an exodus to Palestine, the United States, and the British Commonwealth. The rise of the Nazis in the 1930s caused another rush to escape. Six million or more of the Ashkenazim who remained behind died in the Holocaust. A culture and a language died with them, and Eastern Europe was almost entirely emptied of Jews.

Under the crescent Some visitors assume that Sephardim are Arabs, something to which the Sephardim would not take kindly. Most are refugees from Arab countries. The Sephardim, after a long medieval Golden Age

during the Arab occupation of Spain, remained only slightly affected by Europe's intellectual developments, until they arrived in Israel in the late 15th century. A more cohesive, traditional society, the Sephardim brought to Israel a resistance to secularism, allied to a more easy-going and accepting approach to Jewish traditions. They have also given Israel its best food. They remain largely on the lower rungs of society, but that is changing.

Sefarad means Spain, a place where Jews lived since biblical times, and where the Sephardi culture evolved during 680 years of Muslim domination (711–1391). When Christians completed the conquest of Spain, in 1492, all Jews were forced to renounce their religion or face expulsion. Most Jews followed the Muslims to North Africa and to other areas of the Mediterranean, such as Turkey, Greece, the Balkans, and Palestine. Under Islam, Jews suffered discrimination but rarely outright persecution. They lived in their own districts, with the official status of *dhimmis* (second-class citizens). Persecution increased in the 20th century, however, and when the State of Israel was created, most were forced from their homes.

Jews with other background Most other Israelis fall into one of two conspicuous groups, both of which arrived en masse in big rescue operations. Mizrahim (though they are also called Sephardim) come from Muslim countries, farther to the east, often from the Yemen. They have brought ancient tradition, ethnic color, and superb oriental cuisine. The black Jews of Ethiopia (no longer called "Falashas," or strangers, a hated name in Ethiopia) add yet another dimension to Israel's extraordinary cultural and ethnic diversity.

Children of Israel Half the population of Israel was born in the country, and one-third of its children now have mixed Ashkenazi/Sephardi parentage. The effect has been dramatic in creating a new culture. It is also remarkable how alike Ashkenazi and Sephardi children have become in appearance, mannerisms, and outlook after growing up in the sunshine of Israel. Without the pressures of being a minority population, and after going through school in Hebrew and doing army service together, they emerge as young adults, neither Ashkenazi nor Sephardi, but truly Israeli.

ASHKENAZIM DOMINANT
Modern Israel was created by Ashkenazim. They dominate government and institutions in Israel, and have been credited with giving the country its idealism, secularism, democracy, and know-how, but also its red tape and bureaucracy. However, their role has given way to the increasing influence and numbers of the Sephardim—Jews of the Mediterranean, whose cultural roots pass through the Islamic world.

WORLD POPULATIONS
In 1933, there were 16.5 million Jews in the world, 90 percent of them in Eastern Europe. Of today's 12 million Jews, only 2 million now live in Europe, over 4 million live in Israel and 6 million in the U.S.A.

Happier here than in Ethiopia

BRITISH RULE IN PALESTINE
In December 1917, an emotional General Allenby entered Jaffa Gate on foot and walked to the eastern steps of the Citadel (today's main entrance). Standing on the steps he read his Proclamation to the People of Jerusalem formally announcing the start of British rule in Palestine.

The Tower of David bears the name of Jerusalem's founder

►►► History of Jerusalem Museum (Citadel, or Tower of David) *51A2*

Beside Jaffa Gate (tel: 02-6265310)
Open: see panel opposite. Admission: expensive

The History of Jerusalem Museum is housed in the city's ancient Citadel. Four possible quick itineraries through the museum are indicated at the entrance: the Exhibit Route (2 hours), the Excavation Route (1½ hours), the Observation Route (1 hour), and the Short Route (40 minutes). The entrance charge for the museum includes a 1½-hour guided tour (in English) each morning at 11 AM. The museum and tour provide a uniquely informative, entertaining, and accessible overview of Jerusalem and its history.

Herod's Citadel One of the most imposing and evocative landmarks of the Old City is the high, slender Tower of David, rising from within the massive defenses of the superb medieval fortress known as the Citadel. This stands alongside the powerful stonework of Jaffa Gate. Despite the name, nothing but myth connects this magnificent structure with King David, the city's founder. The Citadel, standing on the Old City's highest point, was in fact constructed much later, by King Herod in the 1st century BC. Archeological exploration points to the presence of major fortified structures here as early as the First Temple period (950–538 BC). Herod's fortress was even more imposing than today's mainly medieval building. His fortress had three monumental square towers, one more than 130 feet high, named after his brother, his close friend, and his wife—Phasael, Hippicus, and Miriam.

Through the centuries After crushing the Second Jewish Revolt (AD 132–135), the Romans ordered Jerusalem be razed to the ground. Only the Citadel and its tallest tower, Phasael's (the bulky square tower, beside Jaffa Gate), were left standing. Roman troops were stationed inside the fort. In later centuries, it served as a garrison for Arabs (who built a smaller—now ruined—fortress within the Citadel), Crusaders, Mamelukes, and Ottomans. It was the ferocious Mamelukes who, in 1310, restored the Citadel and rebuilt the walls that stand today. Under the Ottomans, it was similarly reconstructed in 1610, and it was they who erected a mosque within the fortress. This slender stone minaret became known romantically to many a 19th-century visitor as the Tower of David.

In 1917, under British rule, the fortress retained a nominal military function. For the most part, it has been transformed into a cultural and historical site, with performances and exhibitions. It has maintained this meaningful use.

On the roof From the flat roof of the Phasael Tower, restored in 1987, there is an impressive panorama over the Old City. The dominant position of Temple Mount, a huge lofty plateau elevated above the town's warren of crowded alleys and streets, gives a powerful impression of its importance in Temple times. Today, the beautiful blue-walled and gold-crowned Dome of the Rock occupies the site. From the elevated point, the building can be appreciated in all its glory. The Mount of Olives rises magnificently behind. Within the city, a surprising number of buildings have black and white stripes, a Mameluke style. The astonishing number of fine churches testifies to centuries of Christian devotion in Jerusalem.

Inside the museum The Citadel's ancient halls, rooms, cellars, and outdoor terraces today house a superb and extensive museum of Jerusalem's history. The structure forms a five-sided enclosure around a large central open-air archeological site. Using films, maps, attention-grabbing pictures, dioramas, holograms, life-size fiberglass statuary, superbly detailed models, and numerous other types of displays, as well as thousands of the historic objects found here, the museum leads room by room, age by age, through the long and intricate Jerusalem story, allowing even the most casual visitor to grasp something of its scale and scope. The final stages are presented with genuine film footage and modern artifacts.

As it was: Stefan Illes's 1872 model of the Old City

TOWER OF DAVID/ HISTORY OF JERUSALEM MUSEUM OPENING HOURS AND EVENTS:
Open: summer, Sun–Thu 9–4, Fri–Sat and day before public holidays 9–2; winter, Sun–Thu 10–5, Fri–Sat and day before public holidays 10–2. *Closed:* Yom Kippur (late Sep or early Oct).
On summer evenings an entertaining son et lumière is put on in the Citadel courtyard. Under the stars in the dramatic setting of the fortress, it tells the story of the city and its citadel. Shows in English take place at 9:30 PM on Monday and Wednesday, and on Saturday at 10:30 PM.

CITY CENTER
In Jewish prayer, the name "Jerusalem" is still synonymous with the Temple, the vast gilded palace of sacrifice and worship that dominated the life of the city for over 1,000 years (950 BC to 70 AD). Even though the Temple has been destroyed, it remains the theoretical center of Judaism: at morning services in synagogues throughout the world, sacrifice instructions used in the Temple are read aloud as part of the prayers.

JERUSALEM REDEEMED
"Break forth into joy, sing together, ye waste places of Jerusalem: for the Lord hath comforted his people, he hath redeemed Jerusalem."
—Isaiah 52:9

▶▶ Hurva Square 51B2

This pleasant, paved plaza lies at the heart of today's Jewish quarter. A calm, peaceful atmosphere prevails, with children playing and parents quietly chatting. The square is surrounded by interesting historical sights: on one side soars the memorial arch over the **Ramban Synagogue** and the ruined **Hurva Synagogue** (see below); on the opposite side, the square is overlooked by the attractive **Wohl Archaeological Museum▶▶** (see page 80). Several streets lead off, including HaKaraim Street, named for the Karaites. **Anan ben-David Synagogue** (built 1400) was damaged and looted during the Jordanian occupation, but has been repaired and rededicated. Facing it are handsome remnants of the **Tefillat Israel Synagogue**, a 19th-century edifice and former Old City landmark that was destroyed in 1948.

▶▶ Hurva Synagogue 51B2

Hurva Square
During the 19th century, this was the principal synagogue in Jerusalem. Its ruins can be reached by descending steep steps from the roof terrace of the Ramban Synagogue in

Relics of Hurva Synagogue's former glory

front. Construction began in the early 18th century on Crusader ruins, but the building remained incomplete and fell into disrepair—hence *hurva*, or ruin. In 1856 the Jewish community received permission to complete the building. The result was, by all accounts, splendid, but it was destroyed in 1948. In 1977, sensitive restoration work preserved the ruins while making the site delightful, with a paved marble floor, walls of massive stone blocks, and arched windows. The blue sky makes a lovely roof. A delicate high arch symbolizes its former grandeur. Diagrams and pictures show what a fine structure the Hurva once was.

▶ Israelite Tower *51B2*

Plugat HaKotel Street
Admission: inexpensive
This remnant of a tower of the First Temple period was once part of the city walls. Inside is a small museum. Beside it stand remains of another tower, dating from the 2nd century BC.

▶ Old Yishuv Court Museum *51B2*

6 Or HaHaim Street
Open: Sun–Thu 9–2. Admission: inexpensive
Yishuv refers to the Jewish community living in Palestine before the creation of the modern State of Israel. When Jordan invaded the Old City in 1948, Rivka Weingarten had the foresight to gather together all kinds of objects that would give an impression of life in the Jewish quarter. Subsequently returning to restore her home, a courtyard with simple family dwellings built around it, she created a museum. Each room has a particular theme, illustrating the trades, the crafts, and the different lifestyles of Sephardim and Ashkenazim.

▶ Rachel Yanait Ben Zvi Center *51B2*

Plugat HaKotel Street
Open: Sun–Thu. Admission: moderate
This educational and research center has a museum and a permanent exhibition on Jerusalem in the First Temple period (950–538 BC). There's a model of the city as it was at that time.

▶ Ramban Synagogue *51B2*

Hurva Square
Open: for prayers only, 2 or 3 times daily
Alongside Hurva Square, and beneath the slender Hurva Arch, can be found this attractive little synagogue. Probably the oldest in Jerusalem, it was founded in 1267 by Ramban, the respected medieval Rabbi Moshe ben Nahman, also known as Nahmanides (see panel). It was built on top of Crusader-era ruins. The city's Muslims destroyed the building in 1474, but it was rebuilt to became Jerusalem's main synagogue. Muslim opposition to its presence continued. A mosque was built alongside (there is still one there today) and, in 1588, Jewish prayer was prohibited in the area. Abandoned, the synagogue became a workshop, remaining so until 1967. It was then fully restored and rededicated as a synagogue. The building has a roof terrace with a view directly onto the Hurva Synagogue ruins (see opposite).

NAHMANIDES
Rabbi Moshe ben Nahman, better known as Nahmanides or Ramban, was born in 1194 in Spain, and is acknowledged as one of the greatest Talmudic scholars of his era. Like Maimonides (see page 204), who died when Nahmanides was 10 years old, he wished to simplify and interpret the scriptures and formalize a Jewish "creed" to stand against those of Christianity and Islam. As Rabbi of Gerona, he took part in a public debate (almost a trial) with a noted Jewish convert to Christianity, Pablo Christiani, in the presence of King James I of Aragon at Barcelona in 1263. Accused of blasphemy during the debate, Nahmanides had to flee from Spain, making his way to Jerusalem, where he founded the Ramban Synagogue before meeting his death in about 1270.

HOLY ROCK AND WAILING WALL
"Until 688 AD Jews met yearly, to mourn over and anoint the 'Stone of Foundation,' on which the Holy of Holies once was raised, and which is now covered by the old Arab Dome of the Rock which was erected in 688 AD. In later times they were only able to wail at the outer wall of Herod's great temple enclosure, and they have continued to do so down to our own times."
Palestine Exploration Fund Lectures, 1892

"And it came to pass in the four hundred and eightieth year after the children of Israel were come out of the land of Egypt, in the fourth year of Solomon's reign over Israel, in the month Zif, ... that he began to build the house of the Lord" (I Kings 6:1). Though the Temple has gone, it remains at the very heart of Judaism.

GOD AS A CLOUD
According to II Chronicles 6:13–14, when Solomon's Temple was complete it was dedicated by placing the Ark in the Holy of Holies. During the ceremony, hundreds of men in white linen played trumpets, cymbals, and other instruments. As they did this a cloud filled the building "so that the priests could not stand to minister by reason of the cloud: for the glory of God had filled the house of God."

Top: Holyland Hotel's model of the Second Temple
Below: the building of the Temple

The center of a nation The First Temple was completed in 950 BC, the 11th year of his reign, by King Solomon, son of King David, the Israelite ruler who took Jerusalem from the Jebusites and proclaimed it the capital of Israel. In Solomon's Temple was placed the Ark of the Covenant —the gold-encrusted chest containing Moses' Tablets of the Law—and other sacred objects that the Jews had carried with them in their exile. The Temple became the focal point for the Jewish people, and, wherever they lived, adult males were obliged to come to it for three annual festivals: Pesach (Passover), Sukkot (Tabernacles), and Shavuot (Weeks or Pentecost). Destroyed in 586 BC by Nebuchadnezzar, it was rebuilt as the Second Temple between 538 and 515 BC, being enlarged and aggrandized on several occasions afterward, especially under King Herod in the decades before his death in 4 BC. After the First Jewish Revolt, this Second Temple was reduced to rubble by the Romans in AD 70. Jerusalem's most spectacular landmark, the Dome of the Rock, a Muslim holy place, now occupies the site. Part of the Temple Mount outer wall survives as the Western Wall, the holiest place of prayer for Jews.

History and myth Tradition has it that Mount Moriah was the place where Abraham bound Isaac and prepared to sacrifice him (Genesis 22:2–14; Sura 37, Koran), though there is no mention of this event in II Samuel 24:16–25, describing David's purchase of the threshing floor on which the Temple would stand, nor in II Chronicles 3:1, describing the Temple's construction. In 167 BC, the Maccabees drove the Syrians out of Israel and had to rededicate the Temple: the festival of Hanukkah commemorates their victory and the miracle of a single day's lamp oil being sufficient to light the Temple menorah (candelabrum) for eight days, as required for the rededication. The Temple is featured several times in the life of Jesus: when he remained for three days in learned discussion with the elders at the age of 12 (Luke 2:46); when he overturned the money changers' tables (Matthew 21:12), and when he predicted the Temple's total destruction (Matthew 24:2). Finally, it was mentioned when the Temple veil was torn in two at the moment of Christ's death (Matthew 27:51).

Lamentation and longing The destruction of both the First and the Second Temple is commemorated on the ninth day of the Hebrew month of Av. By coincidence, the

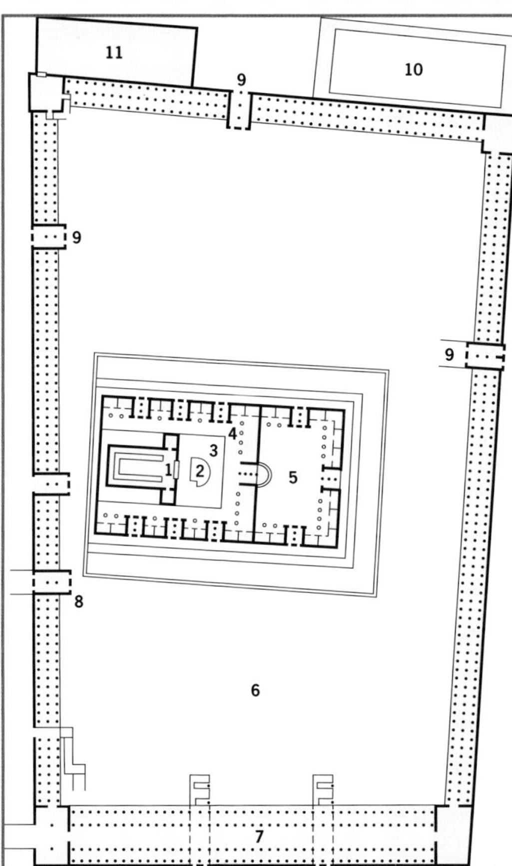

**THE SECOND TEMPLE—
KEY TO PLAN**

1 Temple
2 Altar
3 Court of Priests
4 Court of Israel
5 Court of Women
6 Court of the Gentiles
7 Royal Portico
8 Bridge and gate
9 Gate
10 Pool of Isra' il
11 Antonia

Jews were expelled from Spain on the same day. When the Arabs conquered Jerusalem, they allowed Jews to visit Temple Mount for just one day in the year, to mourn their lost Temple. That day, also, was the ninth of Av (Tisha b'Av in Hebrew). Today it is also a day of fasting, of not wearing leather, and for reciting, in a wailing tone, the Book of Lamentations. In later centuries, the Jews were permitted only to come as far as the Western Wall, and only on that day. Thus, the Western Wall became known as the Wailing Wall because of the Jewish practice on that day. This ceremony can still be seen every year, on Tisha b'Av (mid- to late July).

All that now remains: the Western Wall below the Al-Aqsa mosque

The Third Temple Much of today's synagogue service takes the form of a temporary substitute for Temple practice. At every Orthodox service, prayers are said for the rebuilding of the Temple. But many Jews have doubts about the wisdom of this; if it were rebuilt, Temple practices like animal sacrifice would have to be resumed. Some say it can only be rebuilt when the Messiah comes. There are those who wish to begin at once. For others, it will be rebuilt when the time is politically right, which is not just yet. Some Israeli parliamentarians have referred to the State of Israel itself as the Third Temple.

MUSLIM GATES
Non-Muslims may only enter Temple Mount through Bab el-Maghrebeh (the Moors' Gate) and Bab el-Silsileh (the Chain Gate). Both pass into the enclosure on either side of the Western Wall. Muslims may enter or leave by any of the other gateways. The other Temple Mount gates are (on the western side) Bab el-Masatarak, Bab el-Qatanin, Bab el-Hadid, Bab el-Nazir, Bab el-Ghawanima, and (on the northern side) Bab el-Atim, Bab Hitta, and Bab el-Asbat.

►►► Temple Mount (Arabic: Haram esh-Sharif) 51C3

Open: Sat–Thu 8–noon and 1:30–3.
Admission: Temple Mount is free, but mosques require a ticket (expensive) from Temple Mount entrance

The star of the Old City is the glorious Dome of the Rock, on Temple Mount. It is just one of several fine Muslim Islamic constructions within the ancient Temple Mount enclosure, which is entered at the end of Street of the Chain (through the Chain Gate; Bab el-Silsileh in Arabic) or on the ramp from Western Wall Plaza (through the Moors' Gate; Bab el-Maghrebeh in Arabic). Inside, the grand enclosure is partially shaded by trees. Ahead rises the exquisite blue-tiled facade and golden dome of the Dome of the Rock. To either side stand arches and minarets, and two fountains where Muslims wash before prayers.

Claims to holiness Sura 17 of the Koran states: "Glorified be He Who carried His servant by night from the Inviolable Place of Worship to the Far Distant Place of Worship, the neighborhood whereof We have blessed, that We might show him of Our tokens!" Although Muhammad never visited Jerusalem, Muslims came to believe that Temple Mount was "the far distant Place of Worship" referred to. The legend developed that Muhammad traveled on a winged horse with the Angel Gabriel to the Temple Mount. He then ascended through the seven heavens and met God, before awaking back in Mecca.

Gilded magnificence: inside the Dome of the Rock

Principal sights Mosques and museums are closed to non-Muslims during prayer times (five times daily). Before entering, remove your shoes and leave all bags and cameras with the attendant. The **Al-Aqsa Mosque►►►**, considered by most Muslims to be their third holiest shrine (after Mecca and Medina), was extensively restored in 1948. Jerusalem's main place of Islamic prayer is sumptuous with marble columns, fine carpets, stained-glass windows, and an impressive gilded wooden ceiling. Adjacent is the **Islamic Museum►** containing a collection of artifacts from several mosques.

The Dome of the Rock►►► (Arabic: Qubbet el-Sakhra) is an awesomely beautiful, symmetrical, octagonal structure of blue tiles topped by a gleaming dome of gold. The building is reached by broad flights of steps on each side, over which are triple arches built by the Crusaders.

Inside, the combination of elegantly simple design, finely carved wood and marble, and intricate decoration is thrilling. The air is evocatively filled with echoing prayer and music and soothing light filtered through stained-glass windows. Exquisite mosaic covers the interior of the dome. The huge black stone beneath the dome,

Burnished bronze and azure blue

the impressive rock for which it is named, has an indentation that Muslims believe was made by Muhammad's flying horse as it leapt to the sky.

Smaller, attractive structures within the enclosure include the **Dome of the Chain▶**, the **Dome of the Ascension▶**, and the **Islamic schools▶**. Also inside are the sealed **Golden Gate▶** and the other **gates▶** that lead into the Muslim quarter (see panel opposite).

History and politics Having destroyed the Temple, the Romans erected their own temple on the site. In the 6th century this was replaced by a church. After the Arab conquest in 638, Caliph Omar visited Temple Mount to pray at the black rock. It is said that here Abraham laid his son Isaac for sacrifice. The present Dome of the Rock was built under Omayyad rule in 691. The church was converted into the Al-Aqsa mosque in 715.

Crusaders took Jerusalem in 1000 and made Al-Aqsa into a residence that became the headquarters of the Knights Templar (who took their name from the site). The Templars renamed Al-Aqsa the Temple of Solomon. The Dome of the Rock became known as the Temple of the Lord. The sites were taken by Islam in 1187, and the Mamelukes built new structures there.

Following the 1948 war, Arab states took great interest in Temple Mount, and the Dome of the Rock was restored jointly by Jordan, Egypt, and Saudi Arabia. After reconquering Jerusalem in 1967, the Israelis allowed Temple Mount to remain under Islamic administration. Since that time, the legend of Muhammad's night journey has led the Arab world to lay claim not just to Temple Mount, but to the whole city of Jerusalem. This creates yet more friction between the Jewish and Arab communities.

NIGHT RIDE

In real life, Muhammad did not visit Haram esh-Sharif (Temple Mount), and the Koran's reference to his "being carried by night" makes no mention of angels, or flying horses, or of leaping to heaven. The importance of the legend lies in its metaphorical meaning: that Muhammad, as the last of the prophets, with a mission to take the word and laws of God (or Allah) to the entire world, had taken over Judaism and replaced it. Judaism at the time had suffered dispersion and defeat. It was almost logical for Muslims to view the sanctity of the Jewish holy site as subsumed into the newer, conquering sanctity of the Prophet.

Contemplation

Israel's population of 5.9 million includes nearly one million Arabs. Arabic is one of Israel's two official languages. Arabs have full citizenship, send their children to Arab-speaking state schools, and elect Arab members of parliament (who address the Knesset in Arabic).

THE POPULATION OF ISRAEL:
80.0 percent Jewish
14.9 percent Muslim
2.1 percent Christian
1.6 percent Druze
1.4 percent others

Gentile populations The Israelite conquest of Canaan was never total and—despite a biblical injunction—the non-Jews (Gentiles) were not wiped out. Numerous biblical references show that the land of the Jews always had its minority of Gentiles. Big population changes followed each subsequent conquest. It was Roman policy to dilute difficult peoples. After the Jewish Revolts of AD 70 and 135, non-Jewish settlers were brought into the area around Jerusalem and the coastal towns. Subsequently, the legalization of Christianity encouraged its followers in the Near East to move to the Holy Land.

New religion, new empire In 630 Muhammad and his followers forcibly converted Mecca to the new Islamic religion. Forced conversion (except of Christians and Jews) was part of Islam's creed, and just six years later Muslim forces swept up the Arabian Peninsula and into Palestine. Some settled, and the non-Jews of Israel were converted by the sword. By the middle of the 8th century a vast region—extending from Spain, across North Africa and the entire Middle East to the Indus valley—had been brought under Islam's yoke. The whole empire was ruled from Mecca by the Umayyad dynasty. The administration of Palestine was centered on Damascus, in Syria. People then moved freely over the border, and Israel's Arabs still speak the Syrian dialect.

A Muslim Israel The defeat of the Umayyads by the Abbasids meant a transfer of power from Damascus to distant Baghdad. Apart from the brief Crusader kingdom, Israel was to remain under Muslim rule for many centuries—under the Egyptians, Persians, Mamelukes, and, for 400 years, as part of the Ottoman Empire. Each ruler brought changes, to the cost of Palestine. When the British took over in 1917, the land was largely uncultivated, with inadequate water and extensive areas of desert, rock, dunes, and swamp. The population stood well under one million.

Face of Palestine, citizen of Israel

The fight against Zionism British rule was benign, created work, and improved the country. Arab workers drifted in from surrounding lands to take advantage. From the 1880s onward, Jews also flocked to Palestine, but for a different reason. By 1936, the population of Palestine had risen to 1,367,000—of whom 384,000 were Jews. The Arabs were uneasy. Jews traditionally held low status in

Muslim society. Muhammad had said that their time was over, their religion supplanted. Yet the Jews were purchasing land, displacing Arab tenants, forming settlements, and draining swamps, all in pursuit of their avowed aim of creating a Jewish state. During the 1920s and 1930s, riots and attacks against the newcomers were frequent. When the State of Israel was declared in 1948, the Arab nations joined with the Arabs of Israel to crush the new country. To their surprise, they failed; many then fled across Israel's borders into Gaza and the West Bank, joining those who had left in advance of the war. Jews call this the War of Independence. Arabs call it the Catastrophe. Some 700,000 Arabs fled, leaving about 200,000 who stayed and became Israeli citizens.

Israeli Arabs Not all Arabs opposed Israel, and in particular not the Christians or the Druze. Many who fought against Israel also stayed. Israel's largest Arab town is Nazareth. Other main centers of Arab population are Jerusalem, Haifa, and Akko, with communities in Ramla, Jaffa, and several small towns in Galilee. At first sight, they appear to have come out on the winning side. Under no Arab regime do citizens have anything like the rights and freedoms of Israelis: all religions and sects enjoy full freedom of worship, and Arabs are exempt from military service (though some, the Druze in particular, have chosen to accept conscription). Yet there is discontent, as Israeli Arabs compare themselves not with the Arabs who fled, but with their Jewish fellow citizens. Undoubtedly there is discrimination against Israeli Arabs—as against non-Jews generally (though most Israelis deplore this). And of course, they will forever be seen as a minority: Gentile citizens in a Jewish land.

IN THE EYE OF THE BEHOLDER

"Palestine, a country scarcely superior to Wales either in fertility or extent."
—Edward Gibbon, *Decline and Fall of the Roman Empire* (1776)

"A bare limestone country of little natural beauty."
—Charles Doughty, *Travels in Arabia Deserta* (1888)

"A good land and a large, flowing with milk and honey."
—Exodus 3:8

Arab schoolchildren in the souk

TO BE A PILGRIM

Pilgrimage was rare during the first 200 years of Christianity. Early Christians did not worship the physical Christ or revere the ground where he had walked. As Christianity moved westward into pagan Europe, it met an increasing tendency to worship places, objects, and relics. Pilgrimages to the Holy Land began in the 4th century, when persecution ceased. Later, Christians began to venerate Christ's mother and an increasing number of saints. The church taught that sinners could be absolved by visiting a holy site, that contact with parts of the bodies of saints and martyrs resulted in miracles. These were eagerly sought when the great era of pilgrimage began in the 10th century.

►►► Via Dolorosa 51B3

The "Sorrowful Road" passes through the Muslim quarter to the Church of the Holy Sepulcher. It is honored as the route taken by Christ as he carried his cross to Golgotha, where he was crucified. Along the way, the Stations of the Cross—the different stages on his journey to death—are marked.

History The idea of the Stations of the Cross arose in the Middle Ages. Popular notions of what had happened to Jesus on the way to Calvary, additional to the Gospel accounts, passed into folklore and church tradition. In response to the demands of pilgrims, sites for the Stations of the Cross were first chosen in the mid-18th century by the Franciscans. In the 19th century, the route of the Via Dolorosa was altered to its present course.

Spiritual journey Most Christian communities take the view that Christ's suffering was spiritual and symbolic as well as physical, and that it is not essential to know the actual route Jesus followed. However, tens of thousands of pilgrims of all denominations walk the Via Dolorosa each year. They believe that, in spirit if not in fact, they are stepping in Christ's footsteps.

The route *I—Condemnation:* the first part of the way is relatively wide and quiet. The First Station is the courtyard of the **Omariye Islamic College (El U'mariya College)►**, which some claim as the site of the Praetorium, where Jesus was sentenced. A minaret has been fancifully named Antonia Tower, after Herod's Antonia Fortress, which once stood here. Historically, it is more likely that Jesus was sentenced at the Citadel. It would have been most unusual for the Temple priests to be involved, as recounted in the Gospels, since the day of his trial was the first day of Passover.

II—Taking up the cross: across the street the ancient paving or **Lithostratos►** in the Franciscan Churches of the Condemnation and the Flagellation is said to be where

Top right: Jesus Meets His Mother (Station IV)
Below: the Via Dolorosa, the Sorrowful Road

Jesus was mocked, crowned with thorns, and given his cross to carry. A stone archway, or buttress, spanning the street here is called **Ecce Homo Arch▶**. Traditionally, it is thought to mark the spot where Pilate said of Jesus: "Behold the man" ("*Ecce homo*"). In fact, the arch was erected in AD 135, as a support for Herod's fortress.

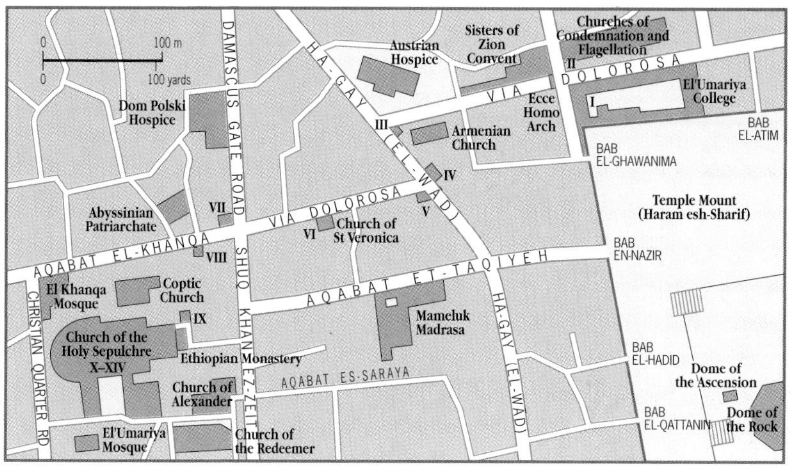

III—Jesus falls: continue to the Austrian Hospice and turn left onto busier El-Wad Street. Here a plaque shows where Jesus fell under the weight of the cross. The route passes Arab shops and tea shops.

IV—Meeting Mary: on the left (opposite a right turn), a shrine marks the place where tradition claims that Jesus saw his mother. Turning right, the street is again called Via Dolorosa.

V—Simon helps Jesus: take the turning, and straight away on the corner is where Simon the Cyrenian is said to have taken the cross from Jesus to help him (see panel right). Narrower and climbing, frequently in steps, the route passes souvenir shops.

VI—Veronica wipes the face of Jesus: a door leads down to **St. Veronica's Church▶▶** in Crusader vaults. The story that a woman named Veronica (the name simply means "true image") wiped the face of Jesus arose in the 7th century. A cloth, said to have belonged to Veronica and marked with the image of a man's face, is kept in Rome.

VII—Jesus falls again: the route reaches a junction in the midst of the crowded shopping streets of the Arab souk (market). Here, believers say, Jesus fell again.

VIII—Speaking to the women: the site (marked by a Latin cross on the wall of a Greek monastery) lies a few paces ahead. Here Jesus urged the women of Jerusalem to weep not for him but for themselves and their children.

IX—Jesus falls again: return to the junction, turn right along the covered Souk Khan ez-Zeit. A right turn leads off the souk to a Roman column at the back of the Holy Sepulcher. Here, the faithful say, Jesus fell for a third time.

X—XIV—Golgotha: return to the souk. Via Dolorosa turns right, passes the Lutheran Church of the Redeemer, and reaches the Holy Sepulcher. The remainder of the Stations are inside the church (see pages 60–61).

VIA DOLOROSA—KEY TO PLAN

I Condemnation
II Taking up the cross
III Jesus falls
IV Meeting Mary
V Simon helps Jesus
VI Veronica wipes the face of Jesus
VII Jesus falls again
VIII Speaking to the women
IX Jesus falls again
X Jesus is stripped
XI Nailed to the cross
XII Jesus dies on the cross
XIII Taken down from the cross
XIV Laid in the tomb

THE WAY OF THE CROSS

"They took the robe off from him, and put his own raiment on him, and led him away to crucify him. And as they came out, they found a man of Cyrene, Simon by name: and him they compelled to bear his cross. And when they had come unto a place called Golgotha, that is to say, a place of a skull, they gave him vinegar to drink mingled with gall: and when he had tasted thereof, he would not drink. And they crucified him."
—Matthew 27:31–35

Temple remnant: the Western Wall

▶▶▶ The Western Wall (also known as the Kotel, HaKotel, Kotel Ma'aravi, or the Wailing Wall) *51C2*

The Western Wall is revered by Jews because it is the last remnant of the only sacred place in the world, the Temple. Two millennia of prayer and tradition have sanctified this link with Temple times, making it the holiest place of prayer in the Jewish world. In addition, its relative proximity to the Holy of Holies (which was at the western end of the Temple) confers an additional claim to reverence. Today, as always, every Jew in prayer, anywhere in the world, faces the Holy of Holies inside the Temple on Temple Mount in Jerusalem—even though it physically no longer exists.

The stonework The Western Wall is the western section of the outer retaining wall of the Temple compound that, until 1900 years ago, entirely covered Mount Moriah, or the Temple Mount. The Wall was not part of the Temple building itself. The Second Temple, completed in 513 BC, was reconstructed by Herod in about 30 BC. The Wall's massive blocks of limestone were put in place. The visible part of the Wall reaches 59 feet in height, while a further 59 feet extends below the present-day ground level.

Visiting the Wall A visit to the Western Wall can be one of the most thought-provoking, interesting, and satisfying experiences in the schedule of Old City sightseeing. After Israel recaptured the Wall in 1967, a vast plaza was created, enabling thousands of people to gather for festivals or special occasions. The exposed length of the Wall has been cordoned into two sections, one for men and the other for women, in keeping with Orthodox practice.

A low barrier a few paces from the Wall keeps sightseers apart from the area reserved for prayer and religious ritual, which is carried out in the open under the gaze of tourists. Any man, Jew or non-Jew, may enter the men's enclosure so long as he is wearing a head covering (even a baseball cap will do), just as any woman may enter the

WESTERN WALL (OR HASMONEAN) TUNNELS
"The Western Wall epitomizes recollections of the Jewish past and the hopes and aspirations of the Jewish future" (sign in Western Wall Tunnels). The tunnel tour starts in the medieval basement from which archeologist Charles Warren set out in 1867 to make the first exploration of the underground remains of the Temple Mount. Additional excavations since 1967 have exposed a 1,470-foot stretch of the Wall (one stone alone weighs 44 tons). You enter the area through a secret passage, come to stairs that date from the time of the Second Temple, and enter a large hall behind Wilson's Arch. A long stroll through a tunnel beside the Wall reveals part of a Herodian street, a quarry, an ancient aqueduct, and a pool. There's also an impressive model of Jerusalem in Second Temple times. The final section emerges onto the Via Dolorosa.

women's section. Most who do, come to recite prayers or simply to take a closer look at the Wall whose gaps are filled with tiny scraps of paper. Inscribed with people's simple wishes, prayers, and blessings, these have been crammed into every cranny by devout souls who believe the Wall is directly scrutinized by God. Good times to visit the Western Wall are Monday and Thursday mornings, when the Torah is read by barmitzvah boys in family ceremonies; Shabbat mornings and all Jewish holidays; and at night, when the Wall is floodlit and the plaza empty.

Beside the Wall Off the men's section (so there is no access for women), the Wall continues into the structures abutting it. These consist of **two rooms▶** beneath the arches that support the Street of the Chain. These are synagogues, with shelves of prayer books and, attached to the Wall, arks containing Torah scrolls that are constantly being taken out and read by groups of men, while crowds of visitors file in to have a look around. The first narrow chamber has a glass-covered opening in the floor providing a view to the lower levels of the Wall. Beyond, in a larger room thought to date from 100 BC, is **Wilson's Arch▶**, the ancient vaulted structure that used to support the original access road to the Second Temple. At the foot of the arch, illuminated openings give a view to the Wall's lower levels.

Off the plaza On the north side of the plaza an entrance leads into the **Western Wall Tunnels▶▶** (Kotel HaIdra). To view these you must sign up for the guided tour (*Book three days ahead; some tours in English. Admission: moderate*) which passes through the underground passages that run along the excavated Wall for several hundred yards. At the western side of the plaza, the **northern passage▶** runs beneath the Street of the Chain, linking the plaza with El Wad (or Hagai) Street. Its roof is composed of an arch of massive stones, dating from the 8th to the 11th centuries. On one side of the floor, openings reveal Roman paving below today's ground level. At the far end, steps climb to the Street of the Chain close to the Temple Mount entrance.

WALL ETIQUETTE

Be prepared for hassle at the Wall. The enclosure is technically a synagogue, so modest dress and behavior are required and on Shabbat it is forbidden to eat or smoke there, or take photographs. Begging is also forbidden, but religious beggars harass visitors constantly (sometimes while they are praying), asking for "donations."

Jewish visitors can seek assistance at one of the stands within the men's section, where volunteers will help you to put on the *tefillin* and say the blessings (there is no charge).

Praying at the holiest place in the Jewish world

The uniform of the ultra-Orthodox Hasidic Jews

JEWISH BATHS
Mikvehs, or, more correctly, *mikvaot*, are ritual baths, that are filled with rainwater. Religious law requires immersion in the *mikveh* for men before a number of Temple rituals, but since the destruction of the Temple, these are no longer required. Women have to immerse themselves at the end of each menstrual period. Before marriage, both bride and groom enter (separately!). Converts to Judaism immerse themselves to complete the conversion process. Some *mikvaot* in the Herodian Houses have separate entrances and exits (unusual today), allowing the person to enter impure on one side and leave purified on the other. Immersion is total with the body upright, entirely clean and naked and without any jewelry.

►► Wohl Archaeological Museum (Herodian Houses) 51B2

HaKaraim Street off Hurva Square
Admission: inexpensive (joint ticket with Israelite Tower and Burnt House)

The Wohl Archaeological Museum preserves in situ the extraordinary discoveries made when this handsome religious institution, built in pale Jerusalem stone, was being constructed. From the small, unassuming museum entrance, steps lead down to the preserved area, which lies 10 feet below the street level and 2,000 years back in time. Here the floor-level rooms of ruined houses of the period are displayed in a remarkable state of preservation.

History The Jewish quarter of today covers the remains of the Upper City of 37 BC–AD 70. In AD 70, during the crushing of the First Jewish Revolt, the Romans totally destroyed the Temple and buildings surrounding it. Then they drove the population, including the priestly class, out of the city. The whole area was set alight in a vast fire, which was described by the 1st-century historian Josephus Flavius. Seventy years later the city was transformed and given new buildings, new ramparts, and a new, non-Jewish name—Aelia Capitolina. On the site of ruined Jewish homes new houses were erected.

The museum The Wohl Museum stands on an archeological site where part of a prosperous residential district of the Herodian period has been exposed. Here wealthy families of the Jerusalem aristocracy and priesthood used to live in fine homes overlooking Temple Mount. A wide low-ceilinged room has been built around the ruins of six of these 1st-century houses, including the largest ever found in the Upper City, the 6,500-square-foot Mansion. Their state of preservation varies; what can be seen are ground floors and basements, with sections of the ground floor walls standing as much as 8 feet high in parts. In some cases, original mosaic floors and wall decorations survive in good condition. In one house, a mosaic of the Herodian period was discovered when drains were installed for later Byzantine dwellings.

Steps lead down to the next level following the ancient walls as they descend the hill. Walkways enclose the house ruins, giving an excellent view into the rooms, and descriptive diagrams indicate the significance of everything that can be seen. A great many artifacts were discovered among the ruins, and it has been possible to give some idea of the furnishing and decor of the houses. In the museum there are displays of the numerous luxury and household items found, as well as a detailed model of the Mansion.

The houses Built close together on the hillside facing Temple Mount, the houses are constructed of large pale blocks of the local Jerusalem stone still used today. The interiors of the homes bear a startling resemblance to modern well-to-do interiors in today's eastern Mediterranean countries. In fact, the similarity to Greek houses gives an insight into the Hellenism that influenced life before and during Herod's reign. The impression is of uncluttered elegance and plenty of cool stone and plasterwork. Houses are divided into large and small rooms, some with attractive mosaic floors. Patterned mosaic often features in the middle of the room, with an undecorated area around the edges. Walls are decorated with paintings and stucco.

The occupants The wealth of the inhabitants is shown by the spaciousness of their homes, the fine quality of the stucco, and the excellence of the mosaic work. Inside, they have private bathrooms and their own *mikveh* (ritual bath), an indication that they were quite religious Jews. It is clear that rooms were often redecorated, old frescoes being painted over with new.

Step down 10 feet and back 2,000 years at the Wohl Archaeological Museum

CITY OF DAVID OPENING TIMES
Note that a visit involves a lot of steep walking outside in the sun. *Open:* all parts of site Sun–Thu 9–4, Fri 9–2. *Admission: inexpensive.*

COMPUTER CONTROL
An enjoyable feature of the Bible Lands Museum is the interactive computer system, which provides information through touch-sensitive screens. The museum's gift shop offers a good range of reproductions of the ancient artifacts displayed in the museum.

The New City

Despite Jerusalem's 3,000-year-old history, nearly all of the city outside the walls is less than 100 years old—and most is under 50. This New Jerusalem spreads in every direction except east, a fact that is critically confusing since Jerusalem has a large Arab district known as East Jerusalem. In fact, East Jerusalem lies north of the Old City walls, while to the geographical east of Jerusalem rises the Mount of Olives. There is another Arab district just to the south of the City Walls, but the rest of the city, including the modern city center, consists of Jewish districts.

All buildings in New Jerusalem must be constructed of the attractive traditional golden sandstone, called Jerusalem stone.

▶ Ammunition Hill *46C4*

Eshkol Boulevard (northeastern edge of the city)
Admission: moderate
On the site of a Jordanian army position captured after a long battle, this is the city's principal memorial to the liberation of Jerusalem in 1967. Now an outdoor museum, the preserved battleground is dedicated to the 183 Israelis who died. Beneath it, the underground Jordanian command post has also been preserved as a museum.

▶ Bethany

See page 209.

▶▶ Bible Lands Museum *46A2*

Museum Row (between Knesset and Shrine of the Book)
Open: Sun–Tue, Thu 9:30–5:30, Wed 9:30–9:30 (1:30–9:30 in winter), Fri 9:30–2, Sat 11–3. Admission: expensive
With remarkable displays of thousands of superb archeological finds, this bright, attractive museum explores Near East ritual and religion throughout the 6,600-year period from Abraham to the Byzantines.

Right: Roman mosaic in the Bible Lands Museum

▶ Bloomfield Science Museum *46A2*

Museum Boulevard, Hebrew University, Givat Ram campus
Open: Mon–Sat. Admission: expensive
This is an imaginative and highly entertaining hands-on science museum with fascinating displays, talks, exhibitions, and workshops geared for different age groups.

▶▶ City of David (Hebrew: 'Ir David) *47E2*

Open: see panel, page 82

This Jebusite settlement, once conquered by King David, lies along the Ofel (or Ophel) Ridge. Here he constructed the first Jewish capital in 1004 BC, later acquiring a threshing floor on Mount Moriah as a site for the Temple. Under Solomon the city grew north to encompass the Temple area. In 1978 a project was established to bring together all the finds from the area and to create a single Ancient Jerusalem Archaeological Park. So far, 25 layers of civilization have been discovered, dating back to 4000 BC. Work is still in progress.

What to see Outside Dung Gate, take Ofel (or Ophel) Boulevard down to the excavations and restorations of the fascinating **Ophel Archaeological Garden▶▶▶** (see side panel), beside Herod's Temple wall and the city's south wall, below Al Aqsa mosque. The Ophel site reveals what was once a busy access to the Temple for people coming from the City of David. You can see remains of Roman and Byzantine houses, 2,000-year-old *mikvaot* (Jewish ritual baths), and a paved street of the same period. Turn right down Observation Point Path to reach the **City of David Archaeological Garden▶▶**. Here too are impressive ruins, including Israelite houses destroyed by Babylonians in 586 BC and the foundations of David's fortress. Some 100 yards downhill is **Warren's Shaft▶▶**, the ancient city's underground water system. This tunnel and well shaft were used to pull water up from the sporadic gushing **Gihon Spring▶**, inside a cave. David's men managed to invade the Jebusite town by climbing up the interior of the shaft (British soldiers did the same thing in 1910).

Continue on to **Hezekiah's Tunnel▶**, built 700 BC. Dug from both ends at once, it stretches 1,500 feet and was used to channel water from the Gihon Spring to the **Siloam Pool▶**. The pool acted as a reservoir within the city walls. Jesus healed a blind man here by rinsing his eyes. The water still flows, and visitors are welcome to wade from one end of the tunnel to the other. It's quite an adventure, takes half an hour, and requires suitable clothing and footwear. And bring a flashlight!

OPHEL ARCHAEOLOGICAL GARDEN

Open Sun–Fri 9–4.
Admission: inexpensive.

Part of this interesting excavation area at the foot of Temple Mount lies within the city walls. Just south of the Western Wall can be seen Robinson's Arch, a broken stump that is all that survives of an arch that once supported a flight of steps up to the Temple platform. The main attraction along the south wall is the remaining stairway, which gave direct access to the Temple via Hulda's Gate: tens of thousands of people coming here in Second Temple days would have climbed these steps, including Jesus. A two-story palace discovered on the site was that of the 1st-century AD Queen of Adiabene who converted to Judaism (see page 85).

David's City in ruins

OUTDATED DEFINITIONS
In 1967, after Israel had recaptured East Jerusalem from the Jordanians, the total population of the city was about 267,000. Some 70,000 Arabs lived east of the former border, and 197,000 Jews to its west. Today, those sharp divisions have been blurred. Owing to the influx of population from both sides, new housing developments, people moving around within the city, and a redefinition of the city limits, Jerusalem's total population has more than doubled to about 570,000. The districts east of the 1948 border now have just as many Jewish residents as Arab—about 150,000 of each.

►► East Jerusalem 47D4

Lying to the north, rather than east, of the Old City walls, this mainly 19th-century area is Jerusalem's principal Arab district. The neighborhood is bounded by Hatzanhanim and Suleiman boulevards, beside the Old City wall, Shivtei Israel and St. George boulevards, curving northeastward to the American Colony, and the slopes of Mount Scopus to the east. The busiest thoroughfares are Sultan Suleiman and Salah ed-Din, both just outside the Old City's Herod's Gate. The whole densely populated area has a fascinating Oriental atmosphere.

Archeology and caves In the eastern part of the district is the **Rockefeller Museum►►►** (*Open* Sun–Thu 11–5, Fri–Sat 10–2. *Admission: moderate*), a substantial building beneath a large tower at the end of Suleiman Street. It houses one of Jerusalem's leading archeological collections. In a sequence of well laid-out rooms set around a central courtyard, its displays cover the full range of human history, from man's origins almost to the present day. Among the most interesting and impressive items are the Galilee skull (dated 200,000 BC) and other very early human remains found in Israel. Also on display is ancient jewelry (some over 4,000 years old), a board game (of about 1600 BC), and ancient Egyptian and Mesopotamian items found in Israel. There are especially interesting reconstructions of a 7th-century Islamic palace and baths. The free guided tours by qualified volunteers are an additional attraction for visitors.

The Old City wall leads to **Zedekiah's Caves►**, a group of subterranean tunnels, probably former quarries, that run for some 200 yards beneath the streets. Among various stories about the caves, it is said that Zedekiah, together with hundreds of other Jerusalemites, hid here at the time of the Babylonian conquest.

If you continue along the wall, you will reach the lively area in front of **Damascus Gate►►►** (see page 53). Cross the road and head up the busy Nablus (or Shehem) Road, turning right for the **Garden Tomb►►** (see page 86), the calm and attractive spot that many Protestants believe to be the true place of Christ's crucifixion and resurrection.

Heading to the western edge of the district, a left turn along Nablus Road leads to the interesting **Tourjeman Post Museum►**, located at the junction of narrow Hayil Handassa Street and wider Antara ben Shadad and HaNevi'im streets. The museum building stands beside the old Mandelbaum Gate (named after the Mandelbaum family whose house once stood alongside). This was the only crossing point between the eastern and western sectors of Jerusalem during the Jordanian occupation of 1948 to 1967. Farther down HaNevi'im Street, the **St. Polyeuctus House Chapel►** is an Armenian establishment with an exceptionally beautiful 5th-century mosaic floor.

On the north side of the Arab district, the **Tombs of the Kings►**, at the top of Salah ed-Din Street (close to the intersection with Nablus Road), form a majestic complex

Ancient art, the Rockefeller Museum

AMERICAN COLONY
This district, part of East Jerusalem, was founded by American Christians in the 1880s. It still has a strong Western and Christian presence and its buildings include the U.S. Consulate, a Y.M.C.A., the American Colony Hotel, and St. George's Anglican Cathedral of 1898.

Understated elegance, the American Colony Hotel

of catacombs, now known to be the 1st-century AD burial place of two unlikely converts to Judaism—Helena, Queen of Adiabene (present-day Kirkuk, near Baghdad), and her son Izates. The queen took the name Sarah and became a distinguished benefactor of the Jewish people. She actually died in her homeland, but wished her remains to lie in Jerusalem. The sarcophagi from the tombs are in the Louvre, in Paris.

Just behind the tombs is the **American Colony** district, built in the 1880s. The **American Colony Hotel▶▶** is one of Jerusalem's best-known hotels. Formerly the grand, opulent palace of a Turkish pasha, handsomely restored, it is now the favorite haunt of the many foreign correspondents based in the city.

Trade flourishes before the Damascus Gate

CHAGALL MASTERPIECES
The Russian artist Marc Chagall (who was Jewish) created a great deal of work for Israeli institutions. Particularly fine are his 12 stained-glass windows in the synagogue of the Hadassah University Hospital, just south of En Kerem. They show, in his typically vivid, other-worldly style, Jacob blessing his sons, the founders of the 12 tribes of Israel.

Above: En Kerem, birthplace of John the Baptist
Below: the Garden Tomb

► En Kerem *206B2*

This picturesque village on the city's western edge is believed to be the birthplace of John the Baptist, where the Virgin Mary visited John's mother, Elizabeth. The reverence for the village dates mainly from the Crusader period. Barluzzi's modern **Sanctuary and Church of the Visitation►►** and the 17th-century **Church of John the Baptist►►** are attractive buildings honoring these events.

►► Garden Tomb *47D3*

Access from Nablus (Shehem) Road
This supposed site of the burial and resurrection of Jesus was chosen by British General Charles Gordon in 1883, and has been acknowledged by several Protestant denominations. Gordon was concerned that the accepted site, inside the Church of the Holy Sepulcher (see page 60), stood within the city walls, in contradiction to the Gospels. In fact, the city walls at the time of Christ took a different course, and Holy Sepulcher does lie outside those walls. For all that, this hill looks like a skull (the Gospel description of Golgotha), has a fine rock-hewn burial tomb adjacent, and is in a garden location. Other high-quality rock-cut tombs found nearby, for example the Tombs of the Kings (see pages 84–85), suggest that this was a burial area preferred by the wealthy. Christ was laid in the tomb of Joseph, a rich man of Arimathaea.

► Holyland Hotel Model *46A1*

Off David Nezer Street, Ramat Sharett
This superb miniature model of Jerusalem at the time of Christ, built on a scale of 1:50 and covering 2.4 acres, has been laid out on the grounds of this hotel.

►►► Israel Museum *46A1*

Ruppin Road (near the Knesset)
(tel: 02-6708811; www.imj.org.il)
Open: Sun–Mon, Wed–Thu 10–5, Tue 4–10 PM, Fri 10–2, Sat 10–4. Admission: expensive
This large modern museum is the nation's leading showcase for history, anthropology, art, and cultural heritage, and places Israel within its regional and global context. A full appreciation of its exhibits would take several days; in a short visit, it is better to concentrate on highlights. The museum provides free daily **guided tours in English** of the most important and interesting exhibits. The

famous Dead Sea Scrolls are housed in the **Shrine of the Book▶▶▶** (see page 98). It is a striking structure, separate from the rest, and takes some time to visit.

Highlights Outside the main complex there are 55 modern sculptures set in the **Art Garden▶**, including works by Henry Moore. The main part of the museum is a huge arrangement of rooms and halls. Of special interest are the **Ethnography and Judaica Wing▶▶▶**; the **20th-century Art Pavilion▶▶▶**, with works by Picasso, Chagall, van Gogh and other seminal modern artists with important Impressionist works and a remarkable donation of over 750 works of Dada and Surrealism; the **Israel Art Pavilion▶▶**, where artists such as Reuven Rubin are displayed; and the **Archeological Galleries▶▶**, where the main discoveries made in Israel are exhibited.

Exhibitions, concerts, and talks The Israel Museum is exceptionally good for its packed program of "extracurricular" activities. There are always special exhibitions in progress here on a wide variety of themes in fields such as design, photography, or the art of America, Asia, or Africa, often on loan from other leading museums. The **Youth Wing** offers activities and special exhibitions for children. Concerts, mainly of classical music but also of jazz and Jewish genres, are given during the day and in the evening. Frequent lectures and talks cover a wide range of subjects of academic, Jewish, or general interest.

JUDAICA
The Israel Museum's Judaica section has the world's most complete collection of Jewish ceremonial art and ritual objects, gathered together from every part of the world in which there have ever been Jewish communities. The Ethnography section includes, among the varied displays, the costumes of Jewish brides in Yemen, Bukhara, Morocco, and other Islamic countries.

The Art Garden, Israel Museum

An Israeli meal is served from a melting pot of cultures, with cooking styles from around the world. The robust, filling Ashkenazi (East European) and more delicate, tastier Sephardi (Mediterranean and Middle Eastern) cuisines are both well represented, together with American and international dishes, and more exotic options like the exquisite spicy food of the Yemenite Jews.

HOW TO EAT FALAFEL IN PITA

The easiest way to spot a tourist is by the amount of mess they make when trying to eat this awkward, overflowing hand-held snack. The trick is to nibble from the top, not the sides. Use the wrap-around paper to hold the whole snack together as you gradually eat downwards. Israelis can eat this without dropping even a shred of lettuce. After a couple of weeks' practice you will be almost as good as the locals.

Falafel, commonly served with salad in pita bread

Salad days Israelis may be the only people in the world who start the day with a salad. Not just as a little accompaniment to something else, and not just a slice of tomato and a leaf of lettuce, but a huge pile of chopped green peppers, radishes, and grated carrot, topped by a generous helping of yogurt-like cheese. In fact, a salad appears at every meal, and in huge quantities. It can vary from something roughly cut and thrown together, to a superb mix of finely cut vegetables, all at the peak of freshness, ripeness, and color, in a delicious olive oil dressing. Then there is hummus (chickpea purée), served in vast amounts with a big splash of olive oil and a delicious condiment called *za'atar* (hyssop and sesame). Similar dishes include avocado purée and *salat khatzilim* (eggplant purée with tomatoes, lemon juice, and onion). They are mostly eaten with pita bread.

Milk and honey Milk, it seems, can be made into more variations on the theme of cottage cheese, cream cheese, sour cream, and yogurt than most of us ever dreamed of. A breakfast or lunch buffet can include half a dozen soft or semiliquid white cheeses, some bland, some flavored with herbs and spices, some mouth-watering, some more of an acquired taste! Generically, they are known just as *leben*, literally "white." One particular plain white cheese, moist with a cuttable consistency, could be regarded as one of the country's staple foods; it is called simply *gvina lavana*, white cheese. Of course, because of Jewish dietary laws, milk products are never eaten at the same meal as meat in kosher restaurants.

One falafel or six The basic snack meal is falafel in pita with salad. Flexible enough to be either a quick bite or a full sit-down meal, it is also utterly delicious. The falafel itself is a deep-fried ball of seasoned chickpea paste (plus wheat flour, onions, and garlic). Usually four or five of them are crammed into the bottom of a cut-open pita with as much diced salad and chopped vegetables as will fit. All this is then smothered with hummus and tahini (sauces made of chickpeas and of sesame seeds with olive oil respectively) and, optionally, either sweet mango sauce or

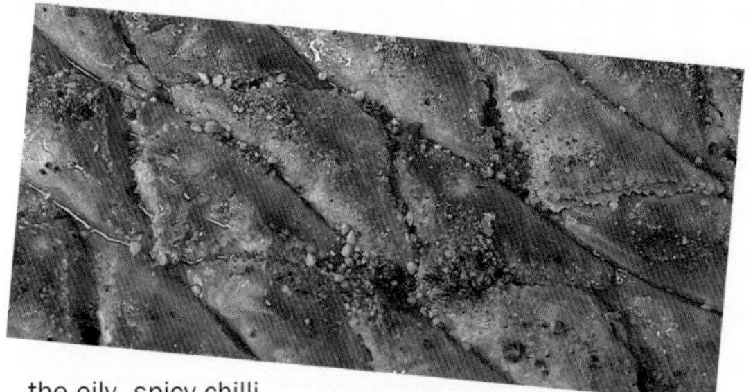

Lebanese delicacy: a honey-soaked dessert

the oily, spicy chilli pepper sauce called *zehoug*. Falafel in pita is available everywhere. In the cheaper places where you serve yourself, you can refill as often as you like.

Meat and fish Plain grilled meats and delicious fresh fish, served with French fries, *hamutzim* (pickles), and (of course) fresh salads make a good, typical meal. Succulent stews with plenty of beans and pulses, especially *ful* beans, are widely seen. *Shwarma* (slices cut from pressed mutton roasted on a vertical spit) is ubiquitous, popular, and (when stuffed into a pita with salad) provides a mobile carnivorous alternative to falafel. Menus often feature *schnitzel*, but in Israel it is usually made of turkey or chicken, not veal. Blintzes (stuffed rolled pancakes) can be filled with meat or cheese, sweet or savory, and can make a good snack, a filling meal, or (especially a cheese blintz sprinkled with sugar) a gorgeous dessert. Chunky little wedges of baklava, the super-sweet honey and nut strudel, also make a good finish to any meal. Israeli ice cream and yogurt desserts are great too.

So eat! Wherever you eat, the portions served are huge. Cooking reaches a decent level almost everywhere, though rarely exceeding it. Most Israeli restaurants lack finesse and imagination, though some now truly merit the ubiquitous "gourmet" label. The bread served is beautifully fresh and the fruit, vegetables and fish can be wonderful. Many resataurants in Israel serve seafood, although seafood is not kosher, and much of it is imported or is imitation seafood, made from fish. The widespread admiration in Israel for the rough-and-ready, and the down-to-earth, works against refinement. Diners are not especially discerning, and they generally care little about the finer points of cuisine, but they expect properly prepared, good quality food, and plenty of it. That is what they get.

VEGETARIAN TREATS
Salads and delicious vegetable dishes are the norm everywhere and the numerous meat-free "dairy" restaurants (which also serve fish) supply a wealth of interesting choice. However, despite the excellent salads, you might get tired of the factory-made vegetarian *schnitzel*—the automatic response to a request for a vegetarian hot dish in a meat restaurant. Mealtimes are flexible. Many Israelis eat early, with breakfast at 6–8 AM, lunch around noon, and an evening meal at 7 PM. Some restaurants are open from 11 AM to 11 PM.

A barrow of bagels

Waiting for Judgment Day: tombs in the Kidron Valley

HEROD'S FAMILY TOMB
Behind the King David Hotel is a tomb of the Second Temple period, now known to contain the graves of members of Herod's family—many of whom he murdered. The opening still possesses its rolling stone "door."

Y.M.C.A.
The wonderfully grand building, opposite the King David, seeming even to outclass the famous hotel, is a Y.M.C.A. It was designed in 1933 by Arthur Louis Harmon, architect of the Empire State Building in New York.

▶ Jerusalem Time Elevator *46B3*

Beit Agron, 37 Hillel Street (tel: 02-625 2227; fax: 02-625 2228) Open: Sat–Thu 9 AM–10 PM, Fri 9–3:30. Admission: moderate
Three screens, moving seats, and multisensory sets offer a rip-roaring half-hour trip through the highlights of Israel's 3,000-year story. You'll have virtual encounters with kings, prophets, and conquerors, enter the Temple, and flee from a Jerusalem in flames.

▶ Kidron Valley *47E2*

The dry valley of Nahal Kidron forms the eastern limit of the original City of David. Pious Jews and Muslims both believe that the Last Judgment will take place below the Mount of Olives (see page 94). For that reason, this part of the valley is also known as Jehoshaphat Valley (literally, "valley of God's judgment"), a name used metaphorically in the scriptures for the place of judgment.

Elaborate **Kidron Valley tombs▶**, on the lower slopes of the Mount of Olives, are popularly thought to be those of early biblical characters. These are, in fact, the tombs of wealthy Jews of the 1st century BC and are constructed in typical style of that period. One with a curious conical roof is referred to as the **Tomb of Absalom▶**, a son of King David. Another is said to be the **Tomb of Zacharia▶** and a third is called **St. James's Grotto▶**, supposedly the place where James the Less hid when Jesus was arrested.

▶ King David Hotel *46C2*

King David Street
This dignified 1930s hotel, now equipped with every modern amenity, remains the venue for state banquets and receptions. It is the flagship of the Dan chain, Israel's most prestigious hotel group. The King David entered the pages of Israel's history when the front of its right wing, being used as the military headquarters of the British in Palestine, was blown apart by the Irgun guerrilla group in

Historic hotel: the King David, former headquarters of the British in Palestine

July 1946. Ninety-one people died in that incident. Several other explosions at that time were aimed at persuading the British to withdraw from Palestine.

▶▶ The Knesset *46A2*

Eliezer Kaplan Street (HaKyria district)
Open: parliamentary sessions Mon–Wed 4–7, Sun and Thu 11–7. Guided tours Sun and Thu 8:30–2:30, when parliament is not meeting. Passport needed

The Israeli parliament building of 1966 is a bleak fortress, on a hill west of the center of Jerusalem. This is the focal point of modern Israel. It was built with defense very much in mind: a good deal of the structure lies below ground level. Here, in debates, the nation's divisions are starkly revealed, as is its essential unity. Religious and secular forces, left- and right-wing ideologues, meet, clash, and form pragmatic alliances. Few countries in the world are as wholeheartedly democratic, with a system of proportional representation that permits almost any and every voice to be heard under this roof. The name itself (*knesset* means assembly) reflects this role too, and the name contains an echo of Beit Knesset, the Hebrew for synagogue.

Debate in the chamber (in Hebrew or Arabic) is lively, with startling displays of real temper. The 16-foot-tall bronze menorah outside, a gift from Britain, symbolizes the central place of the Knesset in the Jewish homeland. Tapestries in the entrance hall, showing scenes from Genesis and Exodus and the Entry into Jerusalem, are by Marc Chagall.

KNESSET ROSES
The beautiful Knesset Rose Garden, open to the public, contains hundreds of different varieties of roses. People come here from time to time with placards to voice their concerns.

Heart of Israeli democracy: the Knesset in its hilltop setting

In this neighborhood, strict rules are observed: Hasidic Jews uphold the Orthodox view

HASIDISM
The Hasidic movement was founded by Israel ben Eliezer (known as Baal Shem Tov, meaning "Master of the Good Name") during the mid-17th century in the Ukraine. At the time, following savage persecution by the Church, Jewish life in Eastern Europe was at a low ebb. He taught that communication with God could only be attained through real fervor, whether in study or observance. The dress of the Hasidim, varied according to sub-sects to which an individual belongs, reflects devotion to their 17th-century roots, as does their elaborate observance.

►► Me'a She'arim *46C4*

This downtown district north of Zion Square is a strictly Orthodox Jewish area where Hasidim (see panel) can be seen at leisure. Here they are on home ground, and children play in the streets (boys making sure never to lose their *kippot*, or skullcaps) watched by the men in their *tsitsit* (fringed garments), while the demurely clad women go about their business. Understandably, the residents object to being a tourist attraction, and many streets have been closed off with barriers and signs erected bearing this message: "Entrance for women immodestly dressed, tourists and groups, STRICTLY FORBIDDEN!!! This is a residence area, not a tourist site; please do not irritate our feelings. Neighborhood Council." It is wise to heed this warning, as Hasidim have a reputation for acting violently against those they regard as transgressors. Men or women in shorts will be spat upon, maybe even stoned.

Certain other streets have no such barriers, and it is even possible to go on an organized synagogue tour (ask at the tourist office). Descriptions of this neighborhood as like an East European *shtetl* (Jewish township) are quite misleading—there is almost no resemblance at all. Me'a She'arim's housing, narrow lanes, and overhanging balconies seem as much Middle Eastern as East European. The European *shtetls* were simple and rustic, and long predated the Hasidic movement. Many residents were not especially religious. Nor were there any cars, paved streets, electricity...or signs warning visitors to keep away.

► Monastery of the Cross *46A2*

Hayim Hazar Boulevard
Open: daily 10–1:30

Built in the 11th century on 5th-century ruins, this fortified Greek Orthodox monastery looks incongruous among the modern architecture of the HaKyria district, with its government offices and museums. Much superstition and legend surrounds the site. Hundreds of monks used to live in the monastery, and its library of precious manuscripts (now kept elsewhere) had a considerable reputation. Today it is a college for Orthodox priests.

Tradition has it that it was from among the olive groves in front of the building that Christ's cross was made.

►► Mount Herzl 46A1

Herzl Boulevard winds through western Jerusalem to this hill, which has been turned into a magnificent shrine to the creation of the State of Israel. At its summit rests a massive plain black stone sarcophagus inscribed with no sentiments of praise or pathos, but one simple word: Herzl. Around the tomb, a lovely, serene garden honors the memory of the founder of the Zionist movement, Theodor Herzl.

Without this cosmopolitan, secular Jew from Hungary, who was born in 1860, it is unlikely that the State of Israel would exist. Herzl was suddenly fired into activity when he witnessed the public parade-ground humiliation of the Jewish officer Alfred Dreyfus in France. He decided to devote himself to the creation of a worldwide Zionist movement. He wished to work on all fronts—especially through politics and diplomacy—to win a homeland for the Jews. He convened the First Zionist Congress in 1897, and by the time of his death in 1904, his dream had almost become a reality. When the State was proclaimed by David Ben-Gurion in 1948, a picture of Theodor Herzl hung on the wall behind him. In 1949, Herzl's remains were brought to Israel and laid to rest here.

The tombs of Herzl's parents and many prominent Israeli figures also lie here, including Zeev Jabotinsky (1880–1940: head of the Irgun guerrilla organization), Levi Eshkol (1895–1969: Israel's third prime minister), and Golda Meir (1898–1978: Israel's fourth prime minister). The principal military cemetery is also on this hill, lower down. The **Herzl Museum►►►** (*Open* summer, Sun–Thu 9–6:30, Sat 9–1; winter, Sun–Thu 9–4, Sat 9–1. *Admission: inexpensive*), the first building you reach upon entering the site from Herzl Boulevard, tells the story of the man and his life. It preserves some original documents and other artifacts relating to him in a reconstruction of his well-appointed study.

BUS 99
The easy way to see the sights of Jerusalem beyond the walls is to catch a number 99 bus. Running on a circuit right around the city, it calls at 36 stops, all of them places of interest. You can get off wherever you like, take a look round, and catch the next 99 bus to continue with your tour.

The tomb of Theodor Herzl, founder of Zionism, on the summit of the hill that bears his name

Ancient tombs on the Mount of Olives

THE END OF DAYS
"And the Mount of Olives shall cleave in the midst thereof towards the east and towards the west, and there shall be a very great valley; and half of the mountain shall remove toward the north, and half of it toward the south."
—Zechariah 14:4

"The sun shall be turned into darkness, and the moon into blood, before the great and the terrible day of the Lord come. And it shall come to pass, that whosoever shall call upon the name of the Lord shall be delivered; for in Mount Zion and in Jerusalem shall be deliverance."
—Joel 2:31–32 (3:4–5)

"Beat your plowshares into swords, and your pruning hooks into spears: let the weak say, I am strong. Assemble yourselves, and come, all ye heathen ... Let the heathen be wakened, and come up to the valley of Jehoshaphat: for there will I sit to judge all the heathen round about."
—Joel 3(4):10–12

►►► Mount of Olives *47E3*

White tombs, not olives, cover the steep hillside rising beyond the city wall east of Temple Mount. This slope has long been wreathed in myth and legend.

Fact, fiction, and faith Almost the only time the hill is mentioned by name in Jewish scripture comes after the revolt of Absalom, when his father, King David, is described as weeping while he walks barefoot up the Mount of Olives to pray (II Samuel 15:30). However, the apocalyptic predictions of Joel 3, that the nations shall be judged in the valley of Jehoshaphat (meaning "God's Judgment") has been taken by some to refer to the nearby Kidron Valley. Zechariah's hallucinatory vision (14:4) of the Mount of Olives being torn into two, and the whole world coming to Jerusalem for the festival of Sukkot has also led pious Jews to believe that the Last Judgment will take place here. The notion that the dead will physically rise on the Day of Judgment has caused Jews to attach special value to being buried on this slope, above the Kidron.

Christians know this as the place to which Jesus and the disciples came on the night before his arrest and trial. The "place called Gethsemane" (Matthew 26:36) is assumed to be on the slope. Fine buildings on the Mount of Olives commemorate these events, although, almost without exception, they are based on Byzantine fervor rather than biblical, or historical, evidence.

Down the mountain There is direct access to the mount from the Old City via Lions' Gate. An easier way to visit the shrines and churches is from the top of the hill. Take a bus or taxi to **Et-Tur►**, the Arab village at its summit, and walk past the Church of the Ascension (no entry) to the **Chapel of the Ascension►**, a simple domed structure within the grounds of a mosque converted from a Crusader church. This is claimed to be the place from which Christ ascended into heaven (although Luke 24:50,

The Russian Church of Mary Magdalene, built by Czar Alexander III

sets this event in Bethany, present-day Eizaria). Inside, a mark in the floor is said to be the footprint of Christ. **Pater Noster Church▶**, belonging to Carmelite nuns, recalls Christ's teaching of the Lord's Prayer at a grotto that now forms part of a lovely cloister. Beyond the church, on the left, rises the unsightly Hotel InterContinental. Just below, an **observation point▶▶▶** gives one of Jerusalem's best views.

Another road from the Carmelite church leads down past the so-called **Tombs of the Prophets▶** (Haggai, Zacharia, and Malachi), in reality a much later complex of catacombs, to the entrance of the **Jewish cemetery▶▶**, the oldest, as well as the largest, continuously used Jewish cemetery in the world. Tragically, it was badly damaged during the Jordanian occupation, when graves were smashed or removed for use as building stone.

The curious **Dominus Flevit Church▶▶** (meaning "the Lord wept"), was built in 1953 and incorporates 5th-century ruins. It has a glass wall and is shaped as a teardrop in memory of Jesus weeping for Jerusalem. The 19th-century Russian **Church of Mary Magdalene▶▶**, with its elaborate colored facade and cluster of onion domes topped with prominent Orthodox crosses, is one of the city's more distinctive landmarks. Ironically, it was built by Czar Alexander III, whose savage pogroms in the 1880s inspired the first great influx of Zionists into Palestine.

At the bottom of the hill, a putative **Garden of Gethsemane▶**, pretty with flowers and a few olive trees, recalls Christ's last hours. Some believe the trees date back to those days. The **Cave of Gethsemane▶** is said to be where the disciples slept while Jesus prayed. The **Basilica of the Agony▶**, an attractive modern building on a Byzantine and Crusader site, is decorated inside and out with mosaics and murals.

The **Tomb of the Virgin Mary▶▶**, a mainly Byzantine and Crusader structure, is reached through a fine doorway. It leads to an underground shrine, where various tombs (in reality medieval) are said to be those of Mary's parents, Joachim and Anne, her husband Joseph, and, at the end of a long chamber, Mary herself. This is one of many places, in Israel and in other countries, where the Virgin Mary is said to have been entombed.

THE BIBLICAL MOUNT OF OLIVES

"And David went up by the ascent of the Mount of Olives, and wept as he went up, and he had his head covered, and went barefoot."
—II Samuel 15:30

"Then returned they unto Jerusalem from the mount called Olivet, which is from Jerusalem a Sabbath day's journey."
—Acts 1:12

A BEACON TO THE JEWS

In Second Temple times, the Mount of Olives had, on its summit, the first in a chain of beacons that extended all over Israel and into Babylon, used to inform Jews of the timing of new moons and festivals.

Beneath here lies the Virgin's tomb

THE VALLEY OF THE SHADOW OF DEATH
Encircling the foot of Mount Zion is the Hinnom Valley, called Gehenna (meaning Hell), in the Bible. Its evil associations can be traced back to Canaanite times when the valley was sacred to the cult of Moloch, whose followers sacrificed children by burning them alive. Fires were kept aflame here specifically for that purpose. Incredibly, such a religion had a strong appeal and was widely practiced throughout the region. Even the Israelites sometimes succumbed to it. The Haceldama Monastery along here, in another link with evil, is believed to stand on the Field of Blood purchased with the 30 pieces of silver given to Judas for betraying Jesus.

▶ Mount Scopus (Hebrew: Har HaTsofim) *47E4*

The Hebrew name for Mount Scopus means "Looking Over," as does the Greek translation, Scopus. As a viewpoint over the Old City and the hills beyond, it is hard to beat. Roman legions camped here in AD 70 before moving to crush the Jewish rebels. The Crusaders, too, camped at the summit on the eve of their attack on Jerusalem. In 1917, British forces rallied on Mount Scopus before their descent to the city. In 1948, however, when the Arab Legion assembled here for the advance on west Jerusalem, they were defeated and driven off the peak. The Israelis then held it as a besieged island of Jewish territory east of the ceasefire line until 1967, when normal life resumed.

Much of Mount Scopus was purchased in the 1920s by Jewish organizations. High on the hill, the impressive **Hebrew University▶▶**, opened in 1925, was rebuilt on dramatic lines (tours daily at 9 and 11 AM). Nearby stands the **Hadassah Hospital▶**, also opened in 1925. Just below is the **Commonwealth Cemetery▶**, containing the graves of British soldiers who fell fighting in Palestine during World War I.

▶▶ Mount Zion (Hebrew: Har Tsion) *47D2*

The name Zion, as a synonym for Jerusalem and even for Israel, conjures much passion. The hill called Zion today is the westerly of two small peaks lying south of the Old City. Apart from the Armenian quarter, which climbs the northern slope, Mount Zion lies outside the city wall. It is dominated by churches built over revered religious sites, yet these, more than most, are without biblical or historical provenance.

A place of history In earlier times, Zion was the name given to the easterly of the two hills—the one on which stood the Jerusalem of King David and King Solomon. Nowadays that is called Mount Ofel. Under Hezekiah, the city grew to cover Ofel, Zion, and Mount Moriah (Temple Mount): his city limits remained right up to the time of Herod. Then Jerusalem expanded into the area of today's Old City, except for the northeastern and northwestern corners. By Byzantine times, it filled the whole of the present Old City, plus the Zion and Ofel peaks, and so it stayed until Crusader times. The Soldiers of the Cross erected new defenses, roughly following the city walls as we see them now—this time leaving the Ofel and Zion hills outside their defensive circle.

Mount Scopus is now dominated by the Hebrew University

A place of piety Half the hill is taken up by Christian cemeteries. The pretty **Church of St. Peter in Galicantu▶**, meaning "at the cockcrow," was built in 1931 by Barluzzi on 1st-century ruins, and recalls St. Peter's three denials of Christ before daybreak. It is also claimed as the site of the **House of Caiaphas▶**, the high priest before whom Jesus was brought after his arrest. The 19th-century pale stone **Church of**

SCHINDLER'S GRAVE
Jews and Catholics alike make their way through the Catholic cemetery on Mount Zion to pay their respects to this notorious womanizer, drinker, and wheeler-dealer. He joined the Nazi party and played the Nazi era for all he could make out of it. Oskar Schindler, immortalized in Spielberg's 1994 block-buster, *Schindler's List*, lies buried here. Like many other German business-men, Schindler used Jewish slave labor in his Polish factory, but, while other manufacturers worked their slaves to death, Schindler found ways of helping them escape to Palestine. Some 1,200 owed their lives to him. Schindler died in Germany in 1974 and, at his own request, was buried on Mount Zion.

Lavish gold mosaic work adorns the interior of the Church of the Dormition

the Dormition►, with its conical roof, stands where, according to Byzantine tradition, Mary fell asleep, instead of dying, before being assumed bodily into heaven.

Just beyond is a building that contains **David's Tomb►**, revered by Orthodox Jews as well as Christians even though its location is incorrect. David was buried in the City of David (I Kings 2:10). This present "tomb" is a 4th-century invention within the remnant of a synagogue later incorporated into a Crusader church. It is richly adorned, with an embroidered cloth cover. The room itself contains Torah scrolls and is used as a synagogue. Many Jews pray here on Shavuot, traditionally the day of King David's death. Upstairs is the vaulted **Cenacle►**, the so-called Room of the Last Supper, a location chosen in the 12th century. Inside, a slab of stone shows where Jesus sat during the meal! Facing it is a Muslim prayer niche. This room is also revered as the place where the Holy Spirit descended upon the disciples as they gathered for Shavuot (Pentecost in the Christian church), seven weeks later.

Opposite David's Tomb, the **Chamber of the Holocaust►►►** (*Open* Sun–Thu 9–5, Fri 8–2. *Admission: donation*) may lack Yad VaShem's awesome memorial (see page 102), but this small museum is just as heart-wrenching. A particularly horrifying feature is the display of anti-Jewish material published since the Holocaust.

Sun symbol carved on the facade of the Room of the Last Supper

The lid-shaped Shrine of the Book

▶▶▶ Shrine of the Book *46A2*

Ruppin Street (tel: 02-670 8811)
Open: Sun–Mon, Wed–Thu 10–5, Tue 10–10, Fri 10–2, Sat 10–4. Admission: expensive

This is the permanent home of the Dead Sea Scrolls (see pages 222–223) and other ancient manuscripts, including original biblical texts. The strange white shape of the Shrine of the Book represents the lids of the earthenware jars in which the scrolls were found. The Shrine forms part of the Israel Museum, and stands alongside the main museum complex.

Inside, the unusual roof covers a vast circular room, around which is displayed an unrolled scroll containing a large part of the Book of Isaiah, written in 100 BC. Almost identical in every detail to the Book of Isaiah contained in later and modern Bibles, it is used as evidence that the Jewish scriptures remained unchanged as they were copied faithfully by generations of scribes.

Other rooms downstairs display a range of letters and scripts from the Second Temple period. Also displayed are documents from Masada (AD 70), and others written during the Second Revolt (AD 135), all of which have been of vital importance in enabling scholars to reconstruct the events of this troubled period. The low lighting of the room has a perfectly scientific rationale, yet it inspires a fitting sense of awe and an almost reverential atmosphere. The official guides seem infected, too, speaking with quiet urgency and passion about the writings.

BEDOUIN SCROLL HUNTERS

The first of the Dead Sea Scrolls was found in 1947 by a young Bedouin shepherd. He sold it a few months later to Arab traders who divided the scroll up and offered the parts for sale separately to academics and institutions. In 1949, archeologists and researchers moved in to look for more scrolls. Even while they were conducting their research unsuccessfully, new finds were being made by Bedouins. Of the 10 new caves containing scrolls, most were discovered by Bedouin shepherds, including the two caves that contained the most important of the documents.

▶ Supreme Court *46A3*

Open: Sun–Thu; guided tours in English at noon

Israeli architecture has won few accolades. From 1948 to the 1990s, it can be characterized as bland and functional. A breakthrough came with the opening in 1992 of the new Supreme Court building on a hilltop near the Knesset, to which it is linked by a walkway. Since then several often inspired, imaginative, and satisfying designs have been brought to fruition. Brother-and-sister architects Ram and Ada Karmi were responsible for the Supreme Court. It is a triumph of elegant, traditional simplicity in pale Jerusalem stone which proves that the modern, functional and unpretentious can be beautiful as well. The building was entirely paid for by the Rothschild family and estate.

Misconceptions about the Jewish faith and religion are rife among outsiders, and that has led to wild accusations, prejudice and murderous hatred in the past. Some visitors to Israel may not find Jewish people very forthcoming about their beliefs, and even on an extended visit it is possible to spend time among observant Jews and yet come away with no real idea what they believe or how they practice their religion.

An open book "People of the Book" is an apt description for the Jews. Jewish prayer is formalized and traditional, with set words being read in a set order from an authorized prayer book. Synagogue services are relaxed, amiable, and not especially formal. At morning prayers many men wear a *tallit* (prayer shawl), *tefillin* (two small leather boxes containing scriptural texts, worn every day except Sabbath), and *kippah* as a head covering. At least 10 men (or women, in non-Orthodox congregations) must be present for key prayers to be said. At Monday, Thursday, and Saturday (Sabbath) services, the week's "portion" of the Torah (the first five biblical books) is read aloud by selected congregants from a handwritten scroll while other members of the congregation follow the text in a book (the *Humash*). Much daily ritual, blessing, and prayer, again from the prayer book, takes place at home.

Time and ritual The weeks, months, and years are marked by their own prayers and rituals. High point of the week is Sabbath, welcomed on Friday night with blessings, candle-lighting, wine, and *challah* (Sabbath bread), and followed by a family meal. Annual festivals recall historical events, in accord with biblical precepts and seasonal customs. Pesach (Passover), for example, is a spring festival, decreed in the Torah as a memorial to the Jewish exodus from their enslavement in Egypt.

Getting it right The essence of Judaism is not belief, but behavior. The important thing is to observe the *mitzvot* (commandments) laid down in the scriptures. Numbering 613 altogether, these encompass every area of life from business to bedroom, childbirth to charity.

Traditions For most Israelis, though, the *mitzvot* are not really rules at all, but traditions. Some are considered part of "being Jewish"—like having sons circumcised, keeping the festivals, and not eating pork. Many Israeli Jews consider others are unnecessary—like going in the *mikveh* (ritual bath) after menstruation, saying a blessing over bread before every meal, or having the hairstyle described in Leviticus. Even some observant Jews don't obey all the rules, and those who do are in the minority.

FOR NON-JEWS VISITING A SYNAGOGUE ...

- Any room containing a Torah scroll may be a synagogue.
- Men should cover their heads whether or not a service is in progress. Paper *yarmulkes* (skullcaps) are usually provided for visitors.
- Formal dress is not required but modesty is. Legs should be covered to the knee. Women should not wear pants.
- Do not walk about while the congregation is standing or while the Torah is being read, and do not speak or distract anyone while the silent prayers are being read.
- In an Orthodox or Conservative synagogue, ensure that you remain in the men's or women's section as appropriate.
- Do take a *Humash* (Torah text) and *siddur* (prayer book) from the shelves, but do not touch *tefillin* (leather scroll boxes), as these are sanctified ritual objects.

Top: Torah scrolls
Below: reading the Torah, from right to left

AFTER DARK
After you have seen the Nahalat Shiv'a pedestrianized area during the day, come again in the evening. These traffic-free lanes, between Jaffa Street and King George V, are the city's favorite after-dark hangout. There's a café every few yards, scores of crowded tables in the open air, bookstores, jewelry stores, and snack takeouts open late into the night.

▶ University Library Albert Einstein Exhibition 46A2

Hebrew University, Givat Ram campus
Open: Sun–Thu 9–7, Fri morning. Admission free.
The Hebrew University Library displays its archives on Einstein's life and work in a series of 20 panels. Einstein's personal papers illustrate his multifaceted interests.

▶▶▶ West Jerusalem *46B1 and 2, C1 and 2*

Sir Moses Montefiore built the first new district outside the Old City in 1860. Mishkenot Sha'ananim, as it is called, stands at the southern end of what is now the **Yemin Moshe** district (see page 104). Nowadays, most of Jerusalem's residents (including the Arab minority) live, work, and play outside the walled tourist heartland. The area west of the Old City has become the bustling downtown of today. The second new district was Nahalat Shiv'a. Part of it, a tangle of renovated pedestrianized lanes around **Ben Yehuda Street▶▶▶**, is now the favorite area of Jerusalemites for strolling, browsing, and whiling away the hours at outdoor cafés. In 1886 the city's busy food market was started at **Mahaneh Yehuda▶▶**, a few minutes' walk northwest from Ben Yehuda. Later, broad avenues were laid out linking the new neighborhoods. They have since become the city's traffic-filled main streets. **King George V▶▶** (and its continuation, Keren Ha-Yessod) and **King David▶** are lined with civic and religious buildings, offices, and hotels. The two streets form the arms of a triangle whose third side is **Yafo (Jaffa) Street▶▶**, a hectic, crowded, fascinating thoroughfare.

Above and right: passing the time in the streets of Jerusalem

Walk

West Jerusalem

Allow 3–4 hours for this quick tour of Jerusalem's modern center (for map see page 46B2/C2). From the **Tourist Office** at 24 King George V Street, head along King George and right onto Shatz Street, which reaches HaNagid Street. At No. 12, see the **Jerusalem Artists' House▶**, with galleries and a café, next to the **Bezalel Academy of Art▶** founded about 100 years ago. Turn back to King George and turn right, passing the **Tzavta Theater**. At the **Jewish National Fund** office, you can arrange to plant a tree in one of the forests on the city's perimeter.

The Orthodox **Great Synagogue▶** is well worth a look inside. Beside it, the **Wolfson Museum of Art▶**, specializing in Judaica, shares a building with the Chief Rabbi's office. Then comes **Kikkar Tsarfat (Zarefat)▶** (or France Square, also called Place de France). This is Jerusalem's central square, at the meeting of King George V, Keren HaYesod, Ramban, Aza (or Gaza), and Gershon Agron streets. On one corner stands the main Conservative Synagogue.

A few paces along Ramban Street, an old windmill has become the basis for a shopping center full of fashion boutiques and eating places. Turn left along Gershon Agron and left again into pleasant **Independence Park▶**. Stroll across to Hillel Street. At No. 27 is the interesting **Museum of Italian Jewish Art▶** and a restored 18th-century **Italian synagogue▶**, brought stone by stone from Italy.

Take Angelo Blanchini Street to reach the pedestrianized area. Walk along **Ben Yehuda Street▶▶▶** to another focal point, **Kikkar Tsion▶** (or Zion Square). Head up Harav Kook Street to **Ticho House▶▶**, now part of the Israel Museum. It was once the home of artist Anna Ticho and is full of her artwork. Walk along Jaffa Road and turn left on King George V. This busy section has many stores selling clothing, books, food, and much else.

The Great Synagogue

Independence Park

YAD VASHEM
The name Yad v'Shem means "A Memorial and a Name"—that is, for every victim of the Holocaust.

▶▶▶ Yad VaShem 46A1

Open: Sun–Thu 10–4:45, Fri 9–2. Admission free

The world's leading Holocaust memorial, museum, and documentation center covers a ridge of high ground named Har HaZikaron—literally, the Hill of Memory—rising west of the Mount Herzl summit.

For anyone who has come to Israel for enjoyment and relaxation, a visit to Yad VaShem may seem a daunting prospect. Difficult though the experience can be, it will only heighten an appreciation of the country and its people. Once you have absorbed the awful facts of recent Jewish history, you will view with new eyes the energy and determination of Israelis to enjoy life to the full. For those who have come to Israel to gain greater understanding of the Jews and their land, a morning at Yad VaShem is essential. The site is sprawling, wooded in part, offers broad views westward toward central Jerusalem, and contains several different buildings.

The symbolic Pillar of Heroism

Visiting the site Start by walking the length of the **Avenue of the Righteous Among the Nations▶**, along the south side of the memorial area. This commemorates non-Jews who risked their own lives in order to save Jews during the Holocaust. They are named individually. The avenue is lined with trees planted by the Righteous themselves. This leads to the **Historical Museum▶▶▶**, containing the main permanent exhibition. Here documents and photographs chronologically trace the course of Hitler's "final solution to the Jewish problem." Many dry German government publications and posters are displayed,

The Silent Cry, *one of the sculptures making up Yad VaShem's Art Museum*

THE HOLOCAUST
Holocaust (*shoah* in Hebrew) literally means "burn whole." Until the Nazi era, the word usually referred to religious sacrifices. The Nazi Holocaust burned deep scars in the contemporary Jewish psyche, and the creation of the State of Israel received much of its impetus from the heightened desperation of Jews to find a safe haven, just as much of its international support is due to the moral legitimacy conferred by the tragedy.

The Hall of Names records all known victims of the Holocaust

matter-of-fact material that contrasts with the disturbing photographs of dead women piled in heaps like rag dolls, camp inmates pushing corpses into furnaces, and of laughing German soldiers humiliating or arresting Jewish children. Immediately opposite, the massive, undecorated **Hall of Remembrance▶** is a large, grim chamber containing little but a memorial flame in front of a vault full of victims' ashes. The names of the Nazi death camps are set into the floor.

Ahead is a plaza with a building on the far side. The entrance on the right leads into a synagogue. The one on the left leads to the **Hall of Names▶▶**, where the names of all Holocaust victims are inscribed on plaques after the evidence has been verified. So far, over three million names have been recorded, and more are being added constantly. Below is the access to the **Art Museum▶▶**, a remarkable collection of drawings and paintings made by concentration camp inmates. Farther on is the **Partisan's Memorial▶▶** and, farther still, the wooded, walled **Valley of the Communities▶▶**, the former memorial recording the names of the communities entirely destroyed during the Holocaust.

On the Yad VaShem grounds, several **sculptures▶▶▶** form an integral part of the memorial. Outside the Art Museum the disturbing collection includes *The Unknown Righteous Man Among the Gentiles, Auschwitz, Job, Ultima* and, by the plaza, *Dry Bones*. Across the plaza stands the powerful *Silent Cry*. From here, walk toward the Children's Memorial, pausing at the heart-rending *Korczak and the Children of the Ghetto*. Korczak was a teacher who voluntarily accompanied his pupils to death at Treblinka because he could not bear to see them taken away with no one to care for them.

The underground **Children's Memorial▶▶▶** is in memory of the 1.5 million young children and babies killed in the death camps. Inside, it is dark except for myriad pinpoints of light like stars, each representing the life of a child taken away. A ceaseless, droning tape reads the list of their names, places of birth, and ages.

TIPS FOR A VISIT TO YAD VASHEM

- Come in the morning, giving time to see the whole museum and memorial without haste.
- Avoid coming with a group if possible. Yad VaShem should be seen at your own speed, with time and privacy to reflect on the exhibits.
- However long or short a time you spend here, do not miss the Children's Memorial on any account.
- Don't take children to see Yad VaShem. Although groups of Israeli schoolchildren are taken around the site, most clearly either do not understand its importance or, in a few cases, are very deeply shocked by what they see. Noisy, laughing youngsters also diminish the impact of the memorial for others, dishonoring the Holocaust victims.

Residences in the Yemin Moshe district

HAAS AND SHEROVER PROMENADES
The most spectacular view of Jerusalem, Old and New, is from the Walter and Elise Haas Promenade, a handsome walkway some 2,000 feet long, set on a ridge of high ground in the new southern neighborhood of East Talpiot. The more recent Gabriel Sherover Promenade (more usually called by the Hebrew name Tayelet Sherover), again with superb Old City views, descends through fine landscaped gardens.

▶ Yemin Moshe *46C2*

This charming, picturesque neighborhood, constructed by the philanthropist Sir Moses Montefiore in the 1860s, rises from close to the southwestern tower of the Old City walls. This was the first settlement to be built outside the walls, and it has since attracted a number of artists whose work is sold in the area's galleries. The whole district has a quiet sense of well-being. Its pale stone paving and buildings climb in stepped alleys and lanes, giving glorious views, up to **Bloomfield Gardens▶** and the famous Jerusalem landmark, **Montefiore's Windmill▶**. Intended to provide a means of income for the area's first residents, the windmill has since been turned into a museum dedicated to the life and times of Sir Moses Montefiore (1784–1885), a remarkable, early pioneer of Jewish rights. Born in Livorno, Italy, he made a fortune as a stockbroker in London, became sheriff of the city in 1824, then retired to devote the rest of his life to founding schools and hospitals in Britain and Jerusalem.

▶ Zoo *46A1*

Open: summer, Sun–Thu 9–7, Fri 9–3, Sat 10–6:30; winter, daily 9–5. Admission: expensive

At Manahat (also known as Malka), on the southwestern outskirts of the city, is the modern **Tisch Gardens Biblical Zoo** consisting of 53 acres of landscaped parkland with lakes, waterfalls, and lawns set against a backdrop of desert hills. Animals wander freely, separated from humans by moats or natural earth banks. Here you can see the now-rare animals of the Old Testament, all once native to the region, including lions and tigers.

Israel adores its children. Even more than in other countries they are indulged and forgiven by everyone. Somehow, their exuberance and enthusiasm, their noisy boisterousness, their energy, and their robust good health, all seem to symbolize the state itself. Israel, too, is young and new and vulnerable. But above all, the children of today are alive. Even now, when Israelis look at their children, they are reminded of a dark past, and an uncertain future.

A precious generation Children seem to be everywhere. School groups, sometimes in neat lines, but more usually like a horde of Tartars, are taken to see every monument and memorial to Israel's creation, every museum of importance. They are always accompanied by an armed guard, sometimes a soldier but more often a parent who is an army reservist with full weapons training (the guns are not loaded—bullets are carried separately).

Israeli children enjoy a freedom their parents did not know

Those who died Before the policy of providing guards began in the 1970s, Palestinian attacks on children were common. School parties, school buses, and children's houses in kibbutzim were considered legitimate targets by the P.L.O. Scores of children were murdered. But overshadowing even these tragedies looms the Holocaust. Common images of Holocaust victims are of adults. In reality, a quarter of all Jews killed in the gas chambers were children. For Israelis today, it is a joy to see Jewish children alive and enjoying their liberty.

A new type The *sabra* is a prickly pear cactus, spiny outside, sweet within. That is how the new generation of Israelis looks to outsiders. A third of all Israeli children now have mixed Ashkenazi/Sephardi families. Chattering (or rather, shouting) in fluent secular Hebrew, a language that did not exist a century ago, taller, stronger, healthier than their mothers and fathers, bold and forthright, and with a country to call their own, they are being nurtured as a new type of Jew.

Innocent play

BED AND BREAKFAST
"Good Morning Jerusalem" is the organization that coordinates over 100 bed-and-breakfast guesthouses in the city and environs. Prices are relatively modest, guesthouses are graded by size and comfort, and all the host families speak English. For bookings or information, contact the reservations office in Jaffa Road, opposite Jerusalem's central bus station, tel: 02 6511270.

Accommodations

The key to enjoying this sprawling city is to be in the right part of it. Top choice would be to stay near the attractions of the Old City, though not too near, as it can be noisy and crowded. The vivacious downtown (west Jerusalem) has most of the best hotels in every price range and is an easy walk from the Old City. The smallish Arab district (East Jerusalem) just north of the Old City walls is atmospheric but less modern. A few of the farther-flung districts are also convenient and enjoyable. Of some 8,000 hotel rooms in the city, over 3,000 are graded deluxe, but there is a good range of budget-priced accommodations as well.

Central Jerusalem On the top rung, the King David Hotel (King David Street, or Rehov David HaMelek), built in 1931 (see page 90), is legendary. Due to continuous

King David Hotel is the grandest in Israel, full of historic importance

The Hotel Laromme, with innovative architecture and luxurious accommodations, is the modern style of Israeli hotel

renovation and modernization, it has left behind much of its prewar grandeur. It is supremely comfortable, well located, with excellent food, facilities, and service, and set on considerable grounds that face the Old City. The King David is part of the top-level Dan chain, which also owns the atrium-style Dan Pearl, facing Mount Zion and not far from Jaffa Gate.

Most international names are on, or near, King David, Keren HaYesod and King George V streets. Here you will find the Sheraton, Hyatt, Hilton, Laromme, and Moriah Plaza. Plenty of good places fill the middle and lower price ranges, such as the Windmill (off Keren HaYesod) and Tirat Batsheva (King George V Street). Lower down the scale, the inexpensive Y.M.C.A. (opposite the King David) is almost absurdly grand looking, and the facilities (especially for sports) are very good. There are also several ultracheap hostels in the city, such as the Jerusalem Inn (Histadrut Street, near the pedestrian streets). The excellent new Yitzhak Rabin Youth Hostel (1 Nahman Avigad Street), near the Israel Museum, is for Youth Hostel members.

Neo-Byzantine splendor: the grand but inexpensive Y.M.C.A.

The Old City and East Jerusalem There is a plethora of budget hotels, dorms, religious hospices, and hostels in the Arab districts around Damascus and Jaffa gates and in the Old City Christian and Muslim quarters. Most are rather shabby. The best are in HaNeviim Street. Note that late-night music and noise, as well as early morning muezzins calling the faithful to prayer, can be a nuisance. Up Salah ed-Din (Saladin) Street there is a string of low-priced hotels. In the American Colony you will find arguably the most interesting and atmospheric hotel in the whole city, the Oriental-style American Colony Hotel. A former pasha's palace, it is now a favorite venue for foreign correspondents and Palestinian leaders.

On a limb The original Jerusalem Hilton, the Sonesta, and the huge Ramada Renaissance hotels, all superbly equipped, stand out west on or just off Herzl Boulevard. They are not far from the Knesset and the major museums, and close to the bus station with its regular departures to points all over the country. Farther out, to the southwest, the Holyland Hotel has a superb model of biblical Jerusalem on its grounds (see page 86). In the other direction is the vast and luxurious Hyatt Regency (32 Lehi Street) on the slope of Mount Scopus with a magnificent city view.

Kibbutz near the city One of the best choices on many counts is the hotel at Kibbutz Ramat Rahel (or Rachel). This is quiet and civilized, has good food, extensive grounds, and a pleasant atmosphere; offers full use of the good kibbutz recreational facilities, and enjoys fine views out toward the Judaean hills. The kibbutz passed into both Jewish and Arab lore in the 1948 war, when it was on the front line and focus of ferocious battles. A kibbutz museum (*Open* daily 8–noon) tells the story. The kibbutz stands halfway between central Jerusalem and Bethlehem, 3 miles from each.

JERUSALEM'S ANNUAL FESTIVALS AND EVENTS
Poetry Festival: March
Book Fair: mid-April
Arabic Arts and Crafts: early May
Fireworks: two nights in May
Yom Yerushalayim (Jerusalem Day): three nights of festivities in May
Israel Festival: three weeks in May and June
Film: early July
Arts and Crafts: July and August
Puppet Theater: August
Artists' Week: August
Early Music: September/October
Jerusalem March: October
Marathon: October

KOSHER
The majority of eating places in Jerusalem are kosher (although most in Arab districts are not). Most big hotels offer something special and traditional for the Friday night Sabbath dinner. On Sabbaths and festivals, many Jerusalem restaurants are closed, but nearly all hotel restaurants remain open.

ONE CENTURY AGO
"In 1873 it was calculated that the Jerusalem Jews, who then numbered only a few hundred in all, were increasing at the rate of 1,200 or 1,500 souls per annum. The Russian persecution gave a great impetus to the movement. I suppose that the present Jewish population of the Holy City cannot be reckoned at less than 40,000 souls. And they are no longer a timorous, oppressed minority, but something more resembling the masters of the city."
—*The Future of Palestine*, Major C. R. Conder, 1892

Eating out

Bed and board Almost all hotels offer a magnificent self-service buffet breakfast of hot and cold dishes, salads, fresh breads, and fruit juices. It makes a great start to the day and can take the edge off lunchtime appetite. Bed-and-breakfast is a good option when booking your trip, giving the freedom to eat dinner in or out of the hotel.

On the hoof In the Old City, there are many small, unpretentious café-restaurants. The format is generally the same: frontage open to the street and, within, a display of salads, pastries, sweets and savories, falafels frying, shwarma on the spit, and some wipe-clean tables. Downtown (West Jerusalem) has scores of small restaurants offering hummus, falafels, latkes (potato fritters), omelettes, grilled meats, shwarma or shishlik (lamb or turkey kebab), salads, pizzas, ice cream, cakes, juices, and coffee.

Some wonderful little bakeries can be found on Jaffa and King George V streets near Ben Yehuda Street and on the other pedestrian lanes—Lunz, Rishonim, Ben Hillel, and Nahalat Shiv'a—which are packed with open-air café tables. Most of these are adequate rather than good, though some have more style and reach a higher standard. Well-established favorites include the Rimon and Alno cafés around Ben Yehuda.

Dinner time Most hotels in town have at least one restaurant, usually "dairy" as well as "meat"-eating places. Try the King David and the American Colony. Away from the hotels, better restaurants aim for either a French-Italian or an Austro-Hungarian style, though Yemenite and Arabic restaurants provide a more exotic experience as well as excellent food. Well established are Little Italy (38 Keren HaYesod Street) for homemade pasta, Mishkenot Sha'ananim (Yemin Moshe, below the windmill) for Moroccan and French dishes, El Gaucho (22 Rivlin Street) for grills, and Oceanus (7 Rivlin Street) for fish. For more ideas, pick up *Jerusalem Menus* from the tourist office.

Israeli restaurants are refreshingly informal

Shopping

Where to shop Wandering along David Street and Street of the Chain, in the Old City, is sheer delight, with a cornucopia of products ranging from cheap souvenirs to antique silver. Outside the walls, away from the central shopping district along and between Jaffa Street and King George V Street, almost every other neighborhood has its well-stocked shopping malls and centers. Some are huge. Talpiot (in the southwest) has the big Canyon Israel Shopping Center, and Manahat or Malka (in the west) has the Malka Mall, the largest shopping center in Israel.

What to buy The Druze weavings, olive-wood carvings, and other craft goods make excellent souvenirs. Jewelry and silverware are great specialties. Silver ornaments and modern Judaica are seen in numerous stores throughout downtown and in the souks of the Old City. Necklaces and other jewelry of silver, gold, and precious stones are also widely available at specialist stores, including along the Cardo, in the Jewish quarter of the Old City.

Diamonds are a major Israeli product, and a tour of the National Diamond Center (143 Bethlehem Road) is worthwhile. All sorts of creative jewelry, imaginative and of a high standard, is for sale. Take a look, for example, at galleries along the main downtown streets. The King David Hotel has shopping arcades selling some of the best. Also look for fine fashions, especially swimwear, in which Israel excels (swimwear giant Gottex is based here). Leather goods are another local strong point, including sandals, which are reasonably priced. And don't miss the unique—and effective—skin-care products (by Arava, for example) made of mud from the Dead Sea.

Bargain-price tapes and worry beads

HAGGLING
Haggling is almost unknown in Israel today, though it's possible to try your luck asking for a "discount." Even in the Arab parts of Jerusalem, haggling has all but died out in the last few decades as traders accustom themselves to the more straightforward, take-it-or-leave-it style of Israelis. Certain goods are never haggled over—food, for example—but in Arab areas, at stalls selling souvenirs, clothing, or trinkets, you may (occasionally) find that goods have no fixed price. Then you should respond to the initial asking price with a shrug, a laugh...and a much lower offer. After a few counteroffers, and some dramatic declarations about not making any profit, family to feed, selling below cost price, etc. (designed to weaken your resolve), you and the trader will agree a price, traditionally about 55 percent of what was first asked.

SHOPPING HOURS
Most businesses, including stores, are open Sunday to Thursday 8:30–1 and 4–7. Bigger shopping malls and centers do not close during the day. On Friday, stores open in the morning only; on Saturday some open after dusk.

DRESS CODE
Whatever the event or venue, informal or casual dress is the norm in Israel. It often startles foreign visitors at official events to see Israeli dignitaries without jackets or ties. Televised Knesset proceedings likewise show members of Israel's parliament—including the Prime Minister—wearing open-neck, short-sleeve shirts. For his important treaty-signing ceremony with King Hussein of Jordan, the late premier Yitzhak Rabin wore a baseball cap. However, sloppy, scruffy clothing is not favored, and immodest or provocative dress is definitely considered unacceptable.

WHAT'S ON
For more details of what's on during your stay, ask the tourist office for copies of the current *This Week in Israel, Events in Jerusalem* and *The Jerusalem Tourist Guide.*

Nightlife

Good clean fun It might be thought that this capital city of religion and faith would go to sleep at an early hour. That is far from being the case. There is an infinite choice to entertain you around the clock, however, nightlife does tend to be of a clean and wholesome variety. Raunchy nightclubs are few, and risqué acts frowned upon. Drama, ballet, concerts, and cheerful folklore shows are constantly available. The only exception is the Sabbath (Saturday), when Jerusalem is quieter than many other Israeli towns. The city's leading venue is the Jerusalem Center for the Performing Arts, at 20 Marcus Street (tel: 02-617167).

Evening air The heart of after-dark Jerusalem is the Nahalat Shiv'a area around Ben Yehuda Street and Zion Square. Along the pedestrian streets, crowds stroll in the open air, and outdoor cafés are packed far into the night. From certain doorways comes the throb of popular music—late-night discos appealing mainly to the young.

Top notch Some evening entertainments are unashamedly touristic, but still top quality. The outdoor Son et Lumière at the Citadel (Tower of David) is superb (nightly except Fridays). It tells the history of the city in a magnificently appropriate setting. Take a sweater; tickets from hotels or the Citadel entrance at Jaffa Gate.

Song and dance Slick Israeli/Jewish folklore shows are put on in the big hotels. Often there are specials, such as a dramatized performance of a Yemenite wedding. Folk shows are put on at the Y.M.C.A., on King David Street, and at the Khan Theater, in an old Turkish inn south of Yemin Moshe. Open-air summer performances are staged at the Sultan's Pool amphitheater below Yemin Moshe.

Arabian nights If you have seen the Israeli shows before, or want a change, take a trip into East Jerusalem for clubs and restaurants that put on the Arab version. They feature lilting Oriental music and exotic (not erotic) dance shows.

Nightlife is clean and wholesome

Practical points

Information The Jerusalem tourist office is at 17 Jaffa Road (tel: 02-258844). It has masses of leaflets, ideas for guided tours, and copies of the latest editions of *This Week in Israel*, *Events in Jerusalem* and *The Jerusalem Tourist Guide*. Staff speak English and are helpful.

Getting around The Old City of Jerusalem is compact, with major sights close to each other. Outside the walls, by far the best way to get from one sight to another is on bus No. 99. The bus follows a round-town circular route every two hours (Sun–Thu 10–4; Fri and the evening before public holidays 10 AM and noon). You can get off at any point of interest, take a look around, and board the next No. 99 bus to continue.

City buses in general are frequent and inexpensive. Bus drivers speak English, and stops have brief route details in English. For local bus information tel: 02 304 704 (toll-free, English spoken). Services run from 5:30 AM to midnight, except on Friday (when services stop for the Sabbath an hour before sunset) and on Saturday (no service until after Sabbath ends, an hour after sunset). Services on Jewish holidays are the same as for the Sabbath. From the city's main Jaffa Road bus station, buses leave every few minutes to towns and cities all over Israel. To Tel Aviv costs 11 NIS and takes an hour.

Regular taxis (called "special taxis"), which generally wait outside hotels, are expensive. Agree upon the fare in advance, or insist that the meter be used (Jerusalem cab drivers are notorious for overcharging). Cheaper *sherutim* (singular: *sherut*), shared taxis that stick to a particular route, depart from set locations.

Business hours Banks are open Sunday to Friday 8:30–12:30, and on Sunday, Tuesday and Thursday 4–6. In tourist areas, some open Sunday to Thursday 8:30–5:30, and Friday 8:30–12:30. Main post offices open Sunday to Thursday 8–6. Post office local branches open daily 8–12:30 and 3:30–6, but mornings only on Monday, Wednesday, and Friday.

Emergencies
Police 100; Ambulance 101; Fire 102; Tourist Police 391250.

GUIDED WALKS
Numerous firms offer guided walking tours. Their leaflets are displayed at the tourist office and big hotels. The tourist office itself runs guided walks, free of charge. Ask for dates and times.

RETURN TO SENDER
"How much better informed the public now is than twenty years ago, when my letters were shelved in an English country post office, because they were directed to me at Jerusalem, and the postmistress said in explanation that she thought 'all that was done away with.'"
—Major C. R. Conder, 1892

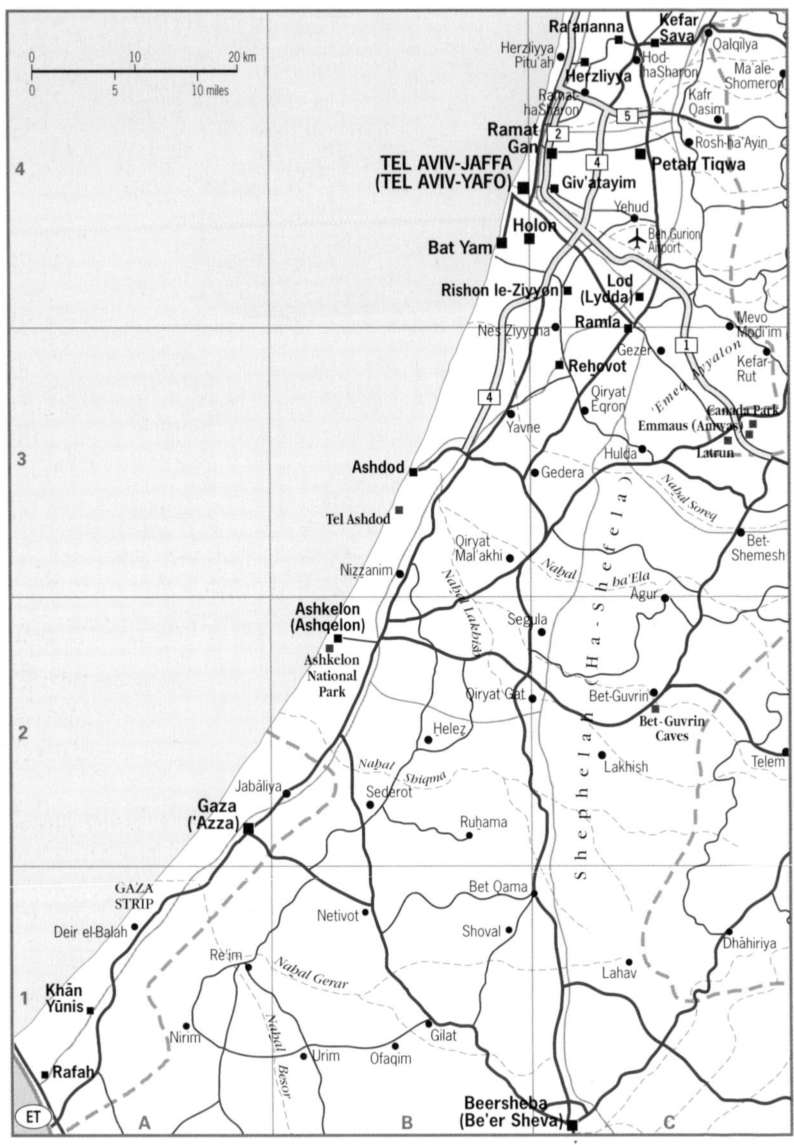

▶▶▶ REGION HIGHLIGHTS

TEL AVIV AND THE COAST The Mediterranean has dominated Israel's life and civilization throughout the ages. Psychologically as well as physically, Israel faces west, for commerce, culture, and communication. Almost the entire population lives on a narrow strip along the coast. Most of Israel's wealth comes from this busy, densely populated strip and from the farms of the well-watered Plain of Sharon, running north to south just inland from the sea. For the visitor wanting to combine beach life with exploration of the country's unrivaled array of ancient sites, it is convenient that (apart from the Negev desert) few places in Israel are further than about 15 miles from a Mediterranean beach.

Tel Aviv and the Coast

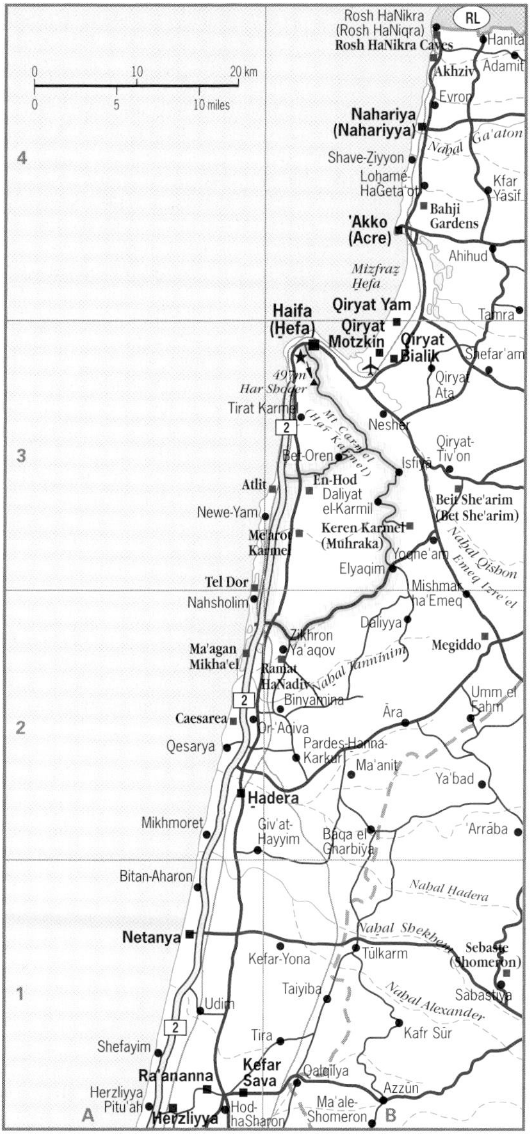

NEW AND OLD RESORTS While Tel Aviv is a big city, bursting with energy, there is a string of quieter resorts, such as Netanya and Herzliya, up and down the coast. Here leisure facilities and accommodations tend to reach a far higher standard than anywhere else in the eastern Mediterranean. It is also possible to stay by the sea without being in town at all—for example, at a kibbutz hotel. Few resorts, whether in the town or the country, date back more than a few decades, and most were designed as resorts in the first place. Yet nearly all have a historical site nearby, remnants of some earlier town—Phoenician, Jewish, or Roman—which stood there thousands of years before, including the star attractions of Caesarea and Akko.

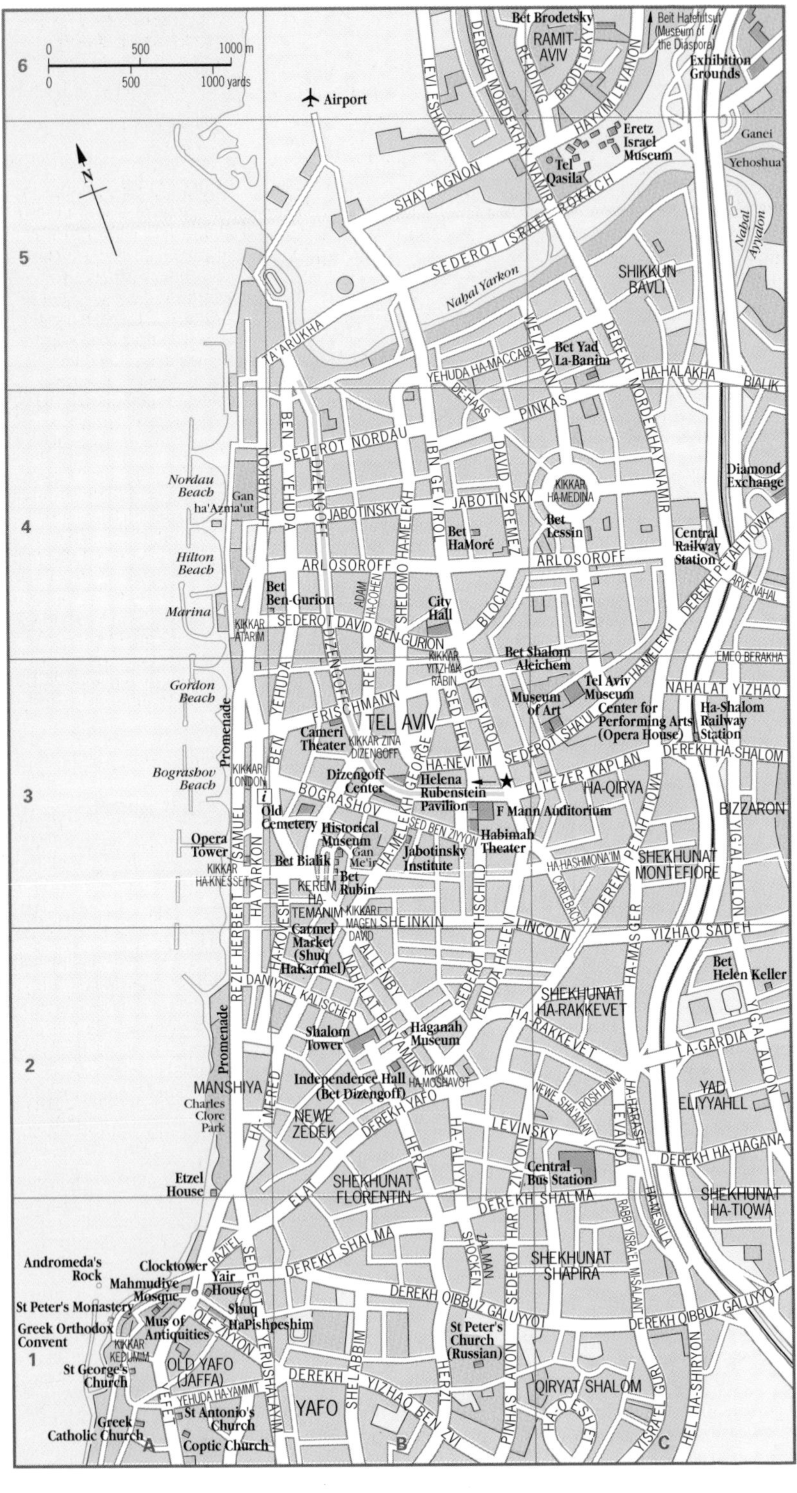
0
500
1000 m
0
500
1000 yards
N
Airport
Bet Brodetsky
RAMIT-AVIV
Beit Hatefutsot (Museum of the Diaspora)
Exhibition Grounds
LEVI ESHKOL
DEREKH MORDEKHAY NAMIR
READING
BRODETSKY
HAYYIM LEVANON
Eretz Israel Museum
Tel Qasila
Ganei Yehoshua
SHAY 'AGNON
SEDEROT ISRAEL ROKACH
Nahal Yarkon
Nahal Ayyalon
SHIKKUN BAVLI
TA'ARUKHA
WEIZMANN
Bet Yad La-Banim
DEREKH MORDEKHAY NAMIR
YEHUDA HA-MACCABI
DE-HAAS
HA-HALAKHA
BIALIK
PINKAS
SEDEROT NORDAU
BEN YEHUDA
DIZENGOFF
IBN GEVIROL
DAVID REMEZ
KIKKAR HA-MEDINA
Diamond Exchange
Nordau Beach
Gan ha'Azma'ut
HA-YARKON
JABOTINSKY
SHLOMO HA-MELEKH
Bet HaMoré
Bet Lessin
Central Railway Station
DEREKH PETAH TIQWA
Hilton Beach
ARLOSOROFF
ARYE NAHAL
Bet Ben-Gurion
ADAM HA-COHEN
City Hall
BLOCH
Marina
KIKKAR ATARIM
SEDEROT DAVID BEN-GURION
KIKKAR YITZHAK RABIN
Bet Shalom Aleichem
EMEQ BERAKHA
Gordon Beach
REINS
FRISCHMANN
SED HEN
Tel Aviv Museum
Museum of Art
NAHALAT YIZHAQ
TEL AVIV
Center for Performing Arts (Opera House)
Ha-Shalom Railway Station
Promenade
Cameri Theater
KIKKAR ZINA DIZENGOFF
KING GEORGE
HA-NEVI'IM
SEDEROT SHA'UL HA-MELEKH
DEREKH HA-SHALOM
Bograshov Beach
KIKKAR LONDON
Dizengoff Center
Helena Rubenstein Pavilion
ELI'EZER KAPLAN
HA-QIRYA
BOGRASHOV
F Mann Auditorium
BIZZARON
Old Cemetery
Historical Museum
SED BEN ZIYYON
Habimah Theater
Opera Tower
SAMUEL
Bet Bialik
Gan Me'ir
Jabotinsky Institute
HA-HASHMONA'IM
SHEKHUNAT MONTEFIORE
YIG'AL ALLON
KIKKAR HA-KNESSET
KEREM HA-TEMANIM
Bet Rubin
CARLEBACH
KIKKAR MAGEN DAVID
SHEINKIN
ROTHSCHILD
HA-KOVESHIM
REZIF HERBERT
Carmel Market (Shuq HaKarmel)
LINCOLN
HA-MASGER
YIZHAQ SADEH
ALLENBY
SEDEROT
YEHUDA HA-LEVI
Bet Helen Keller
DANIYYEL
KALISCHER
NAHALAT BINYAMIN
SHEKHUNAT HA-RAKKEVET
HA-RAKKEVET
Shalom Tower
Haganah Museum
LA-GARDIA
MANSHIYA
Independence Hall (Bet Dizengoff)
KIKKAR HA-MOSHAVOT
YAD ELIYYAHU
Charles Clore Park
HA-MERED
NEWE ZEDEK
DEREKH YAFO
NEWE SHA'ANAN
ROSH PINNA
HA-HARASH
LEVANDA
HA-'ALIYYA
LEVINSKY
DEREKH HA-HAGANA
Etzel House
HERZL
ELAT
SHEKHUNAT FLORENTIN
Central Bus Station
ZIYYON
SHEKHUNAT HA-TIQWA
HA-MESILLA
DEREKH SHALMA
RABBI YISRA'EL MISALANT
RAZIEL
Andromeda's Rock
Clocktower
Yair House
SHOCKEN
ZALMAN
HAR ZIYYON
SHEKHUNAT SHAPIRA
Mahmudiye Mosque
SEDEROT YERUSHALAYIM
DEREKH QIBBUZ GALUYYOT
St Peter's Monastery
Shuq HaPishpeshim
St Peter's Church (Russian)
Greek Orthodox Convent
Mus of Antiquities
OLEI ZIYYON
KIKKAR KEDUMIM
St George's Church
OLD YAFO (JAFFA)
SHELABBIM
DEREKH YIZHAQ BEN ZVI
PINHAS LAVON
QIRYAT SHALOM
HA-Q'ESHET
YISRA'EL GURI
HEL HA-SHIRYON
YEHUDA HA-YAMMIT
YEFET
St Antonio's Church
YAFO
Greek Catholic Church
Coptic Church
A
B
C
1
2
3
4
5
6

Tel Aviv

A century ago it wasn't here. The largest Jewish city ever to have existed has sprung up beside the Mediterranean with dizzying speed. The sense of liberation and excitement in the air is almost palpable. Tel Aviv has pulled fragments of a nation from the world's ghettos and Jewish quarters and, like a crucible, fused them together once again. A quarter of Israel's population lives in the city and its suburbs, which together form a hectic, dynamic metropolis dominating the country's cultural life.

Tel Aviv plays, Haifa works, Jerusalem prays. That is the popular summary of Israel's three cities. It is true that, in Tel Aviv, very few pray: signs of Jewish observance, or of any other religion, are scarce. This is a breezily materialistic, pleasure-loving city. For round-the-clock entertainment and sheer joie de vivre, this is the place.

On the other hand, Tel Aviv at leisure will not appeal to everyone. It is a touch civilized. The city has dozens of first-class galleries and museums. People going out for the evening head to symphony concerts or stage plays, though there are jazz and rock spots too. Performers in the street, almost without exception, play the violin: their repertoire is mainly classical or East European folk music. You probably won't, in any part of town, see anyone drunk. Nightclub acts tend toward satire, not strippers. Day and night, it is the vast beach and its waterside promenade that pull the biggest crowds of all.

An East Mediterranean city Tel Avivians compare their home town grandly to New York or Paris. True, there are chic shops and good restaurants, but the lively avenues and big squares, the generous sidewalks shaded from the sun, the outdoor tables and exuberant (but crime-free) street life, and the little backstreet shops with a prewar feel, add up to an inescapably East Mediterranean feel. A more accurate comparison might be with Athens (but without the level of pollution), for Tel Aviv, like the Greek capital, is newly built, yet echoes with history. And, again like that city, it represents the joyful rebirth of a Mediterranean land swallowed up for centuries by the Ottoman Empire.

PEACEMAKER YITZHAK RABIN (1922–1995)
As Sabbath ended on November 4, 1995, gunshots rang out at the Rally for Peace in Tel Aviv's Kings of Israel Square, killing Prime Minister Yitzhak Rabin as he left the podium. The general who in 1967 led the Six-Day War victory, Rabin, was already a national hero when he pledged to create peace treaties between Israel and her Arab enemies. Many opposed his "land for peace" policies, and the fatal gunshots were fired by an Orthodox student. At the next election, Binyamin Netanyahu was elected Prime Minister on a promise to halt the peace process. In 1999 the new Prime Minister Ehud Barak vowed to complete Rabin's work.

Yitzhak Rabin Memorial Day is on 12 Heshvan, the Hebrew date of his death, and Kings of Israel Square has been renamed Yitzhak Rabin Square.

Mounts of olives

►►► Beaches

114A2–4

A glorious 5 miles of wide, soft white sand runs beside the heart of the city. It is only a 10-minute walk from deckchair to Dizengoff, the main central avenue. More spectacular is the broad beachside **promenade►►►**, paved in swirling patterns, stretching from North Tel Aviv nearly into Jaffa. For most of the distance, busy Herbert Samuel Boulevard runs parallel. From 6 AM to 2 AM, you will see swimmers in the water and joggers on the promenade. And, facing west, the beach and promenade are perfect for sunsets. In the evening, street musicians play the violin, sometimes even joining to form string quartets. Well past midnight, thousands of people still stroll or sit here in the tender night air.

Yet the water looks soupy, the undercurrents are powerful, and the sand is dotted with oil. Join the Israelis, who happily swim and surf under the watchful eye of the lifeguards, and you will need to take a shower at the end of the day, wiping the oil off your feet with detergent-filled brushes provided at beach access points. Use towels, shoes, and clothes that are not special favorites.

North of the main beach The bay by the harbor is dominated by noisy music from a café-bar. Next, Nordau beach divides into enclosed men-only and women-only areas, mainly for the religious (men can use women's beaches if accompanied by a woman). Two more small bays lie below the Hilton Hotel.

Marina and public pool This popular pay-to-enter swimming and sunbathing area, below the Carlton Hotel, has lawns, shade, showers, and snack bar.

FOLLOW THE FLAG
All down Israel's Mediterranean coast, swimming conditions are indicated by colored flags on the beach. White shows that swimming is safe where a lifeguard is on duty. Red shows that swimming could be dangerous, but is permitted at the discretion of the lifeguard on duty. Black means no swimming at all.

ON THE BEACH
Opposite the Dan Hotel, where now sunbathers laze, a ship carrying 850 clandestine Jewish immigrants finally came to rest on August 22, 1939. The overcrowded *Parita* had spent 42 days wandering at sea, avoiding British craft intent on preventing Jews from reaching Palestine.

Space to enjoy a swim or a stroll

Main beach and promenade This starts at **Kikkar Atarim** (or Namir), an ugly plaza with unenticing cafés. About 100 yards beyond, a more agreeable traffic-free section lies below the Sheraton Hotel. Then the boulevard sweeps down to the promenade and a string of upscale sea-view hotels. The low-rise **Dan Hotel**, despite a garish exterior, is considered the city's best. Below it, the gardens of **Kikkar London▶** face the sea, and **Yotvata Dairy Restaurant** attracts big crowds day and night. The **Opera Tower** apartment block is a landmark at busy Allenby intersection. Beach and promenade, less opulent south of this point, fade away just before litter-strewn **Charles Clore Park**.

South of the main beach From here on, the waterfront has a more Arab character. The boulevard turns away from the sea by a mosque, but the promenade continues. Finally there is a pleasant sand beach with a bar, but swimming is discouraged. Here the part-old, part-new **Etzel Museums▶▶** tell the story of the Irgun Tzvai Leumi (see page 119). Where the beach and walkway end, a road continues into **Jaffa** (see page 124).

▶ Ben-Gurion House 114B4

17 Ben-Gurion Boulevard
Open: daily. Admission free

This was the home of Israel's charismatic and powerful first Prime Minister, David Ben-Gurion (1886–1973), and his wife Paula. The small and simply furnished house has been preserved as it was during their lifetime. It is full of personal memorabilia, items of political and historical interest, and a library of 20,000 volumes.

▶ Bialik House (Beit Bialik) 114B3

22 Bialik Street
Open: Sat–Thu. Admission free

Haim Nachman Bialik (1873–1934), revered as the greatest modern Hebrew poet, designed this house, with its Moorish echoes, as his home (1926–1933). Kept unchanged since his death, it contains pictures, letters, and memorabilia that tell the story of his life and work.

▶▶▶ Carmel Market (Shuk HaCarmel) 114B2

This big market (every day except Shabbat) extends along narrow HaCarmel Street (off Allenby Street) and adjoining lanes. Despite the lack of traffic, it is noisy with stallholders' cries and the crush of people walking, talking, and haggling as they look over CDs, shoes, clothes, garlic, fruit, vegetables, and bagels. Some stalls have only nectarines or olives, others lie buried in fresh herbs. In parallel Yomtov and Gedera streets, some are loaded with meat. Here the robust younger generation mingles with graybeards and their headscarfed wives, and Eastern Europe meets Jewish Arabia. In the adjacent run-down **Yemenite quarter▶▶** (or Kerem HaTemanim), many of the simple houses have kept their overhanging balconies and small courtyards.

OPERA TOWER
This prestige apartment tower, with its shopping complex, movie theaters, and restaurants, stands on the beachside boulevard on the site of Israel's first Knesset (parliament building) at 1 Allenby Street. The War of Independence made occupation of the Jerusalem Knesset impossible until December 1949. Later, the Tel Aviv Knesset building was used as the city's opera house, until a magnificent new opera house was opened in October, 1994.

BAUHAUS
Large tracts of 1920s Tel Aviv consists of "workers' residences" constructed by the Histadrut labor union in the inexpensive, functional Bauhaus design. The war destroyed most of Germany's Bauhaus buildings, leaving Tel Aviv with the finest collection anywhere of this 20th-century style—over 3,500 buildings in total. The Museum of Art (see page 129) runs a free weekly Bauhaus bus tour with English commentary. It will pick you up at your hotel—to book, call the Tel Aviv Museum of Art, tel: 03 695 7361.

Who could resist Carmel Market's inviting stalls?

EARLY TOWN PLANNING
When Tel Aviv's avenues were first laid out, they say, the plan was to make them in the shape of a menorah, the seven-branched candelabrum that once stood in the Temple and that is now the symbol of the state. Instead, the builders diverted what is now Ben-Gurion Boulevard toward their favorite beach-side bar.

Traditional crafts at the Eretz Israel Museum

THE FIRST STREETS
Some of the first streets in Tel Aviv were laid on sand just north of Jaffa, in the area called Neve Tzedek, behind the Dan Panorama Hotel. North is one of the city's tallest buildings, the Shalom Tower, in a neighborhood of quiet streets lined by small two-story houses. Many are scruffy and run down, but others have been tidied up as the merits of the neighborhood are gradually being rediscovered.

►► Eretz Israel Museum 114C5

2 University (or Haim Levanon) Street, Ramat Aviv
Open: Sun–Mon, Thu 9–2, Tue–Wed 9–7, Sat 10–2
Admission: expensive. Guided tour in English on Sat at 11

Take a No. 25 bus out of central Tel Aviv to travel north of the Nahal (river) Yarkon to this immense and imaginative national museum, on the site of an excavated tel (settlement mound). Eretz Israel means "Land of Israel," and the museum covers various themes spanning 3,000 years in the history of Israel's material culture and ethnography. An inexpensive site map makes it easy to find your way around, and museum literature recommends two possible routes through the grounds; one short (half a day) and the other long (a full day). Many exhibits were actually discovered here and are displayed in situ. Between the pavilions and the open-air exhibits there are pleasant lawns and trees, plus a good restaurant and snack bar.

Among the best exhibits are **Roman winepresses►**, **Byzantine mosaic paving►►**, and two **ancient roads►** discovered one on top of the other. There is a superb **Planetarium►►**, but the commentary is in Hebrew only.

The **Numismatics Pavilion►►** displays coinage across the millennia from shells to shekels, including biblical weights (of which the shekel is one). The **Nehushtan Pavilion►►** explains ancient mining, with useful information about Timna (see page 251). The **Folklore and Ethnology Pavilion►►** shows the unchanging traditions of Jewish ritual objects and apparel from ancient times to the present day. At the **Man and His Works Pavilion►►**, devoted to traditional hand crafts, you can see a glassblower at work and the workshops of a blacksmith and a potter.

The grounds also include an entire archeological site, **Tel Qasile►►►**, one of several tels on Tel Aviv's northern boundary. This was the first archeological site to be excavated by Israel (in 1949): 12 settlement phases were found dating back to 1150 BC, with remnants of a temple and houses containing domestic objects.

►► Etzel Museums *114B3*

These three museums, known collectively as the Etzel Museums, tell the fascinating story of the Irgun Tzvai Leumi guerrilla organization (1937–1948). They are also known as Etzel, which took on the British Army (except during World War II) and helped to bring about the creation of the State of Israel, by using tactics condemned by the Haganah and official Zionist movement (see page 43). From 1943 to 1948, its leader was Menachem Begin, later Israel's Prime Minister.

The plain white **Beit Jabotinsky (Jabotinsky Institute)►►►** building, opposite the Dizengoff Center, at 38 Rehov HaMelech George (*Open* Sun–Thu 8–4. *Admission: moderate*), covers the pre-1948 history of the organization. Secret operations that attracted worldwide headlines are explained with chilling clarity. Included is the blowing up of the British headquarters in Jerusalem's King David Hotel (July 1946) when 91 people died, the destruction of the British Officers' Club (March 1947) when 17 people died, and the breaching of Akko Fortress (May 1947), when 30 Irgun and Lehi prisoners escaped.

A second museum, by the beach, close to Jaffa, can be found in **Etzel House►** (*Open* Sun–Thu. *Admission: moderate*), restored "in memory of the liberators of Jaffa." It reveals Irgun's activities during the 1948 War of Independence. A third museum in **Beit Yair (Yair House)►**, 8 Avraham Stern Street (*Open* Sun–Thu 8:30–4. *Admission: moderate*), covers the history of the Lehi movement (also known as "the Stern Gang"), the hard-line splinter group that refused wartime cooperation with the British.

► Haganah Museum (Beit Haganah) *114B2*

23 Rothschild Boulevard
Closed Shabbat. Admission: moderate

Beit Eliahu (Eliahu House), home of the founding commander of Haganah, Eliahu Golomb, is a memorial to his life and times. Models and tableaux bring to life the history of Israel's armed forces, from their clandestine origins in 1907, through the creation of diverse undercover groups, to the creation of the Israel Defense Forces in 1948.

► Historical Museum of Tel Aviv–Jaffa *114B3*

27 Bialik Street
Open: Sun–Thu. Admission free

This round-fronted Bauhaus building, once Little Tel Aviv's Town Hall, recalls the creation and growth of the new city (see side panel), using old photographs, models, and a movie.

LITTLE TEL AVIV

The beginnings of Tel Aviv lie in small Jewish neighborhoods that were technically still part of Jaffa. The city really took off in 1921 when it was granted a charter as a separate town. A whole new district was immediately constructed a little farther north, around Bialik Street, the nucleus of the first new Jewish city to be built in modern Israel. Its town hall in Bialik Square later became the Historical Museum. Full of socialist theory, the city's founders declared there would be no commerce or private business at all in Tel Aviv: everything would be run by the municipality. This dream bit the dust as entrepreneurial immigrants flocked in and opened the corner kiosks that are still such a feature of the city. As the town expanded, this original center became known as Little Tel Aviv.

Patriotism rules at the Haganah Museum

A SHADY SEAT

A cross between a public garden and a street, there is a boulevard with a difference that curves right through the heart of Tel Aviv. It starts as Sederot Rothschild (Rothschild Boulevard) close to the Shalom Tower, continues, after Kikkar HaTizmoret and Kikkar HaBimah, as Sederot Hen, and becomes Sederot Ben-Gurion, which turns to reach the sea at Kikkar Atarim. For its entire length, the two main lanes are separated by a broad sandy walkway shaded by leafy trees. Benches every few yards offer a chance to take a break from the noise, from sunshine, and from sightseeing.

▶▶ Independence Hall 114B2

16 Sederot Rothschild

Open: Sun–Thu 9–2. Admission: moderate

The city's first mayor, Meir Dizengoff, lived in this austere bunker-like concrete building. On May 14, 1948, his home was the setting for the historic declaration that brought the State of Israel into being. The house has since become a fascinating museum (part of the Eretz Israel Museum, see page 118) recalling that momentous day and the events that led up to it. Many other exhibits are concerned with the establishment of the city of Tel Aviv.

Among many extraordinary displays is a photograph showing sections of the sand dunes north of Jaffa being awarded, lot by lot, to anyone who wanted one. Another photo is of the United Nations in session in November 1947 voting to partition Palestine, and a third shows the meeting at which David Ben-Gurion announced the creation of Israel. Intriguing maps include one showing which countries voted for partition, and another showing the borders of the Jewish state as proposed by the U.N.—which was to consist of three small sections located between Tel Aviv and Haifa.

Alongside the hall in which the proclamation was made, the **Hall of Documents▶▶▶** is a small annex displaying a collection of original documents. One shows the draft proclamation with the name of the country still undecided—just days before the announcement. Penciled-in possibilities included Zion and Western Eretz Israel.

In the street outside, the white memorial and fountain is known as the **Founders' Monument▶**. It names those who founded the city and depicts the story of Tel Aviv in three bas-relief panels. The first shows laborers leveling the sand by hand, and starting to build while harassed by snakes and jackals. A second depicts important early landmark buildings, including the first Hebrew secondary school. The third captures the modern city showing the port, art museum, theater, the home of the national poet Bialik, and apartments behind.

Commemorating the founding of Israel

Walk

Dizengoff Street

No downtown avenue typifies the life and atmosphere of Tel Aviv so well as Dizengoff, named after the city's first mayor. To walk the full length—stopping to window-shop and see the sights—could take a morning. It could require longer still if you break for refreshment—maybe a falafel-in-pita lunch, or a fresh juice at one of the many snack bars. As it continues northward, the street's character changes to reflect different faces of the city and its people. The street's shaded west side is the more appealing (for map see page 114).

Multicolored fountain at the center of Dizengoff Circle

Dizengoff starts behind the modern **Mann Auditorium▶**, home of the Israel Philharmonic Orchestra, and the national **Habimah Theater▶**, focal points of the city's thriving highbrow culture. **Dizengoff Center** is Tel Aviv's main indoor shopping center. **Dizengoff Circle▶▶▶** (correctly, Kikkar Zina Dizengoff, named after the mayor's wife) is a popular, often crowded, plaza with movie theaters and cheap eateries. Here is also an area raised above the street where a gaudy multicolored **fountain▶** puts on a weird fire-and-water show to computerized music (11–1 and 7–9 daily).

From the Circle northward for several blocks, the street has a pleasant atmosphere. It's busy and crowded, lined with snack bars, juice bars, fashion boutiques, and jewelry stores and shaded by large trees.

After crossing **Arlosoroff**, things quiet down as Dizengoff enters the more prosperous **North Tel Aviv** area. There are more food stores, clothes stores take on a pricier, more exclusive look, and cafés become cooler and more stylish. Beyond the pleasant **Nordau** intersection, Dizengoff narrows. Near the street's north end, by the **Yirmehahu** intersection, there is another little cluster of stylish boutiques and eating places. Just beyond this point, the Nahal Yarkon (Yarkon River) marks the official city limit.

Along Dizengoff's northern stretch

Little over a century ago, Hebrew was not a spoken language at all. Most non-Jews thought it was a dead language like Latin, and most Jews reserved it for prayer and ritual. Then Eliezer Ben-Yehuda arrived in Palestine from Lithuania. For him, it was imperative that Jews speak their ancestral tongue in their own land.

ONE OF THE PEOPLE
Eliezer Ben-Yehuda was not the only East European Zionist who wished to reestablish the Hebrew language. Russian Zionist Asher Ginsburg (1856–1957) also had a vision of Hebrew as the everyday language of the Jews, wherever they lived in the world. He ardently wanted the State of Israel to be created, but only as a spiritual and cultural center for world Jewry. He himself did not envision moving there, although he eventually did so in 1922. His vision attracted few followers, and he was an aloof, wealthy character, living an almost aristocratic lifestyle—in contradiction of his pen-name of Ahad Ha'Am, literally "One of the People." He is buried in Tel Aviv's Old Cemetery.

Nobel Laureate, Shmuel Yosef Agnon

Max Brod

Ben-Yehuda's "crazy idea," as some described it, struck a chord with many people. By 1910, there were demonstrations calling for Hebrew to become the Palestinian Jews' official language. In 1924, the first Hebrew university opened. In 1966, a novelist writing in Hebrew, S. Y. Agnon, won Israel's first Nobel Prize for Literature.

New language, old language Today, as you walk in the bustling, lively streets of Israel's cities, passing newspaper stands piled high with different dailies and weeklies, all expressing varied viewpoints, or as you browse in the popular bookstores, listen to the radio, or watch television, you will encounter Hebrew everywhere.

The early Zionists assumed that Yiddish, the Jewish language based on medieval German and spoken by two-thirds of all Jews before the Holocaust, would be Israel's national language. True, the country does have some

Yiddish publications, just as it has Russian and English papers. But, above all, the life of Israel is conducted in Ivrit, as modern Hebrew is called. This is so closely based on biblical Hebrew that any Israeli schoolchild can read the ancient scriptures with ease. Similarly, Moses, King David, or Solomon would be able to read a modern Israeli newspaper. Yet Ivrit includes many European constructions and English-based vocabulary, making it a functional modern working language for everyday use.

The revival The inspiration behind Hebrew's renaissance was Eliezer Ben-Yehuda (1858–1922), who came from Lithuania to Palestine in 1881. This fanatic announced on arrival that he would not talk to his Yiddish-speaking wife and child except in Hebrew. He spoke to puzzled storekeepers in Hebrew, wrote the first Hebrew dictionary, and in 1890 founded the Hebrew Language Committee. Later the committee became the Academy of the Hebrew Language, final arbiter on all matters of vocabulary. At first dismissed by the Zionist authorities as a crank, he eventually led a mass movement they could not ignore. By 1900, many East European Jewish writers were using Hebrew with great effect, notably Chaim Bialik (1873–1934), the brilliant poet, fiction writer, and translator who moved here from Russia in 1925.

Dots, capitals, roots A Semitic language, written from right to left, Hebrew has no upper or lower case (capital or small letters), and words such as "the" ("Ha") are joined to nouns as prefixes. Also, it has in effect two alphabets—one used in printing and one for handwritten script. Then, more difficult, the all-important dots and dashes underneath consonants, used to indicate vowel sounds, are rarely shown. Lastly, there is no agreed way of expressing Hebrew sounds in English. The guttural *h* is often written *ch*. The sound *ei* is also written *e* or *eh* (as in Eilat). The letter *tzadik*, pronounced *tz*, is often written as *z* or even *s* (as in Sefat or Masada). The common word *beit*—a house or institution—can be written *bet* or *beth*.

A nation of readers and theater-goers Israel has more bookstores per capita than any other nation. A U.N.E.S.C.O. survey showed that the proportion of Israelis who "regularly buy books" is among the highest in the world, way ahead of the U.S.A. and Britain. The world's literature, classic or modern, is avidly read in Hebrew translation. Shakespeare is constantly performed on the stages of Tel Aviv and Jerusalem, as are other great playwrights and contemporary Israeli works. The longest-running play on the Israeli stage was not a comedy, but Arthur Miller's *All My Sons*.

Writers of today Israel has produced a crop of novelists, dramatists, and poets of its own (though few were born in Israel). In 1966, Shmuel Yosef Agnon (1888–1970), writing in German, Yiddish, and Hebrew, was the first Israeli to win the Nobel Prize for Literature. A far better-known Israeli author is Amos Oz (born 1939), whose Hebrew novels and short stories have been widely translated. Other distinguished Israeli writers include Max Brod (1884–1968) and Ephraim Kishon (born 1924).

ON THE STAGE
HaBimah means "the stage." The platform on which the Torah is read aloud in a synagogue is also called the *bimah* and Israel's national theater is called simply Habimah Theater. It is housed in a large round modern building (in Kikkar HaBimah) beside the Mann Auditorium, the superb 3,000-seat concert hall (in Kikkar HaTizmoret) that is home to the renowned Israel Philharmonic Orchestra.

Israeli author Amos Oz

POT LUCK
Inside the Jaffa Museum you can see a copy of the Harris Papyrus, which describes the conquest of the town in 1500 BC by the men of Pharaoh Thotmes III. Under their general, Tehuti, they entered the town by ship, concealed in hundreds of large earthenware cargo pots. Tehuti ceremonially announced himself to the governor of Jaffa, saying he had fled Egypt with a huge stolen treasure. Delighted, the governor invited him to a banquet while the pots of treasure were unloaded. Tehuti accepted, killed the governor over dinner, and seized the palace, while his men attacked the city.

מקור מנהלת נמל יפו
עוסק מורשה מס' 545000283
רשיון כניסה חד-פעמי להולכי רגל
חשבונית מס'/ קבלה מס' 129421
1.00 שקל חדש
המחיר כולל מע"מ
עפ"י תקנה שפורסמה בק"ת מס' 5152 מיום 12.12.88
הרשיון מותנה בתנאים שמצד שני
תאריך ________

▶▶▶ Jaffa (Yafo) 114A1

The oldest working port in the world has become a suburb of Israel's newest city. Approached along the seashore promenade or boulevard, Jaffa lies only a short distance from its neighbor Tel Aviv. Inland, the two are joined and, since 1950, have been a single municipality. In 1960, the Jaffa Development Corporation set out to revive the squalid remnant of the town, and turned it into a place of entertainment and leisure. On Friday and Saturday evenings the atmosphere can be wonderfully vivacious and exciting. The crowds gather by the Clocktower, or in Kedumim Square, to stroll, to talk in the balmy air, or to eat at outdoor restaurants. The view along the seafront to Tel Aviv is superb.

Modern Jaffa conveys little sense of its long history. The earliest remains here date back to the 18th century BC. In the 12th century BC, Jaffa became part of the Israelite kingdom, and the Old Testament makes mention of the town several times. Under Solomon it was developed as the principal port for the Jewish capital, Jerusalem. The 12th and 13th centuries AD saw frequent invasion as successive Crusaders, including Richard the Lion-hearted, were beaten off. From that time up until the British entered Jaffa in November 1917 (with the exception of Napoleon's destructive foray in 1799), Jaffa was resolutely Arab and, despite its ups and downs, a busy port up until modern times.

The 20th century led to far-reaching change, in some ways bringing Jaffa's history to an end (other than as a leisure district of Tel Aviv). By the start of that century, a few Jewish refugees had settled among the Arabs of Jaffa. They were made unwelcome, and, in any case, they aspired to better housing.

In 1909, a group called Ahuzat Bayit built a suburb on barren sands north of the port, the start of Tel Aviv. From then on, the building never stopped. In 1921, 1929, and 1936 Jaffa's Arabs rioted against the Jews, each time killing several people. The response of the British Mandate authorities was to cut avenues through the tangle of narrow streets in order to control civil disturbances. A new port was constructed in Tel Aviv, which soon replaced the port at Jaffa; within months of the 1936 riots, the ancient port was closed down.

The bizarre 1947 U.N. Partition Plan placed Jaffa in an Arab state and Tel Aviv in a Jewish one. Following the

The historic port city of Jaffa

Archeological finds date Jaffa's origins to the 18th century BC

DOCKLANDS
Jaffa's historic docks, famous throughout the ages, have been turned into a curiously downscale, but atmospheric, pay-to-enter family entertainment area. The quays are lined with big old waterside warehouses, some of which have been converted to contain cheap stores and stalls or restaurants overlooking the harbor. In the water are pleasure boats (some with eating places on board) and a few fishing trawlers.

1948 Proclamation of the State of Israel, Jaffa's Arabs launched a military attack on Tel Aviv. They were defeated and many fled. Large areas of unsanitary alleys and lanes were swept away. Today only a minority of residents are Arabs—Christian and Muslim—but Jaffa retains an Oriental flavor. Much of this comes from the many Jews from Arab countries living here.

The center of activity is **Kedumim Square►►►**, a pleasant open plaza paved in pale stone. Around the square are places of entertainment, a nightclub, eating places, and a large Catholic church. Steps dive below street level to the **Visitor Center►►►** (*Open* Sun–Thu 9 AM–10 PM, Fri 9–2, Sat 10–10. *Admission free).* It is, in fact, a simple little museum revealing what lies under the square—mainly walls and structures dating from around 300 BC. Off the square is the **Artists' Quarter►►►**, a strangely quiet, picturesque district of narrow lanes with attractive Turkish-style dwellings.

The green **Abrasha Park►►**, rising from the square, is part of Tel Jaffa. At its summit, there's an observation point with fine sea views. There is more history at the small **Jaffa** (or **Antiquities**) **Museum►►** Rehov Mifratz Shlomo (*Open* Sun–Thu. *Admission: moderate*) part of the Eretz Israel (see page 118). This museum has an astonishing range of finds spanning the millenia, though it is difficult to follow the layout of the five halls and their contents. Just below, close to the waterfront, rise the minaret and two colorful domes of **Mahmudiye Mosque►**. Nearby stands the un-Arabic looking **Clocktower►**, Jaffa's famous landmark, erected in 1906 to honor the rule of Turkish sultan Abdul Hamid II.

On the other side of Yefet Street are the squalid but busy streets of nontourist Jaffa. Off Beit Eshel Street, and near the Clocktower, are the atmospheric alleys and lanes of the extensive **flea market** (Shuk HaPishpeshim)—which is Jewish, not Arab (*Closed* Shabbat).

Attractive Turkish-style dwellings in Jaffa's Artists' Quarter

WHO RETURNED?
Although every Jew has the right to choose to live in Israel, in practice most immigrants have been refugees, driven from their homes by force or under pressure of persecution or discrimination. Some 61 percent have come from Europe, and 18 percent from Africa, almost all of them from North African Arab states that expelled Jews from their homes. Others left South Africa after the start of apartheid. Some 15 percent came from Asia, notably those who fled penniless from Yemen. Only 6 percent have come from the Americas. Currently the population is being increased by thousands of new arrivals every year migrating from the former Soviet Union. Between 1989 and 1998 (latest figures) about 800,000 former Soviet Jews settled in Israel, adding over 13 percent to the total population of the country.

OLD AND NEW
Tel Aviv was the Hebrew title of Theodor Herzl's seminal Zionist work, *Altneuland* (literally, "Old-New Land"). The name is a play on words: a tel is a mound made by civilizations piled one upon the other. The word implies great antiquity. *Aviv* means springtime and newness. So the city's name could mean Hill of Spring, or Old and New. According to the Bible (Ezekiel 3 and 15), this is not the first town to be called Tel Aviv: there was one in ancient Babylon.

▶▶▶ Museum of the Jewish Diaspora (Beth Hatefutsut) *114C6*

At Tel Aviv University (Gate 2), Ramat Aviv
Open: Sun–Tue, Thu 10–4, Wed 10–6, Fri 9–1.
Admission: expensive

Ranging over several floors of an unattractive modern building, but set on pleasant parkland in the university grounds, this museum is mandatory viewing during a visit to Israel, illuminating both the country and its people. It takes a full day to visit—perhaps longer.

In a succession of rooms, each dedicated to a particular theme, visitors wander down the generations, glimpsing the life of Jews in 80 different nations around the world (and "speaking 100 different languages," according to a display caption), scattered since the destruction of the Temple in AD 70. The overall theme is the combination of Jewish diversity with Jewish commonality. The thesis of the museum is that tenacious adherence to traditions—especially observance of the Sabbath, rituals, and festivals, and the constant focus on the idea of Eretz Israel—enabled the Jews to remain as a single people and eventually to return to their homeland. Hand in hand with this uniformity of tradition and belief, a great deal of diversity developed in the different Jewish communities.

This "uniformity with variety" is explored in scores of intriguing displays of ritual objects and clothing, books, photographs, models of housing and synagogues, videos, sound recordings, and much else. The rooms are entitled **Family▶** and **Community▶▶**, **Faith▶▶** and **Culture▶▶**, **Among the Nations▶▶**, the **Return to Zion▶▶▶** and **Remembrance▶▶▶**. There is also an interesting room devoted to the theme of **Synagogue Architecture▶▶▶**. More recent periods are covered in **Jewish Theater▶▶** and **Jews in Arts and Sciences▶▶**. In many exhibits, modern Jewry and Reform Judaism are contrasted with more ancient forms; frequently the links and similarities are striking.

A variety of other **short films▶▶▶** deal with Jewish life in Eastern Europe, Greece, and Morocco. A longer audiovisual show, called the **Chronosphere▶▶** (lasts about 30 minutes), explores the Jewish Wandering, or Diaspora. Other films are shown on such subjects as Yiddish and the other Jewish languages. Fascinating and ingenious

push-button displays and tableaux bring to life important episodes in Jewish history.

A number of sections on the Yiddish-speaking world in **Eastern Europe Before the Holocaust▶▶▶** are painful to observe, revealing, as they do, the vibrant population and culture that was eliminated by the Holocaust. The **Jewish music▶▶▶** of different places and periods can be heard, including the rousing pioneer songs of the socialist Second Aliyah (1904–1914).

Within the museum, the **Dorot Jewish Genealogy Center▶** runs an ambitious project to record the family data of as many Jews as possible from all over the world. For the benefit of future generations and for the purpose of reuniting dispersed family members, the project will give people the chance to see if anything is already known about their family and its history.

For deeper research, there are also study areas where you can view films on topics related to diaspora life. (Note that photography is not allowed and you must leave cameras at the door). The museum can also advise on particular subjects, and has a musicologist on the premises.

On the ground floor there's a pleasant, clean, self-service cafeteria with good food. Customers are frequently entertained by traditional Jewish music, played by invited performers. The museum's shop sells an interesting and unusual range of CDs and tapes of Jewish music.

THE RIGHT TO RETURN

"Every Jew has the right to immigrate to Israel."
–*The Law of Return*, July 5, 1950

Zodiac signs and mystical symbols adorn the ceiling of this mid 17th-century synagogue from Poland

TOWER OF PEACE
The curiously named Shalom Tower (Migdal Shalom, or "Peace Tower") is an unattractive skyscraper dominating southern Tel Aviv. Consisting mainly of offices, it also has shops and snack bars on the ground floor and a top-floor observatory (433 feet) with a restaurant. On the fourth floor is the Israel Wax Museum, with over 100 models of figures from Israel's past.

▶ Old Cemetery *114B3*

Trumpledor Street, off Pinsker
Closed Shabbat. Admission free

A high wall of stone blocks encloses the city's original cemetery, founded in 1903. Many Zionist leaders and politicians—Nordau, Arlo, Zoroff, Dizengoff, for example—as well as poets Bialik and Tcherninchovsky, lie here. The tombs, packed close together, can be hard to locate as the inscriptions are in Hebrew, as are the dates, which, in the Hebrew form, use letters instead of numerals.

▶ Rubin Museum (Beit Rubin) *114B3*

14 Bialik Street
Open: Sun–Thu. Admission: moderate

Bialik Street is the heart of the 1920s district known as Little Tel Aviv. This former home of the distinguished artist Reuven Rubin (1893–1974) is now an enjoyable museum of his curious, dreamlike, highly personal paintings and drawings, with frequent temporary exhibitions.

Old Cemetery, Tel Aviv

Walk

Old Jaffa

This is an easy stroll around a small area. Old Jaffa today exists mainly as a tourist attraction, yet it has plenty of charm and plenty to see. You could enjoy a full day of unhurried strolling and exploring (for map see page 114).

Start at the 20th-century Ottoman **Clocktower▶** (see page 125), in Yefet Street, which looks like an incongruous piece of Victoriana. Around it there is a strong Middle Eastern feel, yet many of the "Oriental" snack bars, such as the Tunisian café, turn out to be Jewish and kosher. Turn right at a sign to the "Old City of Jaffa." Pass by the domes of the **Mahmudiye Mosque▶**. Mifratz Shlomo (no entry for vehicles) rises up, with a wooded park on both sides. To one side lies a little square with the **Jaffa Museum▶▶** (see page 125) in an old stone building. Behind it, pass the old **Hammam▶** (Turkish bathhouse), now a theater-restaurant, and climb to **Abrasha Park▶▶**, on the slope of a tel (settlement mound) excavated 1955–1974. Descend the hill, crossing a wooden bridge, to the traffic-free and beautifully paved **Kedumim Square▶▶▶** (see page 125).

Meander through the **Artists' Quarter▶▶▶**, off the square. Street names here are based on zodiac signs: for a simple route, follow Mazal Dagim (Pisces) to the end, and double back on Mazal Arie (Leo), which reaches a length of **ancient city wall▶▶**. Emerge at the foot of broad steps, but cross straight over to narrow Shimon Habursekai Street. Follow this, passing "Simon the Tanner's House" at No. 8, home of a family who claim that St. Peter stayed in this house.

Go downhill on Mazal Keshet (Sagittarius). To visit the **port▶** (see page 125), turn left at Nativ HaMazalot (Zodiac) and go down covered steps to the waterside. Return along Nativ HaMazalot, below lofty buildings, including the Greek Orthodox church and Catholic St. Peter's. Take a path into the delightful **HaMidron Gardens▶**, passing below the domed former Jews' hostel (now a restaurant) and above the evocative pale minaret of the **Sea Mosque**. Reaching the Mahmudiye Mosque, return to the Clocktower.

Old Jaffa's traffic-free lanes invite unhurried exploration

HEALTHY TAKEOUTS
Fresh juices are made to order at dozens of stands in downtown Tel Aviv. The "menu" generally runs the gamut of fruit varieties, including watermelon, peach, kiwi, prickly pear, orange, or a cocktail of several mixed together.

Expressionist mural, Helena Rubinstein Pavilion

▶▶ Tel Aviv Museum of Art *114C3*

27 Shaul HaMelech Boulevard
Open: daily. Admission: expensive (includes Helena Rubinstein Pavilion)

The imposing modern building of Israel's leading art museum is a world-famous showpiece of 20th-century art and aesthetics. From the architecture of the museum itself—with its exterior sculptures and light, open interiors—to the distinguished exhibitions of 20th-century painting, video, photography, music, and film, this is an important focal point of modern high culture. **Permanent exhibitions▶▶▶**, representing the major 20th-century schools of painting, are arranged in a series of rooms, and include works by Braque, Klimt, Kandinsky, Picasso, Léger, and Mondrian. **Temporary exhibits▶▶▶**, often long-term,

The Tel Aviv Museum of Art specializes in 20th-century art and sculpture

cover contemporary painting and photography, on loan from leading international galleries and museums. There are also **special exhibitions▶▶▶** covering subjects relevant to Israel's history and culture.

Despite specializing in the modern, the museum does not ignore everything that occurred before 1900. There are collections, temporary and permanent, of the art of past centuries, and many of the evening **concerts▶▶▶** feature classical music—while others feature jazz. The **Helena Rubinstein Pavilion for Contemporary Art▶** (6 Tarsat Boulevard) is part of the Museum of Art. It shows work by guest artists from Israel and abroad.

As an unusual diversion from the typical museum visit, the Museum of Art offers a free guided **Bauhaus tour▶▶▶** by bus through the 1930s areas of Tel Aviv, a showcase for this simple and functional architectural style. The tour takes all morning (the bus will pick you up at your hotel). Although the tour is free, the museum will charge its usual entrance fee; after the tour, you can visit the museum without further payment. Tel Aviv is a fascinating city of many architectural styles,but it is these modernist (or Bauhaus) apartment complexes, many influenced by Le Corbusier, that give their character to the "White City."

Visitors soon notice certain obvious facts about Israeli music: most street musicians play classical violin music and most of Israel's contemporary pop music is terrible. More interesting, traditional Jewish folk rhythms from Eastern Europe, North Africa, and the Middle East are fusing with other Mediterranean styles and are beginning to create a genuinely new Israeli music.

A mix of traditions When Jews fled to Israel from Eastern Europe, North Africa, and Arabia, they brought their instruments and musical traditions with them. Indeed, they have come from every continent, bringing the multitude of diverse styles that can be heard today in Israel.

Perhaps the most recognizably Jewish music is the lilting clarinet-and-fiddle of *klezmer*, the sound of celebration and festival in the destroyed Jewish world of Eastern Europe. Few of the old players have survived, but the style lives on. Most *klezmer* today comes from America, though you will hear plenty of it in Israel, including a variant called Hasidic rock. Similarly, traditional Oriental Jewish music has settled in Israel, become more upbeat, and is growing in popularity.

New sounds After a slow start—with a repertoire often limited to rousing, sing-along tunes from religious, kibbutz, and army life—Israel has started to produce world-class pop and rock. Apart from the bland harmonies of the annual Eurovision Song Contest, won in 1999 by flamboyant Israeli transsexual star Dana International, the country produces talented rock singers like Noa (known as Achinoam Nini in Israel), an intriguing mix of Yemen and New York rock-blues artists like Shlomo Artzi, and outstanding folk-rock singer-songwriters like Chava Alberstein. Another influence comes from nearby Greece. You'll often hear Israeli recordings that join traditional Jewish musical ideas to a Greek sound, reflecting Israel's East Mediterranean location.

A symphony of orchestras In classical music, Israel really excels. People say, only half in jest, that every police station and every factory has its symphony orchestra. Certainly there is an astonishing number (the Tel Aviv suburb of Ra'anana, for example, has its own), including several of high standing. At the national level, Israel's Chamber, Symphony, and Philharmonic orchestras, and its National Opera, are all acclaimed worldwide—a remarkable achievement, since the population of Israel is only six million.

MUSICAL MOVEMENTS
Music is such an integral part of life in Israel that almost every community has its orchestra, often reaching professional standards. One Israeli joke has it that two in every three Russian immigrants arrive with a violin case tucked under their arms. What about the third? He's the pianist.

Classical street entertainer

SHABBAT AND FESTIVALS
Although things grind to a stop for Shabbat (Sabbath) each week from Friday afternoon to Saturday evening, and also on certain festivals and holy days, the one place where you can still expect to find things working more or less as normal is a hotel. Only at religious hotels (which make a point of informing guests of the restrictions on arrival) will you find that there are no reception staff on Sabbath —but even here you will usually be able to get a meal.

Hotels line Tel Aviv's coastal road

Accommodations

Comfort plus a sea view Altogether, Tel Aviv and its suburbs have a total of over 6,000 hotel rooms, ranging from the deluxe to the budget, most close to the seashore. This is a new city, and almost all its hotels are modern, comfortable and well-equipped. At most of them, a superb buffet breakfast comes as standard. Some Tel Aviv hotels aspire to (and reach) a high level of service and facilities while remaining relaxed and informal—children are welcome. Widely accepted as the best in the city is the Dan Tel Aviv (on the corner of Frishmann and HaYarkon). This is the best location, for beach access, eating out, entertainment, and downtown shopping. Even if you cannot afford the Dan, it is a good idea to stay in this area.

In the right place The main hotel district lies along HaYarkon Street, between Trumpledor and Ben-Gurion. Here you will find the Dan Tel Aviv, Carlton, Moriah Plaza, Ramada Continental, and Sheraton hotels among others. These are all on the sought-after west side of HaYarkon. But there are also hotels on the other side of the street, or in side streets. Among the best are the Basel, Astor, and City. Although a few paces farther from the beach, they are nevertheless comfortable, convenient, and more modestly priced.

Off the beaten track A few beach hotels lie outside this hotel district. A little farther from the center of things, they can represent good value. Examples are the Hilton, north of the main beach but overlooking a sandy bay, and the family-oriented Dan Panorama, opposite Clore Park at the southern end of the main beach. A free shuttle minibus connects the Dan Panorama to the Dan every few minutes throughout the day.

FRIDAY-NIGHT SPECIAL
Many hotels, even those that are not especially observant of Jewish ritual, offer something special for Friday-night dinner, the big meal of the week for Jewish families. Usually, there are candles by the entrance so observant Jews can light them at the start of Shabbat (Sabbath). *Challah* (the tasty Sabbath bread) and *kiddush* wine will be on the table. Typically, the main dish will be *cholent* (pronounced chilunt), the meat stew popular on Friday night among East European Jews. In the larger hotels there are also Shabbat elevators, programmed to stop automatically on every floor so the observant does not have to push buttons—"work" is forbidden during Shabbat.

Eating out

Out and about Sightseeing, strolling, or shopping, you will pass dozens of places—some upscale, some simple—offering cakes, pastries, and falafel, or shwarma, in pita crammed with salad. Acclaimed for cakes and snacks, Café Levana (182 Ben Yehuda) is a youthful favorite. The many juice stands are a delight, and offer a delicious and healthy liquid meal. Street nibbles include bagels, bigger and breadier than the familiar Ashkenazi bagel, and nuts—plain, salted, or honey-roasted.

Dinner Most big hotels have restaurants. In the hotel area—near Dizengoff Circle, in Ben-Yehuda Street, and along HaYarkon—eating places span the range from elegant French cuisine, to cheap-and-cheerful eateries. Spicy, tasty Yemenite cooking can be sampled in the Yemenite quarter, for example at Shaul's Inn (Eliashiv Street). Beside the sea, lines form at Yotvata Dairy Restaurant. The huge outdoor London Restaurant fills the pedestrianized section north of Frishmann—its prices reflect the lovely setting. It has a big menu, big portions, friendly service, and live music.

Shopping

Where to shop, what to buy Tel Aviv's main shopping streets are Dizengoff and Ben-Yehuda, and there are indoor shopping centers like Dizengoff Center (on Dizengoff) and Opera Tower (corner of Allenby and the promenade) with fashions, music, jewelry, and high-quality Judaica for sale. Kikkar HaMadeina, the big circle in the north of the city, is a designer-label zone. For creative, elegant clothes, jewelry, and Judaica, check out boutiques in northern Dizengoff Street. The southern part of Dizengoff is good for shoes and sandals. If you are wealthy enough to want diamonds, there is no better place than the Israel Diamond Exchange, Maccabi Boulevard, Ramat Gan. At the opposite extreme, try Bograshov Street for low-cost street fashion. For unusual gifts and crafts, take a stroll in Carmel Market.

NOT KOSHER, BUT TASTY
Only a handful of Tel Aviv eating places attain a really high standard, despite the ubiquitous "gourmet" boast. Even so, most are perfectly adequate for an enjoyable evening out, and a surprising number offer live entertainment. Observant Jews need to know that the majority are not kosher. The tourist office has restaurant listings, such as *Tel Aviv Menus.*

Cheap and cheerful cafés line Dizengoff Street

NIGHT OWLS
Like other big cities, Tel Aviv has its share of all-night stores and services. Five supermarkets, a dozen gas stations, and (more surprisingly) half a dozen little confectioners who specialize in nuts and candies stay open in the Tel Aviv area. There are also a dozen different locations where you can rent a video for 24 hours from an automatic machine. Details and addresses of late-night stores are listed in *This Week in Tel Aviv*, obtainable from the tourist office or in hotels.

Tel Aviv's nightlife is livelier than in the capital, Jerusalem

JUST HANGING AROUND
For an easy and relaxing evening, sometimes the best thing of all is to walk, talk, and sit outdoors. Scores of cafés and bars (often misnamed "pubs") open until well after midnight on Dizengoff, Ben-Yehuda, HaYarkon, and the waterfront promenade.

Nightlife

Nightclubs The racy end of late-night Tel Aviv is mainly concentrated in the south and east of the city center, along and off Allenby Street, and close to Jaffa Port. There are some 20 nightclubs for the youth market, offering disco, techno, and house music, and most kick off after midnight. Another 20 or more specialize in ethnic music styles—generally Oriental, Turkish, or Greek—and are aimed at adults, rather than disco-hungry teenagers.

Live music Most big hotels have bars with easy-listening live music (often just a piano) until the small hours. For something more special, there are performances almost every evening by the New Israel Opera (Tel Aviv Performing Arts Center, 19 Shaul HaMalech Boulevard, tel: 03 692 7777), the Israel Chamber Orchestra and Israel Music Conservatory (19 Streiker Street, tel: 03 546 6228), or the Israel Philharmonic (Mann Auditorium, tel: 03 528 9163). Other important spots for concerts are the Tel Aviv Museum of Art (tel: 03 696 1297) and the Noga Theater (7 Jerusalem Boulevard, Jaffa, tel: 03 681 6427). Big-name rock concerts are often staged at Yehoshua Gardens (close to the university, tel: 03 521 8210).

Dance and drama Tel Aviv is home to most of Israel's quality theater. Simultaneous English translation (on headphones, every Tuesday) makes a play at the Cameri Theater (on the corner of Dizengoff and Frishmann, tel: 03 527 9888) enjoyable and accessible. Performances here consist of classics and serious modern drama. Yiddish-speakers will enjoy the Israeli Yiddish Theater, frequently on stage in Tel Aviv, usually at the ZOA House (tel: 03 695 9341). The Habima Theater (Habima Square, tel: 03 526 6666) is the home of Israel's National Theater Company. For performances of modern or classical dance, find out what is on at the attractive Suzanne Dellal Center, home of the Inbal and Bat Sheva dance companies (tel: 03 510 5656). The Hasimta Theater, in Old Jaffa (tel: 03 683 4709), puts on performances by Israeli artists in a café-theater ambience.

Practical points

Information The tourist office, at the New Central Bus Station (tel: 03 639 5660), can provide information, free maps, and assist with bookings. Racks display information leaflets, including copies of the latest editions of *Tel Aviv Today* and *This Week in Tel Aviv*. both of which contain useful listings, telephone numbers, and advertisements.

Getting around Buses, into or out of town, are inexpensive. Rides within Tel Aviv cost about 5 NIS. Bus stops have brief route details in English,·and all bus drivers speak English. For local bus information call Dan Buses, 03 639 4444 (English spoken). Services run between 5 AM and midnight, except on Friday (services stop an hour before sunset for the Sabbath) and Saturday (no service until the end of Sabbath, an hour after sunset). Buses leave every few minutes from the city's two bus stations to towns and cities all over Israel. A return ticket from Tel Aviv to Jerusalem costs 27 NIS (enquiries to Egged, tel: 03 537 5555).

Far more expensive are taxis, called "special taxis," which wait outside hotels. Agree the fare in advance of your ride, or, insist that the meter be used. Check before setting out, for instance at your hotel desk, what the fare should be to your destination. It takes some time to work out the routes of the cheaper *sherutim* (singular: *sherut*), or shared taxis, but they are convenient and can be hailed on main streets anywhere along their set route.

Emergencies Unlike almost any other city in the world, crime is not a problem in Tel Aviv. Violence is very rare. Do take precautions, nevertheless, against simple theft (for example, of bags on the beach). Noisy, horn-tooting young people are probably the worst hazard you will encounter. In an emergency, call: Police 100; Ambulance 101; Fire 102; Rape Center 03 523 4819.

PEOPLE OF THE BUS
Amazingly, Israel's main bus line, despite being a workers' cooperative and operating solely within Israel, is the world's second-largest bus company (after Greyhound). Over a million passengers a week pass through Tel Aviv's New Bus Terminal in Levinski Street. That's about a fifth of the country's entire population. They catch comfortable if crowded air-conditioned buses that depart very frequently to destinations all over Israel from 5 AM to midnight. Tel Aviv likes to boast that the New Bus Terminal (opened 1993) is the largest bus station in the world, but that's because most of the multistory building is in reality a down-market indoor shopping, com-merce, and entertainment center. If not the biggest, the terminal could claim to be the most chaotic and confusing. As if that were not enough, Tel Aviv has two bus stations! The other. a simpler terminal, is beside the train station.

Popular transportation

While the whole world may have heard of the Ten Commandments, few realize that the scriptures contain a total of 613 commandments (or mitzvot*) concerning every aspect and nuance of behavior. Attempting to obey them is "religious observance." Ignoring them completely is to be "totally secular." Most Israelis fall somewhere in between, and regard the* mitzvot *not as commandments but as traditions.*

OBSERVANT ISRAELIS

16 percent of women regularly attend *mikveh* (ritual baths).
22 percent of men keep their head covered at all times.
25 percent regularly wear *tefillin* (prayer boxes containing scriptures).
55 percent read from a prayer book sometimes.
66 percent mark Sabbath with some kind of ritual, usually the lighting of candles.
66 percent eat only kosher food at home.
71 percent fast all day on Yom Kippur.
72 percent light Hanukka candles.
78 percent attend a *seder* (ritual dinner) at Passover.
90 percent keep kosher part of the time.
92 percent circumcise their sons according to Jewish ritual.
98 percent have a *mezuzza* scroll on their doorpost.
—Guttman Institute of Applied Social Research (1994)

Religious observance Tel Aviv's Diaspora Museum suggests that religious observance facilitated nationhood by preserving Jewish identity during the diaspora. In today's Israel schools recogfnize Jewish holidays and teach the Bible (albeit as part of the nation's annals rather than as Holy Writ). Yet many Israelis know little about traditional Judaism, and the many immigrants from the former U.S.S.R. are overwhelmingly secular. Even so, Israelis are proud of their heritage. And religious political parties' show of strength in 1999 elections, bouyed by broadening support, underscores the continued importance of Judaism in Israel.

A secular Zion In the early years of the twentieth century, the pioneering Zionists who made the journey to settle in Palestine and struggled to re-create the Jewish homeland were, almost without exception, socialists and atheists. They wholeheartedly rejected religion, just as they rejected every other inheritance from the past, even family life. They considered the Jewish people to be no more, and no less, than a nation exiled from its land, and defined Jewishness in purely cultural, historical terms. Instead of the biblical injunction to be "a light unto the nations," they wished only that Israel would be "a nation like any other."

The people of Israel The existence of Jews as a separate people rests on their attachment to Israel, which lies at the heart of the Jewish religion. Unlike Christianity, which is based on belief (of God in Man, the Messiah), Judaism is literally a question of getting down to earth. At the cornerstone of the religion is Abraham's perception of Israel as the promised land, the land to which the Jews returned after the exodus from Egypt, the land conquered by Joshua in fulfilment of God's promise. These events are not mythical but historical (if embellished). The only sacred place in the world, for Jews, is Temple Mount in Jerusalem. Synagogue prayers, today as always, refer to the Jews simply as Israel. For millennia, Israel meant the land of the Jews, of the Jewish religion, and of the Temple. That is why Diaspora Jews wanted to return to Israel, and why even the

Burning yeast before Passover

most secular Jews in Israel are part of, and the product of, a religious heritage.

The not-so-great divide A recent nationwide survey of Hebrew-speaking Israeli Jews showed that 21 percent consider themselves to be "totally secular." About 39 percent are "strictly observant" or "observant to a great extent." In between are the roughly 40 percent who pick and choose which customs to keep and which to ignore. To some extent, the division is illusory, because Jewish festivals, such as Hanukka, Pesach (Passover), Purim, Sukkot, are now as much national as religious holidays, observed even on secular kibbutzim. Shabbat (Sabbath) still brings the country to a standstill—for religious and secular alike. Survey figures show that being religious or secular is not an absolute: most Israelis obey some religious commandments, seeing them simply as part of their inherited traditions.

A cause for conflict The big Sabbath shutdown rankles some Israelis, especially in a predominantly nonreligious city like Tel Aviv. There is resentment that the Orthodox authorities, backed by religious political parties (which generally hold the balance of power in the Knesset), can wield such a pervasive influence over the life of the secular. Examples range from the lack of any form of civil marriage to the fact that El Al, the state airline, cannot fly on the Sabbath. But no government that depends on religious party support can risk liberalization. Anger about this has led many Israelis, including the many who are observant to some degree, to regard "the religious" with contempt. The antagonism is mutual.

A VOTE FOR PLURALISM
It is partly due to Israel's electoral system that the religious/secular divide is so sharp. The ultra-Orthodox, who routinely hold the balance of power in the Knesset, have used this position to win government funding and to ensure their grip on certain areas of life. This works against Judaism's non-Orthodox Masorti and Reform streams which are denied funding or places on local religious councils, and whose rabbis are not recognised. If the proportional representation rules are altered, requiring parties to garner a certain minimum percentage of the vote before gaining a Knesset seat, ultra-Otrthodox representation in the Knesset would lose most of their seats and their influence. Non-Orthodox and partially observant citizens would then be in a position to win much-needed civil rights and respectability.

Lighting Hanukka candles

SWEET CONSUMPTION
One thing that Israel's Jews and Arabs have in common is a sweet tooth. Israelis are the world's largest consumers of halva, the hard, sugar-packed sesame confectionery. They consume a phenomenal 3.3 lbs. per person per year on average. Most of the country's Arab neighbors are not far behind in the halva consumption league.

►►► Akko 113B4

This large, industrial Arab town (population 38,000), sitting on a spit of land projecting from the Galilee coast, contains at its heart a striking Old City with thick, sturdy fortifications and imposing towers. These superb 18th-century **ramparts►►►** (free access), now breached by newer roads, were originally entered only through the Land Gate, not far from the shore, or the Sea Gate, on the harborside. Today, access to the top of the walls is from the steps by the law courts.

The historic waterfront quarter, a mass of stone structures, beautiful archways, evocative alleys, and green-roofed mosques, makes a magnificent sight. There is squalor too: you will find groups of youths hanging around, and unwashed children in the dirty squares and alleyways. In the past, Akko (known to the English as Acre) figured large on the map of the world and even today carries the mark of its former standing. Above all, though later restored and reconstructed, the walls and stonework recall an era of bloodthirsty medieval struggles between the Crusaders and the Arabs for control of the land of Israel.

Akko's history dates back far beyond those times. Remnants of a Canaanite settlement on the site of the **Tel►** (settlement mound) about a mile inland have been dated to 3000 BC. Taken, lost, and retaken by Egyptian pharaohs, it became a Phoenician city. Joshua, the Israelite leader, was unable to conquer it in 1300 BC, and the Israelite tribe of Asher, in whose territory Akko was, also failed. The Phoenicians were eventually expelled in 640 BC. The town passed between Persians, Assyrians, and Egyptians, and, in 219 BC became part of the Seleucid kingdom of Syria,

Akko: modern port and Crusader city

Akko's Gothic arches have lasted much longer than the fragile Crusaders' Kingdom that built them

which wisely allowed it to remain an independent city-state. When the Hasmoneans forced the Syrians out of the rest of Israel in the 2nd century BC, they too were unable to take Akko, which survived as a non-Jewish town. Rome succeeded in conquering it, and the town served as their campaign base for crushing the First Jewish Revolt (AD 66). Akko remained a busy port under the Byzantines, and after the 7th-century Arab conquest became the seaport of Damascus.

After years of trying, the Crusaders eventually took Akko in 1104, made it the stronghold of the Knights of St. John, and renamed it St. Jean d'Acre (Saint John of Acre). When the Arabs took Jerusalem (1187), Akko became capital of the Crusaders' Kingdom of the Holy Land. The town's finest spectacle is still the wonderfully preserved **Crusader city▶▶▶** (*Open* daily. *Admission: moderate*) headquarters of the Knights Hospitallers. It is a vast, impressive complex of offices, halls, refectory, and hospice, all now lying underground because the 18th-century Citadel was raised on top of it. Built largely in the 12th century, in the transition from Romanesque to early Gothic, the Crusader city's stone-paved floors and vaulted ceilings retain a simple but majestic elegance and dignity.

From antiquity, Akko flourished as a port, and for a thousand years it was the biggest and busiest in the eastern Mediterranean. It was also notorious as a place of vice and decadence, which worsened under the Crusaders as the town grew. Densely populated, it was divided into quarters given over to different "nationalities"—in fact mostly Italians from the city-states of Genoa, Pisa, Venice, and Amalfi. These districts were often in conflict, sometimes breaking into open warfare. The population was mainly Christian, and there were dozens of churches.

In 1187, Salah ed-Din wrested Akko from the Crusaders but in 1191 it was reconquered by Richard the Lionhearted. When the Fifth Crusade reached Palestine in 1290, full of naïve zeal about driving Islam out of the Holy Land, they slaughtered the Muslim traders resident in Akko—much to the chagrin of the town's Christian citizens, who were more interested in commerce than conquest. The massacre caused the Mameluke Sultan Qalawun to attack the city mercilessly, carting off thousands of Christians as slaves. The Knights Templar fought

THE GREAT ESCAPE
During the British Mandate, the authorities put Akko's medieval citadel to use as a high-security prison for Jewish guerrillas: several were hanged here. In a spectacular raid on the citadel in May 1947, the Irgun group dynamited a hole in the ancient wall, went inside, overpowered the guards, and freed 30 Irgun and 11 Lehi prisoners. The citadel now contains the Museum of Heroism, honoring the prisoners who were held or executed here.

AKKO'S BEACHES

Just outside the walls, Akko has one extremely dirty and unappealing public beach. For something a little better, head farther south from the city to Hof Argaman (or Purple Beach). This lies a 15-minute walk along the seafront. Alternatively, you can drive along the Haifa road as far as the Argaman Motel. You must pay to use the beach, but it has good facilities and an excellent view of the city.

Above and below: Ahmed al Jazzar Mosque

on until the massive wall of their fortress was brought crashing down, symbolizing the end of two centuries of Christian rule in Palestine.

From 1291, Akko was resolutely Arab, sinking into almost total obscurity and poverty. Druze emirs revived it in the 17th and 18th centuries, and between 1775 and 1805, under Ahmed el-Jazzar (literally, "the Butcher"), there was much grandiose building. The Crusader city was covered and above it the mighty **Citadel►** (*Closed* Shabbat. *Admission: inexpensive*) was constructed. Later, the British used this as a prison for Jewish guerrillas: a poorly arranged **museum►►** inside contains photographs, papers, and the gallows on which the Jews were executed. Beside the Citadel, on the site of the Crusaders' Cathedral of the Holy Cross, stands the **Ahmed al Jazzar Mosque►** (*Closed* during prayers. *Admission: inexpensive*), with its geometric marble patterns, tall minaret, and rococo architecture. Close by in Ahmed's handsome **Turkish baths►►** (*Open* daily. *Admission: moderate*), a museum covers the story of the town, explaining how, in 1799, the British came to Ahmed's aid helping to repel an attack on the town made by Napoleon.

Under Ottoman rule, the walls of Akko were restored and new defenses were constructed. Despite this, the British seized Akko in 1918. The residents staunchly defied both the British and Jewish presence in Palestine. In 1948 Akko came fully under Jewish control.

Around the Old City, you will find much of interest: the **souk►**, the narrow streets full of fragrances; the huge *khans* (enclosures built as caravansaries), notably the columned **Khan el-Umdan►►** by the water, with the landmark clocktower beside it; the **quayside►►** with its fish restaurants. Also most enjoyable is the Strauss Ice Cream Factory, south of the town (tour and free sample). Just over a mile north of Akko, the exquisite **Bahá'i Gardens►►** (*Open* daily 9–4. *Admission free*) contain the burial shrine of Bahá'u'lláh (literally, "God's glory," 1817–1892), the title of the founder of the Bahá'i religion. Here, too, is the cottage in which he lived during his last years, having been exiled to Akko in 1868. The shrine is the holiest place in the world for members of the Bahá'i faith (see page 152).

The new country of Israel was won after a hard struggle, involving determination, courage, even ruthlessness. Born of centuries of yearning, Israel is still grateful to the men and women who brought it into being. Some were intellectuals, others soldiers, others farmers who tackled swamps and deserts. They are honored everywhere. Streets, towns, kibbutzim, hills and valleys, not to mention children, have been named in their memory.

Creators of a nation The rebirth of Israel is regarded by many Jews, and not a few Christians, as one of the greatest events to have occurred in two millennia. For some, it is nothing less than the hand of God at work. Others see it as the result of painstaking struggle by individuals of courage and vision. And for yet others, it is a combination of both of these. After all, according to the Bible story, even when God gave the Land of Israel to the Jews, they still had to go out and conquer it for themselves. All those who made this modern, political, and diplomatic miracle happen tend to be regarded with sincere admiration by Israelis.

Above: Vladimir Jabotinsky
Left: Theodor Herzl

The early days Few towns are without a boulevard, main street, or central square named after Theodor Herzl (1860–1904), founder of the Zionist movement. His successor as Zionist leader, Chaim Weizmann (1874–1952), who became the first President of Israel, also has many mentions. The hard-liner who led the Revisionist group within the movement, Vladimir Jabotinsky (1880–1940), is also recalled as a hero, as is Josef Trumpledor (1880–1920), founder of the Hehalutz Zionist movement in Russia, decorated for bravery by the Russian and British armies, who died defending a Galilee farming settlement from Arab attack. More recently, David Ben-Gurion (1886–1973) was the tough and shrewd Zionist veteran who became Israel's first Prime Minister. All were born in Eastern Europe.

Writers and scholars Eliezer Ben-Yehuda (1858–1922) gained huge admiration for reviving and revitalizing the Hebrew language. Shmuel Yosef Agnon (1888–1970) was the first Hebrew writer to win the Nobel Prize for Literature. Haim Nachman Bialik (1873–1934), author of many early Zionist songs and also considered the greatest modern Hebrew poet, is another name held in the highest esteem by Israelis.

THE FOUNDER OF ZIONISM

Theodor Herzl (1860–1904), born in Budapest, grew up to be cosmopolitan, intellectual, and entirely nonreligious. He spoke several languages and studied for a doctorate at Vienna University in a period of daily anti-Jewish rioting in the city. Finding work as a journalist, he was made Paris correspondent of the Austrian *Neue Frei Presse*. In 1895, he witnessed the public humiliation of the Jewish army captain Alfred Dreyfus, who—in a wave of anti-Jewish feeling that swept France—was convicted on a trumped-up charge of treason. The evidence is known to have been forged. The sight had an electrifying effect on Herzl. He at once wrote *Der Judenstaat* (*The Jewish State*) and in 1897 convened the first Zionist Congress. This called for "the creation for the Jewish people of a home in Palestine." He campaigned tirelessly to further that cause until his untimely death. Within 50 years his extraordinary dream had come true. His body was transferred to Mount Herzl, in Jerusalem, in 1948.

►► Ashkelon and Ashdod 112B2–B3

These two modern, rapidly growing, industrial beachside towns (with a combined population of 165,000) were founded in the 1950s on the sand dunes not far from the Gaza border, and are major absorption centers for new immigrants. There is a boomtown feeling in the air, as construction work carries on at a frantic pace (often using Arab labor from across the frontier). Ashdod's successful port is now second only to Haifa's.

Similarly, the two towns also have a long history. Both were among the five Philistine cities on Israel's Mediterranean coast (Joshua 13:3). When the Philistines captured the Ark of the Covenant, they took it first to Ashkelon, then installed it in the temple of Dagon in Ashdod. A multitude of conquerors came and went during the centuries, including Egyptians, Assyrians, Persians, and Romans. The towns were taken by the Crusaders in the 12th century and, when retaken, largely destroyed in the process.

Ashdod►► has a beach and a couple of modest hotels, but plans to turn it into a big vacation resort seem fanciful. Its earlier settlements were at **Tel Ashdod►**, 3 miles south. Later it became an Arab village, hostile to Jewish immigration, with a British army base. During the 1948 War of Independence, the Egyptians advanced this far into Israel before being forced to retreat.

Between the two towns stretch 9 miles of dunes and citrus groves. **Ashkelon►►**, though sprawling, has more appeal for visitors. Its pleasant sandy beach and waterside hotels lie at the southern end of town near **Ashkelon National Park►►**, a popular picnic area with remnants of several periods. The ruined churches, fortifications, and collapsed towers, whose rather forlorn fragments of stonework lie on the sand, were built by Crusaders. Within the site, the earliest remains date back to Canaanite and Israelite times, and there are Roman ruins. North of the park is a 3rd-century Roman tomb.

This part of Israel's Mediterranean coast lies surprisingly close to the desert and to southern Israel, which are within easy reach for day trips.

GAZA

Just down the coast from Ashkelon and Ashdod is another ancient city of the Philistines that regularly features in the news. Gaza (Azza in Arabic) is a noisy, crowded, and squalid city. Its principal sight is the Great Mosque, originally a 13th-century Crusader church, and several modern hotels can be found on the beachfront near the port. Even if you wanted to see this, Gaza is not recommended for a visit. Despite its "independent" self-governing status as part of the Palestinian Autonomous Authority, the whole Gaza Strip remains dangerous and troubled, hostile to Israelis and Jews and anyone who might be thought Israeli. Measuring 30 miles by 3.5 miles, the Gaza Strip consists of dry, near-desert terrain and yet is one of the world's most densely populated areas. Most of the 650,000 residents are the people (and their families) who were on the losing side in Israel's 1948 War of Independence, or as it is known to the Arabs, "The Catastrophe." Many fled their homes, or were driven from them at the end of that war. In the 1967 Six-Day War, the Arabs again lost, and Gaza was occupied by the Israelis until 1994, when the Autonomous Areas came into being.

Right: Ashkelon
Below: Roman statue of Isis

Atlit's sunset beauty belies its tragic history

►► Atlit (also known as Ma'apilim Atlit Camp) *113B3*

About half a mile from the sea, around 5 miles south of Haifa beside an exit from Highway 2 (signposted "Apilim").

Notorious Atlit Camp was the British detention center, established in 1938, used for holding illegal Jewish immigrants to Palestine during the pre- and postwar period. When Jews were trying to escape from Nazi Europe, a succession of more or less unseaworthy and overloaded ships put ashore on Israel's beaches. The occupants were rounded up by the British authorities, brought here, and held in crowded dormitories until they could be deported. Tens of thousands of would-be immigrants passed through the camp.

You can walk between the high barbed-wire fences where Holocaust survivors, including children whose parents had died in the extermination camps, were detained. Some were returned to Germany or other parts of Europe, and many were forwarded to other British prison camps in, for example, Cyprus or Mauritius. This camp was restored in 1970, but of the original 80 dormitory huts only two remain. These are filled with models to give an idea of the life and conditions endured by the inmates. The camp is dominated by the Disinfection Building, where detainees were stripped naked on arrival, segregated by sex, and herded in to be sprayed with disinfectant liquid from showers, in an uncanny echo of the procedures at the Nazi gas chambers. Also on the site is a ship in which some of the illegal immigrants arrived.

Atlit is geared to group visits, of which there are many, but individuals are also welcome with advance notice. A very moving audiovisual is shown to visitors.

► Bat Yam *112B4*

This beach resort, 3 miles south of Tel Aviv, is a suburb of its larger neighbor. It has an attractive setting, a nice, well-maintained beach, and many recreational facilities including a sports center, swimming pools, three art galleries, and several moderately priced hotels.

THE LAST CASTLE

Now within a military base, the huge ruined castle that can be seen perched on a promontory near Atlit was built by the Templars in 1200 following their expulsion from Temple Mount in Jerusalem. They called the new fortress Pilgrims' Castle. After the loss of Akko in 1291, the Templar presence in the Holy Land looked unlikely to survive. The fall of Tortosa Castle, in Syria, in the same year left only Pilgrims' Castle at Atlit in their possession, and the Templars decided to leave before being driven out. The castle subsequently fell into ruins. It was excavated in the 1930s, but is not open to the public.

ALEXANDER ZAID
The statue of Alexander Zaid, on the highest point of Beit She'arim, honors a founder of HaShomer (the Watchman), the undercover organization that provided armed guards for Jewish farmers and that evolved into the Haganah (see page 42). Zaid is said to have discovered the Beit She'arim necropolis while secretly patrolling in 1936. He was eventually killed during the 1938 anti-Jewish riots.

▶ Beit She'arim 113B3

Closed Shabbat. Admission: moderate

This archeological site at the foot of Mount Carmel, some 12 miles east of Haifa, contains the remnants of a Galilean town that acquired enormous importance in Jewish religious life in the centuries after the destruction of the Temple in Jerusalem. With the crushing of the Bar Kochba Revolt in the 2nd century AD, Beit She'arim grew to be a large, religious town. Rabbi Yehudah Hanassi moved here with his seminary, and under him it became the seat of the Sanhedrin, the "supreme court" of Jewish law. Hanassi spent his time here writing and codifying the Mishna (still known today as the Oral Law), which was to become part of the scriptural works that Orthodox Jews believe to be God-given.

Hanassi was buried in the **Necropolis▶▶** (or Necrophos), which is a remarkable network of underground tunnels, stairways, and caves. These catacombs were already well known as a burial site, but after Hanassi's burial they became the most important Jewish burial place in Israel, taking over from the Mount of Olives, which the Romans had closed to Jews. The Necropolis was, and is, entered through landscaped courtyards. Of the 20 burial chambers inside, two are currently open to visitors. Inside, it is eerie and atmospheric. The decorated sarcophagi—now empty—have inscriptions in Hebrew, Aramaic, and Greek. There is also a museum inside the larger of the two catacombs.

Above ground, there are traces of private dwellings and other structures, all dating from the 2nd to the 4th centuries AD. They include ruins of a **synagogue▶**, a large **basilica▶**, a **glass factory▶**, and an **oil press▶**. These are all that remain of the city, which was almost completely destroyed by the Romans in the 4th century.

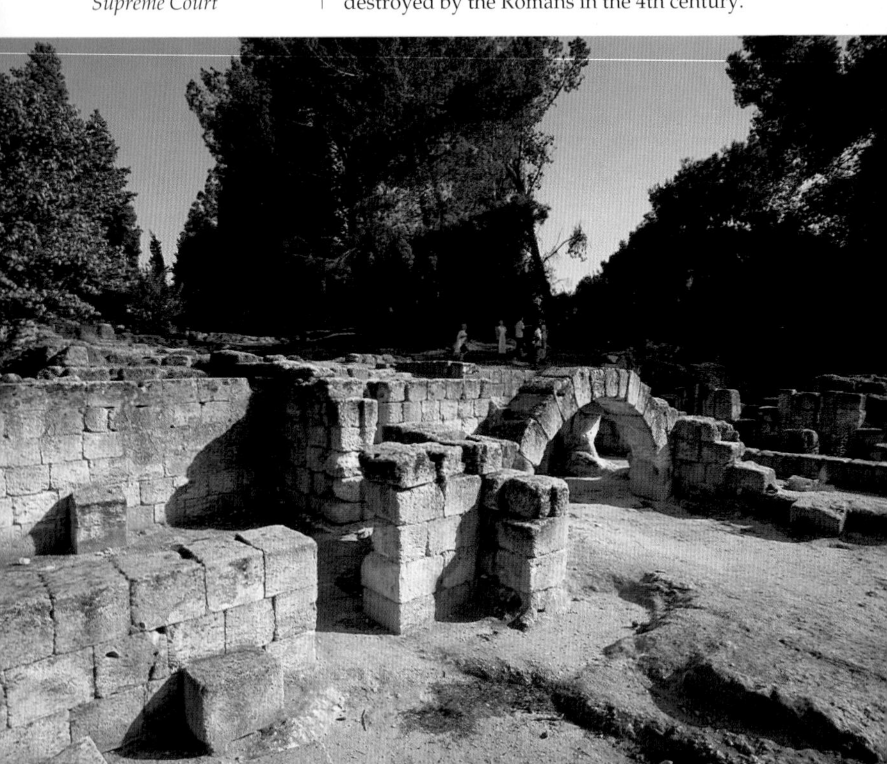

Beit She'arim, site of the Sanhedrin, or Jewish Supreme Court

Some Jewish holidays date back to the Bible, others commemorate events in Jewish history. Many are national holidays celebrated by all Israelis, both religious and secular. Dates vary from year to year. Christian festivals also attract crowds of visitors, as do Muslim festivals, although to a lesser extent.

Spring and summer Pesach, or Passover—the seven-day festival of abstinence from bread and other leavened food, commemorates the Exodus from Egypt. It is mainly a family affair. The big moment is the *seder* ritual festive meal, when the Haggadah, a text containing the Exodus story, is read aloud. Christian Holy Week, with processions along the Via Dolorosa in Jerusalem, and Easter occur at about the same time—Jesus' Last Supper was a *seder*. Holocaust Day, Remembrance Day, Independence Day, and Jerusalem Day, recalling the pain and joy of 20th-century events, follow soon after. Lag b'Omer (April/May) is a day of picnics, one month after Pesach. Shavuot, 49 days after Passover, celebrates Moses receiving the Torah; it is traditional to eat dairy products. The Tisha b'Av fast (July), when people gather at the Western Wall, is the day on which both the First and the Second Temples were destroyed.

Autumn The month of Tishri (September/October) starts with Rosh Hashanah (New Year), a happy but thoughtful time. The 10 Days of Awe that follow are also a time of reflection, ending with the solemn fast of Yom Kippur (Day of Atonement). A joyous note returns with the seven days of Sukkot (Tabernacles), a harvest celebration that commemorates the years spent by the Jews wandering in the wilderness after the Exodus from Egypt.

Winter Hanukah ("Dedication") recalls the Maccabean victory in 167 BC, and the miracle that occurred when the Temple was rededicated (one day's lamp oil lasted for eight days). People light *hanukkiot*, the eight-branched candelabrum, lighting one candle each evening until all eight are lit. Latkes (fried patties), donuts and other fried foods are eaten at this time.

Christmas draws huge crowds, especially to the city of Bethlehem. Purim (February/March), a zany day of fun, recalls the Jewish escape from an ancient Persian plot to kill them. The story of Esther is read in synagogues, and children try to drown out the name of the villain, Haman.

MERRY CHRISTMASES

In Israel, Christmas does not come just once a year: it is celebrated on different dates by different Christian denominations. The Catholics, Latin churches, and Protestants proclaim the birth of Christ on December 25. The Eastern Orthodox churches celebrate his birth on January 6 and 7. The Armenian Church has its Christmas on January 18 and 19.

Top: lilies for Christ's Resurrection
Left: the fruit and palms for Sukkot, the Jewish harvest festival

ANYONE FOR GOLF?
For visitors or Israelis who crave a round of golf, Caesarea Golf Club has no rival—not because it is so good, but because it is the only golf course in Israel. Established in 1980, the club has an 18-hole course covering 395 acres, including 62 acres of grass—no mean achievement in this terrain. The course is open all day, every day of the week, including Saturday. In fact, Saturday is the most popular day, and reservations are advisable.

EIN SHEMER
A short drive inland from Caesarea, lying just off the cross-country road that runs from here to the Sea of Galilee (via Afula), Ein Shemer is an interesting kibbutz, still with the protective enclosing wall that all kibbutzim once had. Calling itself The Old Yard, Ein Shemer has a museum and video about the history of the settlement. One of the kibbutz members is the famous artist-blacksmith Hofi, who can fashion a little work of art out of iron in just a few minutes.

Caesarea: Corinthian capital (right) and theater (below)

▶▶▶ Caesarea 113A2

Closed Shabbat. Admission: moderate

One of the great cities of the ancient world, Caesarea was a port from the 4th century BC onward, and the Roman administrative capital of Judaea for hundreds of years. As an archeological site, it is dramatic, extensive, and accessible. Excavations began within three years of the founding of the State of Israel, and still continue. Today, one sees an area of superimposed walled cities—Herodian, Roman, and Byzantine—overlaid in part by the Gothic remains of a medieval Crusader fortress town. The best-represented periods, dominating the site visually, are the Roman and Crusader cities. A short distance from the archeological site, modern Caesarea consists of a coastal area of high-quality vacation and leisure facilities, including hotels and restaurants, as well as some of Israel's best and most expensive private housing.

The first port at Caesarea was set up by the Phoenicians and conquered 100 years later by the Greek army of Alexander the Great. In 22 BC, the Roman city was born under Herod. This large walled town encompassed the 20,000-seat **hippodrome▶** (or racetrack), which remains unexcavated, and a splendid **theater▶▶▶**. Water was carried in on a fine beachside **aqueduct▶▶** its ruins remain impressive. Through taxes and trade, the town became a source of wealth for Herod and for Rome. It drew large numbers of Jews and pagans, and was above all a cosmopolitan, commercial town. From AD 6, Judaea became a Roman province, with Caesarea as its administrative center. It was here that, in AD 69, Vespasian was proclaimed emperor. At about this time, according to the Acts of the Apostles, St. Philip baptized the Roman centurion Cornelius and later established a Christian community. In 135, following the defeat of the Bar Kochba Revolt, the great scholar Rabbi Akiva was tortured to death at Caesarea.

Minaret in Caesarea, relic of Turkish rule

The town continued to be an important Christian center, and the seat of a bishop, right through the Byzantine period. New walls were erected, enclosing a much more compact area, and the port town prospered. The **Byzantine street▶▶**, lined with shops, is the evocative remnant of this era.

After the Persian invasion of 614, the commercial life of the town came to a complete end, and it fell into obscurity. A succession of Muslim rulers held the town until the arrival of the Crusaders in 1099. Two years later, in 1101, the Crusaders turned their attention to Caesarea, moving in and reviving the site. They constructed numerous substantial new buildings, reusing many pieces of Roman and Byzantine masonry. In 1254, the Crusaders, under the French King Louis IX, constructed their imposing **fortifications▶▶▶**, of which the splendid walls and moat of the Crusader citadel survive. They enclose only a small, rectangular part of the ancient Caesarea, which can be reached by passing through a Gothic gatehouse into the ruined city. Dusty walls and arches, vestiges of houses with their water cisterns, and skeletal remnants of other buildings are sufficient to kindle the imagination. The three apses of the Crusaders' cathedral remain standing.

The Crusaders' presence was abruptly terminated in 1275 by the Mamelukes, and again the city fell to ruin. During the four centuries of Turkish rule, until 1917, there was increasing decay and destruction, apart from an odd episode in which Muslim refugees from Bosnia were accommodated on the site. They built the 19th-century **mosque** beside the Crusader cathedral and put up warehouses by the **Old Harbor▶▶**, which had originally been constructed by Herod and was later reconstructed by the Crusaders. Today, the attractions of the harbor district include several inexpensive eating places and a pleasant pay-to-enter beach area.

A TALE OF TWO CITIES

"If you hear that Caesarea thrives, but Jerusalem suffers—believe it. If you hear that Jerusalem thrives, while Caesarea suffers—believe it. But if you hear that both Jerusalem and Caesarea are thriving—don't believe it." This ancient saying reflects the rivalry between the two great "capitals" of Judaea. Jerusalem was the spiritual, Jewish capital. Caesarea was the temporal, Roman capital. Caesarea attracted pagans and was devoted to wealth and luxury. Jerusalem was pious and dominated by the Temple. Caesarea became an early stronghold of Christianity. Jerusalem was the bastion of Judaism. Even today, Jerusalem remains the religious and national capital, while Caesarea has the country's wealthiest inhabitants, best housing, and most secular atmosphere.

The widespread use of the word kosher—as in "a kosher business deal"—is very close to the real meaning. Other words related to kosher mean such things as honest, wholesome, to legalize a doubtful situation, to be worthy of an honor, to succeed. "Kosher" refers to more than food. It means that things are right, correct, as they should be, and in particular, that they satisfy the requirements of Jewish law.

FORBIDDEN FOODS
"The camel, because he cheweth the cud but parteth not the hoof, he is unclean unto you. And the rock badger, because he cheweth the cud but parteth not the hoof, he is unclean unto you. And the hare, because she cheweth the cud but parteth not the hoof, she is unclean unto you. And the swine, because he parteth the hoof and is cloven footed, but cheweth not the cud, he is unclean unto you. Of their flesh ye shall not eat, and their carcass ye shall not touch. Whatsoever hath no fins nor scales in the water, that is a detestable thing unto you. And these ye shall have in detestation among the fowls; they shall not be eaten, they are a detestable thing..."
—Leviticus 11:4–13

A right way The body of Jewish law and ritual concerning food and drink is called *kashrut*. On restaurant menus and in food stores, you may notice the three Hebrew letters of the word "kosher." That is to let people know, especially religious Jews, that all the food sold there is acceptable to eat. If it is not kosher, food is usually called *trefa* (or *treif*, in Yiddish), meaning impure, incorrect.

Some examples *Kashrut* forbids certain foods entirely, such as pork and shellfish. Commercially prepared foods may be acceptable if free from forbidden ingredients—they generally require the seal of rabbinical approval. Meats must be from animals killed in the prescribed manner so that they have not a drop of blood in them. Jews must never consume any blood. *Kashrut* also reflects the biblical injunction that "You shall not seethe a kid in its mother's milk." Perhaps this was meant to be taken literally; perhaps it was meant metaphorically as a way of saying that, even when animals are killed for meat, they should not be humiliated or treated with contempt. Over the years, however, this has come to be defined as a law that forbids eating dairy products and meat products at the same time—or even within several hours of each other. For the strictly Orthodox, they cannot even be cooked in the same pans. For the more strict, they may not be eaten off the same plates, and for the stricter still, the utensils may not even be cleaned in the same sink or dishwasher. It also means that cheese cannot be made with animal rennet that you cannot put milk in your coffee after a meat meal.

Top: Sabbath bread
Above: sign of approval

Bon appetit You probably won't notice any of this unless you simply cannot live without a chicken breast sauteed in butter or a shrimp cocktail. You won't find them easily, and there is very little call for cheeseburgers in Israeli fast-food bars. However, food in Israel, despite *kashrut*, tends to be very good, and the whole country is equipped with a wide range of vegetarian or "dairy" restaurants (where fish and other seafood are usually served as well).

▶▶ Haifa

150/151

Undoubtedly the most appealing of Israel's three large towns, Haifa is full of views and is beautifully situated on a promontory that projects into the Mediterranean, rising steeply to the south, on the slope of the Mount Carmel upland. A popular Israeli saying has it that Jerusalem prays and Tel Aviv plays, but Haifa works. The city has industrial areas on the northeastern side, a university, a science and research institute of worldwide importance at the top of the Carmel slope, and a major port near the town center.

Haifa is also a town with a mixed population. Predominantly Jewish, it also has many Druze, Muslims, and Christian Arabs. Between the different groups, there seems to be no strife or friction at all, merely a pragmatic desire to work together amicably and have a peaceful life. The city is also the world center of the Bahá'i community (see page 152), whose Shrine of the Bab, with its gilded dome, makes a striking landmark.

Haifa also has attractions of considerable interest to the visitor. The Mediterranean shore, extending alongside the western sections of the town, has a good, long **beach▶** and promenade, within sight of the Haifa–Tel Aviv highway. The beach curves around the headland, almost reaching the **Old City▶**, a mainly 18th- and 19th-century harbor district at the foot of the hill. Up the slope lies **Hadar HaCarmel▶▶▶**, the center of Haifa. Here you will find scores of inexpensive eating places, including Sephardic snack bars selling Middle Eastern dishes.

Downtown Herzl Street is the busy main thoroughfare, for shopping or eating. Parallel to it runs a pleasant pedestrian mall, Nordau Street, which has a quieter atmosphere and scores of open-air restaurant and café tables. As the city heads up the steep Carmel hill, a striking feature is the **stepped alleys** linking street to street. Farther up, near the crest of the hill, **Central Carmel▶** is the more stately, well-to-do, residential and academic neighborhood. A **funicular railway▶** with six stations, from Kikkar Paris at the bottom to the hotel district of Central Carmel at the top, joins the three sections of the city center.

History Archeological studies show settlements on and around present-day Haifa dating back to the 10th century BC. The busy port town with a large yeshiva (a school devoted to the study of sacred texts) was taken by Crusaders in 1099 and largely destroyed.

Haifa survived only as a quiet village until the 19th

Haifa, city of views

HERZL'S DREAM

Theodor Herzl, the 19th-century founder of Zionism, once said that he had a dream—no metaphorical Utopian vision, but a real sleeping dream—in which he saw Haifa transformed, with white buildings rising up the hill and great liners in the harbor. His dream has come true with astonishing accuracy, though in Herzl's fantasy, the liners were cruise ships. In today's Haifa, a century later, they are cargo vessels laden with goods.

THE TECHNION

Another dream of Herzl's was that Israel would one day possess a center of scientific research that would be the envy of the world. Haifa's Technion (the Israel Institute of Technology), the country's first university, opened in 1924, with Albert Einstein as its first president. Even before the creation of the State of Israel, the Technion had made major leaps in knowledge and technology in the fields of construction, water management, and agriculture. In 1954, the Technion moved to its present Mount Carmel campus. Since then it has made great advances in aviation, chemistry, agriculture, electronic communications, and medicine. Its medical school, engaged mainly in developing new techniques, is a world leader.

Map: Haifa

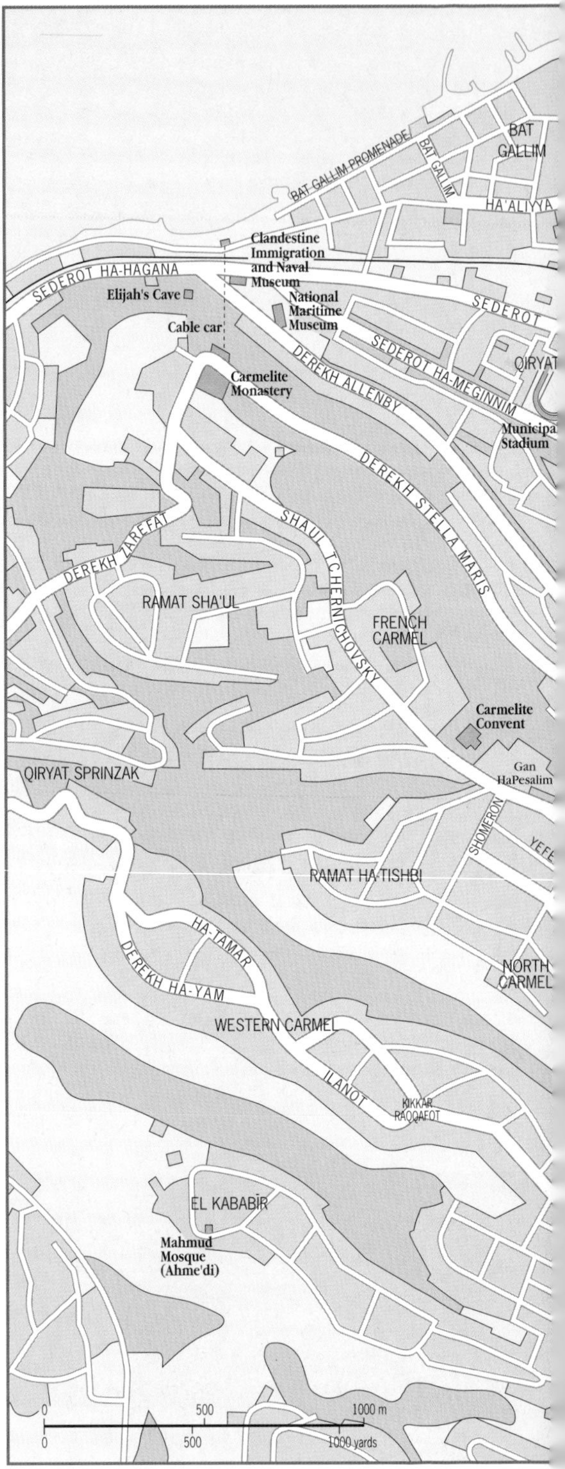

EXODUS

Originally called *The President Warfield*, the 2,000-ton river steamer was renamed *Exodus*. Packed with Holocaust survivors, it set sail for Palestine in early July 1947, from the French port of Sète. On July 18, on the approach to Haifa, British sailors boarded the ship and overcame the crew, killing three passengers and injuring 28. The British government ordered all passengers returned to the French port. On arrival, the refugees refused to disembark, and the French refused to use force against them. They stayed on board until the British decided to take them back to Germany. Here they were forcibly removed from the ships in September and transferred to camps for displaced persons.

Bahá'i Shrine, Haifa

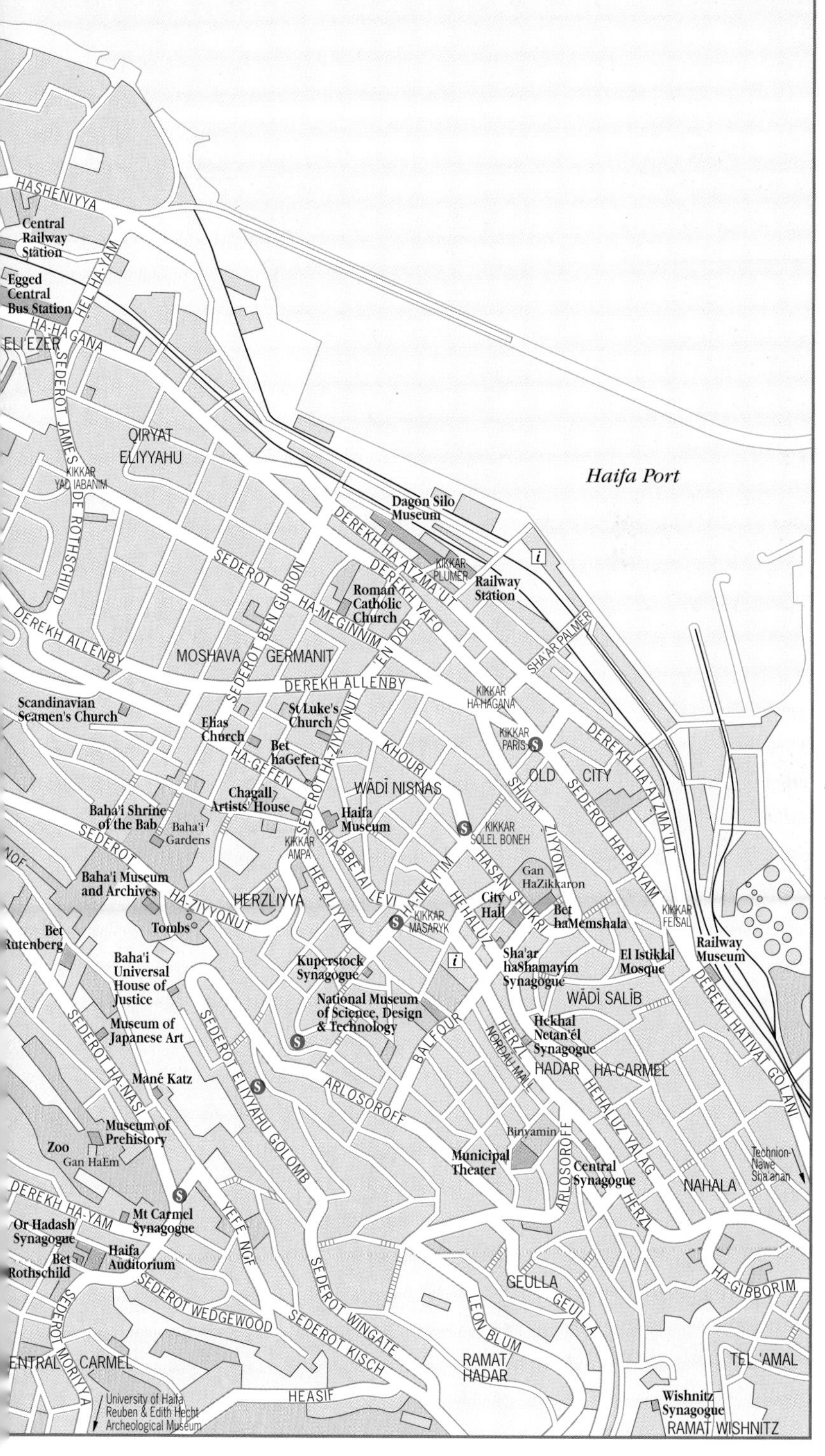
HASHENIYYA
Central Railway Station
Egged Central Bus Station
HEL HA-YAM
HA-HAGANA
ELI'EZER
SEDEROT JAMES DE ROTHSCHILD
QIRYAT ELIYYAHU
KIKKAR YAD LABANIM
Haifa Port
Dagon Silo Museum
DEREKH HA'ATZMA'UT
KIKKAR PLUMER
Railway Station
SEDEROT HA-MEGINNIM
DEREKH YAFO
Roman Catholic Church
SEDEROT BEN GURION
EN DOR
SHA'AR PALMER
DEREKH ALLENBY
MOSHAVA GERMANIT
KIKKAR HA-HAGANA
Scandinavian Seamen's Church
St Luke's Church
Elias Church
Bet haGefen
HA-GEFEN
KHOURI
KIKKAR PARIS
OLD CITY
WĀDĪ NISNAS
Chagall Artists' House
SEDEROT HA-ZIYYONUT
SHIVAT ZIYYON
SEDEROT HA-PALYAM
Baha'i Shrine of the Bab
Baha'i Gardens
Haifa Museum
KIKKAR SOLEL BONEH
KIKKAR AMPA
SHABBETAI LEVI
HERZLIYYA
HASAN SHUKRI
Baha'i Museum and Archives
HERZLIYYA
HA-NEVI'IM
Gan HaZikkaron
City Hall
Bet haMemshala
KIKKAR FEISAL
Tombs
KIKKAR MASARYK
HE-HALUZ
Railway Museum
Bet Rutenberg
Baha'i Universal House of Justice
Kuperstock Synagogue
Sha'ar haShamayim Synagogue
El Istiklal Mosque
WĀDĪ SALĪB
National Museum of Science, Design & Technology
Hekhal Netan'el Synagogue
DEREKH HATIVAT GOLANI
Museum of Japanese Art
SEDEROT HA-NASI
SEDEROT ELIYYAHU GOLOMB
BALFOUR
NORDAU MALL
HERZL
HADAR HA-CARMEL
Mané Katz
ARLOSOROFF
HEHALUZ YALAG
Museum of Prehistory
Binyamin
Zoo
Gan HaEm
Municipal Theater
ARLOSOROFF
Central Synagogue
Technion-Nawe Sha'anan
NAHALA
DEREKH HA-YAM
Mt Carmel Synagogue
YEFE NOF
HERZL
Or Hadash Synagogue
Bet Rothschild
Haifa Auditorium
HA-GIBBORIM
GEULLA
SEDEROT WEDGEWOOD
SEDEROT WINGATE
LEON BLUM
GEULLA
SEDEROT KISCH
SEDEROT MORIYYA
CENTRAL CARMEL
RAMAT HADAR
TEL 'AMAL
HEASIF
University of Haifa Reuben & Edith Hecht Archeological Museum
Wishnitz Synagogue
RAMAT WISHNITZ

THE BAHA'I FAITH
Followers of the Bahá'i religion believe in a single deity, in the essential unity of all human beings and religions, and in the continuous revelation of an evolving, yet fundamentally unchanging, divine truth through a series of prophets ("Divine Educators"). In particular, adherents pay homage to the "Martyr-Herald" (or "the Bab"), who announced his beliefs and his mission in Persia in 1844 and was executed in 1850 (aged 31) as a result, and the "Founder of the Faith" ("Bahá'u'lláh"), who was exiled to Akko in 1868 and died there under house arrest in 1892. Haifa is the administrative capital of the religion, and the Universal House of Justice is its supreme institution. But while the magnificently beautiful Shrine of the Bab is in Haifa and is seen by more visitors, the lovely Shrine of Bahá'u'lláh, at Bahjá, near Akko (see page 140), is actually the more sacred site.

CARMELIM—A NEW REGION
The warm, green, and wooded Mediterranean hills of Mount Carmel, the wine country around Zichron Yaakov, and the narrow coastal plain flanked by a long ribbon of sandy beach have together been dubbed Carmelim by Israelis. This beautiful part of Israel's coastal strip, reaching from Haifa to Caesarea, contains an exceptional legacy of history and culture.
For tourist information tel: 04-984 5239; web: www.carmelim.org.il.

century when its port grew to accommodate steamships. The first half of the 20th century saw a huge amount of Jewish settlement. The Technion, the scientific research institute, was founded (see page 149) and various Zionist-run commercial and manufacturing enterprises were opened. Histadrut, the all-pervasive workers' union, to this day a pillar of the Israeli establishment, based itself in the town. Haifa also became the principal entry port for clandestine Jewish immigrants to Israel.

The seafront areas are the oldest part of town. Behind Haifa's slightly seedy **port**, crowded little **Wadi Nisnas▶** Arab district centers on its busy market streets. Along Ben-Gurion Avenue, the quaint **German Colony▶▶** of red-roofed stone houses was founded in 1868 by a German Christian sect. German family names are still inscribed over some doors. Today the area is being restored, with shops, cafés, and restaurants opening.

The **Clandestine Immigration Museum▶▶▶** (*Closed* Shabbat. *Admission: inexpensive*) at 204 Allenby Street catches the eye of every passing motorist. This building, close to the beach and a little out of the heart of town, envelopes an entire ship. It combines the functions of memorial and archive, recording, through displays and documents, the organized struggle that brought 107,000 "illegal immigrants," including Holocaust survivors, to Israel from Europe during the years 1934 to 1948. Heartrending exhibits include the story of the 1947 clandestine ship *Exodus* (see page 150). The ship on display shows what the interior would have been like.

Almost next door, is the **National Maritime Museum▶** (198 Allenby Street), a record of shipping throughout the ages (*Open* Sat–Thu. *Admission: moderate*). Opposite, on the other side of Allenby and up steep steps, is the atmospheric, if historically dubious **Elijah's Cave▶** (*Closed* Shabbat. *Admission free*).

A steep staircase of 300 steps cut into the hillside continues up and across an attractive heath with superb sea views to the handsome **Carmelite Stella Maris Monastery▶▶▶** (*Open* Mon–Sat. *Admission free*). Inside, a circular domed chapel encloses another reputedly holy and miraculous cave where Elijah is said to have lived and died. Across the road, the Stella Maris Lighthouse stands on a 19th-century Ottoman villa. The easy way to reach the monastery is to take the cable car from close to the Clandestine Immigration Museum.

The conspicuous gilded dome rising grandly over central Haifa belongs to the exquisite **Shrine of the Bab▶▶▶** (*Open* daily 9–12; closed most of Aug. Gardens 9–5. *Admission free*), completed in 1953. This is, without doubt, the best cared-for and most elegant holy site in Israel. The rather meditative, private style of worship takes place in two small and silent white rooms, laid with rich carpets. The shrine stands in immaculate gardens looking across Haifa.

Haifa Museum▶ (26 Shabtai Levi Street) brings together a wide range of exhibits on ancient and modern art, folklore, ethnography, and Jewish ritual art (*Open* daily in morning, Tue, Thu and Sat afternoons also. *Admission: moderate*). Almost opposite is **Chagall House▶** (*Open* Sat–Thu. *Admission free*) another art museum hosting special exhibitions of work by contemporary artists.

▶ Herzliya *112C4*

Named after the "Father of Zionism," Theodor Herzl, Herzliya is a busy working town. Quite separate is its small beach development, correctly called Herzliya Pituach. This has a wide white beach backed by hotels and apartment houses.

▶ Lod (Lydda) *112C4*

Beside Ben-Gurion International Airport, Lod dates to the Israelite conquest in 1300 BC. Its subsequent history includes centuries of rule by Greeks, Maccabees, and Romans. The Acts of the Apostles records that St. Paul miraculously healed a bedridden man here. It is also claimed as the birthplace of St. George, the Roman tribune sacred to Christians and to Muslims. He is buried here, in a building that is both church and mosque, on the site of a 6th-century basilica and 12th-century Crusader church.

▶▶ Lohamei HaGhetaot *113B4*

Tel: 04-995 8044. www.gfh.org.il
Open: daily, early closing Fri. Admission free

The name of this kibbutz, built beside a Byzantine aqueduct on the edge of Akko, means "The Ghetto Fighters." It was founded in 1949 by Holocaust survivors and former ghetto resistance fighters. At the entrance is their massive, gaunt **Holocaust Memorial and Museum▶▶▶**. This deals in clear displays with the Jewish history of Lithuania, the growth of Zionism there, Jewish youth movements, the Warsaw Ghetto Uprising, and much more. A display on the Nazis' death camps includes a large-scale model of Treblinka, and deals with the extermination of two different historic Jewish communities, the Dutch and the community of Salonika in Greece. Among the disturbing photos on display are the terribly sad faces of child victims of Nazi medical "experiments." **Yad Layeled (The Children's Memorial)▶▶▶** is housed in a separate building, an award-winning structure in which visitors follow a spiral of vivid exhibits that evoke the Holocaust through the eyes of its child victims. Yad Layeled is suitable for child visitors.

BEHIND THE SCENES

Perceived by most visitors simply as one of Israel's quieter beach resorts, Herzliya has a successful "clean industries" zone generating an income of U.S. $300 million, and accounting for 25 percent of Israel's science-based exports.

153

Lod, claimed as the birth and burial place of St. George

DUNES AND SWAMPS
Israel's coastal strip is a region of infertile dunes that, apart from the Carmel upland, used to be backed by the hot swampy Plain of Sharon. Right into this century, the area was notoriously unhealthy and unworkable. On top of the other problems, it was inhabited by crocodiles. The great Levantine highway of the ancient world, later to become the Romans' Via Maris (the Coast Road), had to divert away from the swampy, treacherous coastal hinterland. The British Mandate authorities were the first to set about drainage and bridge-building to make the area more accessible. With the founding of the State of Israel, a mammoth effort was made to build new towns along the coast. The marshes were drained and the main north–south highway put through. The Sharon Plain has since been turned into one of the world's most productive citrus-growing areas.

►►► Mount Carmel *113B3*

Some of the most beautiful countryside in Israel falls within the Carmel National Park. The Carmel range—consisting of the Carmel escarpment itself and the smaller Mehallel, Shoker, and Sumak peaks—rises from the surrounding coastal lowlands in the form of a triangle. The triangle's northern apex pushes into the sea at Haifa and its sides plunge down to the Kishon Valley and Yizre'el Plain on one side and to the Mediterranean Sea on the other. The base of the triangle fades gradually into the lower Sharon countryside, creating an attractive landscape of rock and abundant, varied scrub rolling across the Mediterranean hinterland.

Despite the name, Mount Carmel is no mountain. The highest point, only 1,791 feet, hardly projects above the rest of the Carmel ridge, along which runs the road from Haifa. The range covers a tiny area (14 miles from end to end, and only 6 miles at the widest). Yet it has the feel of a world apart, with a character and history distinct from that of the lower-lying country all around.

In Canaanite times, these hilltops were adorned with shrines dedicated to Ba'al. The cult's appeal was such that it continued to thrive long after the Israelite conquest. Its end in the 9th century BC is described in the biblical account (I Kings 18) where Elijah wins a public contest to see whose god could make spontaneous fire for their sacrifices. He called on the people to slaughter the 450 "prophets of Ba'al" and turn instead to the God of Israel. Since then, Elijah's name has been associated with Carmel—interestingly more among the Christians and the Muslims than among the Jews.

Right and below: Carmel National Park

Drive

Carmel scenery

Mount Carmel's Mediterranean countryside, of limestone hills covered with fragrant evergreen vegetation, is full of historical and human interest. There are Druze towns to visit, plus religious and historical sites, an artists' village, and local wine to taste (for map see page 113). *Allow all day.*

From **Haifa**, take the steep road to the **university**, dominated by the intrusive **Eshkol Tower**, a monstrosity designed only to be as tall as possible. Leave the city on the tranquil hill road to **Isfiya▶**, a small town of Christians and Druze. The road winds steeply down to larger **Daliyat▶▶**, where the people's dress and local architecture are more noticeably Druze. Its main street has a fascinating Middle Eastern atmosphere, with open-fronted stores and snack bars. **Oliphant's House▶**, a memorial to Druze soldiers who died for Israel, was the 19th-century home of an Englishman whose Jewish secretary, N. H. Imber, wrote *HaTikva,* Israel's national anthem. A turn leads to the hilltop monastery at **Muhraka▶** (or Keren Carmel), traditional site of the meeting between Elijah and Ba'al's prophets. Follow the main road to **Zichron Ya'akov▶▶** (see page 160), where wine-tasting and a tour of the cellars is available at the Winery Visitors' Center.

The open-fronted stores of Daliyat's main street

Traditional Druze skullcaps for sale in Daliyat.

On the coast, **Kibbutz Nahsholim▶** has a museum, in a former wine-bottle factory. The kibbutz also offers simple beachside accommodations. The archeological site of **Tel Dor▶** was a Phoenician port town thousands of years ago. Take the Haifa highway, and turn into the **Nahal Me'arot Reserve▶▶▶**, where several big caves were inhabited by humans as far back as 200,000 years ago. These can be toured with a guide. The reserve also offers a choice of marked hiking trails through lovely natural vegetation.

En Hod▶, to the north, is a hillside "artists' village" of meandering lanes, scattered houses, pretty gardens, art galleries, and open-air sculptures. A left at the crossroads leads to **Atlit▶** (see page 143) while the right turn winds through beautiful rocky hills to **Carmel Forest▶▶**. The sign to **Hai Bar▶** leads down a dirt road to a reserve where once-indigenous animals are being reintroduced. Continue to the intersection and take a left to get back to Haifa.

In ancient Israel, wine in moderation was the usual drink before, during, and after meals. Jewish coins of the Second Temple period depict bunches of grapes. Grapes or vine leaves can often be seen in the mosaics and stone carvings of post-Temple synagogues. With the return to Israel, the winemaking industry has been revived with great success, and is currently flourishing.

WINE AND RITUAL
"Blessed are you Lord, our God ruler of the world, who created the fruit of the vine." This blessing over wine is said (in Hebrew) before every meal on the Sabbath, starting with the Friday night dinner. A glass of kosher wine is then drunk—usually just a tiny glass of the extra-sweet Kiddush wine.

Sacred and profane Israelis are not big drinkers. There is no breath-testing here for motorists, simply because excessive drinking is almost unknown. Observant Jews thank God for the fruit of the vine on the Sabbath, yet no one could be more abstemious. Things have obviously changed since biblical times when the people of Israel grew grapes in abundance, were fond of wine, and—to judge by references in the Scriptures—sometimes drank a great deal of it.

Jews are supposed to drink only kosher wine. Rabbis decided that any contact with a non-Jew would render wine nonkosher unless the wine was boiled. Of course, boiling is not the ideal way to preserve a wine's finest qualities, and kosher wine came to be regarded with derision by wine-lovers. There is also an ultrasweet blended wine specially produced for Kiddush, the ritual blessing that sanctifies all sorts of occasions. Such wine seems to be intended to dissuade drinking—yet when the sages decreed that the Sabbath be sanctified over a cup of wine, the reason given was precisely that wine brings joy and festivity.

Products of the Golan Heights Winery

The new approach Even Israelis do not think of themselves as a wine-producing nation. They are mistaken, for in recent decades Israel has rediscovered its great wine tradition. In keeping with the Talmudic injunction to ensure that the wine is kosher, only Jews may be involved in its production at every stage. The most modern techniques are used, and many different grape varieties have been planted, crossed, or combined, in the search for higher quality and an authentic Israeli style of fine wine.

Some have been a great success, especially the elegant dry white Chardonnay and Sauvignon Blanc and the classic, full-bodied red Cabernet Sauvignon. Blander and sweeter Emerald Riesling is the most popular with Israelis. Richly sweet Muscat is grown, as is the tangy California

variety zinfandel. The main wine areas are in southern Carmel, the district south of Tel Aviv around Rishon-l'Tsion, and the Golan Heights, with smaller wineries around Ashkelon and Beersheva. Less expensive labels include the Segal and Baron wineries.

Mural celebrating Baron Rothschild's introduction of viticulture to the Carmel region

Carmel It is said that the name Carmel probably means God's Vineyard (Kerem El). A century ago, Baron Edmund de Rothschild had the whole area, from Zichron Ya'akov down to Binyamina, planted with vines, under the direction of French agronomists. The Carmel Mizrachi Winery in Zichron Ya'akov is now the country's largest wine producer, and visitors are welcome for tours and tasting.

Rishon l'Tsion The name (also spelled Rishon le Zion) means "First In Zion." It means, in other words, the first Jewish settlement of modern times, established in 1882. Five years later, the struggling pioneers were bailed out by Baron Rothschild, who again planted vineyards, with tremendous success. The Carmel winery here, recently modernized, offers guided tours and tasting. Its wines have improved enormously in recent years.

Golan Heights Winery Acclaimed as Israel's best are the wines produced on the Golan Heights, just outside Katzrin. The vineyards, tended by settlements and kibbutzim over a wide area of the Golan, are run as a cooperative together with the winery itself. This launched Israel's dramatic rediscovery of winemaking, and it's the only winemaker in the world to have won the Chairman's Trophy of Excellence at the trade's important Vinexpo exhibition three successive years. Golan's soils and drainage are perfect for wine, and, because of poor rainfall, the water supply is controlled by irrigation. The wines, in a wide range of styles, are marketed under three labels: Yarden (the best), Gamla, and Golan. The winery, the only one in Israel growing Merlot grapes, also makes a fine sparkling dry white.

Netanya's beach

Open-air entertainment

SUMMER NIGHTS
Open-air entertainment takes place in Netanya's main square every night of the week (except Friday) right through July and August. The atmosphere is jolly, participatory, and good-humored. In a typical week you could expect a disco on Sunday, folk dancing on Monday and Saturday, magicians, puppets, and clown shows for children on Tuesday, and community singing on Wednesday and Thursday.

▶ Nahariya *113B4*

The waterfront area of this resort on Galilee's Mediterranean coast, 20 miles north of Haifa, enjoys a good beach, a pleasant frontage, a wide range of leisure amenities, and a calm, tranquil air. Farther back from the sea lies a busy working town, founded in 1934 by Jewish refugees from Germany. **Museums▶** of art, archeology, and local history can be found in the town hall. Nahariya resort makes a good base for excursions and tours. About 3 miles north are the seashore ruins of ancient **Akhziv▶▶**, now a national park. It was once an important Canaanite, Phoenician, and Israelite town and renowned for the purple dye produced from some of its shellfish. Some 2 miles south of Nahariya, 4th- and 5th-century Byzantine mosaics and other archeological finds can be seen at **Kibbutz Evron▶** and at **Moshav Shavei Zion**, which also has a good hotel.

▶▶ Netanya *113A1*

Spreading itself comfortably alongside the seashore, but not going far inland, this large, likeable, and unpretentious town is peaceful, almost sedate, and has dozens of decent mid-range hotels and moderately priced eating places. The parklike cliff-top walk gives magnificent views out to sea, and there is a 6-mile sandy beach to enjoy.

One focal point for visitors is **Kikkar HaAtzma'ut** (Independence Square), which fronts onto the cliff top above the main central section of the beach. Another gathering place is the main street, **Rehov Herzl**, where tourists and locals alike stroll in the pleasant evening air. Behind this leisurely facade, Netanya is a productive commercial town. Diamonds have been among its most lucrative specialties since World War II, when the jewelers of Antwerp moved here to escape the Nazis. The **National Diamond Center▶▶** at 90 Herzl Street shows an interesting video about diamonds, gives a guided tour of a diamond factory, and offers a chance to buy at discount prices (*Closed* Shabbat. *Admission free*).

▶▶ Ramla 112C3

Almost unique in that it came into being during a period of Arab rule, Ramla was founded in 716 by Caliph Suleiman and became a large city of Muslims, Christians, and Jews. In 1936, the Jews were forced out by the Arabs, who in 1948 largely fled in fear of reprisals. The population of 50,000 now consists mainly of Jews driven in turn from their homes in Arab countries, along with several thousand Israeli Arabs. It is also a center of the Karaites, a small Jewish sect that accepts the Torah but rejects subsequent rabbinic comment. The town is attractive and friendly, with a strongly Middle Eastern character.

The **Great Mosque▶** (off Herzl Street), reflecting the town's mixed history, is a 12th-century Crusader church topped by a white minaret and transformed into a mosque. The landmark **White Tower▶▶**, a substantial Gothic stone structure, is gaunt, square, and 89 feet tall. Napoleon, who in 1799 stayed overnight in Ramla, enjoyed the view from the top, and General Allenby, in 1917, found it useful as a military observation post. Also known to Christians as the Tower of Forty Martyrs, and to Muslims as the Tower of the Prophet's Companions, it was built in 1267 by the Mameluke Sultan Baibars. It adjoins an extensive walled area, along one side of which are remnants of a **mosque▶** that dates to the founding of the town by Caliph Suleiman. Below the walled courtyard are three large vaulted crypts. Just off Herzl Street, **St. Helena's Pool▶** in fact has no connection at all with St. Helena—it is an impressive 8th-century reservoir.

▶ Rehovot 112C3

Zionist leader Chaim Weizmann (1874–1952), Israel's first President, lived here at the end of his life. In his honor, the distinguished **Weizmann Institute** research center was founded in 1944 (tours by arrangement), near **Weizmann's home▶** (open to visitors). He died here and is buried in the garden.

CHAIM WEIZMANN (1874–1952)

Besides being a leading Zionist, Chaim Weizmann also persuaded Balfour to write the famous Declaration (pledging Britain's support in setting up a Jewish homeland), was president of the World Zionist Organization, and first President of Israel. Born near Pinsk, in Russia, he studied chemistry in Germany and Switzerland, and in 1916 was made director of the British Admiralty Chemical Laboratories. Although devoting much of his energy to diplomacy and politics, he had an international reputation in the scientific world for his discoveries in organic chemistry. He made historic advances in the study of carcinogens, and his many other discoveries included the making of synthetic rubber from organic substances.

Independence Square, Netanya

DOR
Located on the coast close to Zichron Ya'akov and next to Nachsholim, Dor was a Phoenician port in 2000 BC. Though seized by the Israelites and then by the Assyrians, it was recaptured by Phoenicians and remained an independent city until the Roman conquest. From the 4th to 7th centuries it was a Christian town, destroyed in the Arab conquest. Crusaders built a castle on the shore here in the 12th century, but within a hundred years it had been destroyed by the Mamelukes. Dor was revived in 1949 as a *moshav* (cooperative village) set up by immigrants from Greece. It has a beautiful beach and plenty of reminders of its long history.

The white cliffs of Rosh HaNikra

►►► Rosh HaNikra *113B4*

The coastal hinterland climbs as it approaches the Lebanese border, which runs along a high ridge in Israel's northwestern corner. Rosh HaNikra is essentially just a frontier post on this ridge of mountain whose white cliffs plunge straight down into the blue Mediterranean. At the top, thrilling views run far down the country's Mediterranean shore. The border bristles with defenses, and both United Nations and Israeli soldiers continually cross through the gate here.

The area's biggest attraction is the **Rosh HaNikra Caves►►►** at the bottom of the cliffs, which can be reached, except on Shabbat, by an expensive cable car. Here the sea has eaten into the soft pale sandstone like moth grubs into wool. The cliffs are riddled with little holes and tunnels that wind through the rock from one opening to the next—and at each the azure water hammers in as if to bring the whole cliff tumbling down into the waves.

►► Zichron Ya'akov *113B2*

The name means "In Memory of Jacob" and refers not to the biblical character but to the 19th-century banker, Jacob de Rothschild. The town was named in his honor by his son, Baron Edmond de Rothschild (also known as Benjamin or Binyamin). A pleasant small town on high ground at the edge of the Carmel hills, it looks down toward the sea in one direction, and into the Valley of HaNadiv—"The Benefactor"—in the other. The benefactor in question was Baron Rothschild, who purchased this valley and its surrounding country in the 1880s in order to establish new settlements and bail out existing ones. His intentions were Zionist but not always entirely philanthropic. The settlements were run as business concerns and expected to pay their way and cover their costs.

Zichron Ya'akov was founded in 1882 by Romanian Jews, who floundered and fell into serious difficulty. Half of them died, and the others were ready to quit. Rothschild then came in with an offer to buy up the settlement lock, stock, and barrel and employ the residents on a salaried basis. They agreed. The baron then brought in non-Jewish agronomists from the south of France and asked them what could be produced there successfully. Their answer was wine. Other Jews came and, desperate for work, were employed here. Zichron Ya'akov became the most important of the little winegrowing towns of Israel. Today, the main attraction for visitors is a tour of the cooperatively owned **Carmel Oriental** or **Carmel Mizrachi Winery▶** (*Closed* Shabbat. *Admission: moderate*). After a visit to the cellars, you can taste the several varieties of wine made here. The town center is also worth a stroll. On the main streets, HaNadiv and Mayasdim, pioneer houses can still be seen and, at the central intersection, the pioneers' synagogue. **Beit Aaronsohn▶** (*Closed* Shabbat. *Admission: inexpensive*) was the home of the distinguished agronomist and botanist, Aaron Aaronsohn (1876–1917). He created and led, with his brother Alexander and sister Sarah, the Nili spy ring, which operated for the British against the Turks in World War I. The group was eventually uncovered by the Turks, who captured and tortured Sarah for several days before allowing her to commit suicide. Alexander was executed. Aaron later died in a plane crash. Their home, on Mayasdim Street, the ring's headquarters, has been preserved just as it was in 1917.

Memorial to Rothschild, "the Benefactor," who turned Zichron Ya'akov into an important wine town

The road south leads through vineyards to another wine settlement, **Binyamina**, named from the baron's Hebrew name. Between the two towns, an access road leads to **Ramat HaNadiv▶▶▶** (Hill of the Benefactor), the beautiful memorial park dedicated to Baron Edmond de Rothschild and his wife. In the park is their massive and dignified burial chamber. The two lie under a single slab of black marble in a mausoleum open to the public.

Cable car to Rosh HaNikra caves

▶▶▶ REGION HIGHLIGHTS

See drive page 173
See drive page 194
See drive page 198

RL
5
4
3
2
A
B
Rosh HaNikra (Rosh HaNiqra)
Rosh HaNikra Caves
Hanita
Zar'it
Eilon
Adamit
Goren Park
Netu'a
Biranit
Bar'am
Avivim
Dovev
Montfort
Hila
Nahal Keziv
Evron
1006m Har Adir
Sasa
Ma'alot Tarshiha
Nahariya (Nahariyya)
Nahal Ga'aton
Hurfeish
Gush Halav (Jish)
1208m Hare Meron
Yehi'am
Meron
Shave-Ziyyon
Peqi'in
Buqei'a
Har Meron Nature Reserve
Lohamé-HaGeta'ot
Kfar Yāsīf
Yirkā
Bahá'i Gardens
'Akko (Acre)
Rama
Amirim
Ahihud
Karmi'el
Mifraz Hefa
Maghār
Galilee
Sakhnin
Tamra
Qiryat Yam
Yodefat
Kinneret-Negev Conduit
Eilabūn
Qiryat Bialik
Qiryat Ata
Shefar'am
Lavi
Tur'an
Nesher
(HaGalil)
Bet-Lehem-haGelilit
Zippori
Kfur Kana (Kafr Kannā)
Kafr Kamā
Qiryat-Tiv'on
Nazareth (Nazerat)
Nazerat 'Illit
Isfiyā
Bet She'arim
562m Mount Tabor (Har Tavor)
Mt Carmel (Har Karmel)
Migdal-ha'Emeq
Nahal Qishon
Yoqne'am
Ma'agar Kefar Barukh
Gazit
Elyaqim
Yizre'el Valley ('Emeq Izre'el)
'Afula
Ramat-haShofet
Moledet
Daliyya
Megiddo
'En-Harod
Avital
Nahal Harod
Umm el Fahm
Beit-Alfa (Bet-A'lfa)
Âra
500m Hare Gilboa
Jenin
Ya'bad
'Emeq Dotan
Bāqa el Gharbiya
'Arrāba
Qabatiya
Rāba
Nahal Bezeq

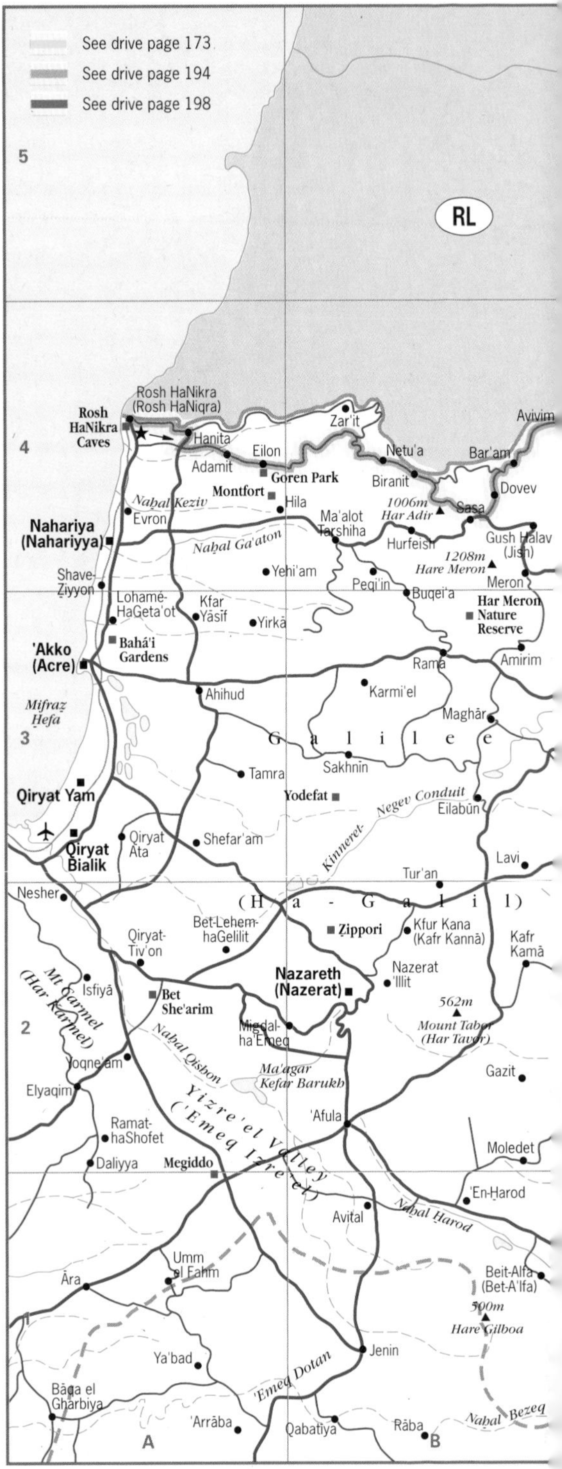

Galilee and the North

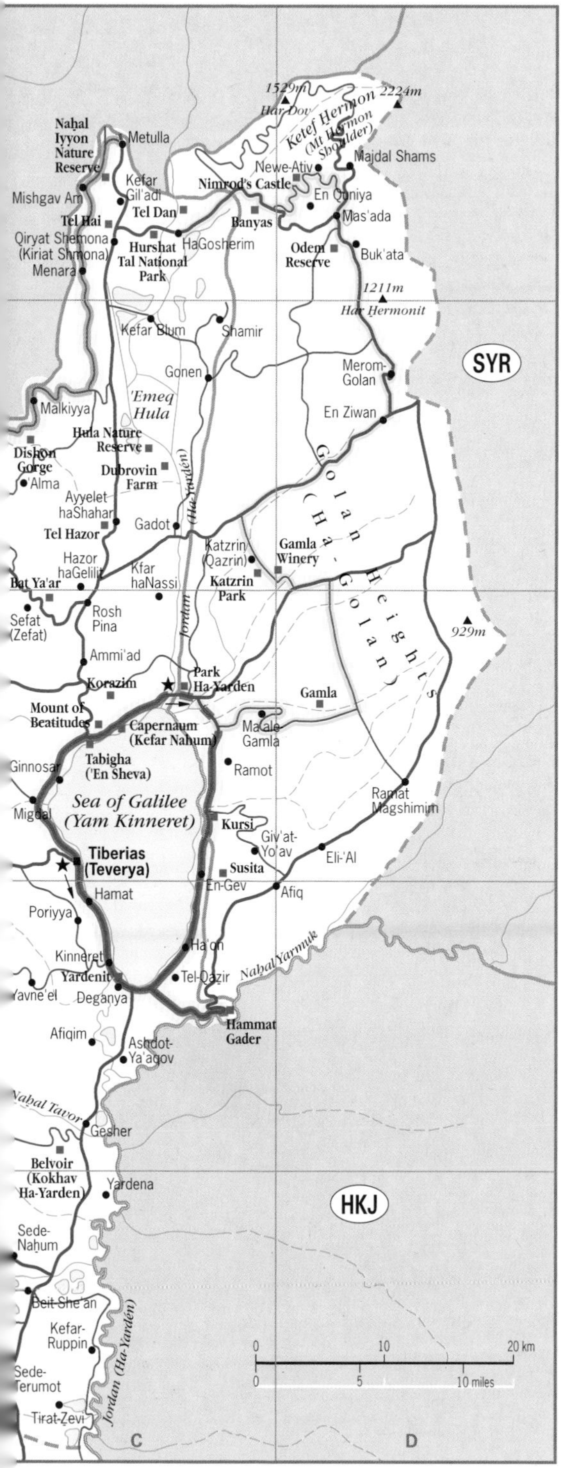

1529m
Har Dov
Ketef Hermon (Mt Hermon Shoulder)
2224m
Nahal Iyyon Nature Reserve
Metulla
Majdal Shams
Newe-Ativ
Kefar Gil'adi
Nimrod's Castle
En Qiniya
Mishgav Am
Tel Dan
Tel Hai
Banyas
Mas'ada
Qiryat Shemona (Kiriat Shmona)
Hurshat Tal National Park
HaGosherim
Odem Reserve
Buk'ata
Menara
1211m
Har Hermonit
Kefar Blum
Shamir
SYR
Gonen
Merom-Golan
'Emeq Hula
Malkiyya
En Ziwan
Hula Nature Reserve
Dishon Gorge
'Alma
Dubrovin Farm
Ayyelet haShahar
Gadot
(Ha-Yarden)
Golan (Ha-Golan)
Heights
Tel Hazor
Katzrin (Qazrin)
Gamla Winery
Hazor haGelilit
Kfar haNassi
Bat Ya'ar
Katzrin Park
Sefat (Zefat)
Rosh Pina
Jordan
929m
Ammi'ad
Korazim
Park Ha-Yarden
Gamla
Mount of Beatitudes
Capernaum (Kefar Nahum)
Ma'ale-Gamla
Ginnosar
Tabigha ('En Sheva)
Ramot
Migdal
Sea of Galilee (Yam Kinneret)
Ramat Magshimim
Kursi
Giv'at-Yo'av
Tiberias (Teverya)
Eli-'Al
Susita
Hamat
En-Gev
Afiq
Poriyya
Ha'on
Kinneret
Nahal Yarmuk
Yardenit
Tel-Qazir
Yavne'el
Deganya
Hammat Gader
Afiqim
Ashdot-Ya'aqov
Nahal Tavor
Gesher
Belvoir (Kokhav Ha-Yarden)
Yardena
HKJ
Sede-Nahum
Beit She'an
Kefar-Ruppin
Jordan (Ha-Yarden)
Sede-Terumot
Tirat-Zevi
0 10 20 km
0 5 10 miles
C
D

Sign advertising the Jordan River baptismal site

Galilee and the North The hills of Galilee, on Israel's warm, northern borders, are startlingly green. Here, the rocky landscape is clothed in natural or planted forests. Farms produce an extraordinary range of crops. The northeast corner, around Dan, on the slopes of Mount Hermon and in the upper Hula Valley, enjoys a wealth of plant, bird, and animal wildlife.

Images of Israel as a Middle Eastern country can be misleading. Essentially, this is a Mediterranean land, tied by history, culture, geography, and climate entirely to the waters of the classical, Mediterranean world, rather than to the sands of Arabia. No part of Israel strikes the eye as so utterly and familiarly Mediterranean as the Galilee.

The Galilee forms a narrow band stretching from the sea in the west to the Jordan River. The east is dominated by the Sea of Galilee, while to the south it is bounded by the Jezreel Plain. The region is blessed with an exquisite climate that is a few degrees cooler than in the beach resorts farther south. Snow falls on the heights in midwinter, but fine weather lasts from May through October.

A place of pilgrimage The fact that Jesus lived in Galilee—and walked on its waters, miraculously fed the multitudes, taught that we should love one another, and recruited his disciples from among the Galilee fishermen—is accepted by Christians around the world. Many travel to see the spots where all this happened. The fact that the sites have been disputed, or are symbolic rather than historically proven, seems not to matter. Stand beside the tranquil shore of the Sea of Galilee, and it is easy to believe that you are indeed standing where he stood, seeing the serene landscapes where he wandered in prayer and in thought. Dozens of simple churches and grand basilicas commemorate the significant events of his three-year public ministry.

It is now more widely understood among Christians that Jesus was an observant Jew, learned in the Scriptures and concerned only that his fellow Jews should obey the spirit, rather than just the letter, of the Law. Galilee, far from the Temple in Jerusalem, was perhaps an ideal place for his teachings. Yet within a few years of his death, after the crushing of the First Jewish Revolt and the destruction

THE DISTRICT

The Hebrew name for Galilee, HaGalil, simply means "the District." Originally it was HaGalil HaGoyim, meaning (more or less), "the Non-Jewish District." That is because, from the 8th century BC to the Hasmonean conquest in the 2nd century BC, the region was not part of the Israelite kingdom. Instead it was a possession of the Assyrians, Babylonians, Persians, and Seleucids. Under Roman rule it was reunited with Judaea. Yet the name has rarely been accurate. Jews have always been numerous here, and this northern region has historically been a stronghold of Jewish nationalism as well as a center of Jewish religious learning.

Right: Christ recruited his disciples from the fishermen of Galilee
Below: Christians from around the world come to trace Christ's ministry

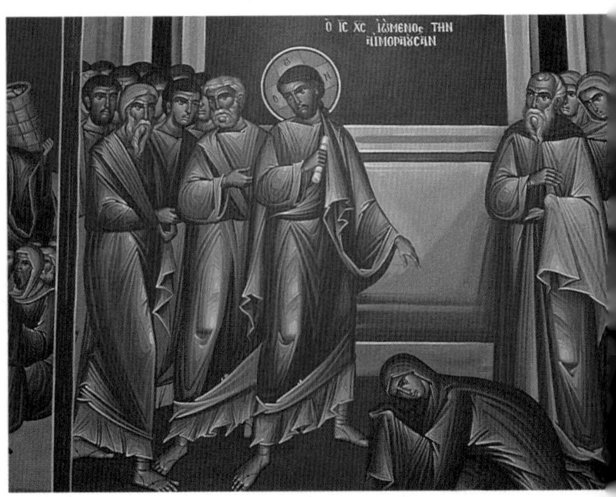

The Sea of Galilee

of the Temple, the eastern Galilee was to become the greatest center of Jewish learning. The Mishna and Talmud (commentaries on the ancient Scriptures) were both written here. Two of the four Jewish holy cities—Sefat and Tiberias—are in Galilee. The region again became the focal point of Jewish culture after the expulsion of the Jews from Spain in 1492. The tombs of the great Galilean scholars and sages of the biblical and medieval periods attract numerous Jewish visitors.

Golan Mediterranean scenery also rises to the east, in the Golan hills. These sparsely inhabited uplands rise to a high plateau overlooked by the majestic snows of Mount Hermon. All this countryside formed part of the biblical land of Israel and has extensive remains from that era. Coming under Arab control in the Middle Ages, Golan formed part of Syria until Syria invaded Israel in 1967. Six days after the invasion, Syria was defeated and driven east. Israel took the Heights and created a buffer zone, which Syria still claims as its own.

Cultural diversity For more than a century, Jews have been drawn to the Galilee as an ideal place to settle and cultivate. Many of their most difficult struggles, both with the land and with the Arabs, have taken place here. Today, there is a good degree of harmony between the different cultural groups, and certainly for a tourist it is safe (and interesting) to visit Israel's non-Jewish communities. The largest Arab town in Israel is Nazareth, where most of the residents are Christian. Several other Galilee towns have a Christian Arab population, though of course many other smaller Arab towns and villages are Muslim. Almost all the members of Israel's 40,000 Druze population live in the western Galilee and on the Golan Heights.

WHERE'S THE BEEF?
Israel has an exceptionally large proportion of vegetarians, and the Galilee, in particular, seems to have become the capital of the meatless lifestyle. Jewish dietary laws require meat and milk to be kept separate—to the point where some believe they cannot be eaten within several hours of each other. For many, the problem of keeping meat and milk apart could be avoided most easily by becoming vegetarian. That is why nearly all factory cafeterias in Israel are vegetarian. Many other Jews chose to become vegetarian for reasons of compassion toward animals, which is a biblical precept. As well as its famous vegetarian village, Amirim, the Galilee has a good meat-free hotel (the Sea View, near Rosh Pina) and an unusual cheese restaurant (Ein Camonim, near Parod).

Byzantine-era frieze in the Golan Archaeological Museum

WHO ARE THE DRUZE?
Bnei Maruf, the Children of Grace, is how the Druze refer to themselves. Members of this distinctive community wear striking black-and-white attire and live in their own well-kept villages scattered over Galilee and Golan. They originated as an 11th-century breakaway group from Ismailism, a branch of Islam. The tenets of the religion are kept a closely guarded secret, with a body of arcane knowledge known only to the initiates or the *Ukal*. The rest of the Druze population are the *Juhal*, the ignorant.

Israel's Druze have been keen supporters of the Jewish state because it gives them full religious freedom, unlike any of the Islamic countries where the Druze are to be found. As a community, they have accepted the obligations of army service (for which, as Arabs, they could have asked to be exempt), and many have distinguished themselves fighting to defend Israel.

▶ Amirim *162B3*

High in the Galilee hills (Amirim means "Treetops") this tranquil agricultural *moshav* (cooperative village) is entirely vegetarian. Just a short drive from historic Sefat, it offers tremendous views to west and east, as well as south to the Sea of Galilee. Half of Amirim's 60 families take paying guests (including some or all meals), and the vegetarian restaurant is very popular.

▶▶ Banyas National Park *163C5*

Open: daily 8–5. Admission: inexpensive

At the foot of Mount Hermon, this lush, delightful park is one of the sources of the Jordan River. With gushing waters, shaded picnic tables and benches, and extensive classical ruins, it attracts many visitors. An enjoyable footpath (about 1½ hours' walk) makes a circle through rich vegetation, crossing and recrossing the turbulent Banyas stream on wooden walkways, with an optional extra half-mile walk to a lovely waterfall that thunders into a pool enclosed by greenery that is perpetually moist.

Banyas was once perhaps the most important pagan shrine in Israel. The park entrance opens into an impressive Greek archeological site, with pools and statuary. Previously sacred to the Canaanite god, Ba'al, the shrine was rededicated to Pan (Paneas in Greek, from which the name Banyas is derived) when it became part of the Hellenistic kingdom of Antiochus III of Syria in the 3rd century BC. In those days the spring poured from the mouth of a cave above the shrine; now it emerges from a crack below. Niches around the cave originally held statues, and scores of Greek carvings have been found here.

The Romans, on taking control of Palestine, rededicated the site to Pan and Zeus, greatly enlarging it. Herod's son Philip made Banyas his capital, renamed it Caesarea Philippi and turned it into the biggest city in northern Israel. It later passed into Arab hands and the city died away. It was held by Crusaders, from 1129 to 1135. By the 1967 Israeli takeover, its population was just 200.

The Gospel of Matthew (16:13–20) relates that, while

Gushing rivers and ancient caves in Banyas National Park

A LONG TWO WEEKS
In late 1948, Israeli forces, fighting desperately against invading Arab armies, arrived at the Christian Arab villages of Biram (now Bar'am) and Ikrit, on the Lebanese border. The Israelis were welcomed and, to assist the soldiers, the villagers agreed to leave for an estimated period of two weeks. But the continuing state of hostilities after the war left the Israeli government wary of Arab villages on the border, and the residents were never allowed back. Ikrit was destroyed in 1951 and Biram in 1953. Many of the villagers, and now their children, live in nearby Rama and Jish, but they have not abandoned hope of returning to their homes and lands.

The remains of Bar'am synagogue

visiting Caesarea Philippi and walking beside the water, Jesus asked his disciples who they thought he was. Simon for the first time declared Jesus to be the Messiah (Christos in Greek), whereupon Jesus called him Petrus, saying, "...upon this rock I will build my church." Banyas remained important to Christians and was the see of a bishop from the 4th to the 7th century. The white-domed Weli el-Hader on the hillside, built in honor of the prophet Elijah, is sacred to the Druze (see panel, page 166).

▶▶ Bar'am National Park *162B4*

Open: summer, daily 8–5; winter, daily 8–4.
Admission: moderate
Dating from the 2nd century AD, the well-preserved remnants of the fine synagogue here include two walls of huge stone blocks, sturdy stone columns forming three aisles, a handsome flagstone floor, and an arched entrance facing Jerusalem.

Until the 1948 War of Independence, the synagogue was part of a small Maronite Arab village and friendly to the Jewish forces. During the fighting—which was intense at this point, so close to the Lebanese border—the residents were asked to leave "temporarily." Instead, their homes were largely destroyed. Not far from the synagogue, on higher ground, is the villagers' church and their ruined houses. Their children, now grown up, still use the church for weddings and ceremonies, and have campaigned to have the village returned to them. Many distinguished Israeli personalities have supported their cause, and the authorities now seem likely to grant the request.

SOMETIME, NEVER
Among the sayings and legends attached to Banyas is the Talmudic statement that the Messiah will come only "when the Banyas turns red." This seems to relate to the old Yiddish expression, that you can have the gift you want or do the thing you want "when Moshiach (the Messiah) comes."

MARRIAGE MADE IN HEAVEN
Not far from Bat Ya'ar, in a pretty vale of pine and olive groves outside Amuka village, stands a small domed building housing the tomb, blackened with candle flame, of Rabbi Yonatan ben Uzziel. The building is divided into men's and women's sections. Here Hasidim and Sephardim flock to pray for a marriage partner or that they might become pregnant. Obscure and tenuous rabbinical remarks account for the practice. Yonatan himself was very preoccupied with the importance of the marriage bond, and later rabbis commentated that the need for a wife, and the way to find one, was "deep" (*amuka*—which happened to be where Yonatan was buried). You might think that only a few hopeless cases would be found here, but among the worshippers are many pretty young women and handsome young bachelors. Glances between the men's and women's sections lead to many a friendly conversation later, and often subsequently to a wedding—thus proving the efficacy of a prayer at the tomb.

▶ Bat Ya'ar 163C3

(tel: 06 692 1788; fax: 06 692 1991)
Open: daily 8–2. Admission free
This popular activity center, close to Amuka, Sefat and Rosh Pina, is set in a clearing in the midst of Israel's largest forest, the Birya. All planted by the Jewish National Fund, these tall, refreshing woodlands consist mainly of Jerusalem pine, cedar, and cypress. Offering activities and excursions ranging from an hour to a week, by pony, jeep, or on foot, Bat Ya'ar is well placed for off-road tours into the Upper Galilee countryside. The 3-hour jeep tour (*Admission charge*) travels through farmland planted with crops ranging from apples to bananas; wildlife encounters could include anything from foxes to gazelles to bee-eaters.

The center also stages children's entertainment, dance, and open-air music shows. It attracts many lunchtime visitors to its ranch-style restaurant, which serves generous salads, steaks, and homemade breads, with a view across the Hula Valley to the snowy summit of Mount Hermon.

▶ Beit Alfa 162B1

Located between Heftsiba and Beit Alfa, two neighboring kibbutzim at the foot of Mount Gilboa, 25 miles from Afula, the ruins of the Beit Alfa synagogue were discovered in 1928 during the digging of a kibbutz irrigation channel. Its beautiful mosaic floor is divided into three panels. One depicts religious emblems and the Ark of the Covenant. Another shows a zodiac circle with the astrological signs named in Hebrew, the moon and the stars, four women symbolizing the seasons, and a youth riding a horse-drawn chariot. The third represents the sacrifice of Isaac, as described in the Bible. Unusually, the work is dated with an Aramaic inscription: "This floor was laid down in the year of the reign of Emperor Justinus." Justinus ruled Palestine from AD 518 to 527.

▶▶ Beit She'an 163C1

Open: Sat–Thu 8–5, Fri 8–3. Admission: moderate
This charmless little town seems modern but has, in fact, been inhabited for 5,000 years. It is the site of Scythopolis, mentioned in Egyptian documents as long ago as the 19th century BC. Its excavations are among Israel's most impressive. In the middle of the new town, a large site contains remnants of a **Roman theater▶** in white stone, and a 5th-century **Byzantine street▶** in black. Of the amphitheater's original 12 rows of seats (enough for 6,000 spectators), three rows have survived to this day.

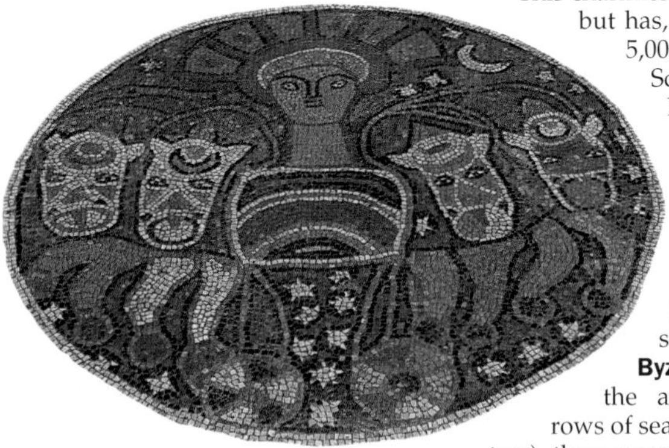

Downhill lie the remarkable principal **Scythopolis excavations**, where work is still in progress. Steps lead to the summit of the **tel▶▶**, where 18 successive towns have been unearthed. A circular trail gives a good overview of the whole site, and the remains of the imposing buildings that

The Chariot of the Sun, Beit Alfa synagogue

Byzantine main street, Beit She'an

once stood in the center. White and black stone make a dazzling contrast here as well. White columns, now being re-erected, lined the black-paved Byzantine **cardo**▶▶▶ (main street). Black walls enclose a superb white **Byzantine amphitheater**▶▶▶ (also seating 6,000), and there is a huge 4th-century **bathhouse**▶▶, with marble columns rising from a mosaic floor. Tragically, an entire 6th-century mosaic floor was stolen from the site in 1989.

▶▶ Belvoir (Hebrew: Kokhav HaYarden) *163C2*

Open: Sat–Thu 8–4, Fri 8–3. Admission: inexpensive

A steep side road climbs to these substantial hilltop ruins of a powerful French Crusader castle, with views across the Jezreel Plain and the Jordan Valley to the Jordanian mountains. The remains consist of a five-sided outer wall, seven towers, and a wide moat on three sides. Inside, a square inner castle has the remains of the storerooms, kitchen, and dining room. Built by Knights Hospitallers in 1168, the castle was twice attacked unsuccessfully by Salah ed-Din in 1182–1183. A third seige, from 1187 to 1191, ended in victory for the Muslims, who allowed the Crusaders safe retreat to Tyre. The Sultan of Damascus then astutely ordered the castle to be partially dismantled. Crusaders returned in 1241, but were unable to reconstruct it.

CONSERVING WATER

The Jordan Valley, from Belvoir to Beit She'an, and the valley of the Beit She'an, a tributary of the Jordan, have been chosen for a massive water conservation program. Water shortages are the biggest threat to Israel's future life and livelihood. Most of the country's water comes from the Sea of Galilee, but this is proving inadequate. Winter downpours result in huge runoffs into the Jordan. The Jewish National Fund has been building a network of 40 reservoirs in the two valleys designed to capture this water. Hopefully it will solve some of the problems, and add some 13.2 billion gallons to the country's water supply.

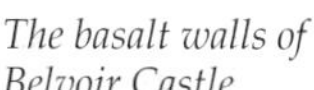

The basalt walls of Belvoir Castle

Greek Orthodox church, Capernaum

JESUS AND CAPERNAUM

"Now when Jesus had heard that John [the Baptist] was cast into prison, he departed into Galilee; and leaving Nazareth, he came and dwelt in Capernaum, which is upon the sea coast, in the borders of Zabulon and Nephtalim."
—Matthew 4:12–13

"After [the wedding at Cana] he went down to Capernaum, he, and his mother, and his brethren, and his disciples."
—John 2:12

▶▶ Capernaum (Hebrew: Kfar Nahum) *163C3*

Open: daily 8:30–4. Admission: inexpensive

Little remains of "the town of Jesus," except for the ruins, enclosed within black basalt walls. It has been excavated by Franciscan monks for the last 100 years. According to the Matthew's Gospel (4:12–14), Jesus moved to Capernaum, from Nazareth to fulfill the words of the prophet Isaiah (9:1–2). John's Gospel (6:42) implies that Jesus was already well known in Capernaum, as were his parents (see side panel). Here, all the Gospels agree, Jesus encountered first Simon and Andrew, then James and John, all of them fishermen working on the nearby Sea of Galilee. They became his first disciples. He then began preaching "in the synagogues throughout all Galilee," as Mark's Gospel tells us, but mostly in and around Capernaum, where he performed numerous miracles.

Enlarged by refugees from Jerusalem after AD 70, the town thrived until it was devastated during the 7th-century Arab conquest. Franciscans acquired the ruins in 1894 and began a program of excavation that continued into the 1960s. Today the site is an open-air museum. On the right, inside the entrance, is an impressive frieze of carved white stone, and on the left the ruins of simple

houses► in black stone. Ahead rises the ugly modern roof of the octagonal **St. Peter's Memorial**, erected over the black-stone ruins, below ground level. The monks claim this is the **home of St. Peter►►**. All around are traces of several similar dwellings, all from about 200 BC to AD 700.

Adjacent to St. Peter's is the substantial reconstructed ruin of a fine **synagogue►►►**. It is imposing in black and white marble, with Roman-style facade, pillars, and carved capitals and lintels. The stonework depicts Jewish symbols, such as the Star of David and the seven-branched menorah (candelabrum), as well as non-Jewish images, such as a half-man, half-fish. The synagogue, dating from the 2nd century AD, is not old enough to be the one where Jesus urged his neighbors to "eat of my flesh and drink of my blood" (John 6:54), though it probably stands on the same spot. For their skepticism, Jesus said the people of Capernaum faced eternal damnation.

► Deganya "A" Kibbutz *163C2*

On the Sea of Galilee's southern shore, by the Jordan outflow, Deganya "A" (founded in 1909) is Israel's oldest kibbutz. At the gate stands a small **Syrian military tank►►**, one of a whole column that was halted by kibbutzniks armed with old rifles and Molotov cocktails during the 1948 War of Independence. Within the kibbutz but entered from the main road, the **A. D. Gordon Institute►** (*Open* Sun–Thu 9:30–4, Fri 8:30–12, Sat 9:30–12. *Admission: inexpensive*) is a museum and study center devoted to local history, archeology, and natural history.

►►► Gamla *163D3*

Open: summer, daily 8–5; winter, daily 8–4.
Closed during military exercises. Admission: moderate (ticket gives discount at Qasrin Antiquities Park)

A rough 1½-mile driveway leads to this dramatic, soaring, exposed site. Its name—meaning "the camel" in Aramaic—derives from the humped terrain. The viewing area beside the parking lot gives a stark impression of the ruined city on its barren hill. Difficult trails lead up to the ruins. Gamla was one of many Golan towns founded after the Maccabean revolt against the Seleucids (168 BC). Some 250 years later, during the First Revolt against Rome, the people of Gamla supported the rebel Zealots. As other Judaean towns were subdued or surrendered, Gamla's population of 5,000 doubled as Zealots flocked here. Some 15,000 Roman troops gathered below, but most were slaughtered in the first battle, which resulted in a surprising victory for the rebels. Three more Roman legions (60,000 men) arrived to besiege the fortress town for a month before unleashing a second attack. This time Gamla was taken. Thousands of residents and rebels were captured and killed, but 4,000 others chose suicide. Gamla was totally destroyed. To see artifacts from the site and a film about Gamla, visit the Golan Archaeological Museum in Katzrin (see page 183).

►► Ginnosar Kibbutz *163C3*

Beside the western shore of the Sea of Galilee, the kibbutz is home to the **Yigal Allon Museum of Man in the Galilee►►** (tel: 06 672 1495. *Closed* Shabbat. *Admission: moderate*) with its **2,000-year-old fishing boat►►** (see side panel). Nof Ginnosar Kibbutz Hotel, next door, has superb grounds.

BEIT GABRIEL

Almost opposite Degania, "the mother of kibbutzim," stands the attractive Beit Gabriel. On the main road beside the Sea of Galilee, this is a cultural center open to the public, with a theater, restaurant, and auditorium for concerts and a variety of other performances.

THE ANCIENT BOAT

The small fishing vessel found at Ginnosar gives a great insight into biblical passages in which the disciples are described fishing or cowering during a storm, or in which Jesus is described preaching from a boat to a crowd assembled on the shore. The boat is 20 feet long and 7.5 feet wide. It is made entirely of wood, the planks being held together by mortise-and-tenon joints. The frames were installed after the hull had been constructed, rather than the more usual practice of building the hull around the frame.

It appears that the boat was crewed by five people, using a sail and two pairs of oars.

HA'AM IM HAGOLAN
All over Israel you will see bumper stickers, posters, and even banners hanging from apartment balconies declaring, in Hebrew, Ha'Am im HaGolan (The people are with the Golan). The slogan opposes any deals with Syria that might involve giving back any part of the Golan region. Opinion polls show that only 5 percent of Israelis are willing to return Golan in its entirety, but a majority would be prepared to let Syria have some of the territory.

Basalt columns in the Hexagonal Pool at Nahal Meshushim, in the Golan Heights

►► The Golan Heights *163D3–D4*

The high, rolling Golan hills, often known as the Golan Heights, rise steeply from the Sea of Galilee (656 feet below sea level) to the Mount Avital plateau (3,949 feet above). Airy and open, these agreeable uplands have spacious, uncultivated areas of heath and grassland cut by deep plunging wadis, as well as some pretty farming districts and important historical sites. A popular outing is to the Kuneitra viewpoint, which looks deep into Syria.

From 1948 until late 1994, Syria officially maintained a state of war against Israel. Until the Six-Day War of 1967, Syrian big guns located on the Golan Heights regularly bombarded kibbutz homes in Israel. When Syria invaded Israel in 1967, it rapidly lost control of Golan. An attempt to regain it in 1973 caused Syria to lose even more ground. In 1981, Golan was formally annexed by Israel. However, Syria still vigorously lays claim to the territory, and the Golan Heights remain a bargaining chip in Israel's quest for lasting peace with its neighbor.

In 1967, the population of the region stood at 12,000 and was almost entirely Druze (there are no Muslim or Christian villages). The establishment of new kibbutzim, and the town of Katzrin, have since attracted 12,000 Jews to the Golan, which has a considerable Jewish heritage. To the surprise of many visitors, there is no tension here, and no danger—though hikers should, of course, not climb into fenced-off military enclosures and training grounds.

A shepherd works in the Golan Heights—a scene unchanged for centuries

Drive

The Golan Heights

(for map see page 163)

Israel's influence on the lower slopes, close to the Sea of Galilee and the Hula Valley, is now complete. There are well-established communities, large and small, productive farms, and tourist facilities. Higher altitudes remain relatively deserted, and the presence of army and United Nations personnel is a reminder that Syria is not far away. *Allow a full day.*

Cross the Jordan River into Golan on the unceremonious **Arik Bridge**, a simple army construction of wooden planks. Beyond the bridge, an access road on the left leads into the pleasant **Jordan River Park▶**, where you can rent a kayak, have a picnic, or visit the excavations at **Tel Bethsaida**. At a fork, turn right (marked "Bet Shean, En Gev"). At the next left, turn uphill. Reaching higher ground, pass the new settlement of Ma'ale Gamla, press on to an intersection and turn left onto the Golan's high plateau road. Soon after, an unpaved road leads to the impressive, rugged site of ancient **Gamla▶▶** (see page 171).

Just before Katzrin, and indicated simply by a sign saying "Industry," is the outstanding **Gamla Winery▶▶**. It is collectively owned by Golan's winegrowing kibbutzim and produces some of Israel's best wines, under the Gamla, Yarden, and Golan labels. Feel free to drop in for a tasting. **Qasrin Antiquities Park▶▶** (see page 183) lies in woods off the road. New **Katzrin▶▶** (see page 183), a pleasant, planned modern town, is Golan's capital, containing half the region's Jewish population. Do not miss its excellent **Golan Archaeological Museum▶▶**. The delightful **Dolls Museum▶**, opposite, uses little models to portray Jewish history.

Drive up to **Kuneitra Viewpoint▶**, at the crest of Golan, to gaze across the now abandoned village of Kuneitra, toward Damascus, 25 miles away. Israel seized Kuneitra in repelling Syria's 1973 attack, but has since given it back. The U.N. base separating the two nations can be seen in the foreground.

Turn north toward snow-streaked Mount Hermon, rising in the distance. You will skirt the lovely oak forest of the **Odem Reserve▶** and pass the **Druze villages▶** of Buk'ata, Mas'ada, and Ein Kuniya. Zigzagging across the foot of Hermon, you will reach **Nimrod's Castle▶▶** (see page 195), **Banyas▶▶** (see page 166), and **Tel Dan▶▶▶** (see page 203), enjoying extensive views over the **Hula Valley**, before leaving Golan.

Important warning

❑ If you get out of the car and walk in the Golan border areas, do not be tempted to climb over fences. And never enter an area with a blue triangle warning sign—this signifies the presence of unexploded mines. ❑

View to Mount Hermon

The kibbutz (plural, kibbutzim), surely Israel's best-known institution, is dedicated to shared effort, mutual aid, communal ownership, and the simple life. Only some 2 percent of the population live on kibbutzim, yet many top army officers, government ministers, and senior officials in all fields have been drawn from a kibbutz background.

KIBBUTZ HOTELS
Around 50 kibbutzim, most of which happen to be in resort areas, have opted to make tourism a major part of their income. Thirty of these are members of the highly professional Kibbutz Hotels Chain, which has its own Tel Aviv head office. Some, like Ramat Rachel in Jerusalem, offer top-notch accommodations not unlike other city hotels. Others are simpler guest houses in rural settings.

Above right: A typical kibbutz canteen, where kibbutz members eat all their meals together

Many young visitors first encounter Israel through working as a "kibbutz volunteer." For some this is rewarding; for others it is a shock to find that this is no easy-going vacation with time off. Kibbutz life involves hard work and few luxuries. These tightly knit communal villages are run on principles very different from those that reign beyond their metal gates and sturdy perimeter fences.

For outsiders who do not really want to roll up their sleeves and earn breakfast by the sweat of their brow, another way to glimpse kibbutz life is as a paying guest. Most of Israel's 270 kibbutzim have tourist accommodations, which vary in style, quality, and price from basic guest rooms to large, high-quality hotels.

To look at, a kibbutz is an assortment of unostentatious dwellings and public buildings. Within its grounds are footpaths rather than roads, while all around lie its fields and orchards, cowsheds, banana plantations, and orange groves. Many also have a theater, museum, and other visitor attractions, marked on tourist maps.

The kibbutznik, though partly a figure of fun for having such plain and unsophisticated ways, is almost everywhere revered as the ideal Israeli. Kibbutzniks are forthright and hardworking, the product of a pioneer movement that literally drained the swamps, watered the desert, and settled the land. Since the earliest days, kibbutzim

have played a vital security role because of their strategic locations, public shelters, and good defenses.

Origins The kibbutz movement started during the Second and Third Aliyahs (1904–1914 and 1919–1923). Thousands of socialist Russian Jews fled to Palestine under often cruel and difficult conditions—some came all the way on foot. They were ardent Zionists who believed just as passionately in the ideals of shared ownership and the virtue of labor. The egalitarian communes they created were not like anything seen before in the world. Decisions were made communally, no one possessed any private property, and children lived together separate from their parents. Though keenly aware of their Jewish identity and heritage, these early kibbutzniks were fiercely antireligious. The first kibbutz was founded at Degania in 1909 and is still going strong (see page 171).

Even today, new kibbutzim are being established. In fact, more have been established in the last 25 years than in the first 25 years of the movement. Though still based on common ownership, free education, health care, child care, laundry, and free meals in a communal dining room, they have diversified from farming into dozens of other ways of earning a living, including manufacturing and tourism. "Children's houses" were scrapped as children have been found to thrive better with their parents. A tolerant attitude to Jewish traditions has replaced strict secularism—and several observant religious kibbutzim have been set up.

The *moshav* However, communal living is not for everyone. In 1920, the first *moshav* (literally "seat," plural, *moshavim*), or cooperative village, was started. Today this is the commonest form of village or rural community in Israel. By the standards of any other country, even the *moshav* is Utopian. *Moshav* members are paid by the community for their work, and live as families on their own income. They lease, rather than own, their homes and land, and are not allowed to employ hired labor. *Moshavim* are run by elected committees, and many free services are provided for the community by its members. A *moshav* is not the same as the similarly named *moshava* (plural, *moshavot*), which is more like an ordinary noncommunal village.

BEYOND THE KIBBUTZ
The kibbutz movement has its own institutions of higher education and scientific research. It also boasts its own chamber orchestra, theater groups, highly acclaimed dance group, art galleries, and large publishing houses. This enables kibbutz members to bypass the private sector in many areas.

Farm workers on a kibbutz in the 1930s express the pioneering spirit of the original movement

BLESSINGS AND CURSES
The track that rises from the Roman spa baths to the 5th-century synagogue ruins passes the burial site of the local Arab ruler who was given Hamat Gader in 1918 by the British Mandate forces. The inscription on his tomb reads: "He who honors Hamat Gader shall be blessed in eternity. He who desecrates Hamat Gader shall be cursed in eternity."

▶▶ Hamat Gader 163C2

Open: Mon–Thu 7 AM–9:30 PM, Fri 7 AM–11:30 PM, Sat–Sun 7–6:30. Admission: expensive

According to the Byzantine empress Eudocia, these were the finest spa baths in the whole Roman world. Even the ruins are considered among the most impressive anywhere, and as there are also modern hot baths, eating places, picnic tables, and other attractions, this is a popular place for a day out. Located in the Yarmuk Valley at the meeting point of Israel, Jordan, and Syria, the area bristles with army patrols. From the main parking lot, hiking trails lead through the parklike grounds.

Steps descend to the extensive **Roman and Byzantine spa▶▶▶**, for six centuries (2nd to 8th) a grand bathing resort. Much survives of the opulent bathhouses built in black and white stone, with numerous pillars, vaults, and statues. You can walk from one pool room to the next, passing the small Lepers' Pool, the well-preserved Oval Pool, the imposing Pilaster Hall, with huge windows in the form of a triumphal arch, and others. An outdoor pool beside the bathhouses contains oily-looking water from a hot spring, veiled in sulfurous steam.

Four mineral springs and a freshwater spring emerge at Hamat Gader. A few paces from the Roman baths are the attractive **modern hot baths▶▶**, laid out as a series of open-air swimming pools, also smelling strongly of sulfur. The hottest is a constant 108°F, and bathers are officially advised that it can be dangerous to stay in for longer than 10 minutes.

Remnants of an **ancient synagogue▶** stand beside a high **observation point▶**. The abandoned mosque is recent. In front of it is a children's play area. As an added amusement, mainly for children, there is also an interesting **alligator farm▶** at Hamat Gader. A wooden walkway crosses an area of naturally warm

Roman baths, Hamat Gader

CROCODILE CREEK
"The crocodile still lingers in one corner of Palestine, at the northeast corner of the Plain of Sharon, under Carmel, in the marshes of the Wadi Zerka (Crocodile Wadi). One was brought to me measuring 11 feet 6 inches. I still possess its head and bones. This is the only spot beyond the limits of Africa where it is found."
The Natural History of Palestine, by the Rev. Canon Tristram, F.R.S., 1892

water, where dozens of alligators and crocodiles can be seen basking.

▶ Ha'on Kibbutz 163C2

(tel: 06 757 555)
Closed Shabbat. Admission: moderate
This pleasant kibbutz, noted for its flowers and palms, is set on the Sea of Galilee's southern shore. Ha'on contains a popular tourist village, restaurant, and an ostrich farm. The birds on display are also sold for their meat!

Reared for meat, feathers, and entertainment: ostriches at Ha'on Kibbutz

▶▶ Hatzor National Park (Tel Hazor) 163C4

This, the largest *tel*, or settlement mound, in Israel, consists of separate Upper and Lower sections and overlooks the southern Hula Valley. In total, 21 layers of civilization have been uncovered here and key biblical passages verified. Joshua, leading the Jews into Canaan after the years of desert wandering, set about conquering the "promised land." In the 13th century BC, having destroyed other Canaanite city-kingdoms, he took on Hatzor, the largest city in northern Canaan. Its king, Jabin, rallied other local chiefs against the Israelites. He chose the difficult Hula swamps, with which only his men were familiar, for a pitched battle. Against the odds, the Israelites won a phenomenal victory, killing Jabin and destroying Hatzor by fire. Later, the Jewish king Solomon restored the town as a fortified royal residence.

That much can be read in Joshua 11, Judges 4, and I Kings 9. Each part of the biblical accounts has been confirmed in the excavations, led by Professor Yigael Yadin between 1955 and 1959. He also uncovered Canaanite temples. Traces of structures dating back as far as 400 years prior to Joshua were found. By comparison, the constructions made by Solomon appear almost recent. Perhaps the most remarkable discovery was King Ahab's tunnel, built in the 9th century BC. It is reached by 123 spiral steps down a 125-foot deep shaft. The Bible records (II Kings 15) that in 732 BC the Assyrians completely destroyed the town. A large number of finds from the site, including beautiful carved stonework and ivory, is on display at the **Hatzor Museum** (*Closed* Shabbat. *Admission: inexpensive*) on the other side of the road beside Kibbutz Ayelet Hashahar (which has good hotel accommodations).

PRAYING FOR RAIN
If there is a drought while you are in Hatzor, go along to the Cave of Honi HaMe'agel, near Ayelet Hashahar. Named for a famous "rainmaker" of Second Temple times, the cave is still considered by the credulous as one of the most effective places to pray for a downpour.

JOSHUA'S TRIUMPH
"And Joshua at that time turned back, and took Hazor, and smote the king thereof with the sword: for Hazor beforetime was the head of all those kingdoms. And they smote all the souls that were therein with the edge of the sword, utterly destroying them: there was not any left to breathe: and he burned Hazor with fire. And all the cities of those kings, and all the kings of them, did Joshua take, and smote them with the edge of the sword, and he utterly destroyed them, as Moses the servant of the Lord commanded."
—Joshua 11:10–12

YESUD HAMA'ALA
The first attempt to tackle the problem of draining the Hula swamp was part of a venture of almost reckless idealism. It started at a *shtetl* (Jewish village) in Poland, when several young people decided to leave together for Palestine. They bought a section of the uninhabitable, uncultivated swamp and in 1883 started to build their new village here. They named it, using an evocative phrase from the Bible, *yesud hama'ala*, ("he began to go up"), describing Ezra's first steps on the road to Jerusalem at the head of the Jews returning from captivity in Babylon. Lacking in knowledge, under attack from Arabs, and brought low by the malaria that thrived in the swamps, the young pioneers might have failed if not for the intervention of Baron Rothschild: he suggested, and provided, eucalyptus trees—which can consume vast amounts of water—to plant all around the settlement.

▶▶▶ Hula Valley (Emek Hula) *163C4*

The green landscape of Hula, wide and flat under an immense sky, makes a glorious sight when viewed from the higher country at its margins. From this viewpoint, a number of small lakes can be seen, each lying beside the canalized Jordan River. The most southerly of these, Lake Hula, lies at the center of an interesting nature reserve and has an information center about the region.

The name of the valley is misleading: there is no Hula River, and neither is this a valley. In Hebrew it is more often called Emek Hula; literally, the Hula Plain. The flatland of Hula lies in a rift basin between the steep Naftali and Golan hills north of the Sea of Galilee. Several rivers and streams run into or through the valley. In the Bible it is referred to as "the waters of Merom" and, until the early 1950s, was a huge area of malarial swamp and fetid waterways. The Arabs used to say that through its reeds it was impossible for even a wild boar to make its way. Perhaps this is an exaggeration, for wild boar certainly lived here, as did water buffalo and hundreds of bird species, some rare. The reed varieties included papyrus, this being the northernmost boundary for the wild plant, from which an early form of paper was made.

The draining and cultivation of Hula began in 1883, with the setting up of Yesud HaMa'ala village (see panel and Dubrovin Farm opposite) by Jewish refugees. They drained their settlement by planting eucalyptus. In 1934, the entire Hula valley was purchased by the Jewish National Fund (J.N.F.), which, after the creation of the State of Israel, began to transform the swamps. The work, completed in 1957, involved changing and channeling the course of the Jordan River. The result was nearly 15,000 acres of new land being opened up for cultivation, as well as the eradication of malaria from the region.

But even before it was completed, the original drainage work gave cause for concern about its environmental impact. This brought about the birth of the Society for the Protection of Nature in Israel (S.P.N.I.), now a powerful national pressure group with a decisive consultation role

Hula wetland reserve

Dubrovin Farm, a fortified 19th-century pioneer settlement, preserved and restored

on all major environmental projects. The first act of the new S.P.N.I. was to set aside Lake Hula as a nature reserve. However, the diversity of the region's flora and wildlife was drastically reduced, while the populations of certain other species—rats, for example—exploded. Worse still, the drained terrain was transformed into a dry and peaty organic material, easily eroded by wind and liable to spontaneous fires in summer. The dried-out terrain began to sink at the rate of 3 inches per year, and windblown Hula peat polluted the Sea of Galilee.

In 1994, the J.N.F. rediverted the waters of the Jordan into the drained marshes, deliberately reflooding some 500 acres as part of a wildlife conservation scheme. The reflooding scheme is intended to enlarge Lake Hula, and a further 2,000 acres of land, in a 38-mile-long strip, will be returned to peat bog. There is public access to the area, and there are plans for a large new nature reserve where marsh fowl and animals will be able to breed. The existing **Lake Hula Reserve▶▶** (tel: 06 693 7069. *Open* daily 8–4. *Admission: moderate*), the country's first nature reserve, gives a good idea of how the swampland looked before 1957. There are picnic areas and an easy walking trail—partly on boards over swamp—allowing visitors to see (if they are lucky) wetland species including water buffalo, wildcats, mongoose, beaver, boar, coypu, and numerous migratory and resident bird varieties. From October through March the reserve is full of birds. The **Visitor Information Center▶** has a museum dedicated to explaining Hula's flora and fauna, and shows a short film about the region.

Dubrovin Farm▶ (tel: 06 693 7371. *Closed* Shabbat. *Admission: moderate*), just south of the reserve and originally part of the 19th-century settlement of Yesud HaMa'ala, has been reconstructed to show how a pioneers' fortified farm once looked. The buildings of the farmyard are ranged around a spacious enclosed courtyard. The family home, smithy, and gardens are the main attractions, but many visitors go simply to enjoy the Dubrovin Farmyard Restaurant, specializing in its own smoked meats and trout, where good food is served in a rough-and-ready stone out-building.

KIBBUTZ CONCERTS

In the middle of the pastoral landscape of the Hula Valley, at a plain and simple kibbutz, a week of civilized entertainment is held every summer during the Kfar Blum Chamber Music Days. The Voice of Israel radio station, the Galilee Council, and the Ministry of Education jointly sponsor an annual classical music extravaganza. Nowadays the event has widened, with typically around 25 concerts and some 50 musicians, a choir, and a program that includes baroque music on period instruments, lieder, and even jazz and chamber music. The Chamber Music Days take place usually at the end of July or beginning of August.

The fact that Israel is turning the desert green is a cliché—and one that does not bring fully to mind the many types of terrain that exist here, or the extraordinary transformation that is taking place. Even more startling than desert irrigation are the millions of acres of forest plantations and nature reserves.

WHO OWNS ISRAEL?
Some 92 percent of the land in Israel is publicly owned, to ensure that it remains a possession of the Jewish people as a whole. This has been a deliberate policy since 1901, when the Jewish National Fund (J.N.F.) began to buy land from (mostly absentee) Arab landowners. Almost all of Israel had been purchased before the setting up of the State, and almost all by voluntary contributions from Jews all over the world. The State owns 78 percent of Israel directly, while the J.N.F. owns 14 percent. The J.N.F. also administers most of the rest of the country's nonurban land.

A drive along Israel's border road with Lebanon shows the stark contrast between the wooded hills of Galilee and the infertile rocky landscape on the other side of the frontier, where goatherds lead their animals in the constant search for vegetation. At the time when Israel came into being, the two landscapes were identical.

Jewish households around the world are familiar with the "blue boxes" of the Jewish National Fund (J.N.F.), in which coins have been collected since 1901 to raise money for planting trees in Israel. During that time the J.N.F. has planted 79,000 acres of woodland—over 200 million trees. These forests, mostly of pine, are criss-crossed with public footpaths and bridle paths, often linking places of historic interest, and some provide considerable leisure opportunities. More importantly, their main purpose is to create topsoil and oxygen, to provide a habitat for threatened animals and birds, and to bring about a lasting change in the terrain.

One of the longest forest belts in the country is the 5,000-acre Bar'am, Ein Zeitim, and Biriya woodland, planted by the J.N.F. in the 1950s on treeless mountain ridges surrounding the historic Galilee town of Sefat. It has been argued that it was a mistake to use only pine, and new planting includes many other tree varieties.

Some of the ancient oak trees of Hurshat Tal National Park

The green belt created by the J.N.F. around Jerusalem on the formerly barren Judaean hills, for example, has been planted with acacia, pepper, myrtle, laurel, oak, cedar, and carob, as well as pine. Areas with any natural woodland—such as Goren Park, around Montfort Fortress—are carefully tended and being enlarged.

A popular J.N.F. scheme allows donors to pay for and plant a tree in Israel with their own hands. You can do this at the J.N.F.'s Jerusalem Planting Center, which enables visitors to make a personal contribution to the capital's green belt or to other new forests around the country.

National parks Israel's forests are intended to change the land, the national parks to conserve it. There are 40 national parks in total, scattered across the country from Galilee to Negev and from the Mediterranean shore to the stony banks of the Dead Sea. Some peaks contain beautiful woodlands, but others are stark desert and wilderness. The National Parks Authority mainly cares for areas of great historical interest—major archeological sites, for example. Part of the authority's job is to open up such places to the public while protecting them from the damage that millions of visitors each year might cause.

Most national parks are relatively small, such as the ancient ruins of Bar'am, Nimrod Castle, Kursi, and Tel Hatzor, while others cover larger areas, such as Carmel Park near Haifa, Hurshat Tal, and Masada. Other properties could hardly be called parks at all—for example, the Jerusalem city walls.

Nature reserves The 160 nature reserves in Israel are something different again. Totaling about a million acres, they concentrate on protecting the country's astonishing diversity of flora, fauna, and landscape. This adds up to over 3,000 species of plants (150 exclusive to Israel), 430 kinds of birds, 70 mammals, and as many as 80 types of reptiles. Terrain varies, from lush river valleys and springs like Tel Dan, to the dry, leafless desert of Timna Park.

Access to forests is free at all times, but national parks and nature reserves are supervised and charge entry fees. The reserves are open every day of the year, except Yom Kippur. The parks are well-marked, and equipped with restaurants and picnic areas.

Carmel Park protects sacred sites and a lovely Mediterranean landscape

FOR MORE INFORMATION
If you want to plant a tree while in Israel call the Jewish National Fund (Keren Kayemet l'Israel) toll-free on: 117 022 3484. The head office of the National Parks Authority is in Tel Aviv on 03 576 6888. The Nature Reserves Authority is in Jerusalem on 02 536 271.

White oryx in the Negev desert

The hilltop town of Jish, in the 1st century an important Jewish stronghold, is now a Christian Arab community

►► Hurshat Tal National Park *163C5*

(tel: 06 694 0400)
Open: Sat–Thu 8–5, Fri 8–4. Admission: inexpensive
Located between Tel Dan and the Hula Valley, this pleasant woodland area, whose name means "Forest of Dew," is watered by the Dan River. Scores of mighty, ancient oaks grow here. Legend has it that 10 of Muhammad's messengers paused here for the night and, finding nowhere to tether their horses, stuck stakes into the ground. In the morning they awoke to find their stakes had sprouted into these fine trees. An artificial swimming lake, restaurant, and picnic site, as well as a nearby riverside campground, make this a popular spot. Adjacent Kibbutz Hagoshrim, part of the Kibbutz Hotels Chain, has attractive grounds and offers high-quality accommodations.

► Jish (Hebrew: Gush Halav) *162B4*

This hillside village of Christian Arabs was an important town during the Second Temple and Talmudic periods, associated with the learned Jewish community based around Meron (see page 185). It was also renowned for its olive oil. During the First Revolt against Rome (AD 68), it was a rebel stronghold. Revolt commander Yohanan came from here. The tombs of 1st-century sages Shemai'a and Avtalion lie in a domed building by the road below the village. Remnants of small 3rd- and 4th-century synagogues were found a mile east of the village, and also at the neighboring *moshav* (cooperative village) of Sifsufa.

► Kfar Kana *162B2*

St. John's Gospel names the (now Arab) village of Cana, near Nazareth, as the place of Jesus' first miracle: turning water into wine at a wedding feast. The Franciscans claim that their church, built in 1881, stands on the ruins of the house where the miracle occurred. It does stand on the remains of a 6th-century church or synagogue with a 3rd-century mosaic floor beneath it (an Aramaic inscription honoring the craftsmen who made the mosaic). Other Catholic and Orthodox churches in Kana also claim to be built on sacred sites.

THE MIRACLE AT CANA
"When the ruler of the feast had tasted the water that was made wine, and knew not whence it was (but the servants which drew the water knew), the governor of the feast called the bridegroom, and saith unto him, Every man at the beginning doth set forth good wine, and when men have well drunk, then that which is worse. But thou hast kept the good wine until now."
—John 2:9–10

Daniel in the Lions' Den: Byzantine frieze in the Golan Archaeological Museum

VOLCANIC GOLAN
The Golan summit was volcanic until the Upper Pleistocene period (40,000 years ago), and the terrain is rich in signs of volcanic activity. Massive basalt boulders, areas of lava flow, deep craters, and remnants of volcanic cones characterize the Heights. The Golan's largest extinct volcano is Mount Avital, near Kuneitra. Its crater is now cultivated.

►► Katzrin (Qazrin) *163C4*

This attractive, well-laid-out town, built in 1967, is now the capital of the Golan region. Its population of 6,000 accounts for half the Jews in the Golan. The name derives from the Hebrew version of *castrum*, the Latin word for a military camp, and the town makes a good base for exploring local antiquities. The **Golan Archaeological Museum►►** (*Open daily. Admission: inexpensive*) has extensive displays of relics from all over the region, especially coins, domestic implements, and stonework. There are many relief carvings of menorahs (ritual candelabrum) dating from Temple times and from the Roman and Byzantine periods. It is well worth seeing the museum's short film about the Roman conquest of Golan's former capital, Gamla. Almost opposite is the **Dolls Museum►** (*Open daily. Admission: moderate*) which tells Jewish history through a succession of charming tableaux made of little models.

Just outside the town on the southeastern side, a sign saying "Industry" indicates the way to the **Golan Winery►►** (tel: 06 696 2001. *Closed* Shabbat. *Admission with tasting: moderate*), a leading name in Israel's quality wines. It is open for tastings, but it is wise to phone ahead to check. Nearby are the remains of the 4th-century **Ancient Synagogue►** in the **Qasrin Antiquities Park►►** (tel: 06 696 2412. *Closed* Shabbat. *Admission: moderate*), an open-air museum. There are reconstructions giving an impression of life in Talmudic times alongside the archeological site of the original town of Katzrin.

Talmudic obelisks in Qasrin Antiquities Park

► Kiryat Shmona *163C5*

The name, which means "eight men and women", commemorates Joseph Trumpledor and his seven comrades-in-arms who died defending the nearby Tel Hai settlement in March 1920. Arab attacks on Tel Hai were launched from the village of Halsa. After the defeat of the Arabs, Halsa was transformed into this (rather unappealing) development town. Today it is largely populated by new immigrants.

HONORING RASHBI
Thousands of Orthodox Jewish pilgrims make their way to Meron every year for the joyful early-summer Hilula Rashbi procession. It's held on the eve of Lag b'Omer (the 26th day after Passover). The pilgrims carry Torah scrolls from Sefat to Meron. On arrival, two bonfires, and countless candles, are lit at Rashbi's tomb. Riotous music and dancing and noisy picnics take place through the night. The following morning, three-year-old boys—who, until then, have been allowed to let their hair grow long—receive their first haircut.

MEGIDDO AT THE END OF DAYS
"And he gathered them all together into a place called in the Hebrew tongue Armageddon. And the seventh angel poured out his vial into the air; and there came a great voice out of the temple of heaven, from the throne, saying, It is done. And there were voices, and thunders, and lightnings; and there was a great earthquake, such as was not since men were upon the earth, so mighty an earthquake, and so great. And the great city was divided into three parts."
—Revelation 16:16–19

▶ Korazim *163C3*

Open: Sun–Thu 8–5, Fri 8–4. Admission: inexpensive
Built of dark basalt and now all in ruins, Korazim is located 2½ miles from the Sea of Galilee's northern shore. According to Matthew's Gospel (11:21), this was one of the thriving Galilee towns that Jesus reproached because its citizens refused to repent after he had performed "mighty works" there. The farming town continued to prosper for four centuries more, being much praised for its wheat. Its fine **synagogue▶▶** was constructed in the 2nd century, and substantial remains can still be seen of the walls and floor and of the pillars that divided the building into three aisles. Remnants of **houses▶▶** (some partly restored) and an **oil press** also survive. East of the site, **dolmens** confirm that the area was inhabited in prehistoric times. Abandoned in the 5th century, Korazim was revived as a Jewish village in the 16th century. Just west is the popular riding center and "Guest Farm" tourist complex of **Vered Hagalil▶**.

▶▶ Megiddo National Park *162A1*

(tel: 06 652 2167)
Open: summer, daily 8–5; winter, daily 8–4.
Admission: expensive
The fortified hill of Megiddo is a remarkable tel (settlement mound) where 20 layers of civilization have been uncovered since excavations began in 1903. The museum has an interesting scale model of ancient Megiddo.

The English corruption of Har Megiddo, or Megiddo Hill, is Armageddon. Here, according to the New Testament (Revelation 16), God will gather everyone together at the end of days and pour out his wrath in earthquakes, storms, and a hail of stones. The hill, long considered worth fighting for, controlled a narrow pass on the ancient route between Egypt and Assyria. Of vital military and trading importance, this highway became the Romans' Via Maris. The French (in 1799) and the British (in 1917) both defeated Turkish forces at Megiddo. One of the titles granted to Commander-in-Chief Allenby was Lord Allenby of Megiddo. In 1948, Jews defeated Arab forces here.

About 4000 BC, Canaanites took over the neolithic settlement here and remained for some 2,000 years. A **Canaanite temple▶▶** and **fortifications▶▶** survive. In 1479 BC, Pharaoh Thutmose III attacked the city. Hieroglyphs describing the battle, carved on the walls of his temple in Upper Egypt, are the first historical reference to Megiddo. When Megiddo was conquered by the Israelites under Joshua in the 13th century BC, the name of the town first enters the Bible. Philistines subsequently held the city for 100 years, but it was retaken by King David in 1000 BC. Solomon enlarged the city, and many vestiges remain from that period. After a 9th-century BC Egyptian attack, it was rebuilt by King Ahab, who added an impressive **underground shaft and water tunnel▶▶** 118 feet deep and 213 feet long. On the site of Solomon's Palace he built **chariot stables▶▶** for 450 horses, chariots, and riders. In front is a large circular **grain silo▶** built in the 8th century BC. Conquered by Assyrians in 733 BC, the site frequently changed hands and was abandoned from 538 BC. A Roman camp was later set up on the adjacent site, which became the Arab village of Lejun (from "Legion") and is now the Kibbutz Megiddo.

SACRED NUMEROLOGY
Kabbala is an esoteric Jewish form of mysticism whose aim is reunification with God, achieved by following specific paths to wisdom. One of its mystical practices involves using assigned numerical values of the Hebrew alphabet to discover hidden meanings within the verses of the Torah (e.g. alef = 1, bet = 2, and so on). For centuries, the study of Kabbala was limited to devout married men over the age of 40, to discourage dabblers and self-seeking enthusiasts. A prime kabbalistic work, the *Zohar*, is often attributed to Rashbi, especially by devout Hasidim and Sephardim. But many scholars believe the book was in fact written by several people, probably in medieval Spain, and based on earlier works stemming from Sefat and Meron.

Remains of Roman houses, Korazim

▶ Meron *162B4*

In Second Temple and Talmudic times, Meron became a great center of Jewish learning, as well as a focal point for rebellion against Roman rule. In 1949, a new Meron, an Orthodox religious settlement, was founded in the same place. Several 1st- and 2nd-century tombs survive, including the domed mausoleums, set within a walled enclosure, of the renowned **Rabbi Shimon bar Yochai▶▶▶** (also known by his acronym as Rashbi) and his son, Eleazer. Rashbi is claimed by the Orthodox to be the author of the *Zohar* (one of the principal books of the mystical kabbala). Some scholars assert that Rashbi was not the author of this work although Meron and Sefat can still be considered the birthplace of Jewish mysticism (see side panel). North of the tomb stands the magnificent rock-carved facade of a 2nd-century **synagogue▶**. Little else remains of the building. Several other revered rabbis are reputedly buried in rock-cut tombs here, including the great 1st-century sage **Hillel▶**, his less liberal rival **Shammai**, and the 2nd-century **Rabbi Yohanan** "the shoemaker."

ARMAGEDDON VILLAGE
The settlement of Mishmar HaEmek (literally Guard of the Plain) stands next to Megiddo, or Armageddon. Founded in 1927, it was the first modern community to be established in the Valley of Jezreel. The scene of much prolonged fighting, especially during the 1948 war, it is better known today for its striking Holocaust memorial.

THE GOOD FENCE
Close to Metulla is the only place where civilians (with correct documents) can cross the border between Israel and Lebanon. There are broad views over the Lebanese hills from here. Most of the permitted border traffic consists of Lebanese workers employed in Israel. The name "Good Fence" comes from the Israeli medical post here, which Lebanese citizens can attend free of charge.

A WRONGED WOMAN?
The word "magdalen" has come to mean a reformed prostitute, or a home for such women, through its association with Mary Magdalene. Yet the Scriptures give no reason to suspect Mary Magdalene of being a prostitute. It used to be thought that the"woman which was a sinner" (Luke 7:37), who anointed Jesus' feet and wiped them with her hair, could be identified with Mary Magdalene, but the text does not suggest this and modern scholars reject the idea. Later, Jesus encounters "Mary called Magdalene, out of whom went seven devils," as if for the first time. The name Mary Magdalene means simply "Mary, woman of Magdala."

Spring comes to Mount Hermon: the view from Metulla

▶ Metulla *163C5*

Enclosed on three sides by the northern border with Lebanon (you can see Arab laborers working the fields across the frontier), this small agricultural town has a cool, tranquil hill setting overlooked by the snowy crest of Mount Hermon. Metulla was settled a century ago on land purchased by Baron Rothschild. Since 1976, it has been best known as the HaGader HaTova (the Good Fence), an opening in the border between Israel and Lebanon through which Lebanese people pass freely to obtain medical supplies or even to work in Israel. The town's main avenue, **Settlers Street▶**, gives visitors a chance to glimpse those early days with its Farmer's House Museum and a few surviving older buildings. The town's Canada Center is a modern leisure complex with high-quality sports facilities, indoor and outdoor pools, squash, tennis, and basketball courts, a complete soccer field, and the largest ice-skating rink in Israel. Between the town and the frontier lies the **Nahal Iyon Nature Reserve** (see page 191).

▶ Migdal *163C3*

On a hillside beside the Sea of Galilee and within an hour's walk of Jesus' home at Capernaum lie the ruins of ancient Migdal (the name means "a Tower"). This was the supposed birthplace of Mary Magdalene, the woman from whom Jesus drove out "seven devils" and who became one of his most ardent followers. Migdal was a thriving small town until about the 2nd century. Remnants of paved streets, a villa, a pool, and a synagogue have been uncovered. Above the old village rises the new, which has plenty of guest accommodations.

▶▶ Montfort Castle *162A4*

This majestic ruined Crusader fortress, soaring on a high crest enclosed by an immense natural forest, is best seen from **Mitzpe Monfort▶▶▶** (*mitzpe* means viewpoint) in **Goren Park▶**. The park, located 9 miles inland from Nahariya, is a natural forest of oak, carob, almond, arbutus, and the purple-flowered Judas tree. To reach the castle, you must follow a series of steep narrow paths for about half an hour, first down to the attractive **Kviv stream▶**, then up again to the fortress. It can also be approached on a longer walk, equally steep, from the village of Hila.

Built in the 12th century by French Crusaders, Montfort Castle (*free access*) is the largest ruin in western Galilee. Reconstruction is under way, consisting of the repair of the remnants of inner and outer ramparts, great blocks of fallen stone, roofless sections of sturdy walls, and broken Gothic arches. These vestiges are all that survive of a once huge fortress. Its lofty position provides a stirring view over rolling woodland. Shortly after completion, Montfort (which means "Strong Mountain" in medieval French) was destroyed by Salah ed-Din in 1187. The shell was then sold in 1220 to the Knights of the Teutonic Order, who rebuilt part of the fortress and renamed it Starkenburg (Strong Castle). They occupied it until 1271, when they were expelled by Baibars, the Mameluke sultan. He allowed them to take their archives and treasury, and the castle has remained abandoned ever since.

►► Mount of Beatitudes 163C3

This lovely grass-covered hillside, rising behind the sites of Tabgha and Capernaum, has long been considered the place where Jesus delivered the Sermon on the Mount. The view from the top of the slope, taking in the calm blue expanse of the Sea of Galilee with blue-tinted hills behind, is serene and inspiring.

Did Jesus really preach his sermon here? The weight of tradition points to this as the likely hill. The church at the summit is modern; previously the event was commemorated by a church nearer to Tabgha. The official Catholic view is that the hill, and the church, should be understood only as commemorating the sermon, not marking the site. But for millions of pilgrims, this is the very hill where Jesus inspired the multitudes with his message of purity of spirit, humility, and peace.

The Sermon on the Mount, fully recorded in Matthew's Gospel (chapters 5–7), marks the start of Christianity's departure from Judaism. The nine Beatitudes are Christ's assertion that nine categories of people are blessed and will receive a heavenly reward. He named in turn the poor in spirit, the meek, mourners, those who hunger for righteousness, the merciful, the pure in heart, peacemakers, those persecuted for righteousness' sake, and those persecuted for Jesus's sake.

The remainder of the sermon praises those who lead a simple, virtuous life according to Jewish law. Much of the sermon restates ancient commandments, although he also departs from them by, for example, prohibiting divorce, redefining adultery to include looking lustfully, and warning of hellfire for calling one's brother "Traitor." He adds to the original "Love thy neighbor" the far more difficult precept "Love your enemies." The sermon ends with a Jewish text that sums up his message: "Be ye therefore perfect, even as your Father in heaven is perfect."

Luke's Gospel (chapter 6) briefly describes what is probably the same sermon, but says that it was delivered at the foot of the hill, "in the plain," after Jesus had spent all night on the mountain in prayer, and chosen and named 12 of his followers as Apostles. He then descended the hill with the Apostles to preach to the multitude. Jesus "looked up" to address the crowd, so

HOW TO FEEL TOWARD YOUR ENEMIES

"It has been said that thou shalt love thy neighbor and hate thine enemy" (Matthew 5:43). These words of Jesus during the Sermon on the Mount have caused controversy, since it was *not* part of Jewish Law that people should "hate" their enemies. Leviticus 19:17–18 states: "Thou shalt love thy neighbor as thyself." It also states that it is all right to "rebuke thy neighbor" (though not in public) but "not to take vengeance nor bear any grudge"; and "Thou shalt not hate thine brother in thy heart." Some of the earliest Bible passages urge humanity and restraint with respect to enemies: "If thou meet thine enemy's ox or his ass going astray, thou shalt bring it back to him again" (Exodus 23:4).

they stood on the higher ground, and urged them to "love your enemies and do good to them which hate you; unto him that smiteth thee on the cheek offer also the other."

The **Church of the Beatitudes▶▶▶** (*Open* daily 8–12, 2:30–5) on the hilltop, an octagonal arcaded structure under a dome, belongs to Italian Franciscans. It is one of the most attractive works of Antonio Barluzzi, architect of some of the finest 20th-century Galilean churches and basilicas. Built in 1937 (the date in the church floor being given as Year 15 of the Italian People—in other words the Fascist regime), it elegantly contrasts white and dark stone and stands among palm trees in delightful gardens. Each of eight sides of the church is dedicated to one of the first eight Beatitudes, written in Latin inside the church. The ninth Beatitude (blessing those who suffer persecution for the sake of Jesus) is symbolized by the dome itself, reaching to heaven. Around the altar of the church are representations of the seven virtues (Justice, Charity, Prudence, Faith, Fortitude, Hope, and Temperance).

Close by is the Franciscans' **Mount of Beatitudes Hospice▶**. Glorious views can be had by walking down the slope from the summit of the mount to Tabgha. The walk takes a more circuitous 2½ miles route by road.

THE SERMON ON THE MOUNT

"And seeing the multitude, he went up into a mountain. And when he was set, his disciples came unto him, and he opened his mouth and taught them."
—Matthew 5:1–2

Church of the Beatitudes, atop the mount where Christ laid down some of the basic tenets of Christianity

Mount Tabor's Basilica of the Transfiguration

▶ Mount Hermon (Har Hermon) 163D5

The snow-covered peak of Israel's highest mountain (9,072 feet) is visible over much of Golan and northeastern Galilee. The mount makes a startling and dramatic contrast to the Mediterranean sunshine, landscape, and vegetation below. Only a small slice of the Hermon massif belongs to Israel, the rest forming the barrier between Lebanon and Syria. From its snow and springs originates much of Israel's water supply. **Neve Ativ▶** (or the Mount Hermon Ski Center) is a small winter sports resort high on its slopes. It has a ski lift from 5,412 feet to 6,560 feet, equipment rentals, good accommodations, and reliable snow from December through April. The runs range in difficulty, the longest run being 1½ miles.

▶▶ Mount Meron Nature Reserve 162B3

Occupying a high ridge at the heart of Upper Galilee, the wooded Meron heights can be reached on steep but fairly easy footpaths from near the Druze village of Hurfeish (on the western side) or from Meron (on the eastern flank). The paths climb through attractive but thorny Mediterranean scrub and low woodland, where you may see several of the curious *katalav* trees, with their smooth bark resembling polished copper. At the rocky wooded summit (3,962 feet), you will find a radar base, a tiny stone pool enclosed by a stone terrace (actually a 2,000-year-old winepress), and immense vistas to the north, with Sefat visible to the east.

THE TRANSFIGURATION
"And after six days Jesus taketh Peter, James, and John his brother, and bringeth them up into an high mountain apart, and was transfigured before them: and his face did shine as the sun, and his raiment was white as the light. And behold, there appeared unto them Moses and Elias talking with him. Then answered Peter, and said unto Jesus, Lord, it is good for us to be here: if thou wilt, let us make here three tabernacles."
— Matthew 17:1–4

▶▶ Mount Tabor (Har Tavor) 162B2

This striking fortified plateau, rising from the Jezreel Plain, is taken to be "the high mountain apart" on which Jesus was "transfigured" in the eyes of Peter, James, and John. According to the Gospels, "His face did shine as the sun, and his raiment was white as the light. And behold, there appeared unto them Moses and Elias talking with him. From a cloud came a voice, saying 'This is my beloved son, in whom I am well pleased' " (Matthew 17: 1–5; Mark 9:2–7; Luke 9:28–35). These were almost the same words that a voice from heaven had uttered when Jesus was baptized in the Jordan (Mark 1:11).

Over the centuries, several churches were erected on or near the site of the apparition, especially during the Crusader period, and their ruins now adorn the mountainside. The slopes are covered with vegetation, notably Tabor oak. A twisting road winds up to the top of the hill. At the summit stands the Franciscans' handsome **Basilica of the Transfiguration▶▶** (*Open* Sun–Fri 8–12, 2–5; *closed* during services), with its two sturdy square towers, built by Barluzzi in 1921 and incorporating the remains of 6th- and 12th-century churches. The basilica encloses three grottoes, or chapels, recalling the three tabernacles that Peter suggested should be put here for Jesus, Moses, and Elijah (Elias). The Grotto of Christ contains a mosaic pavement dating from before the year 422 (after which date it was forbidden to put the shape of the cross in any position where it could be walked upon). In the upper part of the church, a fine mosaic depicts the Transfiguration. Close by stands the Greek Orthodox **Church of Elias▶**, built in 1911 on the ruins of a Crusader church. A **Canaanite shrine▶** also stands on the summit.

During the period of the Israelite conquest of Canaan, the judge and prophetess Deborah (12th century BC) gathered 10,000 men here. She led them in a victorious attack on the men and chariots of Sisera, one of the generals of Canaanite king Jabin of Hatzor (Judges 4).

▶ Nahal Iyon Nature Reserve *163C5*

Located 1.2 miles from the small northern border town of Metulla (see page 186), the reserve lies in the Iyon Valley beside the Lebanese frontier. It offers pleasing tree-shaded water pools and seasonal waterfalls. The **Tanur Waterfall▶** can be found half a mile from the town. It is dry in summer, gushing in winter, and its name, meaning "oven," is based on its shape and the impression of smoke given by the fall's billowing misty haze.

NEBI SABALAN

From the village of Hurfeish the path up Mount Meron first skirts Mount Larom. At the top stands Nebi Sabalan, a large structure enclosing a small cave, together with a pilgrims' inn. Sacred to the Druze, this became a holy site in 1948. The Druze claim that their prophet, Sabalan, lived as a hermit in the cave, studying and composing religious texts. One day, Muslims discovered him and dispatched a force to kill him. When they tried to climb Larom from the Kziv stream at its foot, Sabalan prayed for divine assistance. It came in the form of a dam that blocked the stream and caused the area to be temporarily flooded—just long enough to drown his pursuers. When the water subsided, he moved on to Mount Lebanon, where his tomb can be seen today. Every year on September 10, the Druze make a pilgrimage to Nebi Sabalan, where there are lodgings and provisions for slaughter and sacrifice. Non-Druze are not welcome.

Galilee from Mount Tabor

THE CHILDHOOD HOME OF JESUS

The evangelists do not agree as to where Mary and Joseph lived before the birth of Jesus. Luke says that Nazareth was where the angel Gabriel appeared to Mary, and that she and Joseph set out from Nazareth to register in Bethlehem for the census. They also returned "to their own city Nazareth" after presenting Jesus in the Temple. Matthew, on the other hand, implies that Jesus' birthplace in Bethlehem was not a temporary dwelling but the family home of Joseph (a native Judaean) and Mary (by tradition the daughter of a Temple priest, and so living in or near Jerusalem). In his account they fled from Bethlehem to Egypt, then, fearing to return to Judaea, they went to dwell in Gallilee, eventually settling in Nazareth. Mark only states that Jesus, having reached manhood, "came from Nazareth of Gallilee and was baptized of John in the Jordan." John simply has Nathaniel, a Gallilean, astonished to be told that the man the prophets wrote about came from Nazareth.

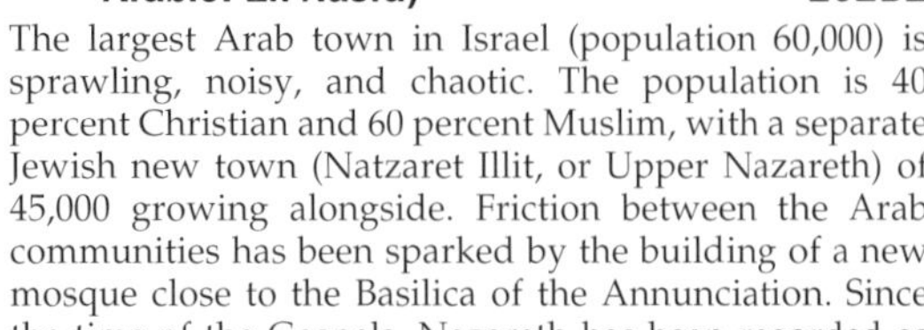

►► Nazareth (Hebrew: Natzerat; Arabic: En-Nasra) *162B2*

The largest Arab town in Israel (population 60,000) is sprawling, noisy, and chaotic. The population is 40 percent Christian and 60 percent Muslim, with a separate Jewish new town (Natzaret Illit, or Upper Nazareth) of 45,000 growing alongside. Friction between the Arab communities has been sparked by the building of a new mosque close to the Basilica of the Annunciation. Since the time of the Gospels, Nazareth has been regarded as the childhood home of Jesus. The town bristles with

churches: but the seeming lack of spirituality, or sense of authenticity, sometimes disappoints Christian pilgrims.

Nazareth gets no mention in Josephus' comprehensive list of towns and villages of the Galilee. Archeological evidence finds scant trace of habitation at the time he refers to, although there are vestiges of older structures on the site dating from 2000 BC. From the 3rd century AD there was a Christian settlement here, destroyed by Persians in the 7th century. It was revived in 1099 by the French Crusader Tancred, then seized by Mamelukes in 1263. All Christians were banished until 1620. Nazareth once again became popular as a center for Christian worship in the 19th century, when it became a focal point for Christian Arabs.

All the Gospels agree in suggesting that Jesus spent most of his childhood in Nazareth, though how many years is unclear. There is disagreement as to whether Joseph and Mary lived there before the birth of Jesus. According to Luke (1:26), they did: he asserts that it was here that the Archangel Gabriel spoke to Mary, telling her that she was to give birth to a son who "shall reign over the house of Jacob forever, and of his kingdom there shall be no end." Matthew (1:18–21) relates that Joseph, learning Mary was pregnant, planned to divorce her but was dissuaded by an angel in a dream.

Early Christians worshipped at this place, which was known later, as the Grotto of the Annunciation. The first of Nazareth's churches was built there, in a style that resembles a synagogue. With the growth of devotion to Mary, and to the image of Jesus as an infant, even greater importance became attached to the grotto where Gabriel addressed Mary.

Three more churches, erected in the 5th, the 12th, and the 18th centuries, were built at the grotto long before today's **Basilica of the Annunciation▶▶▶** (*Open* Mon–Sat 8:30–11:45, 2–5, Sun for services only) was constructed between 1955 and 1969. The main entrance is in Casa Nova Street, the heart of the older part of town. This pleasing modern edifice, by the Italian architect Giovanni Muzio, is built of pale stone, arranged in bands of lighter and darker shade, under a dark conical dome surrounded by delicate white stonework. Some of the walls stand on top of the ruined 12th-century Crusader walls, and the Crusader's triple apse at the east end has been brought into the new building. Thus it ingeniously combines the past—represented by the lower levels and the grotto itself—with the present, the two being linked by stairs at the west end. A large opening in the floor beneath the dome gives a view down through the centuries to the grotto and the relics of earlier churches. The upper church is decorated with images of the Madonna and Child from around the world.

Other churches (*Open* daily) lie nearby, reached via teeming narrow streets and an open-air market. **St. Joseph's▶** (1914), in Casa Nova Street, stands above a grotto known since the 17th century as Joseph's Workshop. **Synagogue Church▶**, stands on traces of a 6th-century synagogue that, despite the date, Greek Catholics claim was the one Jesus attended. **Mensa Christi Church** (1918), west of the Synagogue Church, contains a slab of rock that Franciscans claim was the table at which the risen Christ ate with his disciples. A mile out of town, on the Tiberias road, **Mary's Well▶** or the Fountain of Mary has four waterspouts set in a modern circular stone surround. This is another place where some claim that Gabriel appeared to Mary. Many believe the waters to have miraculous healing powers. This new Mary's Well replaces the older one in the crypt of beautiful **St. Gabriel's Church▶** nearby.

TOURING NAZARETH
The town is hot and crowded, built up a steep hill, bus services are not geared to tourist sights, and the maze of streets is short of signs. If you are not prepaired to deal with these challenges join an organized tour. Hotels and tourist offices all over Galilee can provide details of these.

Greek Orthodox rites at St. Gabriel's Church

Left: Basilica of the Annunciation

Drive

The Northern Road

(for map see pages 162A4–163C5)

The northern road takes a quiet, peaceful course along a crest of forested hills. There are good views into Lebanon, with its relatively barren terrain, and across the Galilee, where a hundred years of tree-planting have sharply altered the scenery. Along the way the drive passes a string of old pioneer kibbutzim and appealing, small-scale relics of history, ancient and modern. *Allow a full day.*

Start at the high chalk cliffs of **Rosh HaNikra▶▶** (see page 160). On the cliff top is the scruffy frontier post with Lebanon, but there are also magnificent views down to the coast. At the foot, reached by cable car, spectacular white caves lie half submerged in the sea. The winding road descends through natural and planted woodland toward **Kibbutz Hanita▶** (founded in 1938), with its small antiquities museum. Among the trees nearby is **Hanita Tower and Stockade▶**, a well-preserved example of the simple wooden watchtowers used by early settlers. The border road continues east beside the frontier. For greater interest take the parallel route through the attractive maple and terebinth woods around **Eilon▶** and **Goren Park▶▶**, south of which rises the Crusader fortress, **Montfort Castle▶▶** (see page 186).

Back on the border, **Netua▶** and **Biranit▶▶** give great views into Lebanon. Cross the high **Har Adir** plateau, descending to the superb ancient synagogue at **Bar'am▶▶** (see page 167). After **Avivim**, where 11 children were killed in a P.L.O. attack on the school bus in 1970, the **Dishon Gorge▶** on the right has a drivable trail at the bottom. Suddenly, ahead you will see a broad view of the Naftali hills, reaching to the Hula Valley. The fence of **Mishgav Am Kibbutz** forms the national boundary. In 1980, five P.L.O. men captured the nursery and ended up shooting a 2-year-old and its teacher in front of the other children.

A landscape under transformation: forests have been planted on the once-barren Lebanese frontier

Continue to **Metulla▶** (see page 186) via the **Good Fence▶▶** border crossing, so named because of the free medical clinic run here for Lebanese citizens.

▶ Nimrod's Castle National Park *163D5*

Open: Sun–Thu 8–5, Fri morning. Admission: moderate

The massive, ruined hillside fortress 2 miles east of Banyas was named after Nimrod, the "mighty hunter" (Genesis 10:8–9). It dates largely from the 13th century. Originally built by Crusaders in 1129, it was immediately seized by Syrian Arabs. Held again by Crusaders from 1140 to 1164, it was taken and enlarged by Ayyub sultans in 1220, by Mamelukes in 1260, and later abandoned.

▶ Peki'in *162B4*

Now mainly Druze, this village claims an impressive Jewish history. The revered 2nd-century Rabbi Shimon bar Yochai (see page 185) lived in a cave here with his son for 13 years, hiding from the Romans. A possible candidate above the village has been marked **Rashbi Cave▶**. Walk down past the ornate village fountain and balconied houses to the attractive **Old Synagogue▶▶**, on its original 2nd-century foundations. It has a simple interior, a floor of huge stone blocks, and fine stonecarving. Other sights in Peki'in include the olive presses, flour mill, and Jewish cemetery. Two snack bars face each other on the main Haifa road. Both make excellent pitas and local dishes.

▶▶ Rosh Pina *163C3*

Its name means "Cornerstone," and this village on Mount Canaan was the first Zionist settlement in Galilee. Head up the steep main street to **Rosh Pina HaAtika (Old Rosh Pina)▶▶▶**. Here the road surface has been stripped off to reveal handsome cobbles (hard to walk on), while to either side restored pioneer houses of pale stone survive from the original hilltop settlement site of 1882. The community today has an arty feel, and some of the old buildings are appealing restaurants. Nearby **Kibbutz Kfar Hanassi** makes high-quality herbal remedies from its own gardens (tel: 06 691 4833). Roadside viewpoints on the way to Sefat include **Mitzpe HaYamim▶**, where both the Sea of Galilee and (hazily) the Mediterranean can be seen.

ECHOES OF THE PAST

When the Israelites conquered Canaan in 1300 BC, the area that would become Galilee was shared between the tribes of Asher and Naftali. The Menasseh tribe had the Golan. The tribe of Dan was given the foot of Mount Hermon. Many of today's place names recall this remote past. The Naftali hills overlook the Hula Plain. Ancient Dan lies half a mile away from the Dan of today. Sefat stands atop Mount Canaan.

Nimrod's Castle, named after the mighty hunter of the Bible

BELOW THE RED LINE
The banks of the Sea of Galilee lie 695 feet below true sea level. From north to south, the lake measures 13 miles, and its width reaches a maximum of 8 miles. The total area is 65 square miles. On average it is 160 feet deep. The lake is Israel's principal reservoir, and the National Water Carrier pipeline pumps water directly from the shore near Capernaum to smaller reservoirs across the country. The "red line" is a theoretical water level below which the lake's surface should not drop—but it has done so frequently in recent years. In the early and mid-1990s, the level has often been about a foot below the red line, causing anxiety about the quality of the water and the effect on its fish.

▶▶▶ Sea of Galilee (Hebrew: Yam Kinneret) *163C2-C3*

Not really a sea, of course, the exquisitely beautiful and tranquil body of water that Israelis call Lake Kinneret astonishes the eye, lying blue under a pearly sky, enclosed by hills that also seem blue-tinted. The name Kinneret comes from *ginnar*, meaning a harp, because of its shape. Certainly its size and shape are ideal. Wherever you stand, whether on a distant viewpoint or on the very shore, the countryside can be seen rising steeply on the other side. All along, the gently lapping waters disappear enticingly around folds in the landscape.

This is, of course, no ordinary lake. It exists as much in faith and legend as in reality, and holds a central place in the hearts of millions of people around the world. This, more than anywhere else, is the land of Jesus. He lived on the lake shores, his disciples were its fishermen, and many of his miraculous works were performed around its banks. If the Gospel account is not a metaphor, he even walked on its waters. What is more, the Jordan River, of hymns and prayers and Gospel songs, that richly symbolic frontier of the biblical Promised Land, flows in one end and out of the other.

Not surprisingly, many visitors find here not only water and sunshine, but also the very spirit of Jesus and echoes of his ministry. However, beware. Many pilgrim sites, even those hallowed by centuries, rest on scant historical evidence. Theologians have decreed that this does not matter, that one should regard the sites as commemorative. But for anyone with simpler, Sunday School notions of "The Holy Land," a few places associated with Jesus could prove quite surprising, and even disappointing. Although many New Testament stories were never intended to be taken literally anyway, shrines, exquisite churches, or opulent basilicas mark every spot.

Yet Israel is not a storybook: it is a real country, inhabited by Jews for whom the greatest miracle is their return to this land after their 1,800-year exile. For them, the most wonderful thing of all about the Sea of Galilee is that it is a vast, clean lake in a Mediterranean country with few other

Still waters of the Galilee shore

CHANGING NAMES
In the early Scriptures, the Sea of Galilee is called Sea of Chinneret. Both Numbers 34:11 and Joshua 13:27 explain that its eastern shore forms the edge of the Promised Land. By the time of the Book of Maccabees—which is not included in the Jewish and Protestant Bibles—the lake is called the Sea of Ginnosar. This evolved to Lake Gennesaret in the New Testament (Luke 5:1), though Sea of Galilee (Matthew 4:18, Mark 1:16) and Sea of Tiberias (John 6:1, 21:1) are also used. Sea of Tiberias seems to have been current in the 1st century—the time of Jesus —as both the Talmud and the historian Josephus use that name.

Oleander in full bloom

sources of fresh water. The sea is full, too, of edible fish—20 different species, notably the unique St. Peter's fish. Its shores are fertile and eager to yield their produce. Most of its shoreline remains wonderfully undeveloped, but kibbutzim and *moshavim* (cooperative villages) are scattered all around the lake. The fields grow the whole gamut of fruit: apples, avocados, beans, and bananas. Most people are involved in fishing or fish farming.

The lakeside kibbutz hotels make excellent places to stay—or merely stop for a meal. They have parklike settings and a more restful atmosphere than conventional hotels. Among the most appealing are the well-placed **Nof Ginnosar** (see page 171), on the northwestern shore and the religiously observant (though non-Jews are very welcome) **Kinar**, facing it on the northeastern bank.

On the whole, the northern half of the lake offers superb tranquility. Most of the places associated with Jesus are here: **Capernaum▶▶** (see page 170) and, within a few minutes of Capernaum, the **Mount of Beatitudes▶▶** (see page 188), **Tabgha▶▶** (see page 202), **Migdal▶** (see page 186), the home of Mary Magdalene, and ancient **Kursi▶** (see page 198).

The southern half of the lake tends to appeal to a livelier crowd. **Tiberias▶▶** (see page 204), Galilee's little capital, stands on the edge of the water and invites you to swim in it, ski on it, or take a trip on it—either in a mock-biblical boat or in a modern pleasure cruiser equipped with disco. Or you can soak in its hot spa, famous since Roman days. At the southern tip of the Sea of Galilee, where the Jordan River pours out of the lake at **Yardenit▶** (see page 205), you can even be baptized in its waters.

WATER FOR PEACE
Under the 1994 peace accord, Israel provides Jordan with 150 million cubic meters of water per year by allowing extraction from the Yarmouk River, which flows into the Sea of Galilee. These days, the amount of water now pumped out of the Sea of Galilee each day to meet the needs of Israel's own population is more than the total for all of 1948.

Drive

The Sea of Galilee

(for map see pages 163C2–C3)

This circular tour of the lake offers plenty to do and see. *Allow all day, and take a swimsuit.*

From the lake's biggest town, **Tiberias▶▶** (see page 204), head south. After 3 miles you pass the Roman and modern spa baths of **Hamat Tiveria▶▶** (see page 205) and, on the hill slope opposite, two beautiful **old synagogues▶**. Nearby is the tomb of Rabbi Meir Ba'al Haness, revered by many Sephardi Jews. Turn right beside the Jordan River to the **Yardenit▶** baptismal park (see page 205). Almost next door, **Deganya▶** (see page 171), founded in 1909, is Israel's oldest kibbutz. A right turn leads from the lake to **Hamat Gader▶▶** (see page 176), site of extensive spa baths and an alligator farm. If alligators are not to your taste, try the ostrich farm at **Ha'on Kibbutz▶** (see page 177).

Kibbutz Ein Gev▶, founded in 1937, lies just within the pre-1967 border.

Green and scenic Galilee, site of many events in Christ's life

This was where the first Jews in modern times cast their nets again into the Sea of Galilee. On the stony hill above is ruined **Susita▶** (Hebrew for "horse," named after the hill's saddle shape), which, as the seat of a Byzantine bishop, flourished until the 7th-century Arab conquest. Nearby **Kursi National Park▶**, the biblical Gergesa, contains what was once Israel's largest Byzantine monastic church. The 5th-century building, partly reconstructed, traditionally marks the place where Jesus cured the man possessed by a "legion" of unclean spirits; they entered a herd of some 2,000 pigs, which promptly ran down to the water and drowned (Mark 5:1–20). **Kinar▶**, a religious kibbutz, has a hotel and restaurant on delightful lakeside grounds.

The road recrosses the Jordan on the wooden planks of **Arik Bridge**, and straight away reaches **Amnun Beach▶**, a very agreeable spot for a dip. Just minutes away, several important places in Jesus' ministry lie close together: **Capernaum▶▶** (see page 170), **Tabgha▶▶** (see page 202), and the **Mount of Beatitudes▶▶** (see page 188 and opposite Walk). Do not miss the **ancient boat▶▶▶** at the **Man in the Galilee Museum▶** which can be found beside the attractive **Nof Ginnosar Kibbutz Hotel** (see page 171). Last comes ancient **Migdal▶** (see page 186), just 2½ miles from Tiberias.

The Chapel of the Primacy of St. Peter

Walk

In the footsteps of Jesus

Most of Jesus' ministry took place within a small area around Capernaum. This attractive countryside, dotted with churches, makes for enjoyable, easy walking. Wear a sunhat, take drinking water, and dress modestly for access to churches. *Allow 1½ hours.*

Start by visiting Capernaum's ancient synagogue and dwellings, including the one said to have been St. Peter's House (see page 170). Jesus lived at **Capernaum▶▶**, where he preached and soundly reproached the townsfolk for not taking his message to heart.

From the site, take the access path back to the main road. Almost opposite, paths lead on through the fields to the **Mount of Beatitudes▶▶** (see page 188), a possible site of the Sermon on the Mount. Climb to the summit (half a mile), where the lovely domed **Church of the Beatitudes** (or Basilica), set in gardens adjacent to the **Hospice**, commands a fine view.

Descend on the path that heads in the direction of Tabgha (half a mile). You meet the road almost opposite the grounds of the **Church of the Primacy of Peter**. Walk to the simple chapel, which stands on the shore of the lake. The chapel was built on the spot where the risen Christ appeared to his disciples, who were fishing on the lake. They did not recognize him until he told them to cast their nets on the other side of the boat, whereupon their nets were full. Peter then miraculously walked on the waters of the lake to reach the shore. Over breakfast Jesus asked Peter three times if he loved him. On replying yes, Peter was made head of the Church.

Turn along the road away from Capernaum. Immediately on the right are remains of the 4th-century **Monastery of the Sermon on the Mount**, held, at that time, to mark the site of the Sermon. Continue for 150 yards to the modern **Church of the Multiplication of the Loaves and Fishes**, the third church on this site. It is traditionally associated with the feeding of the multitudes with loaves and fishes. Return along the road to Capernaum.

THE ARI
Sefat's Ari Ashkenazi Synagogue is supposed to stand on the spot where the nature-loving Yitzhak Luria, known as Our Master Rabbi Yitzhak, or the Ari (an acronym that means "the Lion"), would greet the Sabbath. The six psalms and chanted blessing that he and his followers recited have become the familiar Friday evening *Kabbalat Shabbat*. The Ari also established the popular Tu b'Shvat festival, the "New Year for Trees," now celebrated by Jews all over the world. The Ari was Sephardi, but the congregation today is Ashkenazi—hence the synagogue's name.

▶▶▶ Sefat (Hebrew: Tsfat or Zefat) *163C3*

One of Israel's most picturesque towns, Sefat (see panel for other spellings) stands 3,280 feet high in beautiful hills north of the Sea of Galilee, with superb views. This has been a center of Jewish learning for centuries and was, with **Meron▶** (see page 185), a birthplace of kabbala (Jewish mysticism). It's one of the four holy Jewish cities. Many strictly observant Jews live here, but it is a focus of secular Jewish culture as well. Every July, Sefat hosts its popular festival of *klezmer* (East European Jewish music).

Café-lined **Yerushalayim (Jerusalem) Street▶▶▶**, is the old city's main street and is set on the slope of a steep hill. Pick up a map at the tourist office, located a few paces from the **Davidka▶**, a homemade cannon; its noise alone is said to have helped the Jews conquer Sefat in 1948. At the hill's summit, there is a park and the remains of a **Crusader Citadel▶▶**. On the northern slope, the **Israel Bible Museum▶** (*Closed* Shabbat. *Admission free*) houses art depicting biblical scenes. More interesting, **HaMeira House▶▶** (*Closed* Shabbat. *Admission: inexpensive*) has material on 19th-century Sefat. It is near the top of **Ma'alot Olei HaGardom▶**, a remarkable flight of hundreds of stone steps down the hill. Also at the top of the steps is the **Police Station▶**, built by the British to separate Jewish and Arab neighborhoods. It is still pitted with bullet marks.

North of the steps, wander among the attractive cobbled lanes, stairways, and courtyards of the **Synagogue Quarter▶▶▶**. The ornate little 16th-century synagogues (some rebuilt in the 18th century) are very much in use. These synagogues welcome non-Jewish visitors, though modest dress is expected (see panel, page 99). Do not miss

Sefat's ancient Abuhav Synagogue

the **Ari Ashkenazi Synagogue▶▶▶**, a tiny white stone building in a quiet stone courtyard, with its detailed hand-carved ark. Also not to miss are **Abuhav Synagogue▶▶**, with its three arks, and **Yosef Caro Synagogue▶▶▶**, named after the Spanish-born rabbi who arrived here in 1535. Caro wrote the still-authoritative work on Jewish law, the Shulhan Aruch.

South of the steps lies the charming **Artists' Quarter▶▶**, a former Arab district taken up in the 1950s by an artists' collective. This area is packed with studios and open-air sculpture displays. Farther south is the town's fascinating **Ancient Cemetery▶▶**, which has the graves of many distinguished 16th-century rabbis. Also buried here are the victims of two tragic P.L.O. attacks—the 22 Sefat high school pupils killed at Ma'alot on a school trip, and the 11 younger children from Avivim, whose school bus was attacked.

After the First Revolt (AD 66–73), the town grew as Jews fled here from Jerusalem. Crusaders drove the Jews out

Lions and doves in the Artists' Quarter

and constructed the citadel in 1140 (they dubbed the town Safed—still a popular version of its name). It was taken in turn by Salah ed-Din (1188), the Knights Templar (1240), and the Mamelukes (1266). In 1517 all Israel came under Ottoman rule. Jews returned, including many expelled from Spain in 1492. The new arrivals brought with them a rich culture; they built the synagogues and, in 1578, set up the region's first printing press. An earthquake in 1759 caused great damage, after which many Sephardim (Jews of Spanish origin) moved elsewhere. However, Ashkenazim arrived from Russia and took their place, bringing with them their own mysticism and Yiddish culture. In 1837, another earthquake and epidemic killed over 5,000 people, and the town went into decline. Arabs moved in, and in the 1929 anti-Jewish riots they killed 21 Jews and wounded 80.

In the 1948 War of Independence, Sefat was an Arab stronghold with a population of 12,000 Arabs, including a fighting force of 6,000. When the Arabs entered the Jewish quarter, with its population of 1,500 mainly elderly Hasidim, a group of 35 men in the Palmach elite Jewish fighting force arrived. The fact that such a small number of men managed to defeat the Arab forces and take the whole town is now widely celebrated in Jewish history. It is known as the Miracle of Sefat (see panel).

THE MIRACLE OF SEFAT

When the Jews won Sefat in the 1948 war, the chief rabbi of the town gave it as his opinion that the victory had been due to two things: the natural course of events, and a miracle. The natural course of events was that Jews prayed and God answered their prayers. The miracle was that the Jews were prepared to stay and fight for their city when so heavily outnumbered.

HOW ARE YOU SPELLING THAT?

The name of the hilltop town north of the Sea of Galilee is spelled in Hebrew with the three letters *tsadi, feh, taf,* pronounced approximately as Tsfat. Foreign efforts to say this, or transliterate it into different European languages, have led to a multitude of alternative spellings. As well as Sefat, the town's name is commonly written as Sefad, Safed, Zefat, Sfat and Tsefat.

Modern walls on Roman columns in the Church of the Multiplication of the Loaves and Fishes

► Shibli 162B2

This village on the north slope of **Mount Tabor** (see page 190) is one of several Galilee Bedouin communities. The **Galilee Bedouin Heritage Center►►** (*Open* Sun–Thu 9–4. *Admission: moderate*), arranged mainly in tents and in the open air, explains their culture and tradition. Refreshments include freshly baked pita. It makes for a relaxed, enjoyable, and educational outing not only for interested tourists and Israelis, but also for Bedouin families.

►► Tabgha 163C3

Not a village, but a small, fertile valley on the Galilee lakeshore, its name derives from the Greek *hepta pegon* or "seven springs." The springs emerge by the Church of the Primacy of Peter. Just 2 miles from Capernaum, Tabgha lies at the foot of the **Mount of Beatitudes►►** (see page 188). At the bottom of the hill the **Church of the Multiplication of the Loaves and Fishes►►►** (*Open* daily till 5) commemorates the feeding of the multitudes. This attractive modern building was constructed in 1982 for the German Benedictines, whose 1956 monastery stands next door. The church stands on the site of its 4th- and 5th-century predecessors, and encloses a beautiful cloister in white stone. Inside, visitors must remain quiet, which creates a tremendous atmosphere. In the transepts, exquisite **ancient mosaics►►** retrieved from the two earlier churches depict Egyptian imagery, common in early Christian art. A mosaic in front of the altar shows the two fishes and the basket of loaves (four, not the biblical five) with which Jesus fed the 5,000 (Mark 6:30–44).

Next door, the small, black **Church of the Primacy of Peter►►►** (*Open* daily till 5) built in 1933 on traces of a 4th-century church, marks the site where Jesus appeared to his disciples after his resurrection, according to the Gospel of John (21). The church is in a superb setting on the shore of the Sea of Galilee. Inside, modern colored glass contrasts with the black basalt. The simple interior is built around the waterside rocks, with one great rock emerging from the tiled floor. Known as Mensa Christi, it is claimed to be the "table" at which the risen Christ sat and ate bread with the disciples. Beside the church, steps carved into stone lead down to the water. These steps date from the 2nd century, but many believe that the risen Christ appeared to his disciples on them. On that same occasion, he named Peter head of his church.

JOSEF TRUMPLEDOR

Born in Russia in 1880, Trumpledor served in the Czar's imperial army, lost an arm in battle and was decorated for bravery, and yet still had to endure the anti-Semitism sweeping Russia at the time. He founded the Zionist Hehalutz (Jewish Pioneer) movement, and in 1912 went to live in Palestine. There he founded the Zion Mule Corps. and, despite having only one arm, fought with the British at Gallipoli, after which he was again decorated for bravery. On his return to Palestine in 1917, he joined with others to purchase and cultivate the land they called Tel Hai, the "Hill of Life." In 1920, Arabs attacked the settlement, which was vigorously defended. Eight settlers died, including Trumpledor, whose last words were: "It is good to die for our own country." His grave attracts many visitors, especially on the 11th day of the Jewish month of Adar, which has been set aside for the commemoration of Tel Hai Day.

▶▶▶ Tel Dan *163C5*

The ancient city of Dan, standing on the largest of the three sources of the Jordan River, marked the northern limit of the biblical Land of Israel ("from Dan to Beersheva"). It is now located within a glorious 100-acre **nature reserve▶▶▶**, still on Israel's northern border. Rising above the spring, the adjacent **Tel▶▶** gives a dizzying sense of history. The site of Laish, a city mentioned in Egyptian records of the 19th and 15th centuries BC, it was conquered by Joshua in the 13th century BC and occupied by the Jewish tribe of Dan, which, the Bible notes, had a bad record of idolatry. About 200 years later the city was destroyed by the Assyrian king Tiglath-Pileser III and never rebuilt.

Kibbutz Dan▶, half a mile away on a panoramic ridge, has views of the Hula Valley and the summit of snow-covered Mount Hermonr. The kibbutz runs a field studies center with residential classes and guided walks. Its **Beit Ussishkin▶▶** (*Closed* Shabbat *Admission: inexpensive*) (Ussishkin House) houses an information center and museum of the wildlife of Golan, Hermon, and Hula. The displays and video can only hint at the region's variety of over 2,000 plants and 400 species of birds to be seen here.

▶ Tel Hai *163C5*

North of Kiryat Shmona, Tel Hai (the Hill of Life) is a simple encampment preserved as a museum of the pre-State Haganah underground militia. Josef Trumpledor (see panel opposite) and others of the "eight people" (*kiryat shmona*) died here in March 1920 while defending the land they had purchased in 1917. Trumpledor's grave is at the **military cemetery▶**. To the north, **Beit HaShomer▶** (*Open* daily. *Admission: inexpensive*) at Kibbutz Kfar Giladi is a museum of the HaShomer (literally, "the Watchman"), another early Zionist militia.

JESUS APPEARS

"But when the morning was now come, Jesus stood on the shore, but the disciples knew not that it was Jesus."
—John 21:4

"DAN TO BEERSHEBA"

"And this shall be your north border: From the great sea you shall point out for you Mount Hor; From Mount Hor you shall point out your border unto the entrance of Hamath; and the limits of the border shall be to Zedad; And the border shall go on to Zifron, and its limits shall be at Hazar-Enan; this shall be your north border."
—Numbers 34:7–9

The Tel Dan Nature Reserve, believed by some to be the Garden of Eden

MAIMONIDES
Rabbi Moshe ben Maimon, also known by the sobriquet Rambam, or as Maimonides, was born in Spain in 1135. The leading scientist and physician of his day, he became the personal doctor of Salah ed-Din and wrote important commentaries on biblical matters that have now become standard works. He died on December 13, 1204, and was buried as he wished, at the holy city of Tiberias.

WISH YOU WERE HERE?
In the year 985, Arab writer El-Mukadassi had this to say about life in Tiberias: "For two months a year they gorge themselves upon the fruit of the jujube bush which grows wild and costs nothing, for two months they struggle with the numerous flies, for two months they go about naked because of the heat, for two months they suck sugarcane, for two months they wallow in mud because of the rain, and for two months they dance in their beds because of the legions of fleas."

Modern fishermen follow in the footsteps of St. Peter

►► Tiberias (Hebrew: Tiveria) *163C3*

Galilee's little capital (population 37,000), one of the four holy Jewish cities, runs downhill to the edge of the Sea of Galilee. The traffic-free *tayyelet*, or waterfront promenade, with its palms, strolling crowds, fish restaurants, and Oriental-looking food stalls, has a pleasant, convivial air and a curious mix of the plush and the tacky. There is a lot of entertainment for visitors, including evening lake cruises with dinner and dancing on board. Away from the shore, the town degenerates into squalor and appalling traffic jams. Most residents and tourists live in new districts high above the old city, but even the lakeside old quarter is marred by a mishmash of modern architecture.

History In AD 20, near the ruins of ancient Rakkat, Herod Antipas built an opulent palace and synagogue which soon attracted numerous religious scholars. The Mishnah was compiled here about AD 200, codifying the so-called Oral Law, the traditional interpretation and practice of the Written Law. From then until AD 429 (when it was abolished by Emperor Theodosius II), this was the seat of the Sanhedrin, the supreme court of Jewish law. The Palestinian or Yerushalmi Talmud (Book of Law) might be better termed the Tiberias Talmud, as it was written here around AD 400. Jewish life thrived until the 7th-century Arab conquest. Crusaders took the town in 1099 and Salah ed-Din in 1187. Under the Ottomans, Druze Emir Daher revived Tiberias, resettling it with Jews. The First Aliya (1882–1903) dramatically increased its population, and the town has continued to grow ever since.

Sights Waterfront amusements include the **Galilee Experience►** (tel: 06 672 3620. *Closed* Shabbat. *Admission: moderate*), a stirring multimedia "edutainment" packing the region's 4,000-year story into a shmaltzy 40-minute family show. Remains of the black basalt **Crusader fortifications►** are on the north side of the old town. The handsome **St. Peter's Monastery►** (*Open* daily 8–11:45, 2–5), close to the waterfront, also stands on Crusader ruins. Off the main HaGalil Street, the **tomb of Maimonides►►** (the renowned 12th-century Rabbi Moshe ben Maimon, also known by his acronym Rambam) lies beside a small garden. The tomb is reached by steps lined with black

The tomb of Maimonides

pillars. The large rounded pale stone tomb, set within a black stone enclosure, is unceremoniously covered by a ramshackle metal roof. Rambam's wife's square tomb lies to one side of the enclosure. Beyond are several other imposing rabbinical tombs, including those of 1st-century Yohanan ben Zakai, the eminent scholar and founder of the Yavne Academy. Also found here is the tomb of another revered scholar, 2nd-century Eliezer "the Great". The white **tomb of Rabbi Akiva▶▶**, spiritual leader of the Second Revolt against the Romans (AD 132), can be seen higher up the hill, among newer buildings.

Nearby Romans flocked to enjoy the hot baths at **Hamat Tiveria▶▶**, 3 miles south of town. The spa now occupies a modern complex and the emphasis is more on pleasure than on health. On the hillside opposite, ancient buildings were found; relics can be seen in the **Lehman Building▶**. Drive or walk up the ramp to an attractive paved esplanade to enter the domed interior of an ancient **Sephardi synagogue▶**, still in use. Above, on the slope, is the blue-domed **Ashkenazi synagogue▶**. Both provide access to the low vaulted chamber of the **tomb of Rabbi Meir Ba'al HaNess▶**. This 2nd-century scholar is revered by Sephardim as a miracle worker.

THE *TAYYELET*
Until 1934, the waterfront of Tiberias was densely populated, with houses descending to the edge of the lake. A huge storm in that year caused mud, water, and rock to pour through the city, demolishing hundreds of homes at the foot of the hill. Many people were killed. In the aftermath the ruined homes beside the water were swept away. In their place was constructed the town's *tayyelet*, or waterside promenade.

▶ Yardenit *163C2*

Open: Sat–Thu 8–6, Fri 8–5

Kibbutz Kinneret's baptismal park is on the banks of the Jordan, south of the Sea of Galilee. It has attractive grounds and water terraces, where devout Christians come to be immersed in the biblical river. (The site of Jesus' baptism in the Jordan near Jericho has been closed for several years.)

▶▶ Zipori (or Sepphoris) *162B2*

North of Nazareth, this remarkable **archeological site▶▶▶** consists of ruins from the First Temple period, remnants of a complete pre-Roman Jewish town, and a Roman theater. A reconstructed Roman villa contains its original Dionysian mosaic floor. A woman's face in the design has been dubbed the "Mona Lisa of the Galilee." Zipori's 12th-century **Crusader fortifications▶** are a reminder that the Crusader armies gathered here in 1187, before marching to the Horns of Hittim to take on Salah ed-Din. The former's crushing defeat ended the Second Crusade.

Crusader fortress rising above Roman theater ruins at Zipori

Judaea and Samaria (The West Bank)

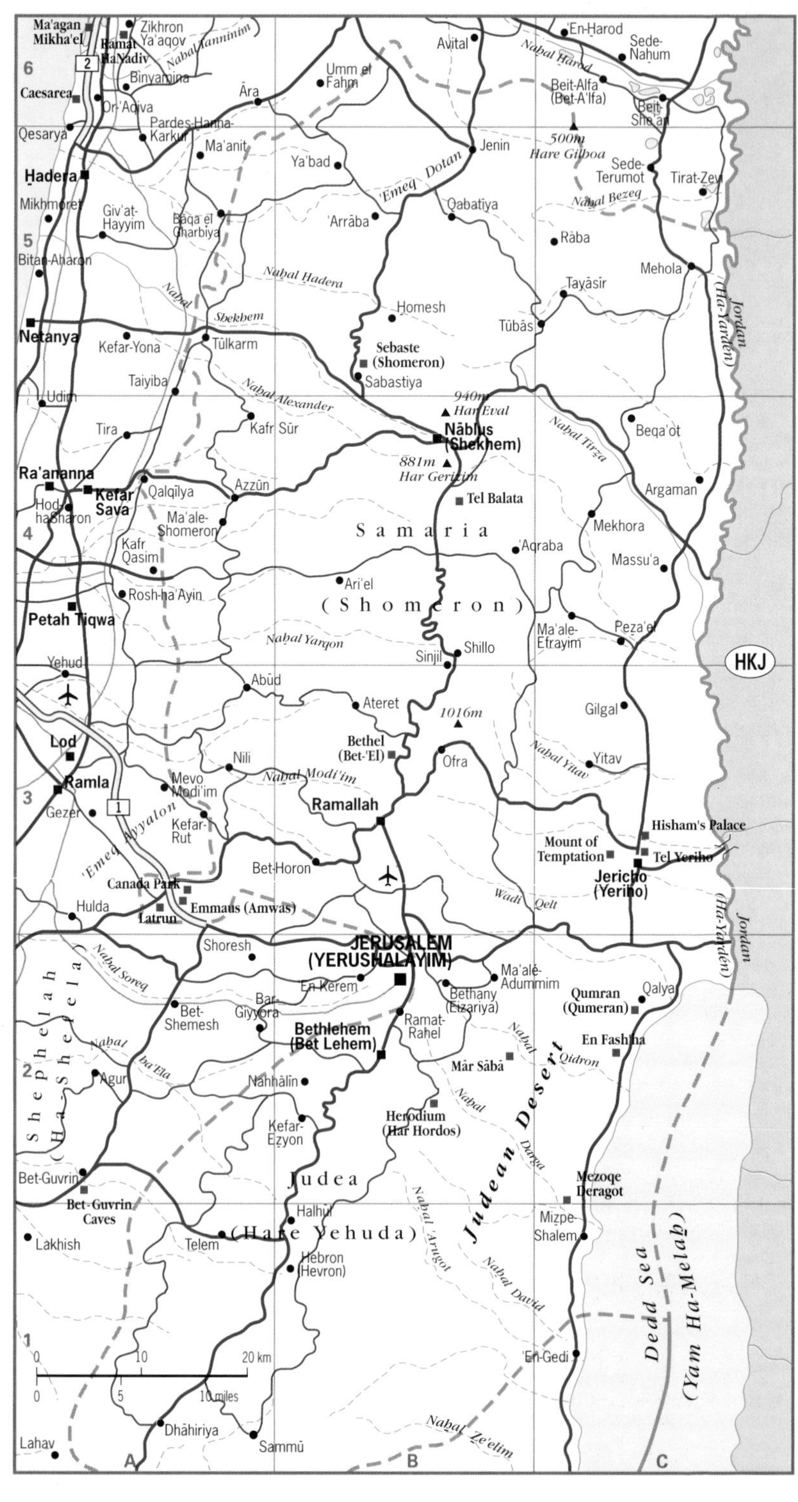

Judaea & Samaria (The West Bank)

Judaea's rocky terrain is cut by wadis that run only in the rainy season

JUDAEA AND SAMARIA (THE WEST BANK) In Hebrew, this region is known as Yehuda and Shomron. By Arab residents the area is referred to as Al Defa al Gharbia, literally, the West Bank. Most of Judaea and Samaria lies outside the State of Israel. These two ancient Jewish kingdoms have been disputed territory since 1948. Technically, the territory belongs to no one and is part of no country, although, since the setting up of the Palestinian National Authority in 1994, most of the region is under P.L.O. administration.

The term West Bank (of the Jordan River) is merely a convenient shorthand; originally it included most of the State of Israel. Currently, "the West Bank" suggests only the land placed under Israeli military rule after the 1967 Six-Day War. Worldwide, it was dubbed the Occupied Territories until the handover to the Palestinian Authority; Israel refers to it as the Administered Territories (or just "the Territories"), arguing that, under international law, only land properly belonging to another country can be described as occupied. Either way, it remains a divided, disputed region, a remnant of Palestine that ended up in neither Israel nor Jordan (see page 209 for travel advice).

A HARD PLACE A narrow ridge of rocky hills, reaching from Galilee to the Negev, passes through Judaea and Samaria and forms the greater part of the terrain. On their eastern slopes the hills fall sharply down into the Jordan Valley. Certain parts of Judaea fall within the borders of Israel proper such as Ein Gedi on the Dead Sea, Masada and Arad, and the capital itself, Jerusalem, which also includes "the mountains that are round about" the capital (Psalm 125:2). "Administered" Judaea lies south and east of Jerusalem,

JUDAEA WEEPS
After quelling the Jewish Revolt and destroying Jerusalem, the 1st-century AD Roman emperor, Vespasian, issued celebratory coins showing a palm tree, a man in chains, and a woman weeping, and bearing the words: *Iudaea Capta* (Judaea taken).

DISAPPOINTMENT
"What public relations can do for a river!"
—Henry Kissinger, on seeing the West Bank of the Jordan River in 1980.

LAND WITH NO NAME
Israelis often talk about "across the Green Line" when referring to the West Bank territories. They are also known officially by an acronym, Yesha, from Yehuda-Shomron-'Azza (Hebrew names for Judah, Samaria, Gaza). The name West Bank, first coined by the American C.I.A., was brought into general use by the Jordanians.

Previous page (bottom, right): detail at the entrance to the Milk Grotto Sanctuary

St. George's Monastery at Wadi Qelt, near Jericho

with Samaria to its north. Together they total only 2,260 square miles (just larger than Delaware). Both districts are stony, mountainous, and largely infertile, though the Samarian hills are terraced and planted with olives and other crops. A large proportion of Judaea consists of harsh uninhabitable desert, yet Judaea and Samaria lie near the heart and soul of Jewish history and heritage. Judaea (in Hebrew, Yehuda, or Judah) actually means "the Land of Jews." This is the country in which Abraham wandered, where he and the other patriarchs—and the matriarchs—of the Jewish nation lived and died. Jewish towns and places of pilgrimage grew around their tombs. Later, some of these became Muslim holy sites as well.

WHOSE LAND? In 1947, as the British were about to withdraw, the U.N. debated the future of Palestine. The Arab Higher Committee in Palestine, chief representative body of Palestinian Arabs, declared that "Palestine is part of the province of Syria." At the same time, the new kingdom of Jordan claimed sovereignty over all of British Palestine, while the Egyptians formed their own All Palestine Government to fill the vacuum left by the British departure. In 1948, the war between the Arab states and Israel left the region partitioned between Jordan, which annexed the entire West Bank, and the new State of Israel. With its defeat in the 1967 Six-Day War, Jordan lost the West Bank, which Israel occupied but did not annex.

After 1987, Israeli rule was challenged directly by the Intifada (literally "Throwing Off"), essentially an uprising of West Bank Arab residents, some opposed to Israel's presence in the West Bank, others opposed to the State's very existence. Partly through their inability to contain the Intifada, Israelis moved toward the idea of quitting the West Bank. Prime Minister Yitzhak Rabin's government was elected in 1992 with a mandate to "trade land for peace." Agreement between Israel and the P.L.O. was reached in 1993, and in 1994 the Palestinian Authority took over Gaza and Jericho as a first step. In stages, more of the land came under Palestinian rule. The argument does not stop there, however. Some Arab guerrilla groups will not contemplate any accommodation with Israel, and some Israelis cannot bear the idea of "giving back" any part of the Promised Land.

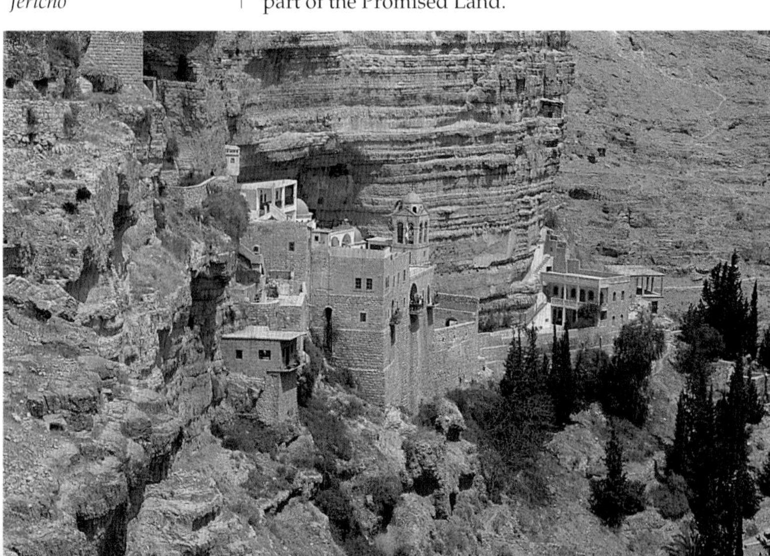

▶▶ Bethany (Arabic: El Azaria, Eizariya) *206B2*

A small town just over the crest of the Mount of Olives, Bethany is only 3 miles from Jerusalem. The Gospels of Luke and Matthew record that, before riding into Jerusalem on his final journey, Jesus sent two disciples to Bethany to fetch "a colt [of an ass] ... whereon yet never man sat." The animal had been tied up for him there—possibly by Lazarus and his sisters Martha and Mary, friends of Jesus who lived in Bethany.

In Aramaic, Bethany means "house (or place) of poverty," but the Arabic name means "The (place of) Lazarus." Lazarus is revered by Muslims as well as Christians. Lazarus had died from an illness, John's Gospel relates, and "lain in the grave four days already" before Jesus arrived. Jesus wept and called out, "Lazarus, come forth." The dead man came out, still bound with strips of cloth (John 11:1–44).

Lazarus' Tomb▶▶,near the mosque, is the principal sight. Difficult steps descend to a dark cavern, which leads to the low tomb where Lazarus is thought to have lain. The area north of the church was a cemetery in the 1st century AD, and the tomb has been popular with pilgrims since the 4th century. Mark makes no mention of Christ raising Lazarus from the dead, although the evangelist does have Jesus and the disciples going to Bethany on that day. In his story, Jesus is hungry and pauses at a fig tree. Finding it without fruit (because, as the Gospel states, Passover is not during the fig season), he curses the tree and tells it that no man shall eat fruit from it forever. Tourists are sometimes shown what is said to be the very tree, although Matthew (21:19) says that after Jesus' curse "the fig tree withered away" instantly.

Jesus stayed with his friends again "six days before the Passover" (John 12:1), on which he was to be crucified. The various Gospel accounts differ in their details of what happened on that day. John's gospel tells of Lazarus' sister Mary anointing Jesus' feet with "a pound of spikenard, very costly," and wiping his feet afterward with her hair. Matthew's Gospel says that a woman came with precious ointment in an alabaster box and anointed his head. These anointments, Christian authorities have claimed, were the ritual verification of Jesus as the Messiah. The word messiah, or *moshiach* in Hebrew, meaning "the anointed," is used several times in the Old Testament to describe Jewish kings or leaders.

In Matthew's Gospel (26:6–13), the anointment of Jesus takes place not at the home of Martha and Mary, but in the home of a leper called Simon. Not far from Lazarus' Tomb is the ruined **House of Simon the Leper▶**. Formerly known as the Castle of Lazarus it was once part of the defenses for a nunnery. The nunnery was founded by Milicent, wife of the Crusader-era King Fulke. Similarly, the so-called **House of Mary and Martha▶** is the remains of the medieval nunnery. A blocked-off recess in the **Church of Mary and Martha▶** forms another entrance to Lazarus' Tomb.

According to Luke's Gospel (24:50), Bethany is also the site of Christ's ascension. There are other Christian associations nearby: about 6 miles out of Bethany, on the Jericho road, is the inn of Jesus' parable about the Good Samaritan (Luke 10:25–37).

▶▶▶ REGION HIGHLIGHTS

Bethlehem *pages 212–214*

Cave of Machpela *page 215*

Herodion *page 214*

Jacob's Well, Nablus *page 220*

Trappist Monastery, Latrun *page 218*

TRAVEL IN THE WEST BANK

Two well-supported, well-funded, and well-armed Palestinian guerrilla organizations are at war with Israel: Hamas and Islamic Jihad. Their presence in the West Bank can make it dangerous to travel here. The stoning of cars with Israeli license plates (including rental cars) is commonplace. Shootings have also taken place, resulting in the deaths of several drivers and passengers.

This being said, the main roads to popular tourist sights are considered safe and have good security cover (for example, the Jerusalem to Qumran and Jericho road, or the Dead Sea road to Ein Gedi). Arab buses will not be attacked, and the Arab-run buses based at the East Jerusalem bus station travel to towns and villages throughout the West Bank. Organized tours, though dull and predictable, are the safest way to see the sights. West Bank tours are usually organized by Arab companies, with Arab guides traveling in Arab buses. The office of the Palestine Ministry of Tourism is in Bethlehem (tel: 02 274 1581, e-mail: Mota@pl.org).

The Palestine Liberation Organization (P.L.O.) was created in 1964 with the aim of destroying Israel. Its leader, Yasir Arafat (known to the Arabs as Abu Amr, Father of War), never seen without his traditional keffiye *headdress and a pistol strapped on to his battle fatigues, became a media figure lauded by Western radical groups and Soviet-bloc client states.*

CHANGING ROLE
"Chairman Arafat is doing his best to be a leader of a people, rather than the leader of a faction."
—Nabil Sha'ath, the P.L.O.'s planning minister and chief peace negotiator (December 1994)

On September 13, 1993, Yasir Arafat took off his gun and held out his hand in peace to the late Israeli Prime Minister Yitzhak Rabin (see panel on page 115) on the lawn of the White House in Washington. In 1994, the Israelis began the process of handing over territory to P.L.O. rule. This has not brought an end, though, to the Palestinian war against Israel. The P.L.O. is an uneasy alliance of guerrilla factions. As boss of the largest group, Al Fatah, Yasir Arafat may be chairman, but his policy is dictated by the need to appease rivals and keep warring factions together. Until 1993, they were bound by a common aim, set out in the P.L.O. Covenant. Its aim: to destroy Israel and set up an Arab state in all of Palestine. The Washington handshake and the repeal of the call to destroy Israel have given birth to a new P.L.O. that eschews terrorism. Meanwhile, no-quarter Islamic groups are winning the hearts of those who have lost faith in the P.L.O. yet still wish to see "the Zionist entity" utterly destroyed. Israel's hope is that the prospect of at last having some land to rule will encourage Chairman Arafat to deal firmly with his opponents.

Top and below: violent scenes such as these have diminished since Palestinian Arabs were granted self-rule

History In the Arab world, resolute opposition to the setting up of a Jewish state in Palestine goes back a long way and runs deep, for psychological, religious, and political reasons. Before and after Israel came into being in 1948, Arab states set up anti-Zionist armed groups. *Fedayeen* (terrorist) attacks ran at a high level through the 1950s. In 1964 the Arab League (a pan-Arab intergovernmental forum) met in Cairo to create the Palestine Liberation Organization as an umbrella for these diverse forces. They declared the P.L.O. was "the sole legitimate representative of the Palestinian people." Al Fatah joined in 1967 and became the dominant faction. Through the 1970s, terrorist acts around the world were sharply escalated. At the same time, the P.L.O. set up humanitarian bodies that won support among the Palestinians. More recently, the P.L.O.'s support for Iraq's invasion of Kuwait backfired as the Arab states allied themselves with the Kuwaitis. At this point, Israel seized the opportunity to work for peace with the weakened P.L.O.

A new era As the P.L.O. finally reaches out for acceptance and compromise, and is duly rewarded with territory to call its own, the unrest continues. In 1987, the Intifada uprising against Israeli rule started in the West Bank, and

Arab prisoners held for acts of aggression against the State of Israel

ON PAPER
Israel is the only Middle Eastern country in which P.L.O. newspapers are freely available. The main Arab newspapers, both published in Jerusalem and distributed throughout the West Bank, are *Al-Quds*, which is pro-P.L.O., and *Al-Nahar*, which is pro-Jordan.

came under the wing of the violent Islamic groups. Hamas (based in Gaza) opposes Palestinian self-government, seeing the region as part of a pan-Islamic state. It calls for the murder of all Jews. Islamic Jihad (sponsored by Iran) sees Israel as an arm of Western imperialism. Members believe that those who die attacking Israel enter heaven at once. The P.L.O. does not wish to antagonize Palestinian Arabs by coming into open conflict with such groups. However, it will have to curb them if it is to continue the peace process and secure an independent state, under P.L.O. rule, for the Palestinian Arabs.

ZIONISM
Arabs hostile to Israel brand it "the Zionist entity." Their influence enabled a vote to be passed year after year in the U.N. Assembly affirming that "Zionism is Racism," a Soviet-sponsored motion only rescinded with the collapse of the Soviet bloc. In fact, Zionism is the political movement whose objective is to create (and, now, to maintain) a Jewish homeland in Israel. Most political organizations and parties in Israel, even those advocating total withdrawal from the West Bank, consider themselves Zionist.

Clashes often involve youths and children

CHRISTMAS IN BETHLEHEM
Those who wish Christmas would come more often should be taken to Bethlehem. The three denominations controlling the Church of the Nativity celebrate the birth of Jesus on different days: Catholics on December 25, Greek Orthodox on January 7, and Armenians on January 19. The Catholic Christmas is a big event but, to prevent crime and overcrowding, visitors are required to have a permit to visit Manger Square, St. Catherine's Church, and the Church of the Nativity on December 24 and 25. Permits can be obtained from Israel Government Tourist Offices in Israel. Seats for midnight Mass in St. Catherine's Church must be booked well ahead with the Christian Information Center, Jaffa Gate, Jerusalem, tel: 02-287647.

SOLOMON'S POOLS
South of Bethlehem, on the main road to Hebron, three large and ancient reservoirs are attributed to Solomon (Ecclesiastes 2: 6). Herod brought water from them to Herodion, and Pontius Pilate ran their waters into Jerusalem.

BEWARE OF TOUTS
On arrival in Manger Square, visitors are usually set upon by groups of would-be guides of all ages, who shout and pull at the tourists while offering their "services." To employ one might be an act of charity, but for a more enjoyable visit to Bethlehem, it is wise to refuse.

▶▶▶ Bethlehem (Hebrew: Beit Lechem; Arabic: Bet Lacham) *206B2*

For devout Christians, a visit to this large Arab town, located 6 miles from Jerusalem, is the experience of a lifetime. The focal point is the Church of the Nativity in Manger Square, known to the world as the birthplace of Jesus and praised in carols, nursery songs, and poetry.

History Bethlehem first appeared in the Scriptures nearly 2,000 years before Jesus as the burial place of the matriarch Rachel, wife of Jacob, who "set a pillar upon her grave" (Genesis 35:19 and 48:7). The events of the Book of Ruth took place locally, and a young shepherd boy from Bethlehem, David, son of Jesse, was anointed King of Israel here by Samuel (I Samuel 16:1–13). The richness of its fields and pasture are reflected in its name: the Hebrew Beit Lechem means "House (or Place) of Bread," while the Arabic name means "House of Meat."

Christian beliefs Jesus' birth in Bethlehem is attested to by two of the evangelists. The Gospels of Matthew (2:1) and Luke (2:4–7) relate what has become the traditional Nativity story (neither Mark nor John refers to the birth of Jesus). They give no details of the exact location, except that Jesus was lain in a manger "because there was no room at the inn" (Luke). Tradition has it that a certain cave was the exact place of his birth as animals were often quartered in such places. Many older Bethlehem houses have caves behind them to this day. According to the 4th-century St. Jerome, the cave and site had, since Hadrian's time (AD 135), been a shrine to Adonis, the youthful "paramour of Venus" who symbolized the winter solstice. Hadrian's choice of this site, it has been suggested, may have been motivated by a desire to interfere with the veneration by Christians.

The first church When St. Helena, the mother of Emperor Constantine, visited in the 4th century, she was shown the cave, told the story and promptly ordered a church to be built. In the 6th century Emperor Justinian replaced this with a larger structure. His church was left standing by the Arab invaders of the 7th century. It also remained untouched in the 11th century when many churches were destroyed by invading Muslims. Jesus is named in the Koran as one of the Holy Prophets, and the destructive force of the ferocious Muslims was quelled by the thought that this was his birthplace. Justinian's church remains essentially that which exists today, except for alterations carried out by the Crusaders, who captured it in 1099. On Christmas Day in 1100, the Crusader King Baldwin I had himself crowned here.

Power struggle When the Crusaders left, the church went into decline. Warring Christian factions divided it into sections and each defended their own patch, while Mamelukes and others took everything of value. Later, in the bitter struggle for ownership of the church, Napoleon intervened on behalf of the Roman Catholics, securing a portion for them. Armenian, Greek Orthodox, and Catholic monasteries and churches were built abutting the Church of the Nativity, with entrances directly into it.

Bethlehem's Church of the Nativity

When the church was damaged by earthquake (1834) and fire (1869), disagreements between the factions made it impossible to carry out repairs or replace lost furnishings. Under British and then Israeli rule, pilgrimages to the church revived. Israeli soldiers have several times had to separate fighting Christians, notably in 1984 when armed Greek and Armenian clergymen fought a fierce battle.

Church of the Nativity▶▶▶ For nearly all visitors Bethlehem's main attraction is this church, believed by millions to stand over the place of Jesus' birth (*Open* summer, daily 5:30 AM–6:30 PM; winter, daily 5:30–5). Despite an unattractive, buttressed, fortress-like Crusader outer wall, the church is a good example of early Christian basilican construction. It is entered by crossing a large paved courtyard to reach the tiny 6th-century doorway, which Crusaders made even smaller, apparently for ease of defense. By contrast, the interior is large and open, almost entirely free of any decoration or furnishing. Inside are two double rows of red limestone pillars beneath an oak ceiling (a gift from Edward IV of England and Duke

HERODION
This magnificent archeological site (*Open* Sat–Thu 7:30–6, Fri 7:30–5. *Admission: moderate*), set on a high hilltop in the Judaean wilds south of Bethlehem, preserves substantial and impressive remains of the palace that Herod constructed for himself in 24–15 BC. He flattened the summit and ringed it with defenses to enclose his luxurious circular Mountain Palace. The Lower Town, at the bottom of the hill, was built for Herod's staff. In both the First and Second Jewish Revolts, the palace was seized by rebels and used as their fortress and operations center. Later, Byzantine monks built a monastery on the slope among the ruins of the palace annexes. From the summit, there is a fantastic view of Bethlehem and the Judaean hills.

Visitors entering the church bow in submission and humility through this low door

The Church of St. Catherine

Philip of Burgundy in 1482). During Crusader times and after, this austere interior was beautifully painted and gilded. Trapdoors in the floor open to show remnants of the **mosaic floor▶** of Helena's original church.

Site of the Nativity Beside the ornate Greek Orthodox altar at the east end, steps lead down to the **Grotto of the Nativity▶▶▶**. The marble-lined cave is small—8 feet high and less than 13 feet across—and rather overpowering, with its warm, heavy atmosphere of incense and lamps. Some visitors are visibly moved. Groups on religious tours often break into carols or hymns. Below the little curtain-fringed Altar of the Nativity, a large silver star overhung with lamps supposedly marks the spot on which Mary gave birth, though the position was chosen much later, in the 17th century. Across from the altar, three steps lead into the **Chapel of the Manger▶**, where Mary is said to have placed her newborn baby. The Grotto, a Greek Orthodox possession, is part of a labyrinth containing altars, chapels, and the tomb of St. Jerome, with separate access from the Catholic side. To the right of the Grotto is the Greek Orthodox Monastery, and to the left the pleasant 19th-century Franciscan **Church of St. Catherine▶** (*Open* summer, daily 5–12, 2–6; winter, daily 5–12, 2–5).

Where shepherds kept watch there is now a modern shrine

The other sights Leading off Manger Square, Milk Grotto Street passes the **Chapel of the Milk▶** (*Open* daily 8–11:45, 2–5) where, it's said, drops of Mary's milk fell while she was breast-feeding Jesus, turning the ground white. Running parallel, Shepherds' Street leads out of town to the cultivated **Field of Boaz▶**, where Ruth gathered the gleanings left by her future husband (Ruth 2). Just over a mile away is the walled **Shepherds' Fields▶**, now an olive grove. A small cave in the center has become the **Grotto of the Shepherds▶**, a shrine stated to be the very place where the "shepherds watched their flocks by night." Located 6 miles farther south, **Herodion▶▶▶** is the well-kept remnant of Herod's majestic hilltop palace (see page 213).

Out of Bethlehem on the Jerusalem side, **Rachel's Tomb▶** (*Closed* Shabbat) is a well-established place of prayer for the Jews. A large tomb here, shrouded in cloth, is supposed to cover the grave of the matriarch, second wife of Jacob. **Beware of youths stoning cars on the way to all of these out-of-town sites.**

▶ Hebron (Hebrew: Hevron; Arabic: El Khalil) *206B1*

Be careful if you intend to visit this notorious trouble spot. It is a town with a large population (70,000) and a devout Islamic center with a tradition of violence (see page 209 for advice on traveling in West Bank trouble spots). Hebron is a harsh town without warmth, bars, or theaters, but it does have a powerful, fervent atmosphere. Among the world's oldest cities, occupied continuously since Canaanite times, this is also one of the four Jewish holy cities. It was here, as Genesis details, that Abraham made his covenant with God, here that Abraham and Sarah, Isaac and Rebecca, Jacob and Leah, founders of the Jewish nation, lived, died, and were buried. Here David was anointed Saul's successor as King of the Jews; he made Hebron his capital before Jerusalem. As a national shrine, the town has been vitally important ever since. The Bible also calls the town Kiryat Arba, and that is the name of the heavily defended, tough-minded new Jewish district (population 5,000). This replaced the old and peaceful Jewish quarter (population 700), emptied by Arab rioters in the horrific 1929 massacre and demolished during the Jordanian occupation.

Sights The town is dominated by the fortress-like structure (largely 13th- and 14th-century, but with Herodian elements dating to 20 BC) built over the **Cave of Machpela▶▶▶** (*Open* Sun–Thu approx 8–4; restricted access Fri and Sat). Also called the Tomb of Patriarchs (in Arabic: Haram el Khalil—literally "Tomb of the Friend"), this tense, divided shrine is where Jews and Arabs both pray. It stands on the south side of town, not far from the busy souk. The cave itself is sealed; 9th- and 14th-century cenotaphs in the building and courtyard are said to stand above the graves of Abraham and Sarah. Koranic script decorates the walls. The shrine has been a synagogue, a mosque, and a church before reverting to the Muslims, who from 1267 to 1967 banned Jews from entering. The Yitzhak (or Isaac) Hall is still reserved for Muslims. A synagogue has been placed between the cenotaphs of Abraham and Sarah. It is quite probable that this really is the site of their graves. Less plausible is the popular idea that Adam and Eve are also buried in the cave. Adam's footprint, Abraham's oak tree, and other doubtful tombs and relics are among the town's sights.

MASSACRE IN HEBRON
Hebron had an almost unbroken Jewish presence for thousands of years up to August 1929, when Arabs besieged the Jewish quarter, killing 67 people and forcing the rest to abandon their homes. After the 1967 Six-Day War a group of Jews returned and created the new Kiryat Arba district. In May 1980, as a group of Jewish students came out of the Cave of Machpela, Arabs opened fire on them, killing six and wounding 17. In 1993 and 1994, following the Israel–P.L.O. accord, there were many attacks on Jews in the Hebron area. In February 1994 a Jewish doctor, Baruch Goldstein—previously considered a dutiful servant of both communities—walked into the Isaac Hall at the Cave of Machpela and opened fire on the Arabs praying there, killing 29.

The cave of Machpela is a place of prayer for both Jews and Muslims

The walls of Jericho come tumbling down

CROSSING INTO JERICHO
The P.L.O.–Israel accord was held up for months by the P.L.O.'s insistence that it should have its own border checkpoint on the Jericho road. Despite this, most travelers approaching the "frontier" of Jericho's autonomous area are simply waved by without so much as a glance at their documents. About 2 miles before reaching the Palestinian line, near the turning for Yered Yeriho, an I.D.F. (Israeli Army) checkpoint adopts a similarly low-key attitude.

Knot window from Hisham's Palace

►► Jericho (Hebrew: Yericho; Arabic: Er Riha) *206C3*

The lowest town in the world (820 feet below sea level), and the oldest, Jericho has a shabby charm and a relatively calm atmosphere. It's a popular, and safe, excursion for Israelis. There are lots of places to eat and a striking abundance of greenery and flowers. It's the main center of Palestinian administration on the West Bank, and was the first town to become autonomous.

History The "oldest town" claims do not really apply to present-day Jericho—only the *tel* (settlement mound) on the northern boundary is ancient. This was, the Bible vividly records, the first town in the Promised Land taken by the Israelites under the command of Joshua. Following God's instructions, Joshua encircled the city, and when the priests blew their trumpets, the walls came tumbling down. He then cursed the city and any man that would rebuild it. All this and more is told in ripping style in the Book of Joshua. The curse was not taken too seriously by his fellow Israelites, who immediately rebuilt Jericho as a Jewish city. Despite a succession of foreign rulers this is how it remained, with a few breaks, right through the millennia up to the Arab conquest in the 7th century AD. Its location has varied slightly.

Jericho makes numerous other appearances in the Bible, and its life seems to have been entwined with that of Jerusalem. Temple priests had homes here, and it was said that trumpets blown at the Temple could be heard in Jericho, 22 miles away. In 30 BC, the city became the personal possession of King Herod, who enlarged and aggrandized it, building a winter palace here. It was the Herodian city that Jesus knew and to which he came prior to the Crucifixion.

Herod's city was virtually destroyed by the Romans during the Second Jewish Revolt, but reappeared on its present site under the Byzantines. Arabs took control in AD 638, then the Crusaders, who were driven out in 1147. The town then dwindled away; at the British takeover it had a population under 3,000. This changed dramatically in 1948, when 70,000 Arabs, fleeing from the new State of Israel, settled here in refugee camps. After 1967, they came under Israeli rule and again fled, this time to Jordan. In 1994, under the gaze of the world's TV cameras, Jericho became the first independent Palestinian city on the West Bank. There's a casino here, and tourists are welcome in town.

Sights Most things worth seeing lie north of modern Jericho. Start with **Tel Yeriho▶▶** (*Open* summer, daily 8–6; winter, daily 8–5. *Admission: inexpensive*), where 23 layers of civilization have been found, dating back to 8000 BC. The whole of the mighty encircling defenses of Canaanite times have been excavated, together with traces of the rampart that fell at the sound of Joshua's trumpet blast. Despite its importance, however, the *tel* does not convey a great deal to the layman. At its foot, and across the road, Elisha's Spring (Nahal Elisha), also known as Sultan's Spring (Ein es-Sultan) provides the abundant fresh waters that have given the area its greenery and fertility. Close by, in a private house, ruins of an **Ancient Synagogue▶▶** (*Open* daily 8–4. *Admission: moderate*) have a lovely 6th-century patterned mosaic floor featuring a menorah (candelabrum) and the inscription "Peace on Israel."

Some 500 yards east, the ruined **Hisham's Palace▶▶** (*Open* Sat–Thu 8–5, Fri 8–4. *Admission: moderate*) was probably built by Caliph Hisham of Damascus as a winter palace in 743. Four years later, it collapsed in an earthquake. Even so, much survives, including massive columns, a sumptuous bathhouse, exquisite mosaics, and delicate stonework. Just over a mile farther north, the **Mount of Temptation▶** is where Orthodox churches claim that Jesus was "led into the wilderness to be tempted of the devil" (Matthew 4:1–11). An impressive Greek **monastery** (*Open* Mon–Sat) hangs onto its barren, rocky slope. West of town, at the start of Wadi Qelt, are the ruins of **Herod's Palace▶**. Here, Herod entertained during the winter months and, occasionally, got up to darker deeds. It was here, for example, that he murdered his 18-year-old brother-in-law, drowning him in the swimming pool.

JESUS' BAPTISM

The Jordan River east of Jericho is where Jesus was baptized by John, according to Matthew's Gospel. The reputed site (chosen by Byzantines), though sign-posted, has remained closed for a number of years. However, a visit is possible for members of the Greek Orthodox Church at Epiphany (January) and for Roman Catholics on the third Thursday in October. The Christian Information Center at Jaffa Gate, Jerusalem, has more details.

This harsh desert is typical Judaean terrain

THE SAMARITANS
A tribe and sect descended from the tribes of Ephraim and Menasseh, which broke away from mainstream Judaism around 400 BC, the Samaritans hold that only the Torah (the first five biblical books) is sacred, rejecting all subsequent oral and rabbinic law. In that respect they resemble the Karaites. However, the Samaritan Torah contains variations from the Jewish text, including its own version of the Ten Commandments, one of which requires God's followers to build his sanctuary on Mount Gerizim. Samaritans say the original holy Scriptures were altered by Ezra, for which there is some historical evidence. There are no lay teachers, and all ritual remains in the hands of the hereditary priests and Levites (assistants to the priests). Savagely persecuted by Romans, Jews, Muslims, and Christians, Samaritans today number only about 600, all living at either Holon or Nablus.

PALESTINIAN POST
In 1994, the Palestinian Authority issued its first postage stamps, initially priced in the British Mandate currency of mils. It was then overstamped in Jordanian currency of fils. Significantly, the Palestinian stamps depicted locations that had not been transferred to Palestinian rule, including Temple Mount and the Tower of David, in Jerusalem.

►► Latrun *206A3*

This monastery, fort, wooded park, and ruined village is located on the main highway, midway between Jerusalem and Tel Aviv, overlooking the Ayalon Valley. It sits in a corner of land that saw some of the worst fighting in 1948. Many lives were lost as Jews struggled to keep the road to the capital open, and Arabs struggled to close it. The abandoned building on the hill above the road was the British police station that had previously overseen this trouble spot. Like many other British military emplacements and police stations, it was handed over to the Arab Legion in 1948. The Ayalon Valley, now blooming with new settlements, has a long history as a battleground. When Joshua came this way and urged the sun and moon to remain still, so as to prolong the day and give him more time to slaughter the Amorites, they obligingly did as he asked (Joshua 10:12).

On the left-hand side of the road (coming from Jerusalem), the attractive French **Trappist monastery►►►** (*Open* daily) of 1927 stands among its flourishing gardens and crops. The monks produce good wine, spirits, and olive oil (on sale by the entrance). Early Christian stonework can be seen in the monastery gardens. On top of the hill behind stand the ruins of a 12th-century **Crusader fort►**. To the right of the road is the ruined village of Amwas, known in the Bible as **Emmaus►**. It was here, according to the Gospel of Luke, that Jesus appeared to two disciples after the Resurrection. The ruins of an old church remain, while above it are a monastery and the ruins of a Crusader-era basilica, erected on the site of a Roman villa. Here, the **Canada Park►** forest makes a pleasant place for a walk and a leisurely picnic.

►► Mar Saba (St. Sabas) Monastery *206B2*

Open: daily 7–11, 1:30–5

The watchtower of this historic Greek Orthodox monastery lies at the end of a long road that passes through barren hills. West of it rises the sheer Kidron Gorge, pockmarked with caves. A sect of hermits used to reside here, each man living in his own cavern. One of them, arriving here in AD 478, was a monk called Sabas, who originally came from Cappadocia. In 492 Sabas founded a monastery on the slope opposite his cave. Sabas became an influential figure, persuading Emperor Justinian to rebuild Bethlehem's Church of the Nativity. After his death in 532, the monastery of St. Sabas, and the saint's grave, both became popular places of pilgrimage.

In 614 the community was attacked by Persians and in 636 by Arabs, but adherents continued to arrive. One of them, in 712, was John of Damascus, who until then had been the representative of the Christians to the Omayyad rulers in Damascus. In the 12th century, Italian Crusaders stole the body of St. Sabas and took the monk's remains to Italy. In 1838, Russians reconstructing the monastery also removed the remains of John of Damascus, and took them to Moscow. In 1965, Sabas' relics were returned by Pope Paul VI.

Only male visitors may enter the monastery. Taken around by a monk, they are shown what is left of Sabas, along with the main church with its painted walls, the skulls of monks killed in the 7th century, and a fantastic view across the valley. Women have to make do with the Women's Tower on an adjacent hill. There is a superb view from here as well!

►► Mount Gerizim *206B4*

The holy place of the Samaritans rises to 2,890 feet just south of Nablus. The mountain gives glorious views over Nablus and the surrounding countryside. Below the summit are dwellings that the Samaritans use at Pesach (Passover), which they observe as a pilgrim festival, fulfilling every detail of the biblical injunctions concerning the sacrificial slaughter of sheep (carried out at a ceremonial site just off the road). On the same mountain, Samaritans believe that Abraham prepared to sacrifice Isaac.

CASTLES AND ROBBERS

The name Latrun has an odd history. For centuries Christians have held that it comes from the Latin *latro*, robber, and that this was the home of the "Good Thief" crucified alongside Jesus. However, Latrun is probably the Arabic form of the medieval French name, Le Toron des Chevaliers (Knights' Hill), so called because of the Crusader fortification built here in the 12th century. Later the fortress ruins became known as Castrum Boni Latronis (Castle of the Good Thief), compounding the confusion.

Surviving against the odds: the 5th-century Mar Saba monastery

SAMARITAN ISRAELIS
Although Samaritans are not considered Jews, their relationship with Israel is a special one, and their religion is closely connected with Judaism. That is why the Israeli High Court has ruled that Samaritans have the right to become Israeli immigrants with full citizenship. The court was responding to a petition from Samaritans wanting to leave Nablus (on the West Bank) and live at Holon (near Tel Aviv), the other Samaritan population center.

▶ Nablus (Hebrew: Shechem) *206B4*

Nablus is a beautifully located commercial and industrial town, the largest on the West Bank (population 75,000). It is also a passionate center of Palestinian nationalism, with a recent history of violent unrest and political killing. **This is a place to visit with the utmost care, after checking the current situation**.

Nablus is the successor to the biblical city of Shechem, demolished by the Romans in AD 70 and replaced in AD 72 by Neapolis, literally the "New City." Its name became corrupted to Nablus after the Arab conquest. The small **Samaritan quarter▶** lies in the western part of town.

Just over a mile southeast of Nablus, **Tel Balata▶▶** is the site of the original Shechem, the place where Abraham was told by God, "Unto thy seed will I give this land." Here Abraham erected his first altar before heading farther south. Returning from Mesopotamia, Jacob set up camp here. An unfinished Greek Orthodox church, built on top of Crusader foundations, now encloses **Jacob's Well▶▶▶** (*Open* daily 8–12, 2–5. *Admission free*), set within an elaborate, arched chamber hung with lamps. This is probably the very same well dug by Jacob, on land where he had pitched his tent outside Shechem (Genesis 33:19). It is also the place where, in John's Gospel (4:1–42), Jesus asked for a drink from a Samaritan woman, who convinced the townsfolk that he was the Messiah. Just a few hundred yards north, a white dome covers the reputed **Tomb of Joseph▶** (Joshua 24:32), whose remains were brought here from Egypt. Formerly closed to non-Muslims, the shrine is now open to all (*Open* daily 8–6).

►► Qumran National Park 206C2

(tel: 02 994 2235)

Open: daily, summer 8–6; winter 8–5. Admission: moderate

Famous as the place where the Dead Sea Scrolls were found in 1947 (see page 222), mystery still surrounds Qumran's archeological site, which lies 12 miles south of Jericho, close to the Dead Sea. Built in 150 BC, destroyed in AD 70, its stonework is well preserved, with several rooms still enclosed by high walls. Its watchtower gives an excellent overview of the site. The scrolls were found in almost inaccessible caves (indicated by signs) in the adjacent hillsides. The mystery is that so little is known about Qumran, and theories and questions abound. Was it a community? There are no bedrooms. Just a library? There is a large cemetery. A military fortress, a religious retreat, a factory? Many of the scrolls detail the practices and structure of a rigid, rule-bound community. The prevailing view is that this was a community of some 200 to 400 Essenes (see panel on page 223), and that they hid their writings in the caves to save them from the Romans.

►► Sabastea 206B5

Open: Sat–Thu 8–5, Fri 8–4. Admission: inexpensive

In 876 BC King Omri founded the hilltop city of Samaria, or Shomron (I Kings 16:24). Capital of the Northern Kingdom and notorious for abandoning Judaism in favor of Ba'al, it was destroyed in 721 BC by Persians, who built a non-Jewish city here. Taken by successive conquerors, it was eventually left deserted. Today there is a small Arab village below the ruins of the ancient city where the most impressive parts date from the Herodian period.

Qumran's ruins continue to mystifiy scholars

MA'ALEH ADUMIM

About 4 miles east of Jerusalem on the main Jericho road, the gleaming white modern blocks of this large new Jewish town (population 20,000) make a stark contrast with the surrounding scenery. At the heart of town is a major archeological site with the dramatic ruins of the Byzantine **Martyrius Monastery►►** (*Closed* Shabbat). The largest such structure on the West Bank, it has a display of well-preserved mosaic floors.

SINJIL AND SHILOH

Between Nablus and Ramallah is the village of Sinjil. It was named after St. Gilles, a small town in southern France, and ruled by Raymond, Count of Toulouse and St. Gilles, who built the fortress here. On the other side of the road, a turning leads to the site of ancient Shiloh, where the Ark of the Covenant was housed in its Tabernacle during the early days of the Israelite conquest. From here the Ark was seized by the Philistines. Little survives from that period, though there are traces of an even older Canaanite temple, as well as some Byzantine mosaic floors.

In 1947, he didn't remember in which month, a Bedouin shepherd boy named Muhammad ed-Dhib scrambled into a cave near the (then unexcavated) site at Qumran and found strange-looking earthenware jars containing fragments of parchment and leather. It was to prove the most dramatic discovery of ancient Hebrew documents ever found.

NOW READ ON...
Scores of books have been written about the Dead Sea Scrolls, some sensational, some academic, some religious. For a balanced, intelligible overview, authoritative and academic yet accessible, read *The Dead Sea Scrolls* by Geza Vermes (Penguin, 1999).

The caves (top) that held the Dead Sea Scrolls and the jars (above) in which they were stored

What are the Scrolls? After the initial find, a dozen more Qumran caves yielded a vast hoard of ancient manuscripts in Hebrew, and occasionally in Aramaic, ranging from scraps to scrolls. Among them were two complete Books of Isaiah, parts of all the other Hebrew holy books (except for Esther), books of the Apocrypha and Pseudepigraphia (both excluded from the Jewish Bible), and other nonbiblical works such as the Book of Jubilees and the Book of Enoch.

There were prophetic and visionary Jewish books not previously known, and biblical commentaries offering unfamiliar interpretations. The Temple Scroll described the Holy Temple in detail. The enigmatic Copper Scroll discusses hidden treasures. Perhaps most interesting, many scrolls—including at least one written in poetic form—spelled out the Qumran sect's customs and beliefs: the Community Rule (beliefs and rituals), Statutes (practices and laws in detail), the War Scroll (concerning the perpetual struggle between Good and Evil), and dozens more.

Important for Jews The discovery of the Scrolls, the oldest Hebrew texts ever found, revealed two complementary and contradictory things. First, that the Hebrew Scriptures have remained essentially unchanged for at least 2,000 years. Second, parts of the Bible have existed in several versions. Some of the Scrolls resemble later Greek editions, some are like the Samaritan Torah, some contain the Masoretic text used today.

The Qumran scribes also worked on and from other scriptural writings that are no longer part of Jewish liturgy. Individual scribes felt free to "reinterpret" or "edit" texts, showing that they considered the Scriptures a product of the human hand and human mind, albeit perhaps guided by God. Only after the destruction of the Temple did a group of Pharisee rabbis set the seal on a limited and censored body of holy literature, conforming to the Pharisee viewpoint. This included compilation of oral traditions, which they then declared to be the word of God. They thus created a unified, unchallengeable "Orthodoxy" that has, arguably, served well as a survival mechanism during the Diaspora years.

Important for Christians At an early stage in the study of the Scrolls, excited attempts were made to read them as Christian documents. Some wanted to believe that Jesus was the Teacher of Righteousnesss mentioned in various Scrolls, others that it was John the Baptist, or Jesus'

Professor Bieberkraut has devoted his life to conserving the scrolls

kinsman, James. Several agreed that Paul was the Wicked Priest. None of these notions stood up to further study. Instead, it became clear that the Essenes—their ideas predating Jesus by a century or more—had many beliefs that reappeared in the New Testament. The hierarchical community devoted to religious study under a learned leader presaged the monastic and church system. The Essene idea of a Holy Spirit became part of Christian doctrine. Jesus' celibacy and his emphasis on sharing and communality—all these echoed Essene dogma.

Essenes practiced baptism to symbolize a new beginning in religious awareness, as did John the Baptist. Miracle cures associated with forgiveness of sins were well-known among the Scroll writers. One of the Scrolls, the Prayer of Nabonidus (set in the 6th century BC), is about just such a cure. To this extent, the Scrolls show that Jesus' ideas were not new. It is interesting, too, that the New Testament reviles all the other Jewish groups but makes no mention of the Essenes. But Jesus himself was no Essene. Their rigid, structured, and exclusive community prepared itself for the end of days, while Jesus opened his arms to the common people and a new age.

THE ESSENES

The Essenes numbered about 4,000 people and they lived in the period 2nd century BC to 1st century AD. Much has been learned about the Essene sect from the contemporary Roman writer Pliny and the Jewish writer Josephus. Both greatly admired their austerity, asceticism, and firmness of purpose. The Essenes at Qumran (see page 221) were vegetarian, probably celibate, and preoccupied with a high degree of ritual purity. They lived communally but under a hierarchy with a Teacher of Righteousness at its head, and believed that they alone were the chosen, the "Sons of Light," who would soon be led by the Messiah to victory over the "Sons of Darkness." They were vehemently opposed to the Hasmonean dynasty, to the Pharisees, the Saducees, the Romans, and to the Temple priests, whom they felt had betrayed and defiled the Temple. They revered the descendants of King David's high priest Zadok as representing the pure line of the priesthood, supplanted by the Hasmoneans.

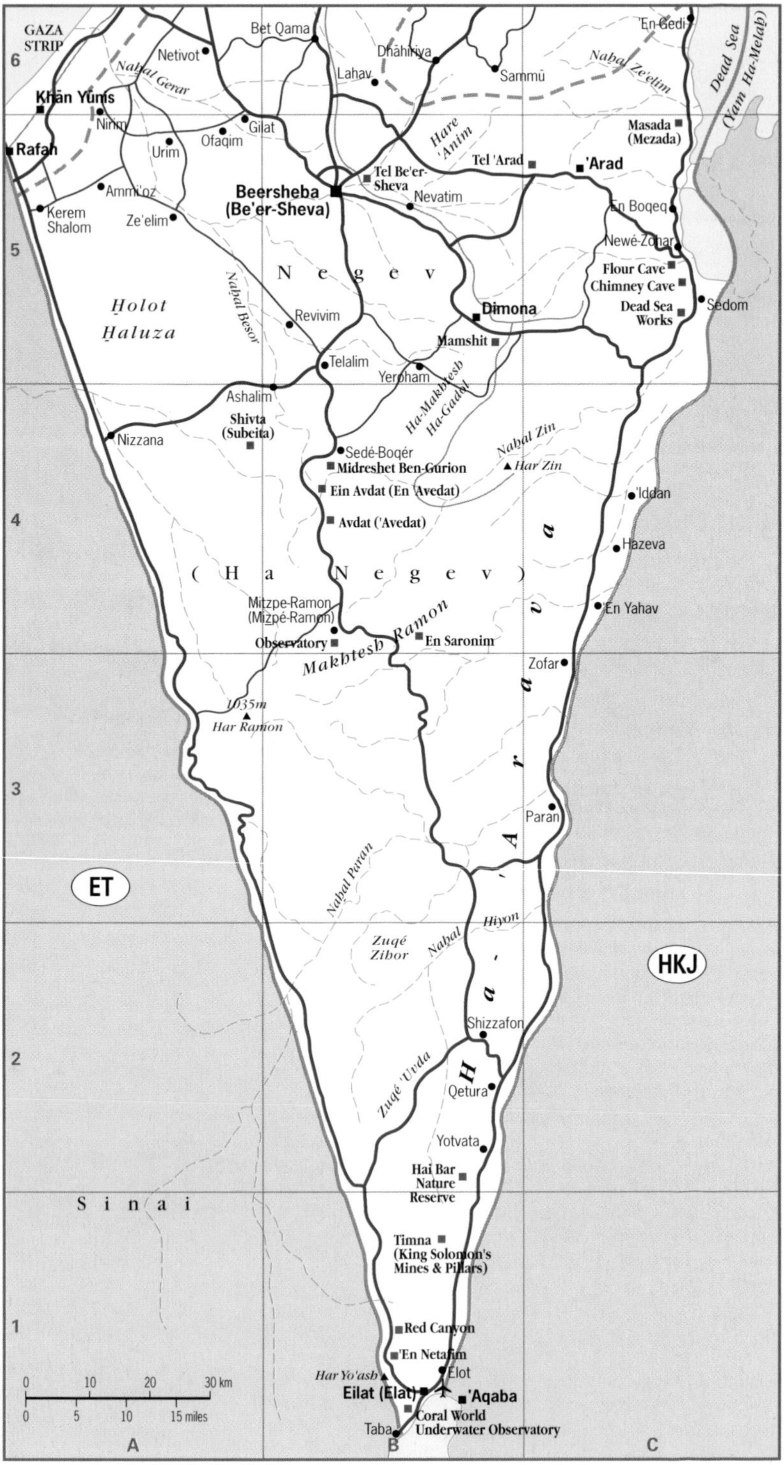

GAZA STRIP
Bet Qama
'En-Gedi
Dead Sea (Yam Ha-Melah)
Netivot
Dhahiriya
Nahal Gerar
Lahav
Sammu
Nahal Ze'elim
Khan Yunis
Nirim
Gilat
Masada (Mezada)
Rafah
Urim
Ofaqim
Hare 'Anim
Tel 'Arad
'Arad
Tel Be'er-Sheva
Beersheba (Be'er-Sheva)
Nevatim
Ammi'oz
Kerem Shalom
Ze'elim
En Boqeq
Newé-Zohar
Flour Cave
Chimney Cave
Negev
Nahal Besor
Holot Haluza
Dimona
Dead Sea Works
Sedom
Revivim
Mamshit
Telalim
Yeroham
Ha-Makhtesh Ha-Gadol
Ashalim
Shivta (Subeita)
Nizzana
Nahal Zin
Sedé-Boqér
Midreshet Ben-Gurion
Har Zin
Ein Avdat (En 'Avedat)
'Iddan
Avdat ('Avedat)
Hazeva
(Ha Negev)
'Arava
Mitzpe-Ramon (Mizpé-Ramon)
'En Yahav
Makhtesh Ramon
Observatory
En Saronim
Zofar
1035m
Har Ramon
Paran
ET
Nahal Paran
Zuqé Zibor
Nahal Hiyon
HKJ
Ha-'Arava
Shizzafon
Zuqé 'Uvda
Qetura
Yotvata
Hai Bar Nature Reserve
Sinai
Timna (King Solomon's Mines & Pillars)
Red Canyon
'En Netafim
Har Yo'ash
Elot
Eilat (Elat)
'Aqaba
Coral World Underwater Observatory
Taba

0 10 20 30 km
0 5 10 15 miles

A B C
1 2 3 4 5 6

The South

Scorched rock eroded by wind-blown sands

THE SOUTH More than half of Israel is desert, including the whole of the southern half of the country, which is taken up with an awesome expanse of scorched rock and raw, naked mountains and scored by arid bone-dry valleys. This is the Negev, picture-book desert, where the harsh dryness, consuming heat, and intense light can thrill you—or kill you. Anyone exploring off the beaten path here, or even stepping out of their car for a quick look around in some desert location, will realize within seconds that it is vital to take precautions.

LIFE Yet the Negev is no sterile, lifeless zone. This part of Israel has its tough and resilient flora and fauna, and it also has a human history. Nations have thrived in the Negev, nourished by a body of practical knowledge—of how man can live in such an environment. This has been all but lost. Three thousand years ago, the trade routes of the Nabateans ran through the Negev between the ports at Gaza and Eilat and the Nabatean capital at Petra, in what is now Jordan. Their camel trains carried perfumes and goods of all types, many imported from Europe.

The Nabateans, originally a nomadic Arab people, built caravansaries, even small towns such as Avdat, in this empty land. Water cisterns were placed in flood valleys to catch the runoff after rare desert rains. It has been estimated that a Nabatean settlement collected enough rain in half an hour to provide water for three years. The Romans, conquering Palestine, took over the Nabatean settlements, then fortified and enlarged them. Following the Arab conquest, civilization here disappeared, leaving only the nomadic, pastoral Bedouin as the last people of the desert. A thousand years later, Jewish kibbutzniks arrived.

The serenity of the desert at dawn

▶▶▶ REGION HIGHLIGHTS

DESERT CITIES

Despite annual rainfall of less than 8 inches a year, five Nabatean cities once thrived in the Negev. Taken over by the Romans and later occupied by Byzantines, they continued to prosper right up to the Arab conquest in the 7th century. Four were destroyed. The fifth, Shivta, was occupied by the Arabs but abandoned two centuries later. Known as the Negev Pentapolis, the five desert cities were Avdat, Kalutza, Nitzana, Mamshit, and Shivta.

LANDSCAPE The Negev is a region within a much larger arid desert zone reaching into Jordan, Egypt, and Saudi Arabia. It is a hard land, consisting mainly of bare granite mountains and dry valleys scattered with sand or stones. The rock faces are streaked through with shades of red, yellow, purple, and even stark black and white. Visually, it is highly dramatic. On the map, the Negev forms a vast upside-down triangle, its point at Eilat on the Red Sea, its base running across Israel from Gaza to the Dead Sea. On its eastern edge, the Dead Sea and the Arava rift valley score a deep frontier between Israel and Jordan. The rather arbitrary border with Egypt's Sinai desert marks the western side. The flatter Arava, where the main road links Eilat to the rest of Israel, is less interesting than the mountainous interior.

LEISURE There is a tremendous amount to see, learn, explore, and experience in the Negev—this is Israel's vast, natural adventure playground. Hiking, bird-watching, climbing, riding, jeep tours, and camel tours—even sightseeing—are excitingly different in this terrain. Although even a quick glimpse can be intriguing, you need something more than the usual brief tour taken by every visitor to Eilat to get the best of it. Far more rewarding is to stay in the heart of the desert itself—for example at Mitzpe-Ramon, or at a Dead Sea spa resort such as the lovely Kibbutz Ein Gedi. Remarkably, there is plenty to see in the Negev, including Roman and Nabatean ruins, and a reserve for rare desert animals such as oryx and addax.

THE FUTURE It is an old Zionist dream that towns will prosper in the midst of the Negev. Several kibbutzim shock the eye with their lush fields lying like vivid green rugs on the rocky desert floor. So far, though, attempts to break and harness the spirit of the Negev have met with only limited success. Some Israelis want to keep it that way. Others would like to see the whole place green and cultivated. Inevitably, some parts of the Negev will be developed. Water conservation will become more advanced so that small towns, industry, and agriculture may indeed flourish here, but this vast area of heat and rock will never be tamed, never lose its haunting spirit.

►► Arad *224C5*

Arad, the town nearest to the Dead Sea, was founded in 1962 as a base for archeologists and for scientists working in connection with Dead Sea industries. The thriving new town has also attracted a lot of medical staff because of the allergy and asthma treatment that goes on here, as well as university people from Beersheva who like living in modern and civilized Arad. In addition, the W.U.J.S. (World Union of Jewish Students) is based here attracting students engaged in Jewish studies.

The town perches on the hilly ridge just west of the Dead Sea. Immediately noticeable is the tangible cleanliness of the air (despite mineral industries on one edge). There is no pollen at all—all planting in the area is controlled—so the place is a boon for asthmatics. The Margoa Arad Hotel has a clinic catering specifically to sufferers.

For visitors, Arad makes an ideal base for touring the northern Negev, the Dead Sea, and the wild Judaean hills. The **Visitor Information Center** is well informed on local antiquities and desert walks. Next door, the **Arad Museum►** (*Open* Sun–Thu 9–5, Fri morning. *Admission: moderate*) displays collections of finds from nearby **Tel Arad►** (see page 250). Around the edge of the town are several Bedouin encampments where, despite the unrelieved aridity of the area, sheep and goats are somehow grazed. The Bedouin, who have very good relations with the locals, find casual work in the town.

►► Avdat National Park *224B4*

Open: daily, summer 8–5; winter 8–4. Admission: expensive
The walled, ruined desert city of Avdat stands on a rocky ridge of high ground just off the main Negev interior road (Route 40), 40 miles from Beersheva. Constructed in 300 BC by the Nabateans (who called it Obodas, after a king they worshipped as a god), it flourished under Roman and Byzantine rule, but—having become a Christian settlement—was abandoned following the Arab conquest in the 7th century. The town has survived remarkably well and has benefited from sensitive and intelligent restoration. It retains superb relics of each period in its history, especially the Roman era, with remnants of streets, dwellings, water cisterns, houses, a Roman bath, temples, basements, and wine cellars. Its irrigation system was studied by the Israelis in 1948 and successfully copied at new Negev settlements.

ARAD FESTIVAL
Arad's usual peace and quiet are broken in July for the huge neo-hippy and hippy-revival rock fest lasting nonstop for four days and four nights. About 200,000 visitors (most aged under 20) gather for round-the-clock Israeli rock and folk music. During the festival, some 120 performances are staged in the town or under the desert stars at nearby Masada.

OPENING TIMES
Opening times differ slightly from those in the north, and many sites remain open on the Sabbath. Museums and attractions in the south are usually open 8:30–4:30, with slightly shorter hours on Friday and Saturday.

Byzantine frieze, Avdat

Avdat's rock-cut wine cellars and basements

ABRAHAM FOUNDS BEERSHEBA
"And Abraham planted a tamarisk tree in Beer-sheba, and called there on the name of the Lord, the Everlasting God."
—Genesis 21:33

The Negev Museum, Beersheva

Abraham's Well

▶ Beersheva (Hebrew: Be'er Sheva) *224B5*

The capital of the Negev stands on the desert's flat northern edge, where irrigation and water conservation have dramatically reduced the aridity. The town's picturesque Turkish old quarter still has a slightly rough and dusty look. However, the sprawling newer neighborhoods around the town, which has mushroomed in the last 10 years and continues to grow rapidly (current population: 170,000), are fresh and modern, if less atmospheric. There is also a university and a desert research center. New Russian immigrants make up much of the population.

The town's roots run deep into the pages of the Bible. Cave dwellings of 4000 BC and an Israelite town of 1100 BC have been found 2.5 miles east at **Tel Sheva▶** (*Open* daily 9–5. *Admission free*) which has a museum. The patriarch Abraham settled at Beersheva and purchased a well for the price of seven lambs (*be'er sheva* means both "well of seven" and "well of the oath"). Here he was called by God to sacrifice his son Isaac, and here he drove out the Egyptian maidservant, Hagar, with his other son Ishmael, who grew up in the desert and married an Egyptian (Genesis 21 and 22). In the next generation, Jacob left Beersheva on his own journey to Egypt. Later, Beersheva was named the southern limit of the Land of Israel (Judges 20:1).

The **Old City▶▶** dates only from 1907, when the Ottoman Turks revived the town as a Bedouin market. After 1948, Jewish settlers were drawn to the place and developed it. Today it is an attractive area of the city, with pedestrian sections, sidewalk cafés, and a marked walking tour. The Old City runs to **Abraham's Well▶** (*Closed* Shabbat. *Admission free*). The well is an Ottoman invention, with no known connection to Abraham. In a former mosque off HaAtzmaut Street, the **Negev Museum▶▶** (*Open* Sun–Thu 10–5, Fri–Sat 10–1. *Admission free*) displays artifacts from the town's prehistoric origins.

The town's most interesting feature is the continuing Bedouin presence. However, the **Bedouin market▶▶**, held every Thursday, has been marred by tourism and modernization. Permanent **Bedouin encampments▶▶** can be seen south of the town: big, dark tents among which human beings, camels, and dogs go about their business together under the desert sky.

Abraham was a nomadic herdsman. To understand something of his way of life, and that of the other patriarchs, take a look at the Bedouin who still wander through the harsh desert scenery, far from food or water and accompanied only by a herd of animals that somehow find enough pasture to survive.

Tribal lands Just as the people of Israel comprised 12 tribes, so too are the Bedouin divided into several tribal subgroups, each with its own territory. In 1946, when the British created the Kingdom of Transjordan (now Jordan), almost 40 percent of its population were described as Bedouin. A report of that year stated: "There are constant seasonal migrations of the Bedouin from Transjordan into Palestine, from Arabia into Transjordan, and back again." The Bedouin are true native inhabitants of these uncultivated regions, former pagans who embraced Islam when it arrived in the 7th century.

Lifestyle Like Abraham, the "nomadic" Bedouin do not in fact wander constantly. They have home ground and they have seasonal territories in which they pasture their herds of sheep, goat, and camels. They move according to the seasons and the needs of their animals. Like Abraham, they live in spacious tents, in extended family groups. They are subject to their own tribal laws, enforced by their tribal sheik (chief), which the state recognizes as valid for minor disputes.

The future The official Israeli view of the Bedouin is that they should be housed in modern, well-equipped dwellings as soon as possible and be offered tempting alternatives to this ancient lifestyle. New Bedouin small towns and neighborhoods have thus come into existence. At the same time, Bedouin culture is changing spontaneously. Many tribes have started to erect their own stone dwellings for more permanent habitation on the desert margins. However, the nomadic way of life is enduring and adaptable, and it is unlikely that the Bedouin will be persuaded to abandon it altogether.

BEDOUIN ISRAELIS
Most Bedouin consider it in their interest to support the State of Israel. They distinguished themselves during the War of Independence and assisted the army in later wartime desert operations against neighboring Arab states.

Above: sociably gathered around a glowing fire
Left: preparing to move on

Pillars of salt

Floating free

THE DEPTHS
At 1,305 feet below true sea level, the shores of the Dead Sea are as low as you can get on the surface of the earth. It is said that the additional 1,300 feet or so of atmosphere filters out enough ultraviolet radiation to help prevent sunburn—but it is not worth running the risk of exposing yourself unnecessarily to find out whether this is true.

▶▶▶ The Dead Sea (Hebrew: Yam HaMelach) *224C6*

Dramatic rocky desert surrounds this blue lake, the saltiest on earth and located at the lowest point on earth, at more than 1,300 feet below sea level. It is so salty that the human body floats like a cork and you can sit in the water reading a newspaper. Try it—almost everybody else does!

The saltiest The Hebrew name means Salt Sea, and it is the high level of salts—nearly 10 times the proportion in the Mediterranean—that makes it the Dead Sea. Life is impossible in these weird waters. The Jordan trickles down from the Galilee to the Dead Sea, and gets no farther. The water evaporates, leaving minerals behind. The process has been going on for countless millennia, so the concentration of salt is greater than ever.

At its southern tip, mushroom-like excretions of minerals have formed a bizarre white landscape. This "salt" is not the table condiment variety, but is composed of a mass of minerals. Salt pans in the south draw off magnesium, potassium, and sulfates for a multimillion dollar industry. In this same location, the biblical cities of Sodom and Gomorrah, synonymous with moral decadence, were located. According to Genesis (18:16–19:29), when God determined to destroy the cities, he first allowed Lot to flee with his wife. She looked back with regret and was turned into a pillar of salt.

The healthiest The mineral-rich waters, together with hot springs, have given rise to a number of thriving spa resorts. These are nothing new: Cleopatra, Herod, and Solomon all visited the Dead Sea for a cure. Their naturally warm waters are a proven help in the treatment of skin and rheumatic problems. It is claimed that the water is beneficial even to healthy skin. Be careful, though, when taking a dip! The salts are painful to the eyes, lips, and mucous membrane. After bathing, the skin feels oily and sticky. Unless you are on a cure, it is far

Mineral-rich Dead Sea mud is good for the skin—and has entertainment value too!

more enjoyable to swim in a hotel pool. As a bonus, this arid zone is almost totally pollen-free—a boon for people with hay fever or respiratory complaints.

South to north The sea measures 47 miles from tip to tip, and is never more than 10 miles across. Half of the Dead Sea's western shore is in Israel's Negev region and half in Judaea. The eastern shore is in Jordan. At the southern tip, erstwhile Sodom has been reborn in different guise as **Sedom**, center of the mineral extraction industry. The bleak little hot-springs spa resort of **Zohar▶** stands on the shore just up the road. From here an empty, uninhabited coast road clings to the shore, with a salty desert plain (formerly under water) and mountains to the left. **Ein Bokek▶** is another small waterside spa resort with hotels and a beach. Beyond the turn for **Masada▶▶▶** (see page 242), there is the concrete and glass **Ein Gedi Spa▶**, with showers, beach access, and Dead Sea mud for sale. A little farther is **Ein Gedi▶▶**, a waterside bathing area.

Above it, **Ein Gedi Kibbutz▶▶▶**, established in the 1950s by concentration camp survivors in the harshest environment they could find, is now a comfortable and prosperous community. It has a popular "inn,"consisting of terraces of small, simple bedrooms in basic centers scattered about the attractive grounds. The self-service restaurant is of good standard. Most guests are here on spa cures. Ein Gedi's fantastic setting, and its amazing achievement—the lush, florid greenery of the kibbutz bursting from a hillside of barren red desert rock overlooking the Dead Sea—make it a remarkable place to stay. Below Ein Gedi, the **Nahal Arugot▶▶** and phenomenal **Nahal David▶▶▶** nature reserves both consist of desert gulleys with hiking trails running alongside their seasonal riverbeds (see side panel).

Beyond here, the road crosses into Judaea. The scene changes little, and there are no further developments or interesting sights on the road until the area of **Qumran▶▶** (see page 221), near the northern end of the Dead Sea.

NAHAL DAVID

In this nature reserve, a footpath follows the narrow *nahal* (seasonal watercourse), which flows with water and bursts with lush greenery in contrast to the barren rocky cliffs either side. After some 20 minutes the path reaches a lovely waterfall splashing down from high rocks. Turn back here, or take a steeper path to the top of the waterfall, which emerges from a spring, close to which there is a cavern, called Lovers' Cave, and some ancient temple ruins. For a longer walk, leaving most other visitors behind, continue up the *nahal* past two more springs and into the desert canyon beyond. A marked path in the "dry canyon" takes all day to complete; above the springs it can be moist and even muddy underfoot, and winter can bring flash floods. Several animal species thrive in the reserve: little hyrax (or rock rabbits) dash across the path, and there is an ibex observation point. Wild leopard live in the western part of the reserve, but are rarely seen.

Dolphin Reef

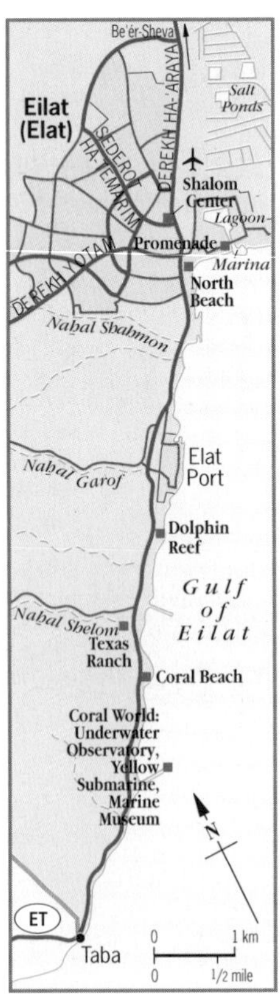

▶▶▶ Eilat 224B1

It's the location of Eilat (pronounced Ay-*lat*) that makes it so special. Jagged rose-tinted mountains rise up on three sides, forming ridge after ridge of barren rock fading back into scorched wilderness. In front lies the sea, reflecting those red peaks under a blue sky like shimmering silk. The desert air is warm and dry, and there is a sense of immense space, of enormous distances. Eilat feels like a land apart, separated from the rest of Israel not just by the Negev desert, or by time and distance, but also by attitude. It is alive, with a taste for pleasure and action. This southern outpost was, for years, a rough and ready place with a Wild West feel to it. Even though Eilat is now a civilized beach resort with a whole string of good hotels, the old pioneering spirit and taste for adventure linger on in the atmosphere, even in the look of the town. Even so, Eilat is not as new as it looks. It even gets a mention in the earliest books of the Bible, for Moses paused here with the Children of Israel when they were wandering in search of the Promised Land. They arrived here, but soon moved on again. Maybe that is why almost everything is open on the Sabbath: Eilat must be just about the least religious town in the whole of Israel.

The town center The heart of Eilat remains surprisingly small and undeveloped, with something of a "settlement" look. Even indoor shopping areas, such as the **Shalom Center▶**, do not rival those in other Israeli towns. In front of it is a plaza with dozens of café tables. Mingling with the locals you will still see a few tough, tanned outdoor types—some have driven in from desert kibbutzim. To discover the finer things in life, look in the hotels and in the beach areas, a little separated from the rest of town.

North Beach Within easy walking distance of the town center, Eilat's main leisure district is **North**

Beach▶▶▶, which runs along the tip of the warm Gulf of Eilat (or Gulf of Aqaba). The beach is of mixed sand and pebble, lined by palm and tamarisk trees, as well as bars and water-sports rental shops. Running alongside is a very pleasant paved promenade, lined for most of its length by good restaurants. North Beach ends at the **marina and lagoon▶▶**. A hump-backed pedestrian bridge crosses the water to another promenade area, which turns to follow the lagoon waterside, with shops and eateries alongside. Most of Eilat's leading and popular hotels are clustered around here. On the seafront beyond North Beach, the two **New Lagoons▶▶** include a swimming lagoon with beaches. The **Royal Promenade▶▶** pushes the resort eastward toward the Jordan border, via the Royal Beach and Dan hotels.

Coral Beach To find Eilat's marine nature reserve, drive out of town and down the Taba road on the western shore of the Gulf. Pass by the **Red Sea Star** restaurant, standing in (and below) the water (*see Restaurants, page 283*). Just after the port is **Dolphin Reef▶▶** (*Open* daily 9–5), a delightful pay-to-enter sand and pebble bay with an enjoyable beach bar-restaurant. There are also several large enclosures in which you can "swim with the dolphins." Or, if you prefer, you can watch from floating pontoons as the endearing dolphins—along with sea lions and turtles—frolic in the water. Farther down the road, on the right, is the **Texas Ranch▶** (*Admission: moderate*), a mock Wild West town that children will enjoy. Just south, the pay-to-enter **Coral Beach▶▶▶** (*Open* summer, daily 9–6; winter 9–5) and its offshore waters form an unusual

PETRA AND AQABA
With the opening of Eilat's Arava border crossing into Jordan, Petra makes a superb excursion. The amazing desert capital of the Nabateans, with its temples, treasury, tombs, amphitheater, and monastery all cut out of the pink sandstone cliffs, can be visited with an overnight stop. Allow time to linger in Aqaba, Eilat's unassuming neighbor on the Red Sea shore, and an entirely nontouristic Arabian town. Inclusive trips from Eilat are bookable through all hotels.

Artistic efforts point the way

Bring the children to Texas Ranch

and important nature reserve, a magnificent underwater garden of coral and warm-water fish (see page 236). This is one of the world's leading sites for diving and snorkeling. A visitor center on the beach is geared up to deal with divers' needs and give instruction (for children too). Marked "paths" under the water lead around the coral reef.

At the southern end of Coral Beach is **Coral World▶▶▶** (tel: 07 637 6666. *Open* Sat–Thu 8:30–5, Fri 8:30–3. *Admission: expensive*), the major Eilat attraction. This comes in several sections, with a recommended route indicated by directional arrows. First come the large and impressive aquariums, including a circular reef tank which visitors view from the middle, and a shark pool.

Coral Beach gives access to the underwater coral reserve

View the creatures of the deep by submarine or underwater observatory

An outdoor pool contains turtles and rays. The walkway then reaches the superb **Underwater Observatory▶▶▶**. This is no ordinary tourist attraction, and should not be missed. Spiral steps descend to viewing areas, where you can literally walk around under the sea, peering through thick windows at a seabed heaving and moving with strange life forms, like a bizarre jungle. There are no barriers or nets to keep the fish in. What you see is really living out there. The Observatory also rises high above the waves, giving magnificent views across the gulf, to the red mountains of Jordan and Saudi Arabia.

Also available at the Observatory, the **Oceanarium▶** (tel: 07 637 6666. *Open* daily) is a virtual trip beneath the waves—a three-screen simulator where spectators move in hydraulically operated seats while watching a spectacular audiovisual show. For the real thing, a trip in the **Yellow Submarine▶▶**, called *Jacqueline* (Mon–Sat from 9 AM. Check in 45 minutes before boarding), takes visitors on a one-hour journey beneath the Red Sea, giving a close-up view of the exotic underwater world. The 75-foot-long, 10-foot-wide submarine descends to a depth of 200 feet, then gradually climbs to 100 feet, beside the coral reef wall.

Finally, walk through the intriguing **Marine Museum▶** for a closer look at some of the species that live here.

Taba The coast road continues from Eilat to the Egyptian frontier, established in 1989 after a long dispute over its location. The beach along this stretch is poor and the location bleak, though the views are dramatic. The Princess Hotel just before the crossing, is one of Eilat's most remarkable resort complexes. The hotel dining room has a huge glass wall that nearly touches the desert's mountainside.

Crossing the border is a nuisance and can sometimes be time-consuming, with queues of backpackers and the usual careful security procedures. On the other side is the Hilton Hotel, constructed when Taba was in Israeli hands. It has a private beach, and hotel guests have special arrangements that speed up the border crossing.

ISRAELI FOLKLORE
Since Israel is hardly a half-century old, its "folklore" is necessarily something of a recent invention, but simple traditional Jewish dances and shows based upon Jewish themes and customs are a popular entertainment. The weekly Israeli Folklore Evening at Kibbutz Eilot, 2 miles from town, makes a good night out. It is held every Saturday evening, and the price includes a typical kibbutz buffet dinner, free drinks, and transportation from Eilat to the kibbutz, as well as a singing-and-dancing extravaganza under the desert stars.

The greatest treasure of Eilat is the water itself. Beneath its surface lies a whole spectacular world of color and coral, home to thousands of exotic fish, looking like rainbow fragments. For a closer encounter, dive in: the water is gorgeously warm (constantly around 70°F). No wonder this is a world capital for scuba and snorkeling.

MARINE RESERVE
Coral Beach is managed by Israel's Nature Reserves Authority. The area was studied over a period of years following the creation of the State of Israel, and declared a nature reserve in 1964.

Dali-esque fish drift among the vividly colored foliage. Tiny silver shoals like iron filings dart past as if toward a magnet. There are fish with pink dots, blue stripes, yellow patches, and long feathery spikes. Is that a plant, a fish, or just a stone lying on the bottom? Seemingly all three, and it is called a stone fish. Whether for experts, amateurs, or complete novices, diving at Eilat is a remarkable experience, and one not to be missed.

The reserve The Gulf of Eilat (or Aqaba), part of the Red Sea, is among the northernmost extensions of tropical ocean. The Eilat coral reef is the most northerly in the world. Starting just below the surface of the warm, lapping waters, the coral reef is 3,900 feet in length, reaches to within 35 feet of the high-tide line, and drops 20 feet to the seabed at its farthest edge. The reserve extends out from this point on to the densely populated seabed, where thousands of species of tropical fish and other sea animals can be seen.

Sea life The surface of a coral reef is a mass of living animals (mainly stony corals), while the rest consists of fossilized or dead corals from previous generations. The corals live for hundreds of years, growing at an incredibly slow rate, as they expand the existing colony or create new ones. Living among the hard corals are several species of soft coral, looking like brightly colored seaweeds, their delicate tendrils waving to and fro.

Eilat's coral reefs throng with colorful fish

Pretty as they are, corals can be dangerous, and it is best to avoid being scratched by them. One variety called fire coral (not a true coral but a similar life form) gives a burning sting that marks the skin. Sharing the seabed with the corals are weird mollusks and other invertebrates, such as giant clams and sea anemones. Other plantlike animals move around at night, including the sea lilies, sea urchins, and different kinds of starfish that hide during the

SCUBA RENTAL
Scuba equipment can be rented from several firms in Eilat, mostly along the Coral Beach area. The tourist office and most hotels have the names of diving rental companies.

WARNING
Wear sneakers or plastic shoes in the water. Swim, don't walk, except where indicated on marked pathways. Don't touch anything at all underwater, whether it seems to be a plant, fish, animal, or rock. Some of these are in fact highly venomous creatures whose poison can injure or kill.

Diving at Eilat (left) leads to close encounters with Dali-esque fish (below)

day. Day and night, the coral throngs with dazzlingly hued fish. Pretty damsels and clowns, butterflies and parrots, blues and cleaners can be seen during the day, while darkness brings out the uglier, highly poisonous varieties, such as the lion, scorpion, and stone fish. Most coral-dwelling fish are exceptionally thin, enabling them to slip in and out of the coral construction.

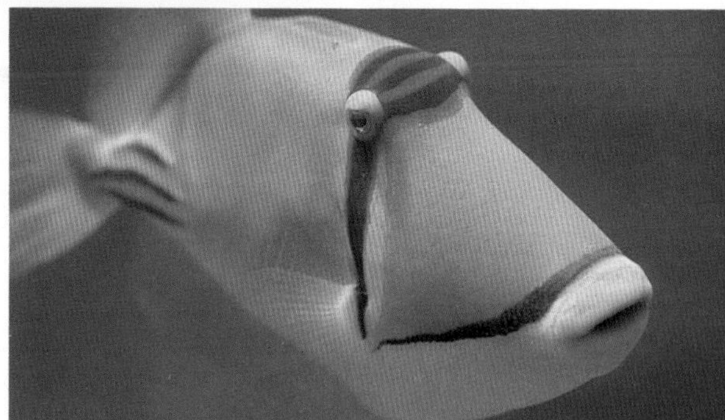

Snorkel and scuba It is possible to get a good look at all these creatures without even getting wet, from the Underwater Observatory (see page 235), the Red Sea Star restaurant (see page 283), or on a glass-bottomed boat tour. For a more intimate look, get in the water at the Coral Beach marine reserve (see page 233–234), one of the best places anywhere in the world for diving. If you want to scuba dive, bring certification card and log book in order to rent equipment. If you wish to learn, bring a medical certificate.

The Negev is no theme park. This is raw and dangerous wilderness, yet majestic and beautiful. No visit to southern Israel would be complete without an off-road excursion into this haunting, rocky terrain. The best introduction is by guided tour in a four-wheel-drive jeep—desert tours and excursions are referred to as "safaris".

WALKING IDEAS
Experienced hikers thinking of tackling a short outing in the southern Negev should ask the tourist office for its free booklet *Routes and Trails in Eilat Mountains.*

If you are hungry for something challenging, rest assured that an all-day trip into the desert, even with a group and a guide, will be something to remember. The vehicles do not offer pampered luxury. The ride is rough, entailing a certain amount of clinging on for dear life. As if that were not enough, there are two-day, even three-day trips, with nights spent under the stars. Trips on horseback, or even by camel, are available. It is also possible to see the desert on foot, perhaps combined with jeep touring; for this, it is even more important to have an experienced guide, except on short marked trails.

Desert encounter On closer inspection, you'll see that the desert is not totally barren. Isolated acacia trees spring from the solid rocks, red-berried mistletoe clings to the branches. Tiny sandbirds dart about. Ibex sprint with ease up near-vertical cliff faces. Caper bushes hang from granite clefts: the edible part is the flower bud, but the caper fruit can be eaten too—it tastes like mustard and, so Bedouin say, improves virility.

Desert safaris reveal that life exists in the wilderness

Around Eilat A quick four-wheel-drive trip into the desert is a popular excursion for Eilat tourists. There are outings that last an hour or two, all morning or all day. Most jeep tours, or "desert safaris," make their way into the wilderness from the Coral Beach area. There is plenty to see, even within just a few minutes: the incongruous, lush spring of **Ein Netafim▶▶** where animals and birds gather; the vivid sandstone of the amazing **Red Canyon▶**, where there is an easy one-hour marked hiking trail between the rock

The majestic landscape of Sde Boker

faces. **Mount Yoash** offers a panoramic view reaching into four countries—Israel, Egypt, Jordan, and Saudi Arabia. Either do-it-yourself or guided trips on noisy "fun buggies"—small motorized all-terrain vehicles—can be a lot of laughs, but you will miss out on the magic, silence, and beauty of the real desert experience.

The Arava Part of the Syrian-African Rift, the Arava is a deep lowland at the eastern edge of the Negev, marking the border with Jordan. A main road runs along it from Eilat to the Dead Sea, and offers the easy way to penetrate the desert while staying on a modern highway, virtually free of traffic. Sights along the way include **Timna▶▶** (see page 251) and, just a little farther north, the **Hai Bar Reserve▶▶** (see page 240). For the more intrepid, there are several simple-to-follow three- to four-hour walking trails that follow desert canyons, signposted off the road, such as **Wadi Sh'horet▶▶**, **Nahal Barak▶▶**, and the **Amran Valley▶▶**. Be aware, though, of current flash flood warnings.

Central Negev Several firms, notably the excellent market leader, Desert Shade (tel: 07 335377), run a range of long and short off-road drives. Some combine with walks through the immense and magnificent Makhtesh Ramon crater. Near Mitzpe-Ramon, you will find Nabatean and Roman ruins, strange flora, the tracks of strange fauna, and other-worldly scenery. Other trips through the desert go to Avdat, the ruined Nabatean city, and to Sde Boker, the desert kibbutz where former Prime Minister David Ben-Gurion once lived. It can be cool in these higher regions in winter, and snow in winter is not unknown.

Eastern Negev Walks and drives from Ein Gedi include explorations of the Dead Sea hinterland and hikes up the steep, stony footpath to Masada (see page 242). There is also a great hike from Ein Gedi along the enclosed valley trail of the Nahal Arugot Nature Reserve to a waterfall and pool in the midst of desert.

TAKE WATER!
On any trip into the Negev, summer or winter, it is essential to carry adequate supplies of drinking water—you will need about one quart per person for every hour spent in the desert.

GET BACK TO WHERE YOU ONCE BELONGED
"At all times one should live in Israel, and not live outside Israel, even in a place the majority of whose population is Jewish."
—Maimonides, *The Laws of Kings* (5:9–12), 1197

"I call upon you, our brothers and sisters in the Diaspora, to send your children here."
—Ezer Weizman, President of Israel, Independence Day speech, 1997

The upper Zin ravine, cut by the Ein Avdat

►► Ein Avdat National Park 224B4

(tel: 07 655 5684)

Open: daily, summer 8–5; winter 8–4. Admission: moderate

The Ein Avdat, or Avdat Spring, runs through the upper Zin ravine in the midst of the Negev. To either side, the ravine walls rise to crests of striking white chalk and dark flint. The spring and its surroundings form an oasis bursting with plant life surrounded by harsh, spectacular aridity. Trees even grow in places around the spring, and at the head of the ravine there is a single 250-year-old pistachio tree. Desert animals and birds gather here for food and drink. Two marked walks provide an opportunity to explore the area thoroughly. The longer route involves some steep climbing and the use of metal ladders. The shorter walk is much easier, but takes in all the main sights.

DINNER GUESTS

Numerous guided trips in the desert offer dinner or tea in a real Bedouin tent with a real Bedouin playing host. The Bedouin consider the whole thing just a game in which they win a few shekels from the gullible tourists, and the experience bears little resemblance to an authentic encounter with nomads. For all that, it is interesting and enjoyable to sit on the floor in a huge tent, eating meat and pita bread or being poured a cup of tea by a Bedouin in full traditional attire.

►► Hai Bar Reserve 224B2

(tel: 07 637 6018)

Open: Sun–Thu 8:30–5, Fri–Sat 8:30–4. Admission: moderate

On the Arava road, 22 miles north of Eilat, a side road on the right leads to this curious desert enclosure that mixes nature reserve and zoo, combining entertainment with serious conservation. Visitors may only explore the reserve by means of guided minibus tours, which include a walk. Most or all of the desert creatures that can be seen, have at some time been native to the Negev. The reserve's objective is to breed these animals for reintroduction into the wild, and to disperse some species throughout Israel's other 280 nature reserves. Many of the species here are not usually found in zoos and most visitors will never have come across them before. For example, you will see the ongar (or Asiatic wild ass), an elegant, nervous little wild donkey like a miniature horse. Also to be seen is the gray Somalian wild ass, precursor to the donkey and the antelope-like oryx and white oryx, that can live for prolonged periods without any water at all. The walk takes you through small carnivore enclosures, where the species include the lovely fennec, like a little golden fox, the sand cat, the ancestral wild cat, and the caracal, like a small lioness. There are also lynxes, wolves, hyenas, and leopards, as well as snakes, lizards, and birds of prey.

▶ Mamshit (Arabic: Kurnub) *224B5*

(tel: 07 655 6478)
Open: daily 8–5. Admission: moderate

Mamshit is the most northerly of the five walled and fortified Negev cities of the Nabateans, located 4 miles from Dimona, southeast of Beersheva. Mamshit was changed little during the Roman and Byzantine periods, and so preserves many elements of its original character. The fine, pale stone ruins still possess a certain grandeur. At Mamshit, there are remnants of the main street, houses, arched lintels, stables, an imposing flight of steps, and two Byzantine churches. Several tomb chambers have been excavated at the cemetery outside the town.

The nearby Camel Ranch is a fun desert-encounter and resort base, providing accommodations in a Bedouin tent. Bedouin hosts entertain with good food and traditional music. Guests can set off with guides to explore the desert by jeep, camel, or on foot.

A well-camouflaged caracal

OVER THE BORDER
The Negev continues, across the Egyptian border into the Sinai, where several intriguing sights can be found within easy reach of Eilat. Highlights are Ein Hudra (a beautiful oasis), the Nawamis (well-preserved Bronze Age burial sites), St. Catherine's Monastery, and Mount Sinai. In the other direction, trips can be made to Petra, the rock-carved Nabatean desert capital (see page 233).

Mountaintop Masada

►►► Masada National Park 224C5

(tel: 07 658 4207)
Admission: expensive

A ruined mountaintop fortress in the desert overlooking the Dead Sea, Masada has become a potent symbol for the state and people of Israel (see side panel opposite). Israeli soldiers are sworn in here with the words, "Masada shall not fall again."

Reaching the top the easy way

Reaching the site From the parking lots, visitors climb dusty Snake Path to the mountaintop—the walk taking about an hour. Alternatively, a cable car carries visitors up the mountain, a marvelous ride with magnificent views, leaving but 80 steps to be climbed to the site entrance.

History The small Hasmonean fort at Masada assumed its present form under King Herod (40–4 BC), who constructed the palaces and fortifications as a desert retreat. He did not make use of it, but a Roman garrison was always stationed here. In AD 66, the knife-bearing Sicari, or Zealots, captured Masada from the Romans at the start of the First Jewish Revolt (AD 66–73). As the revolt was crushed in other parts of the country, Zealots made their way here. Eventually the Romans besieged Masada with 15,000 men, and traces of their camps can be seen at the foot of the mountain. The Zealots and their families numbered about 967. The Romans built a ramp up the western side of the mountain and breached the wall on the first day of Pesach in the year AD 73. They found everyone dead, except for one woman and her children.

She related what had occurred. When defeat seemed

inevitable, the Zealot leader, Ben-Yair, made a rousing speech praising death above defeat and dishonor. Ten men were selected by lot to kill everyone else. Every family group lay down together, and all were killed. Finally the 10 killed each other, one last man killing himself. She alone had decided to choose life.

The Romans occupied Masada again briefly. Byzantine monks resided here in the 5th and 6th centuries, after which the site was abandoned.

Visiting the site Snake Path Gate passes through the citadel's original guardroom into the site, which consists of a vast space open to the sky, steep and rocky in places, with several ruined structures, the whole encircled by ramparts. A black line on the structures shows the height that remained standing until reconstruction work began in the 1980s. Turn right to follow the fortifications; the walls here are low, giving an impressive view across the flat red and white terrain to the Dead Sea. You will reach a small **quarry▶**, spacious **storerooms▶**, that held a year's supply of stores in big jars, and a **lookout▶▶**. Just beyond, projecting northward on a rocky crag, is the **Northern Palace▶▶▶**, Herod's immense private dwelling. Built on three levels, it retains corridors with several large and small rooms leading off. There is also a splendid **bathhouse▶**, with traces of mosaic and frescoes, and several hot and cold pools. In front of the bathhouse, the **upper terrace▶▶** of the Northern Palace villa gives a fantastic view.

The marked path next follows the perimeter of Herod's Northern Palace, above a vertiginous precipice. From here the **Roman ramp▶▶** can be seen (on the Arad side). Leaving the palace on the southwestern side, there is an **administration building▶** and a **mikveh▶** (ritual bath), close to the **storerooms' watchtower▶▶▶**, which gives a clear overall impression of the site.

Now follow the western rampart wall, where there are a number of interesting structures, including a 2,000-year-old **synagogue▶**, the oldest ever found. The **observation point▶** here marks the point where the Roman ramp reached the citadel. This is close to the Byzantine western gate, the point of entry for walkers from the Arad side (the walk up the ramp takes 20 minutes). The **Western Palace▶▶** here has a complex of small rooms, including baths, with mosaic decoration. Close by is a small Byzantine **church▶**.

A longer tour through the large, open southern section of the citadel reaches **bakeries▶**, **large pools▶** for bathing, a neat, circular **columbarium▶** (or dovecote), and a **water cistern▶**, probably all of the Herodian period.

Roman underfloor heating

VISITING MASADA

Signs for Masada lead from near the southern end of the Dead Sea and from the desert town of Arad (28 miles east of Beersheva). It can be approached from either direction, but both roads end at parking lots at the foot of the mountain (after visiting Masada you must return the way you came). Here, stores, eating places, and restrooms are available. A visit to the site takes several hours. Recommended routes around the site are marked. It is a good idea to wear a sunhat and take drinking water. Masada is open daily from dawn to dusk. Walk up, or take the cable car (operates from 8 till 4).

HISTORY LESSON UNDER THE STARS

A son et lumière in the extraordinary setting of Masada is as dramatic as you might expect. Using the latest in light and sound techniques, the show is staged in an amphitheater at the foot of the Masada mountain and brings to life the story of the citadel from Herod's construction to the Roman conquest. The amphitheater lies on the Arad side of Masada, and the show takes place every Tuesday and Thursday in summer at 9 PM.

That Israel has "made the desert bloom" is a cliché. Before Israel was created, much of this land was tough stony heathland, swamp, and dunes. Travelers in the 19th century spoke of the appalling poverty of the land. Early Zionists set themselves the task of reclaiming it, draining the Hula, planting the hills of Galilee and Carmel, and irrigating the Negev.

ISRAEL IN THE TIME OF PLENTY
"For the Lord thy God bringeth thee into a good land, a land of brooks of water, of fountains and depths that spring out of valleys and hills; a land of wheat, and barley, and vines, and fig trees, and pomegranates; a land of olive oil and honey; a land wherein thou shalt eat bread without scarceness, thou shalt not lack any thing in it."
—Deuteronomy 8:7–9

Milk and honey Was Israel ever a land of milk and honey? When the British took it over from the Turks, it consisted largely of infertile and arid terrain, supporting a total population of under 700,000, most of whom scraped the most meager of livings. Yet the Bible records that 3,500 years ago fields of grain, vineyards, and oak forests ran from Jerusalem to the sea. It seems likely that, as the generations passed, more and more forest was cut down to make way for fields. Without the tree cover to bind the soil, storms washed the surface away. Overgrazing by sheep and goats made it difficult for trees to reestablish themselves, and the land became impoverished.

Reclamation The British and the early Zionists together started the process that proved the land could be drained, improved, planted, and cultivated—or, in Zionist terminology, redeemed. The new State of Israel continued the task of reclaiming poor land. Kibbutzim and *moshavim*—communal settlements whose occupants were usually willing to undertake difficult tasks for little reward—played a vital role in this process, and still do. Scientific research has also contributed. The Rothschilds brought in agronomists from the south of France to help replant the Carmel as a vineyard region. Millions of trees have been planted by the Jewish National Fund.

The rewards These efforts have paid off. Israel is now completely self-sufficient in agriculture, and exports large quantities of produce. Previously uncultivated areas are now intensively farmed. The range of crops grown is astonishing, with bananas, apples, avocados, and oranges growing alongside each other. The Sharon Plain has become one of the world's most productive citrus regions. Galilee farmers have prospered with terraced fields of grain. Cotton, cereals, and beet thrive in the

Top: corn, vetch, and poppies—typical roadside wildflowers
Right: turf production

Jezreel Plain. The sunbaked Arava, on the Negev border with Jordan, supports thousands of acres of tomatoes and vegetables. Vineyards again flourish on the slopes of Mount Carmel. Careful planning, mechanization, and skillful use of water account for much of the success.

Water, water everywhere All over Israel, the land is being irrigated, mostly by the underground drip-feed system, which was invented here and is now used all over the world. The system allows tiny drops of water to cover a wide area, being channeled directly to the roots of crop plants. This process makes maximum use of a scarce resource—and water is very scarce indeed. The National Water Carrier pumps water from the Sea of Galilee to reservoirs all over the country. New reservoirs are always being built. Forty new reservoirs, built mainly to catch storm runoff, have been constructed in the Beit She'an and Jordan valley areas, south of the Sea of Galilee. Much of the water used for irrigation is brackish—not clean. It has been found that this actually yields much better results.

Natural riches Land reclamation is not all about agriculture. Israel has some 300 nature reserves and an extraordinary variety of flora and fauna, with more than 2,000 plant species, hundreds of types of resident birds, and almost 100 different kinds of native animals. By setting aside over 600 square miles for wildlife reserves, it is hoped that this abundance and diversity will flourish throughout the country.

MILK AND HONEY
"If the Lord delight in us, then he will bring us into this land, and give it us; a land which floweth with milk and honey."
—Numbers 14:8

Ben-Gurion University research station: testing the tolerance of various plants

The road south of Mitzpe-Ramon crosses the floor of the huge Makhtesh, or crater

▶▶ Mitzpe-Ramon *224B4*

Mitzpe-Ramon means "Ramon Viewpoint." The settlement was built in the 1950s in the optimistic belief that it would grow into a prosperous desert city. It hasn't yet, and remains a rather bleak one-horse town. It does, however, have one astonishing treasure: Ramon Viewpoint.

The Makhtesh The town has a setting that few places can rival, standing on top of a dramatic cliff with an extraordinary view, a sight that simply compels awe. Spread out below the cliff is the immense desert canyon called Makhtesh Ramon, or Ramon Crater. A *makhtesh* is a gigantic canyon-like crater formed not by a river but by huge natural cracks in the Earth's surface. At 154 square miles, it is the world's largest. On the far side, the canyon rises to barren mountainous uplands. The whole scene is raw, vast, and unspoiled. If standing in the open air, on the teetering brink of a 3,000-foot drop, does not appeal, go into the town's cliff top **Observatory and Visitor Center▶▶▶** (tel: 07 658 7392. *Open* Sun–Thu 9–5, Fri–Sat 9–4. *Admission: expensive*). This semicircle of glass, projecting over the cliff edge, gives a glorious opportunity to linger safely over the view. It also houses an excellent exhibition explaining what has been learned from the canyon, together with displays of what has been found in it, and an audiovisual show about its creation.

This gigantic cut in the surface of the globe has been uniquely valuable to geologists, providing a window into the planet's earliest history. The strata at the bottom of the canyon date from 200 million years ago, and successive bands of color on the cliffs show the eons rising to reach our own era. In its dizzying timescale, and in its sheer physical size, Makhtesh Ramon puts humanity into perspective.

HAMSIN
An annoying feature of the Negev climate is the Hamsin, the uncomfortably hot and dry wind that blows occasionally in April, May, September, and October. The name comes from the Arabic for fifty—supposedly the number of days the wind will blow once it starts.

Exploring the Makhtesh For rugged and experienced individualists, well equipped with maps, local knowledge, and plenty of drinking water, there are several hiking trails through the Makhtesh. For a safer adventure, with all the benefits of having an experienced and capable companion at your side, book a guided four-wheel-drive tour, which can be combined with a walk. On a Makhtesh tour, footpaths and tracks reveal the astonishing character of the terrain. One trip passes through a dazzling white limestone ravine, narrow and echoing, the rock slashed and riddled with holes by rough weather in seasons long past. Leopard tracks run across the paths, and multicolored lizards bask on the stones. Bedouin signs, made of stones or tied into a bush, are translated by your guide. Visiting the remnants of past civilization and the natural wonders within the Makhtesh is like finding lost treasure: such places lie all around, but are hard to locate without a guide. **En Saronim▶▶**, not far from the main road, is a 2,000-year-old caravansary. Such camel-train stopovers appear every 15 miles or so, the distance a loaded camel can walk in a day. Nearby is a gracefully arched water cistern, cool and fresh, which once held 28,000 gallons of water. It could still be used today. Another high point is **Ktsra▶▶**, a ruined Nabatean fortress; from the hills above, vistas open up across landscapes of sometimes formless chaos, a world of chalk and flint, black and white swirling shapes, ridges, edges, and clefts, leading to the incongruous sight of snow-covered peaks in Jordan.

Around the town Other sights nearby include the popular **Alpaca Farm▶** (*Open* daily 9–6. *Admission: moderate*), which makes for an interesting outing, entertaining for children. Not just alpacas, but llamas, angora goats, angora rabbits, camels, Pyrenean sheepdogs, and Welsh border collies are reared here. The animals are all harmless, though at times alpacas show their irritation by spitting at visitors!

DESERT DELIGHTS
Hikers in the desert should cover up against the sun and take care to avoid some of the less welcoming inhabitants: highly venomous yellow scorpions, vipers, black widow spiders, and the sand flea, whose bite is said to be able to kill a dog.

The view from Mitzpe-Ramon looks far across an awesome scene of arid desert

Israel lies at the junction of several important bird migration routes between Europe, Asia, and Africa. Literally millions of birds—including birds of prey, storks, and pelicans—pass overhead twice a year, between February and May, and September and November, and one of the best places to come for birds is Eilat.

TAKING TO THE AIR
It is possible to take wing yourself in a motor glider, arranged by Eilat's International Birdwatching Center (tel: 07 374276). With the engine turned off, you drift silently in the sky among the flocks, enjoying a close-up view of the migrating birds.

Bird highway More than 150 different species of bird pass through Israel on their migration routes. Bird-watchers recently counted 750,000 buzzards and eagles alone passing over Eilat—10 times as many as in the world's other great bird-watching area, the Bosphorus. The birds' main "corridor" is the Arava/Jordan Valley, which takes them from Eilat, via the Dead Sea, to the Galilee, after which the different species take different routes into Europe and Asia. The Arava/Jordan Valley forms part of the Syrian-African rift, which guides the birds between continents on their long journey. On reaching Eilat after the unbroken flight from Africa, millions of the smaller birds touch down for a rest on the salt pans beside Eilat and the fields of Kibbutz Eilot, 2 miles from town.

Watching the birds Free bird-watching walks depart from Eilat three times a week, led by a qualified guide. Held on Sunday, Tuesday, and Thursday, they start at 8:30 AM from Marina Bridge; bring a hat, water, and binoculars. The walks last three hours and follow an easy path via the beach to the extensive salt ponds and Kibbutz Eilot fields. For those who prefer to go on their own, a marked trail takes a similar route. The best times to watch bird life are early morning and late afternoon. Numerous small waders and waterfowl, plovers, and sandpipers, some migratory, some resident, will be seen. An interesting colorful bird to look for is the little green bee-eater. Coots, herons, stilts, and flamingos wade in the shallows. Birds of prey, such as kites and hawks, try to pick off the smaller birds. In the Eilot fields, wagtails, warblers, and pippits scamper down below, while millions of swallows and swifts fly overhead.

Pelicans (top); bird-watchers (below)

►► Sde Boker (Sedé-Boqér) *224B4*

This desert kibbutz attracted the attention of Israel's rugged, no-nonsense first Prime Minister, David Ben-Gurion. He and his wife, Paula, became members in 1953. The kibbutz itself is a hardworking community cultivating fields and orchards, and manufacturing adhesive tape. Members, totaling just a few hundred, live in plain white bungalows, some draped with dazzling purple bougainvillaea. The **Ben-Gurions' "hut"►►►** (tel: 07 656 0320. *Open* Sun–Thu 8:30–3:30, Fri 8:30–2, Sat 8:30–2:30. *Admission free*) was originally only slightly superior to those of the other kibbutzniks.

A guided tour of the house, unchanged since the 1960s, reveals the little details of this gigantic character. His library, for example, contains 5,000 volumes on every subject, yet not one novel. In the kitchen is a list, pinned up by Paula, detailing her husband's medication and menus. We see that the pair slept in separate—and very different—bedrooms, his stark and spartan, hers adorned with personal mementoes; a place where she sat dreaming of living somewhere more comfortable.

A 15-minute drive from the kibbutz, you will find **Ben-Gurion College►**, a center for desert studies and part of Beersheva University. Here, the college's solar energy center is open to the public. A pathway leads through a pretty, natural garden, to the **Burial Site of David and Paula Ben-Gurion►►►**. The tombs are marked by massive stone slabs, on a cliff top overlooking the Wilderness of Zin. Here is the barren heart of the Negev, where bleached cliffs plummet to a stony plain riven by wadis. **Ein Avdat►►** begins at the foot of the cliff (see page 240).

THE BEN-GURIONS AT SDE BOKER

Having visited Sde Boker in 1953, David Ben-Gurion wrote to the kibbutz expressing his huge admiration for the enterprise and his envy of the life of its members. Later the same year he retired from politics, age 67, and moved with his wife Paula to Sde Boker, both becoming kibbutz members. He was asked to return to public life in 1955 and agreed to do so, while remaining a kibbutz member. In 1968, Paula died, aged 76, and David returned to seclusion on the kibbutz. He died in 1973, aged 87, and was buried alongside Paula near Sde Boker.

David Ben-Gurion (left) and the cottage (below) to which he retired after 13 years as Israel's Prime Minister

BEN-GURION'S DREAM
"It is possible to settle even millions of Jews in the Negev. Some day two million can be settled there based on agriculture. If so, another three million can be based on industry."
—David Ben-Gurion, 1935

►► Shivta (Subeita) 224A4

Free access

About 40 miles south of Beersheva, this impressive desert site was the only Nabatean city to escape being sacked and destroyed by the Arabs. Like others in the Negev Pentapolis (see page 226), the town was originally founded as a stopover on the Nabatean caravan route to Petra. It was taken over and improved by the Romans, later occupied and Christianized by the Byzantines. By the 4th century it had become a substantial community, despite the arid setting, thanks to the Nabateans' knowledge of water conservation. It continued to thrive until the Muslims invaded in the 7th century and settled here without causing much damage to the existing structures. However, as Nabatean know-how on water and irrigation was lost, the town went into decline and was abandoned completely in the 9th century. Shivta's location, well away from roads, enabled it to survive the centuries relatively unscathed. Buildings survive up to two or even three stories high, each with its water cistern. You can also see a wine press, paved streets, three churches with marble-clad walls, and a mosque.

DESERT FRUITS
Scientists at Ben-Gurion University are working with Negev farmers to use brackish water from deep desert aquifers. The water, previously thought unusable, is proving highly effective for fish farms, tomatoes, and exotic new crops like argan. Argan yields cooking oil, and pitaya is an edible cactus fruit that Israel has started selling to European supermarket chains.

► Tel Arad National Park 224C5

Open: Sun–Thu 8–4, Fri morning. Admission: inexpensive

Some 20 minutes' drive west of the new city of Arad, these remnants of a walled Canaanite and Israelite settlement of 3500–1500 BC lie on a desert hillside set back from the road. This was already an old, handsome, wealthy city when its king joined the struggle to keep Moses and the Children of Israel out of Canaan. Later, Israelite settlements on the site were smaller and simpler. Tel Arad's setting is glorious: gentle, undulating sand and rock, speckled by the dark tents of the Bedouin who administer the site. Ruins of streets, houses, wells, sacrificial altars, a synagogue, and a palace uncovered in two separate excavation areas, vividly illustrate desert life in those times. From here modern Arad looks like a striking blanket of green thrown over the desert.

Timna National Park

Temple used by Egyptian miners, the first to exploit Timna's mineral wealth

►► Timna National Park *224B1*

(tel: 07 637 2542)
Open: daily 7:30–5. Admission: expensive

Renowned as one of the great Arava copper mines of ancient times, Timna was once known as King Solomon's Mines. It is now a huge area (23 square miles) of desert scenery and historic ruins set around the dry Wadi Timna and edged by a semicircle of hills. Lying off the main Arava highway, 20 miles north of Eilat, and reached by a long access road, Timna National Park is desert pure and simple consisting of bare red sandstone and limestone with a few acacia trees and tumbleweed, though an artificial lake has been added as an extra diversion for visitors.

About a mile into the park, turn right to the **mushroom rock►**, so called for its shape, and the **copper smelting plant►**, which dates from the 14th century BC and belonged originally to the Egyptians. Dwellings, workshops, and stores survive, and a temple site of the same period nearby was probably built for the use of miners.

Continuing, the road reaches the extensive **copper mines►►►**, characterized by sandstone arches, caverns, shafts, and tunnels. Archeological work in the 1960s showed that copper had been worked here as long ago as 3000 BC. The Bible records that Solomon exported copper

ISRAEL'S FLAG

Israel's national flag is the same as the Zionist flag raised at the First Zionist Congress in 1897. The design, worked out by David Wolfsohn, subsequently World Zionist Organization president, simply placed the Star of David in the center of a Jewish prayer shawl. "That is how our national flag came into being," he said. "And no one expressed any surprise or asked whence it came, or how."

COPPER AT TIMNA
The name King Solomon's Mines is misleading because, although Solomon exploited this and other mines, Timna was known and used many centuries before (and after) his reign. Copper mining continued at Timna under the Romans, and the Arabs also extracted from the site. Mining was resumed here from 1958 to 1976, but proved unviable. In 1980, copper mining started again at another site about a mile south of Timna, and the mine is still in operation.

YOTVATA IN THE CITY
Sweet and savory yogurts, chocolate milk, flavored cream cheeses...
If you are fond of Yotvata's imaginative milk products, you can also enjoy them in Tel Aviv and Haifa, at the excellent Kibbutz Yotvata restaurants on the waterfront.

from a port at Ezion-geber (near Eilat), and derived great wealth from the proceeds. In a crevice at the bottom of a cliff, reached by means of rock-cut steps from the mine, **rock drawings►►**, attributed to 12th-century BC Egyptians and Midianites, depict war scenes in which charioteers and archers fight with men armed with axes and shields.

The road continues to the artificial lake. Here is a restaurant and picnic area. Beyond is the most enjoyable feature of the park, the natural phenomenon known as **King Solomon's Pillars►►►**. Having nothing to do with Solomon, these rocky structures result from the erosion of a 165-foot-high sandstone hill, at the foot of which, on the east side, is a 13th-century BC temple dedicated to Hathor. The pillars are gigantic columns forming just part of a jumble of weird and weather-beaten rocks, monumental in size and eroded to fantastic shapes, that can be climbed on, in, or through. Steps have been carved up the massive formations, sometimes by man, sometimes by centuries of wind. The red stone is covered with its own red dust. Openings between the rocks suddenly look out onto immense desert mountains and the dry plain. The latest attraction at Timna is **The Tabernacle►►►**, a full-size exact reconstruction of the Israelites' original tabernacle as they wandered in the desert after receiving the Torah. Every detail of the extraordinary portable structure comes from the precise description in the Book of Exodus. An accompanying multimedia show tells the Exodus story.

► Yotvata *224B2*

Many of Israel's favorite milk products come from Kibbutz Yotvata in the Negev desert. Many passersby on the Arava road stop here for a bite in the self-service **Yotvata Tourist Restaurant►**. There's a picnic area and a children's play area. At the **Yotvata Visitor Center►►** is a permanent exhibition on the flora and fauna of the Negev. Set back farther from the road is **Ye'elin Holiday Village►**, with a pool and pleasant chalet accommodations under the shade of acacia and palm trees. Ye'elin has its own big cafeteria, open to nonresidents, and is better than Yotvata's.

King Solomon's Pillars

Travel Facts

Arriving

Getting there

Entry formalities Visitors to Israel do not require a visa, but their passports must be valid for at least six months from the date of arrival. Travelers are normally granted a three-month stay. However, those entering by land from Egypt or Jordan may be allowed only one month (visitors wishing to stay longer must apply for a visa through the Ministry of the Interior; expect a certain amount of delay as Israeli bureaucracy is not fast-moving).

On arrival to and departure from Israel, be prepared for a longish wait at passport control. Allow plenty of time, security is a big issue in Israel, and every visitor is closely questioned by highly trained staff who will also carefully scrutinize all documents. Answer all questions frankly—and do not try to be humorous. For those traveling to or from Israel by air, this formality is usually performed as part of the check-in procedure. If you enter the country by private car, you will also be asked to empty the vehicle of all luggage and the vehicle will be searched. Cameras may be opened, so remove film before passing through security checks. An entry permit—form AL17—will be inserted in your passport, to be returned on departure.

By air Israel has two international airports. Ben Gurion lies 37 miles from Jerusalem and 12 miles from Tel Aviv (known as Tel Aviv Airport). Ovda is located in the Negev desert, about 40 miles from Eilat (bear in mind that Ovda offers few facilities).

El Al, Israel's national airline, offers regular nonstop departures from New York and several other cities in the United States and Canada. Although not always the cheapest option, many travelers choose nonstop El Al flights for security reasons. All the food served on board is kosher. A number of U.S. and other international major airlines also offer scheduled direct flights.

In addition, numerous charter airlines fly from European cities to Israel, many direct to Eilat. July and August, and the periods around the major Jewish and Christian festivals, are the most expensive times to travel to central and northern Israel; winter is the peak season for Eilat.

For details of all El Al flights, call:

- 120 West 45th Street, New York, NY 10036 (tel: 212/768-9200 or 1-800/223 6700).
- UK House, 180 Oxford Street, London W1N 0EL (tel: 020 7957 4100).

For details of all British Airways flights to Israel, call:

- British Airways New York (tel:1-800 AIRWAYS).
- British Airways Head Office, Waterside, PO Box 365, Middlesex UB7 7OGB (tel: 0845 779 9977).

Haifa, the biggest and busiest of Israel's ports

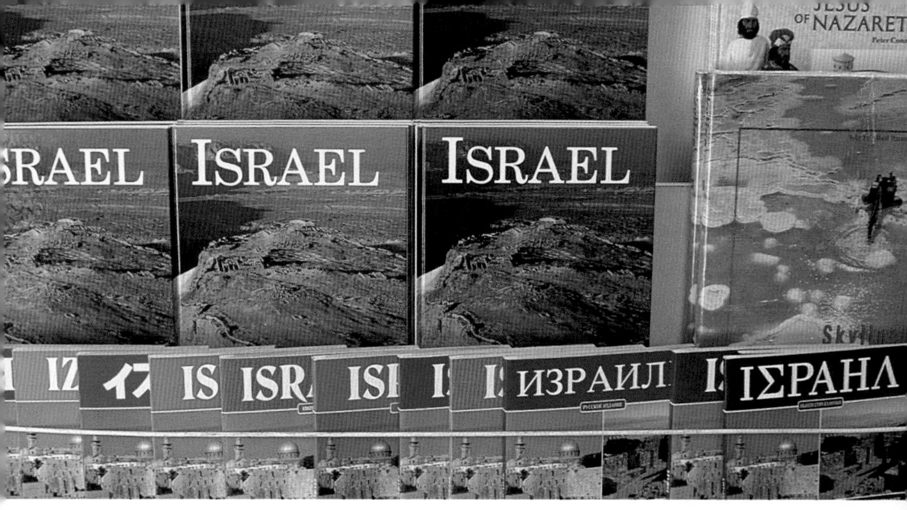

Catering to the visitors who come to Israel from all over the world

By sea Israeli ports feature in the itineraries of cruise ships. There are sailings from ports in Italy, Greece, and Cyprus to both Haifa and Ashdod. The popular sea route from Piraeus, in Greece, takes about 58 hours.

By land There is, as yet, no border crossing between Israel and either Lebanon or Syria. Travelers may cross to and from Egypt at Taba (Eilat). There are three crossing points between Israel and Jordan: Arava (just outside Eilat), the Allenby Bridge (east of Jerusalem), and Sheikh Hussein Bridge (south of the Sea of Galilee). Border procedures are slow, and exit fares are levied.

Departure Air travelers should reconfirm their reservations 72 hours before scheduled departure times. Those traveling with the airline El Al may reduce the long check-in time to just one hour by checking in their hold baggage at certain special El Al offices 24 hours before departure—most notably the office opposite the Tel Aviv North train station.

A departure tax is payable, and this is often included in the price of prepaid tickets. Where this is not the case, it is payable at check-in. Those arriving and departing from Eilat do not have to pay.

VAT repayments On leaving Israel, visitors may claim back VAT paid on individual purchases of greater than US$50 in value, paid for with non-Israeli currency (see Money Matters, page 258) at stores designated by the Ministry of Tourism and displaying a sign to this effect. The cash can be refunded on the spot in U.S. dollars through the Bank Leumi office located in the departure hall at Ben Gurion Airport, and at Haifa Port. The receipt must be produced and the goods should be packed in your hand luggage. At all other points of departure, the amount will be stamped in your passport and mailed to your home address.

The calendar

❑ No fewer than four separate calendars are in use in Israel—the Jewish and Muslim lunar calendars, plus the Julian and the more familiar Gregorian (Western) solar calendars. For everyday and business purposes, the last is used. The remaining three are mainly of religious significance. However, the terms AD (*Anno Domini*, the Year of Our Lord) and BC (Before Christ) are not used. Instead, years are measured as Before the Common Era or during the Common Era (BCE and CE). Fortuntely, the Common Era is deemed to have begun at the birth of Jesus, so there is no need for conversion. ❑

Essential facts

Climate

Climatic contrast is one of the striking features in Israel. The country compresses four climate zones into a space hardly bigger than New Jersey, ranging from Mediterranean to Saharan. All four can be experienced in a 20-minute drive through Judaea.

For much of Israel, the year is dominated by two seasons—the hot, dry summer and the cool, wet winter. January temperatures in Jerusalem can drop to around 40°F. The Galilee enjoys a short and delightful spring (in March and April) before the hills are slowly parched by the sun. Most of Israel's rainfall occurs between November and April, with the Mount Hermon area getting up to 40 inches a year. Eilat receives less than 2 inches.

The hottest areas are Eilat, with winter temperatures around 70°F, the Negev, the Jordan Valley below sea level, and the shores of the Sea of Galilee (in high summer) and the Dead Sea. A strong, dry, easterly wind—known as the Hamsin (see page 246)—blows during the brief spring, and again in the fall, raising temperatures as well as tempers.

Note that the relatively short days of winter, coupled with reliance on solar heating, can leave some accommodations rather chilly.

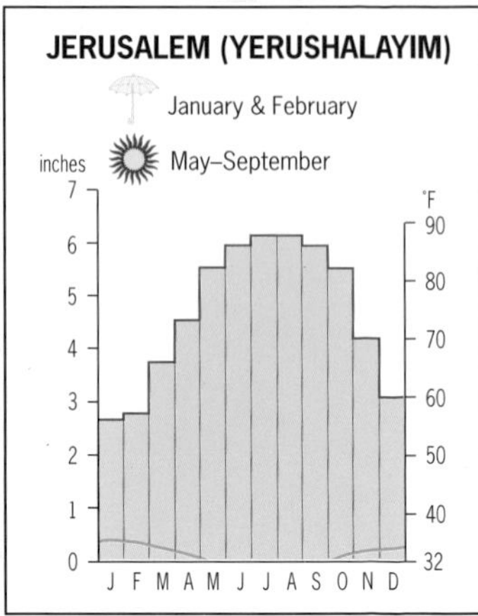

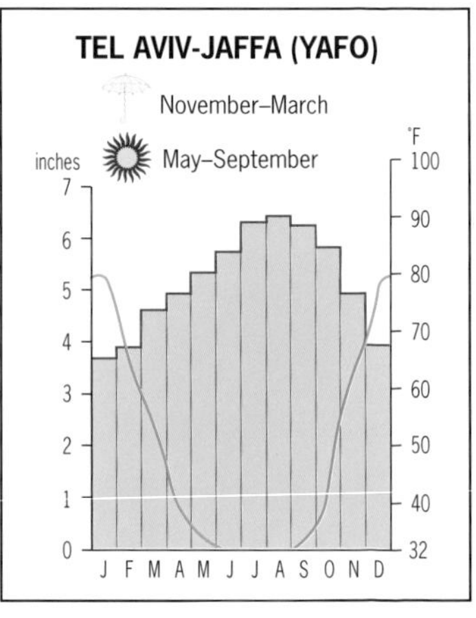

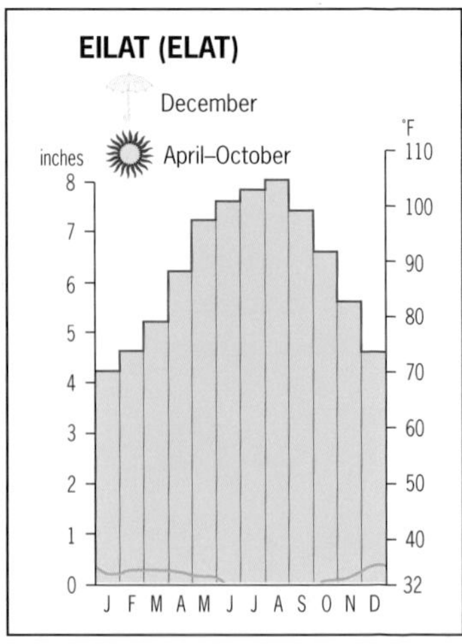

National holidays

The system of public holidays in Israel is complex, as there are Jewish, Christian, and Muslim festivals to be observed. Additionally, there are differences within the Christian community between the observance of Western churches (Roman Catholic and Protestant) and Eastern (Greek and Russian Orthodox and Armenian). Jewish, Muslim, and some Christian festivals are timed according to the lunar calendar, and their dates in the more familiar Gregorian calendar vary from year to year. It is well worth checking for festival dates before you depart for Israel, as a lot of time can be wasted while stores and services are closed. Tourist sites are also frequently affected.

The Jewish Sabbath (Shabbat) almost literally brings Israel to a standstill. The only exceptions to this are the southern resort of Eilat, where many businesses ignore the Sabbath, and, to a lesser extent, Tel Aviv. Elsewhere Jewish stores and services close on Friday afternoon and reopen on Saturday evening or Sunday morning. At these times, there is virtually no public transportation. If you are driving, you should avoid the ultra-orthodox areas of Mea She'arim, in Jerusalem, and Bnei Brak, near Tel Aviv, whose residents are hostile to Sabbath drivers. All Jewish festivals begin at sunset on the preceding day. Likewise, they end at sunset on the festival day. Christian stores and services generally close on Sunday. Muslim stores and services close on Friday.

The following list includes only those festivals when some or all stores and services will be closed. The dates are given according to the Gregorian (i.e. Western) calendar.

January 1 (New Year's Day, Western churches); January 6 (Epiphany); January 7 (Christmas, Eastern churches); January 14 (New Year's Day, Eastern churches); January/February (Muslim New Year); March/April (Good Friday and Easter Sunday); March/April (Pesach, Jewish Passover, first and seventh days only); April (Muhammad's birthday); April/ May (Yom HaAtzma'ut, Jewish Independence Day); 40 days after Easter (Ascension); 50 days after Easter (Pentecost); May/June (Yom Yerushalayim, Jewish Day of Liberation of Jerusalem); May/June (Shavuot, Jewish Feast of Weeks); July/August (Tisha b'Av, Jewish fast commemorating the destruction of the Temple); September/October (Rosh Hashanah, Jewish New Year); September/October (Yom Kippur, Jewish Day of Atonement); September/October (Sukkot, Jewish Feast of Tabernacles, first and eighth days); October (first day of Ramadan); October/November (Id el-Fitr, last three days of Ramadan); December 24 and 25 (Christmas, Western churches); December/January (Id el-Adha, Muslim Feast of Sacrifice).

Time

Israel is seven hours ahead of Eastern Standard Time and ten hours ahead of Pacific Standard Time. Israeli Summer Time, a source of much controversy locally, operates from mid-April to the end of September, roughly in line with America's Daylight Saving Time.

When to go

Although beach resorts are packed in summer, the weather then is not necessarily at its best. It is oppressively humid on the Mediterranean coast, and almost unbearably hot on the Dead Sea and at Eilat. The brief spring and fall are perhaps the most comfortable times to visit Israel. Winter in Eilat can be delightful, with clear blue skies and temperatures usually in the lower 70s. The periods around the great Jewish and Christian festivals are expensive and crowded. Easter/ Pesach (Passover) in spring and Sukkot in fall are both lovely times of year, but go just before or after the festivals to avoid the crowds.

Money matters

Currency The unit of currency is the New Israeli Shekel (NIS), known simply as the shekel, divided into 100 agorot. There are banknotes of 10, 20, 50, 100, and 200 shekels denomination. Coins are issued in denominations of 10 and 50 agorot and 1, 5, and 10 shekels.

Changing money Money may only legally be changed through a bank, many of which have branches in the larger hotels, or through a licensed money changer. Only a few of the latter remain, but in Jerusalem many are to be found near the Damascus Gate of the Old City. They may give a better rate of exchange. The relative weakness of the shekel makes it preferable to change money in small amounts in Israel rather than abroad.

Credit cards Most major credit cards are freely accepted in Israel, and credit card companies usually give a good rate of exchange.

ATMs

Holders of certain credit cards can obtain cash from ATMs at many branches of Israeli banks. Check with your card issuer before leaving home to see if your card will work in Israeli ATMs.

Payment in foreign currency Goods and services may frequently be purchased with foreign currency, although there is no obligation on businesses to accept this. The U.S. dollar is most favored, but sterling and deutsche marks are also readily accepted. Many stores quote prices in dollars. Change will be given in shekels, so it is advisable to bring notes of small denomination. No VAT is applied to hotel, airline, car rental, and other bills paid in overseas currencies, credit cards or by traveler's checks.

Opening times

Stores Traditional hours are Sunday to Thursday, 8:30 AM to 1 PM and 4 PM to 7 PM; Fridays and days preceding Jewish holidays, 8:30 AM to 1 PM. These days, many stay open all day. Additionally, many stores close on Tuesday afternoons, most hairdressers close on Monday afternoons, and travel agents close on Wednesday afternoons.

Banks Generally open 8:30 AM to 12:30 PM Sunday to Thursday, 4 PM to 6 PM on Sunday, Tuesday, and Thursday, and 8:30 AM to noon on Friday. Some banks are open for longer hours in the afternoon, and branches in hotels may keep hours to suit their guests.

Museums and archeological sites Usually open Sunday to Thursday, 9 or 10 AM to 4 or 5 PM. Typically they open mornings only on Friday and are closed all day on Saturday (any exceptions to these opening times are noted in the individual entries in the A to Z section).

Post offices Hours vary considerably. Some main post offices are open from 7 AM to 10 PM, others are open Sunday to Tuesday and Thursday, 8 AM to 6 PM; Wednesday, 8 AM to 1:30 PM; Friday, 8 AM to 1 or 2 PM. Smaller post offices open Sunday to Tuesday and Thursday, 8 AM to 12:30 PM and 3:30 to 6 PM; Wednesday, 8 AM to 1:30 PM; Friday, 8 AM to 1 or 2 PM.

Gas stations These are usually open all day and into the evening. However, only a few stations on main roads remain open on Friday afternoons and Saturdays, so remember to fill up before Shabbat (Sabbath) starts.

Government offices Usually open to the public from Sunday to Thursday between 8:30 AM and 12:30 PM.

Pharmacies A list of pharmacies that take turns to remain open outside normal business hours is published in the *Jerusalem Post*. It can also be obtained from hotels or from Magen David Adom (the Israeli equivalent of the Red Cross).

Customs and courtesies Israelis are remarkably casual in their dress and behavior, though immodesty by both sexes is frowned upon. Many Israeli people seem to regard excessive displays of courtesy with disdain. You should not, therefore, feel affronted if your own attempts to be polite are disregarded. Accept that Israelis do not wait in line patiently or hold doors open for each other.

Do pay attention to the customs of the Jewish Sabbath (Shabbat) and religious festivals. Do not smoke in public on these days, and in certain places where it is prohibited, including the public rooms of some hotels. Observant Israelis leave their cars at home on the Sabbath and on other festival days. For information on conduct in places of worship see page 269. Photography is forbidden within the enclosure at the Western Wall in Jerusalem.

Another feature of life in Israel is that daily life starts early (about 6 AM) and carries on until late (many restaurants and bars are open past midnight).

Getting around

Car rental

To rent a car it is necessary to produce your driver's license and be over 21, with at least one year's driving experience. Many international car rental companies are represented, and it is possible to book a car before departure from home, to be picked up at the point of arrival in Israel. Several Israeli companies also have offices abroad. Rates are seasonal and highest in July and August. Car rental desks at Ben Gurion Airport are open 24 hours a day.

Driving

An excellent road network, lovely and varied scenery, and short distances make touring Israel a pleasure. However, as in all areas of life, Israelis can be impatient and are not afraid to take risks when behind the steering wheel. Be cautious and drive defensively. Rush hours in major cities are hectic, and traffic jams are frequent.

Traffic drives on the right, and the rules of the road are similar to those of North America and Western Europe. Traffic signs are international and easy-to-understand, and street signs are in Hebrew, Arabic, and English (although the type may be small and difficult to read if driving fast) . Seat belts must be worn by all passengers at all times. Driving under the influence of alcohol is prohibited. Traffic approaching from the right has priority, except on main roads marked with a sign bearing a yellow square with a black and white border. These roads have priority over all side roads. All vehicles driving on roads between towns must use their headlights (note that parking lights are not enough) *at all times* between November 1 and March 31.

Emergencies Breakdown assistance can be obtained from the Automobile and Touring Club of Israel (MEMSI). The club offers free assistance to members of affiliated motoring organizations, such as the AAA. Patrols operate around the clock, but a charge is made for assistance given between 5 PM and 8 AM. Towing is free for distances under 25 km (15 miles). Car rental companies are often prepared to include short-term membership in the rental price, or have their own emergency arrangements.

Parking This is strictly regulated in most town and city centers. Cars can be legally parked only in streets where the curbs are painted in blue and white stripes. A parking card (*cartise*) allowing five hours of street parking must be purchased from a

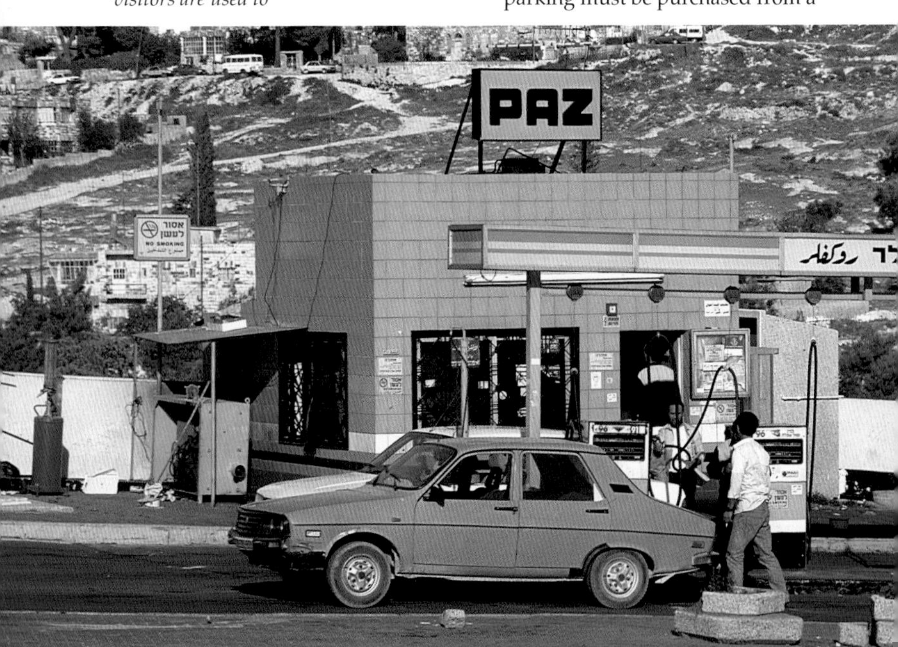

Gas prices are slightly higher than many visitors are used to

post office or street kiosk and displayed on the windshield. Between 7 AM and 5 PM a car may be so parked for one hour. From 7 PM to 10 PM a longer period is allowed, and appropriate parking cards must be displayed. Overnight parking on blue and white striped streets is not regulated—but turn on your alarm clock! Find a parking lot for longer stays in downtown areas. Do not park near red painted curbs: cars will be towed away or wheel-clamped—often within minutes of arrival.

Gasoline Filling stations supply standard grade gas (91 octane), premium grade (96 octane) lead-free, and diesel fuel. Prices are generally much higher than in the United States, and a little higher than in Europe.

Speed limits Built up areas: 50 kmh (30 mph); elsewhere: 80 kmh (50 mph) for cars, 60 kmh (35 mph) for cars with trailers and 70 kmh (40 mph) for motorcycles.

Public transportation:
Air Israel's domestic airline, Arkia, has scheduled flights between Tel Aviv, Jerusalem, Haifa, Rosh Pina, and Eilat. The under-an-hour flights from Tel Aviv to Rosh Pina or Eilat are much faster than the 3–4 hour drive. Chartered flights to other airfields, such as Masada, can be arranged through Arkia and other private charter companies. Consult travel agents and Israel Government Tourist Offices.

Train Train services are run by Israel Railways. The main route links Tel Aviv and Haifa. Some trains continue north to Nahariya. There is a limited service on the line between Jerusalem and Tel Aviv, although the bus is faster. Fares are lower than for bus travel, but stations are often sited away from downtown areas.

Above: a station on Haifa's subway system
Below: Jerusalem train station

Bus Buses dominate public transportation in Israel. The nation-wide Egged bus company (the name means "linked together") provides a low-cost, comprehensive, and efficient network of over 3,000 routes. These connect even the most isolated kibbutzim with the rest of the world. Buses are clean, comfortable, and, for the most part, air-conditioned.

Services start at about 5 AM and continue through the day until early

Bus passes also allow discounts on museum entry and restaurant bills

Traveling by bus is part of the Israeli way of life

evening. Only the major routes between Tel Aviv, Haifa, and Jerusalem continue until 11:30 PM. Services also stop for the Sabbath on Friday afternoon and for religious festivals on the evening of the preceding day. Buses are often full, and it is well worth booking in advance at Egged offices or bus stations. Town buses stop only when required, and passengers wishing to alight must press the bell to alert the driver. Bus drivers all speak at least basic English—it is part of their training.

There are several money-saving ticket options. The Israbus pass (costs vary) allows the holder to travel on all Egged buses for a specified period (7, 14, 21, or 30 days). It also entitles the holder to a range of discounts on tours, car rental, museum entrance fees, and restaurant bills. Multifare discount passes are valid for a month on urban routes only, and permit the holder to make a specified number of rides at a discount price. They can be used by more than one person. A simple round-trip ticket will also give worthwhile savings. Apart from anything else passes save you from having to wait in line for tickets, which can be a time-consuming and frustrating business, well worth avoiding at busy downtown bus stations! Tel Aviv city buses are run by Dan, and Egged passes are not valid here.

Various Arabic bus companies operate from the East Jerusalem bus station, serving Arab towns and villages in Judaea and Samaria (the West Bank). Their buses are painted blue and white, or green and white. Arab buses tend to be crowded, cheap, and rickety, but can be very useful for visiting these areas. They do run on Saturdays, unlike their Egged counterparts.

An easy and inexpensive way to see the sights is by taking an Egged guided tour in English. The national bus company runs trips lasting from half a day to a week, spent visiting all the country's places of interest. For information and bookings, go to any bus station in Israel, or contact Egged's head office in Tel Aviv, tel: 03 537 5555.

Taxi and *sherutim* So-called "Special" (i.e. nonshared) taxis have a poor reputation among tourists and locals alike. The drivers are often unhelpful, and overcharging is frequent. Yet they can be a boon at times, so you will have to adopt strategies for ensuring that you do not get ripped off. One thing you can do to protect yourself is to confirm the correct fare at your hotel, or at a tourist office, before you set out. Insist that the taxi meter be turned on before departure. If the meter is "broken"—an amazingly frequent occurrence—agree upon the fare before getting in.

The *sherut*, or shared taxi, is the preferred choice of locals. These large cars, or minibuses, carry up to seven passengers, plying fixed routes within, or between, towns. All passengers pay a flat-rate fare (usually 20 percent more than the bus) and may alight at any point along the route. *Sheruts* operate from taxi stands and depart as soon as they have collected seven passengers. This usually does not take long, as they are very popular. Fares are officially fixed, with supplements for night travel, and the drivers are generally helpful and honest, if not always friendly. The correct fare can be established by asking fellow passengers, or at the tourist office. *Sheruts* often run on Sabbath and festivals, but expect to pay a supplement. The addresses of *sherut* locations can be found in the local telephone book under "Taxi-cabs."

Beware the taxi driver—some are out to take advantage of the trusting passenger

Boat Regular ferry services cross the Sea of Galilee between Tiberias, Ein Gev, and Capernaum. Excursion boats can be chartered on the lake. For details, ask at local tourist offices. Red Sea excursions can be booked in glass-bottomed boats, and there are ferries between Eilat and Taba. Details can be had from hotels or local tourist offices.

Ferry boats offer tranquil trips across the Sea of Galilee

THE JERUSALEM POST

FRIDAY, MARCH 3, 1995 ● II ADAR 1, 5755 ● I SHAWAL 1, 1415

Communications

Media

Israel has a thriving and extensive press, publishing in Hebrew, Arabic, and many European languages. Papers cover the full gamut of opinions. The *Jerusalem Post* is a right-wing English-language daily news-paper (no edition on Saturday) sold throughout Israel. It carries a full entertainment listings section on Fridays. Left-wing *Ha'Aretz* publishes a weekly English edition. Monthly magazines in Engish include the *Jerusalem Report*, a current-affairs magazine, and the *Israel Economist*. The *International Herald Tribune* and some British papers and magazines are also available. The Arab press produces some English-language publications, which are more readily obtainable in East Jerusalem.

Radio Kol Israel (Voice of Israel) broadcasts news in English every day at 7 AM, 1, 5, and 8 PM on short wave (1170 kHz in the south and 576 kHz in the north). The 1 PM news is followed by a 15-minute magazine program. The Voice of America (1269 kHz) and BBC World Service (1323 kHz) can also be received and are much listened to by Israelis.

English-language news is broadcast by Channel 1 on Monday to Thursday at 6:15 PM, Friday at 4:30 PM, and Saturday at 5:30 PM. In addition, cable television is available in most hotels, usually including BBC World and CNN. TV schedules appear daily in the *Jerusalem Post*. Jordanian television is avidly watched by Israelis to gain an Arab slant on current events.

Post offices

These display a sign showing a leaping white stag on a blue background. As well as stamps, they sell telephone tokens (Hebrew: *asimonim*) and telecards, and they provide fax, telex, and telegram services. International phone calls can be made here, and some post offices also sell street parking cards (they also collect payment of bills and parking and traffic fines).

Main post offices in major cities are open from 7 AM to late (see page 259 for other post office opening

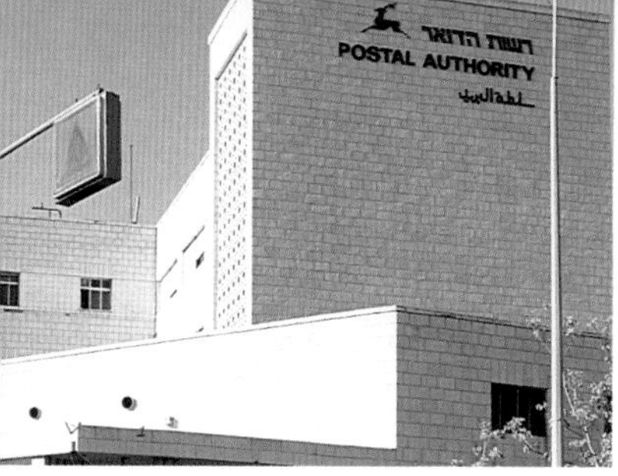

Typical main post office

times), and their fax, telex, and telegram services are often available around the clock. The post office at Ben Gurion Airport is open 24 hours a day. Mailboxes are either yellow (local mail) or red (all other destinations).

Stamps, telephone tokens, and cards can be purchased at hotels and street kiosks. Stamps are also sold at bookstores and stationery and souvenir stores.

Visitors may receive mail through the *poste restante* (general delivery) service offered at main post offices (Jerusalem: 23 Jaffa Road; Tel Aviv: Rehov Mikve Yisrael Street); for details phone the Postal Authority's toll-free number: 177 022 2131.

Telephones
Israel's phone company is called Bezek. Calls from public telephone booths must be paid for with a phonecard which can be purchased from post offices and hotels. Street kiosks sell them at slightly higher prices. Phone charges vary according to the time of day, with the highest rates in the morning. International calls can be made from hotel rooms (very expensive) or from public telephone centers where staff can advise you on the cheapest times to call.

International calls can be dialed from public pay phones by using a phonecard. Collect calls can be made from such phones by dialing 188, which puts you through to the international operator. You must insert a phonecard to get through, but there is no charge for the call. Some Arab states, technically at war with Israel, do not accept collect calls.

Public telephone centers Remember that some public telephone centers are closed on Friday afternoons and Saturdays. Centers are located at 3 Koresh Street and 236 Jaffa Street, Jerusalem; 13 Frishman Street, Tel Aviv; Bezek Offices, Old Commercial Center, Hatmarim Boulevard, Eilat; 14 HaAtzma'ut Square, Netanya; Bezek Offices, Midrehov Promenade, Tiberias.

Telephone services
Information: 144
International operator: 188
Time: 155
Telegrams by phone (up to 50 words): 171.

International dialing codes
United States or Canada to Israel: 011 972
United Kingdom to Israel: 00 972
Israel to the United States or Canada: 00 1
Israel to the United Kingdom: 00 44

When telephoning to or from a foreign country, omit the first zero of the local dialing code.

Language
The official languages of Israel are Hebrew (Ivrit) and Arabic (Aravit), with Hebrew being by far the most widely spoken. Most people dealing with tourists can speak, or at least understand, some English. This is particularly true of hotel staff. If this fails, it is always worth trying another language, as many Israelis are multilingual—French and Russian are very widely spoken, for example.

Street signs are usually in Hebrew, Arabic, and English.

Basic vocabulary

hello (literally: Peace!)	*shalom*
goodbye	*shalom*
yes/no	*ken/lo*
please	*bevakesha*
thank you (very much)	*toda (raba)*
sorry/excuse me	*sliha*
where is ...?	*aifo?*
restaurant	*mis'adah*
museum	*muzaion*
synagogue	*beit knesset*
church	*knaissia*
hotel	*malon*

Emergencies

Crime

Israel is one of the safest countries in the world and experiences very little violent crime. A midnight stroll in any of the major cities is safer than it would be in broad daylight in most North American or European equivalents (although locals are keen to discourage walking alone in East Jerusalem and parts of the Old City after dark). Violence may not be a problem, but theft can be. It pays to take a few elementary and common-sense precautions:

- always carry money and valuables in an inside pocket or in a bag with a secure strap;
- never carry your money and travel documents in the same wallet or bag;
- never leave valuables visible in a parked car or unattended on a beach;
- do not flaunt valuable jewelry;
- pay particular attention to expensive cameras and video cameras.

World headlines give the impression that terrorist attacks are frequent in Israel. In fact, owing to the high level of security, they are rare. Some European countries suffer worse terrorism—and there is very little danger of being involved in such an incident. However, anyone wishing to visit the Israeli-held West Bank or the Palestinian Autonomous Areas should keep abreast of events in order to avoid any local disturbances. It is always a sensible precaution to travel by Arab bus or by local taxi in these areas, rather than in an Israeli-rented car, with its telltale yellow license plates. Almost all of the occasional cross-border attacks on Israel have occured in the far north of the country, around the upper Galilee town of Metulla. It is worth knowing, too, that most of Israel's Arab towns and villages are also in the Galilee.
If you are in any doubt about your itinerary, check with tourist offices (see page 272), hotel staff, or Israeli fellow travelers.

Police

In Jerusalem a special unit of the Tourist Police operates from the Kishle Police Station inside the Jaffa Gate of the Old City. These officers speak English, French, and German and will deal with all problems concerning tourists, ranging from crime to lost companions. They also use the services of volunteers who speak other languages. Unfortunately, this unit operates only in Jerusalem.

Embassies and consulates

Israeli embassies abroad

- 3514 International Drive, Washington DC 20008 (tel: 202/364-5500).
- 50 O'Connor Street, No. 1005, Ottawa, Ontario K1P 6L2 (tel: 613/567-6450).

- 2 Palace Green, London W8 4QB (tel: 020 7957 9500).

Embassies in Israel

- United States: 71 Hayarkon Street, 63903 Tel Aviv (tel. 03 519 7575); 27 Nablus (or Shechem) Road, Jerusalem (tel: 02 253 288).
- Canada: 220 Hayarkon Street, 53405 Tel Aviv (tel: 03 527 2929).
- United Kingdom: 192 Hayarkon Street, 63405 Tel Aviv (tel: 03 524 9171/8); 1 Ben-Yehuda Street, Jerusalem (tel: 02 510 0166).

Emergency phone numbers

Ambulance: 101
Police: 100
Fire: 102

Health

The standard of health care provided in Israel is among the best in the world, and most doctors speak adequate English.
In an emergency, any hospital (Beit holim) will offer treatment. There are hospitals, clinics, and duty doctors in almost every community, no matter how small. You should take your passport, insurance documents, and money for payment with you. Do not forget to keep your receipts so that you can get reimbursed by your travel insurance.

For out-of-hours treatment or, nonemergency medical attention, look for details in the *Jerusalem Post*. This publication lists duty hospitals and pharmacies. Magen David Adom, the Israeli equivalent of the Red Cross, has first-aid stations in many towns.

Lost property

Always report serious losses to the police, who will supply you with a copy of their report for your insurance claim.

Report all lost passports to your embassy; it is a good idea to carry a photocopy of your passport's data page (separate from your passport) to speed the replacement process in case of loss.

Report stolen or lost credit cards and traveler's checks to an issuing bank or the issuing company's emergency telephone number.

Soldiers praying at Judaism's holiest site, the Western Wall in Jerusalem

Other information

Camping
There are campgrounds throughout Israel, offering accommodations in cabins, chalets, and trailers as well as for tents. Facilities usually include stores and/or restaurants, around-the-clock security, showers and a swimming pool. Some have electrical hook up. Information concerning locations, reservation arrangements, and tariffs can be obtained from local tourist offices.

Travelers with disabilities
Israeli attitudes to travelers with disabilities, and facilities provided, are generally good, but fall short of what is expected in some American cities. Ramps, curb cuts on main streets, wheelchair accessible elevators, doorways, hotel rooms, and accessible restrooms are common—but not universal. State-owned sites and museums generally have good wheelchair access. Most inconvenient is that buses and taxis are not equipped for passengers with disabilities. Israel Government Tourist Offices provide a fact sheet entitled *Holidays in Israel for the Disabled* (see page 272 for addresses).

Electricity
The power supply in Israel is 220 volts AC. Wall plugs are of the small three-pin type, and a suitable transformer and plug adaptor are necessary for many American and European appliances.

Places of worship
The many places of worship in Israel represent dozens of different religions. All large Israeli towns have synagogues representing the various orthodox and progressive viewpoints. There are also Masorti (Conservative) synagogues in several towns. The main synagogue in large cities usually follows the Ashkenazi Orthodox rite.

There are numerous mosques in Israel's Islamic neighborhoods.

Most of Israel's Christian population is Greek Orthodox. The Christian Arabs are Maronites. Many other Christian denominations have churches in Israel. Roman Catholics are particularly well represented.

Beautiful menorahs, symbol of the Israeli state and the Jewish faith

Israeli attitudes toward tipping are changing. Tourist-oriented restaurants now expect it

Various Protestant denominations have churches in the main towns. In Jerusalem, for example, Episcopalians, Baptists, Lutherans, and Seventh Day Adventists are represented.

Many houses of worship are also major tourist attractions, and visitors should behave and dress with consideration for worshippers. Modest dress is essential for both sexes: shoulders, arms, and legs should be covered, skirts should be at least knee-length and women should not wear slacks when visiting mosques or synagogues. Men should cover their heads in synagogues (paper caps are provided for those with no hat). Women should carry a hat or scarf to cover their heads, if required, in churches and mosques. When visiting mosques take off your shoes before you enter (see panel page 99).

If you arrive during services you may take part if you wish. Do not interfere in any way with the service.

Tourist offices (see page 272) have details of local churches and times of services.

Tipping
Israelis do not normally expect to give or receive tips. Unfortunately, in some places catering to tourists, that is not the case and serving staff will sometimes even inform you that tips are expected. Ten percent of the bill is more than adequate. Where service is already included, no tip is required. It is not necessary to tip taxi drivers, but it is customary to tip hairdressers.

Restrooms
Public restrooms are rare. Some leave much to be desired and little to the imagination. They are usually marked with the sign "00," plus a male or female symbol. Most restaurants, museums, and movie theaters have modern, clean restroom facilities, as do some of the bigger stores. Often, the best bet is to use the facilities in the larger hotels' public areas. Attendants do not normally expect a tip.

Student and youth travel

For low-cost youth travel to Israel, check out specialist travel operator STA at www.sta-travel.com. Within Israel, an International Student Identity Card gives 25 percent discounts on the country's minimal rail network, and 10 percent reduction on most town-to-town bus fares. The Israel Youth Hostels Association (tel: 02 258 8900; web: www.youth-hostels.org.il) provides over 30 well-managed hostels around the country.

If you want to take part in an archeological dig contact either the Youth Section Promotion Department at the Ministry of Tourism (23 Hillel Street, Jerusalem; tel: 02 623 7311) or the Israel Antiquities Authority (P.O. Box 586, Jerusalem; tel: 02 560 2627).

❑ Working as a volunteer on a kibbutz is an inexpensive and interesting way to see something of Israel and learn about its society. However, be forewarned: it is more work than play. Most of Israel's 300 kibbutzim and *moshavim* use volunteers who get full board and pocket money. They generally do menial labor and unskilled tasks, unless they have some qualification that the community can make use of. For all that, most volunteers come away thinking the experience was valuable. For information contact the Jewish Agency, Kibbutz Aliyah Desk, 110 East 59th Street, New York, NY 10022 (tel: 212/318-6130); or Kibbutz Representative, 1A Accommodation Road, London NW11 8ED (tel. 020 8458 9235). ❑

Hitchhiking

Hitching (called "tremping") is widely practiced by all sorts of people, not just tourists. Vast numbers of off-duty soldiers, carrying weapons as they are required to do, hitch around the country (even though they have free bus passes). Getting lifts is quick and easy, as people who stop usually take more than one person. There are known hitchhiking spots on the major roads—you can recognize them by the soldiers hitchhiking. They are almost like bus stops, with drivers stopping every couple of minutes to pick people up. To hitch a lift, do not hold up your thumb, instead, simply point your index finger.

Women travelers

Women can travel alone safely in Israel, but they should, of course, maintain the precautions they would usually adopt at home. Lone women may occasionally experience a certain amount of comment from male passersby, especially teenage boys. This is best ignored, as a response might be misunderstood. As everywhere, modest dress and discreet conduct will minimize hassle. In Arab areas, women may receive more persistent and unwanted attention from men. Emulation of the extreme modesty of Arab women can be helpful in these circumstances. Wearing a headscarf, in addition to very modest dress, can alleviate the situation. Locals advise against walking on the ramparts of

Jerusalem's Old City alone, though in fact women visitors often do this. Incidents are extremely rare. Women hitchhiking alone, or with another female companion, should maintain a sense of caution. If women do get inside a car with strange men, it is best to behave and talk with great modesty and reserve.

CONVERSION CHARTS

MEN'S SHOES

U.S.	8	8.5	9.5	10.5	11.5	12
U.K.	7	7.5	8.5	9.5	10.5	11
Rest of Europe	41	42	43	44	45	46
Israel	41	42	43	44	45	46

WOMEN'S SHOES

U.S.	6	6.5	7	7.5	8	8.5
U.K.	4.5	5	5.5	6	6.5	7
Rest of Europe	38	38	39	39	40	41
Israel	38	38	39	39	40	41

CONVERSION CHARTS

MEN'S SHIRTS

U.S.	14	14.5	15	15.5	16	16.5	17
U.K.	14	14.5	15	15.5	16	16.5	17
Rest of Europe	36	37	38	39/40	41	42	43
Israel	36	37	38	39/40	41	42	43

MEN'S SUITS

U.S.	36	38	40	42	44	46	48
U.K.	36	38	40	42	44	46	48
Rest of Europe	46	48	50	52	54	56	58
Israel	46	48	50	52	54	56	58

DRESS SIZES

U.S.	6	8	10	12	14	16
U.K.	8	10	12	14	16	18
France	36	38	40	42	44	46
Italy	38	40	42	44	46	48
Rest of Europe	34	36	38	40	42	44
Israel	32	34	36	38	40	42

FROM	TO	MULTIPLY BY
Inches	Centimeters	2.54
Centimeters	Inches	0.3937
Feet	Meters	0.3048
Meters	Feet	3.2810
Yards	Meters	0.9144
Meters	Yards	1.0940
Miles	Kilometers	1.6090
Kilometers	Miles	0.6214
Acres	Hectares	0.4047
Hectares	Acres	2.4710
U.S. Gallons	Liters	3.7854
Liters	U.S. Gallons	0.2642
Ounces	Grams	28.35
Grams	Ounces	0.0353
Pounds	Grams	453.6
Grams	Pounds	0.0022
Pounds	Kilograms	0.4536
Kilograms	Pounds	2.205
Tons	Tonnes	0.9072
Tonnes	Tons	1.1023

Tourist information

Tourist offices

There are branches of the Israel Government Tourist Office (IGTO) in all the larger towns and places of tourist interest. They display a sign showing the letter "i" in white on a blue background. They can provide a wide variety of information in English about accommodations, excursions, local sights, and events. Free town maps are available, as well as a free weekly English-language magazine called *Hello Israel*, which gives news and entertainment listings for the entire country. Offices in major cities also produce their own local listings magazines.

These are the main IGTO offices:

- Visitors Center, 17 Jaffa Street, Jerusalem (tel: 02 625 8844);
- Jaffa Gate, Jerusalem (tel: 02 628 0382);
- New Bus Station, Tel Aviv (tel: 03 639 5660);
- 18 Herzl Street, Haifa (tel: 04 866 6521);
- Arava Highway Corner, Yotam Road, Eilat (tel: 07 637 2111).

There is also an office at Ben Gurion Airport. Addresses and telephone numbers for other tourist offices can be obtained at any of the above.

IGTOs overseas

- Israel Government Tourist Office, 800 Second Avenue, New York, NY 10117 (tel: 212/499-5650; fax: 212/499-5655).
- Israel Government Tourist Office, 6380 Wilshire Boulevard, Los Angeles, CA 90048 (tel: 213/658-7462; fax: 213/658-6543).
- Israel Government Tourist Office, 180 Bloor Street West, Suite 700, Toronto, Ontario M5S 2V6, Canada (tel: 416/964-3784; fax: 416/964-2420).
- Israel Government Tourist Office, U.K. House, 180 Oxford Street, London W1N 9DJ, United Kingdom (tel: 020-7299 1111; fax: 020-7299 1112).

Accommodations & Restaurants

ACCOMMODATIONS

The Israeli Ministry of Tourism lists over 300 places to stay throughout the country, from pilgrim hostels to luxury hotels. Details can be obtained from IGTO offices anywhere in the world (see page 272). There is no hotel grading system, but most hotels in Israel reach high standard, and price is generally a reliable guide to a hotel's facilities and level of service. Hotel prices are usually quoted in U.S. dollars, and it is worth charging all services to your account. Settle your bill in hard currency (again, dollars are the most widely accepted currency) or by credit card, so as to obtain VAT exemption (see page 255 and Money Matters, page 258). Note that hotel pools shut early by U.S. standards. Arrive back in early afernoon for that refreshing dip or you may be disappointed.

Kibbutzim Most of Israel's 300 kibbutzim have guest accommodations. These vary enormously in style, quality, and price. Some only offer a couple of basic guest rooms, while others are comparable to high-class hotels. In the case of the latter, guests are accommodated away from the kibbutz living and working areas. A free tour is always available, giving a glimpse into the day-to-day workings of a textbook utopia.

Some 30 kibbutzim, located in resort areas, are members of the highly professional Kibbutz Hotels Chain, which has its own Tel Aviv head office (see below). These are well placed all over the country and always located within a few minutes of beaches, main towns, historic sites, or resorts. For many people, their peaceful setting, informality, and lack of traffic make them preferable to staying in town hotels. Bookings can be made through travel agents, or direct through the Kibbutz Hotel Chain in Israel (Kibbutz Hotel Reservation Center, 1 Smolanskin Street, P.O. Box 3193, Tel Aviv; tel: 03 5246161); or in the United States (Israel Hotel Reservation Center, 20 South Van-Brunt Street, Englewood, NJ 07631, tel: 201/816-0633).

Apart from these better kibbutz hotels, scores of kibbutzim and *moshavim* (cooperative villages) offer inexpensive guest accommodations on a bed-and-breakfast basis. Most must be booked by calling the kibbutz direct, but a group of about 30, mostly in Galilee, can be booked through the Kibbutz Hotels Chain. Ask for "Kibbutz B and B Country Lodging", or visit the Kibbutz Hotels Chain website, www.kibbutz.co.il. Many are in peaceful, off-the-beaten-track locations, and a car is essential. Tourist offices also have details of other kibbutz accommodations.

Hostels The Israel Youth Hostels Association (www.youth-hostels.org.il) runs high-grade hostels throughout the country offering dormitories and family rooms to guests of all ages. Meals are usually provided, as well as a kitchen for guests' use. To enforce a degree of peace and quiet at night, most hostels close their doors at times varying from around 11 PM to 3 AM—and not even paid-up guests will be allowed back in! Further details can be obtained from the Israel Youth Hostel Association, P.O. Box 1075, Jerusalem (tel: 02 252706).

Christian hospices There are Christian hospices of various denominations near most Christian sights. They offer simple, clean, well-maintained, and very inexpensive accommodations, either with full board or on a lodging-only basis. It is not strictly necessary to be a pilgrim, or even a Christian, to use them. However, it is vital to abide by the rules of the hospice, which often include a curfew and an early start. Advance booking is essential. Full details, including prices and facilities, can be found in the leaflet *Christian Hospices in Israel* published by the Ministry of Tourism, from tourist offices or the Christian Information Center in Jerusalem (tel: 02 272 692).

The big chains The best of Israeli hotels nearly all belong to chains. However, these are not always the familiar international names. While Hilton, Meridien, Sheraton, Hyatt, and Holiday Inn do exist in Israel, the highest standards of all are set by Israeli companies. These include the top-of-the-range Dan hotels, with nine locations (bookable in the U.S., tel: 212/752-6120; in the U.K., tel: 020-7439 9893; or in Israel, tel: 03 527 1430; www.danhotels.co.il); Isrotel, with seven establishments, five of them in Eilat (to book in the U.S., tel: 201/816-0830; in the U.K., tel: 020-8997 6423; in Israel, tel: 03 517 8989; www.isrotel.co.il); and Radisson Moriah, with seven hotels (in the U.S., tel: 800/333-3333; in the U.K. tel: 0800 374 4111; in Israel, tel: 177 353 004; www.radisson-moriah.co.il).

Hotel price grading Hotel rates vary widely according to the week and the season. The price categories given here are an approximate guide, and are per person, per night, sharing a double room, including full Israeli breakfast:

- budget $ less than $50
- moderate $$ $50–$100
- expensive $$$ more than $100

JERUSALEM – OLD CITY

See also page 106.

Within the walls, there are small, very inexpensive Arab hotels and guest houses ($) around Damascus Gate, and Christian hospices ($) in the Muslim and Christian quarters.

Al-Ahram Hostel ($)
Via Dolorosa tel: 02 628 0926
Centrally located on the corner of the Via Dolorosa and al-Wad Street (near Third Station of the Cross), this low-cost hostel offers a choice ranging from basic private rooms to dorms, or rooftop sleeping. There's a good young atmosphere, with a lounge and music.

Hashimi Hostel ($)
73 Souk Khan al-Zeit tel: 02 628 4410
fax: 02 628 4667
Among the best of the low-budget family-run Arab quarter hostels, with a clean airy feel, marble floors, good facilities, and good views. Choose between dorms and private rooms. It's in the souk (market streets) near Damascus Gate.

JERUSALEM—NEW CITY

East Jerusalem

There is a string of low-budget Arab hotels ($) all the way up Salah ed-Din Street.

American Colony ($$–$$$)
1 Louis Vincent Street, Nablus Road
tel: 02 627 9777 fax: 02 627 9779
Arguably Jerusalem's best hotel, despite the variable rooms and slightly less than encyclopedic range of facilities. A former pasha's palace, this beautiful old Oriental building has real charm and style, as well as a good pool, lovely terrace, and superb (nonkosher) breakfasts and buffets.

Capitol ($–$$)
Salah ed-Din Street tel: 02 282 5612
Reasonable rooms and public areas, air-conditioned, facing the Mount of Olives.

Y.M.C.A. (or Capitolina Hotel) ($$)
29 Nablus Road tel: 02 628 6888
Good value accommodation with spacious, comfortable rooms, air-conditioning and plenty of facilities including a swimming pool and squash courts. Located close to the U.S. Consulate, not far from Damascus Gate.

Downtown

Most of the top-class luxury hotels, including members of international chains, are located on King David, Keren Hayesod, and King George V streets.

Beit Shmuel ($)
tel: 02 620 3473
Non-Orthodox Jewish hostel and cultural center (open to all) beside city walls, comfortable, friendly, regular evening entertainment (folklore, etc.), attractive garden.

Dan Pearl ($$$)
Zahal Square tel: 02 622 6666
fax: 02 622 6600
Elegant, attractive stone-and-glass low-rise, one of the most comfortable hotels in the city, close to Jaffa Gate and with good views of the Old City.

Jerusalem Inn ($)
6 Histadrut Street tel: 02 625 1294
Good, clean, low-budget downtown hostel accommodations.

King David ($$$)
32 King David Street tel: 02 620 8888
fax: 02 620 8882
The city's stately and dignified number-one luxury hotel, a legend as well as a piece of Israel's history. The place where you are most likely to see visiting heads of state, stars, and tycoons (see page 90 and 106).

Laromme ($$$)
3 Jabotinsky Street tel: 02 675 6666
fax: 02 675 6777
Modern, popular luxury hotel overlooking Old City; good value in its class.

Radisson Moriah Plaza ($$$)
39 Keren Hayesod Street tel: 02 569 5695
fax: 02 623 2411
Immaculate large comfortable modern hotel, with elegant rooms, rooftop swimming pool, and numerous facilities, 15 minutes' walk from the Old City and the main sights.

Sheraton Jerusalem Plaza ($$$)
47 King George Street tel: 02 629 8666
fax: 02 623 1667
Excellent modern hotel with great views and a superb restaurant.

Tirat Batsheva ($$)
42 King George Street tel: 02 623 2121
fax: 02 624 0697 www.tbs.co.il
Good mid-range modern accommodations in the city center.

Windmill ($$)
3 Mendele Street tel: 02 566 3111
Popular mid-range, comfortable place, 15 minutes' walk from the Old City, 20 minutes from downtown.

Y.M.C.A. (or Three Arches Hotel) ($$)
King David Street tel: 02 625 3433
fax: 02 623 5192 www.ymca3arch.co.il
Standing opposite the great King David Hotel, and arguably just as grand and imposing, the YMCA has basic small but adequate rooms and a good range of facilities, especially for sports. More expensive than other hostels and hospices.

Farther out

Park Plaza ($$$)
2 Ze'er Vilnay tel: 02 658 2222
fax: 02 658 2211
A first-class hotel close to Herzl Boulevard, the Knesset, and the major museums.

Hyatt Regency ($$–$$$)
31 Lehi Street, Mount Scopus
tel: 02 533 1234 fax: 02 581 5947
Dramatic modern building (the six-story atrium has waterfalls and lush vegetation) covering a huge area and overlooking the city from Mount Scopus on the east side. Masses of artwork, luxurious rooms, good restaurants, and superb sport facilities. Relatively inexpensive for its class.

Kibbutz Mitzpe Ramat Rachel Hotel ($$)
D.N. Tsfon Yehuda, 90900 Jerusalem
tel: 02 670 2555 www.ramatrachel.co.il
This excellent, well-equipped hotel (see page 107) is part of the only kibbutz within the city limits (though technically not part of Jerusalem). It makes a green haven after the noise and traffic of Israel's capital. Guests have access to kibbutz facilities, which include a big grassy playground and a heated (all-year) swimming pool, as well as plenty of hotel amenities and its own pampering Health Center. Great views of Bethlehem. Easy and frequent access by bus from downtown.

Neve Ilan Hilltop Resort ($$)
tel: 02 533 9339 www.neve-ilan.co.il
A 15-minute drive along the main Tel Aviv highway, set in a quiet airy location, this pleasant modern hotel has large gardens, excellent sports facilities, and a good restaurant.

Yitzhak Rabin Guest House and Hostel ($$)
1 Nahman Avigad Street tel: 02 678 0101
fax: 02 679 6566
Excellent youth hostel close to the Israel Museum.

Neat, comfortable, modern rooms (some with TV), air-conditioning, and there's also a cafeteria and dining room.

TEL AVIV AND THE COAST

See also page 132.

In Tel Aviv, and right up Israel's Mediterranean coast, there are numerous modern, well-equipped hotels ranged along the beachfronts of popular seashore areas. They do not vary much in architecture, service, and facilities, but standards of comfort are generally high.

Tel Aviv

The main beach and city hotel area is Hayarkon Street, between Trumpledor and Ben-Gurion streets. This is where you will find the main high-quality hotels, as well as several catering to those on smaller budgets. Bargain-basement places and hostels are scattered over the whole area west of Dizengoff Street.

Adiv ($)
5 Mendele Street tel: 03 522 9141
fax: 03 522 9144
This is a low-cost hotel located near the sea, offering simple accommodation

Ambassador ($$)
56 Herbert Samuel Esplanade
tel: 03 510 3993 fax: 03 517 7301
On the corner of Allenby, facing the seafront and opposite Opera Tower, this is a well-placed modern low-rise. Most rooms have a sea-facing balcony.

Astor ($$)
105 Hayarkon Street tel: 03 522 3141
fax: 03 523 7247
Fronting the busy beachside highway and on the corner of Frishmann, this comfortable, well-placed, mid-priced hotel has a good restaurant. Handy for downtown, and across the street from the beach.

Aviv ($)
88 Hayarkon Street tel: 03 510 2784
fax: 03 523 9450
Good, modern, inexpensive hotel with bar downstairs, on very noisy part of Hayarkon, but with sea views and only two minutes' walk from the beach.

Basel ($$)
156 Hayarkon Street tel: 03 524 4161
fax: 03 527 0005
Reliable, well-liked, reasonably placed modern hotel, set back just a few paces from the main beach area.

Carlton ($$$)
10 Eliezer Peri Street tel: 03 520 1818
fax: 03 527 1043 www.carlton.co.il
Set a little north of the main beach, overlooking the yachting marina, this big landmark hotel is in the highest class.

City ($$)
9 Mapu Street tel: 03 524 6253
fax: 03 524 6250
An appealing, popular hotel just a couple of minutes' walk from the main beach area; comfortable and reasonably equipped.

Dan Panorama ($$)
10 Kaufmann Street tel: 03 519 0190
fax: 03 517 1777
A little away from things, facing Clore Park and not near the best part of the beach, this hotel offers luxurious accommodations at lower rates and has a strong bias to children and families. Good food, excellent breakfast buffet. A free shuttle bus runs throughout the day to the Dan Tel Aviv.

Dan Tel Aviv ($$$)
99 Hayarkon Street tel: 03 520 2525
fax: 03 524 9755
Said to have been the city's first hotel, this is still most people's first choice for comfort, service, and convenience. Large and modern, but surprisingly personal, with excellent facilities and superb sea views (rooms on the street side without the sea view are cheaper).

David Intercontinental Hotel ($$)
12 Kaufman Street tel: 03 795 1111
fax: 03 795 1112 www.interconti.com
Very plush, spacious, classy new hotel with huge atrium filled with greenery. Facilities include beauty center, gym, an excellent restaurant (see Aubergine, below), and an internet café. It's close to the beach but not particularly well placed—on the busy intersection facing the mosque, opposite the scruffy Dolphinarium. Reasonable prices though.

Dizengoff Square Hostel ($)
13 Ben Ami Street tel: 03 522 5184
fax: 03 522 5181
Next to Dizengoff Square, this modern, well-equipped hostel, with accommodations from dorms to private rooms (with bath), could hardly be closer to the heart of Tel Aviv.

Gordon Inn Guest House ($)
17 Gordon Street tel: 03 523 8239
fax: 03 523 74119
Something between a small budget hotel and a better-than-average hostel, the Gordon is well placed on a city center corner just a few minutes' walk from the main beach. Choose between basic dorms and simple private rooms. It's open 24 hours a day, and there's a pleasant little coffee bar where breakfast is served. Good value.

Grand Beach ($$)
250 Hayarkon Street tel: 03 543 3333
fax: 03 546 6589
Well away from downtown and feeling a little remote. Not far from the less impressive northern beaches and park, the hotel represents reasonably good value.

Hilton ($$$)
Independence Park/Hayarkon Street
tel: 03 520 2222 fax: 03 527 2711
On a seafront ridge overlooking the shore, but well to the north of the main beachfront area. Not in the best location for either beaches or city. The building has been thoroughly renovated and is a luxury hotel up to the usual Hilton standard.

Isrotel Tower ($$)
78 Hayarkon Street tel: 03 511 3636
fax: 03 511 3666
This well-placed high-rise landmark building close to the seafront combines a comfortable all-suite hotel with unserviced self-catering aparthotel in an unusual concept. Each of the comfortable

two-room suites has two TVs with cable, a stereo CD player, two phone lines. There's no restaurant, but a basement bar provides refreshments. Business-class guests get added benefits.

Mercure Marina Tel Aviv ($$)
167 Hayarkon Street tel: 03 521 1777
fax: 03 521 1770 www.clal-tourism.co.il
The Tel Aviv branch of this popular mid-priced good-quality French chain overlooks the marina at the north end of the main beach. Rooms are spacious and comfortable, and hotel facilities include a pool, private voice mail, and cable TV.

Moss ($$)
6 Nes Ziona Street tel: 03 517 1655
fax: 03 517 1655
Low-priced, mid-range hotel, simply furnished and equipped, in a side road off a busy section of Hayarkon Street. Five minutes' walk from the beach.

Ramada Continental ($$$)
121 Hayarkon Street tel: 03 521 5555
fax: 03 521 5588
High-standard luxury hotel, but located close to Namir Square, at the northern end of the main beach. A moderate walk from the heart of the city.

Sheraton Moriah ($$$)
115 Hayarkon Street tel: 03 521 6666
fax: 03 527 1065
A landmark on the Tel Aviv waterfront, a few paces from the beach, within walking distance of downtown. A top-class luxury hotel.

Travellers Hostel ($)
38 and 47 Ben Yehuda Street
tel: 03 523 2451 fax: 03 523 7281
Small but popular, clean, and inexpensive hostel with attractive garden. Fully equipped kitchens, luggage room, and reception staffed almost round the clock. Easy walk to beach and downtown. Also at 122 Allenby Street (tel: 03 560 6656).

Akko

Argaman Motel ($)
tel: 049 916691 fax: 04 991 6690
Modern hotel on the beach providing comfortable but basic accommodations, with a good view of Old Akko.

Palm Beach Hotel ($$)
tel: 04 981 5815 fax: 04 991 0434
Neighbor to Argaman, above, this better hotel is equipped with good sport facilties, including tennis and squash courts, pool, sauna and jacuzzi, as well as a nightclub.

Caesarea

Dan Caesarea ($$$)
tel: 06 6269111 fax: 06 626 9122
In a green parkland setting, this delightfully relaxed and luxurious resort hotel emphasizes sport—including golf at Israel's only golf course, nearby.

Kef Yam Resort ($$)
Sdot Yam Kibbutz tel: 06 636 4444
fax: 06 636 2211 www.kef-yam.co.il
Set close to the Caesarea beach, this imaginative and lively kibbutz resort, popular with Israelis, offers a wide range of sports, activities, classes, and tours for all age groups. There's a restaurant, and accommodations in family apartments or simpler hostel-style quarters.

Carmel Forest

Carmel Forest Spa Resort ($$$)
P.O. Box 9000, Haifa 31900
tel: 04 830 7888 fax: 04 832 3988
Hidden in a tranquil Mediterranean woodland about a mile and a half south of Kibbutz Beit Oren (near Haifa), this luxury spa hotel offers nonstop pampering and pleasure, rather than the usual health cures and Dead Sea mud.

Haifa

High-quality hotels are clustered in the tiny Carmel Center district up the Carmel slope, above the heart of the city. Top-rung places are the **Dan Carmel** ($$$), *HaNasi Avenue (tel: 04 830 6306; fax: 04 838 7504)* and its near neighbor, the **Dan Panorama** ($$$), *HaNasi Avenue (tel: 04 835 2222; fax: 04 835 2235)* The top floors have fantastic views. Both have an abundance of facilities.

Shulamit ($)
15 Kiryat Sefer Street tel: 04 834 2811
fax: 04 825 5206
An excellent, inexpensive hotel a bit farther from downtown.

Herzliya

Dan Accadia ($$$)
Ramat Yam Street tel: 09 597070
fax: 09 959 7090
Magnificent family resort hotel on the beachfront. Popular and lively. Sport and activity oriented, with lots provided for children. Good buffets.

Sharon ($$)
Ramat Yam Street tel: 09 575777
fax: 09 957 2448
Good, comfortable modern hotel near the beach.

Nahsholim

Kibbutz Nahsholim Guesthouses ($–$$)
MP Hof Carmel tel: 06 399533
fax: 06 639 7614
This kibbutz on the Carmel coast offers accommodations in simply furnished, rather spartan, condominuim style chalets, right on a spectacular beach. The restaurant is below average.

Netanya

There are almost 50 ministry-approved hotels in this town.

Grand Metropole ($–$$)
17 Gad Mahnes Street tel: 09 624777
fax: 09 861 1556
A good-value resort hotel located near the beach.

The Seasons ($$–$$$)
1 Nice Boulevard tel: 09 601511
fax: 09 862 3022
One of the friendliest and best hotels in this popular resort.

Shavei Zion

Hotel Beit Hava ($–$$)
Moshav Shavei Zion tel: 04 982 0391
This quiet *moshav* (cooperative village), 2 miles south of Nahariya, runs a remarkable high-quality modern hotel and restaurant. Immaculate, with good service, attractive grounds, and good facilities, including a large swimming pool.

Shefayim

Kibbutz Shefayim Guest House ($–$$)
Shefayim 60990 tel: 09 595595
fax: 09 959 5555
This kibbutz outside Herzliya runs a big, busy hotel, restaurant, and water park. Used almost exclusively by Israelis. The atmosphere is warm and animated, with functions and events occurring almost every evening. The rooms are well-equipped and comfortable. This makes a good base for much of the coast, including Tel Aviv.

Zichron Yaakov

Radisson Moriah Carmel Gardens ($$)
1 Etzion Street tel: 06 300 111
fax: 06 639 7030
Located on a hilltop close to town, this smart new hotel hosts a lot of conferences, has spacious gardens, a high standard of luxury, and sweeping green views.

GALILEE AND THE NORTH

Amirim

Amirim guest houses ($)
near Sefat tel: 06 698 9571
Several families offer comfortable guest accommodations at this beautifully located all-vegetarian *moshav* (cooperative village) west of Sefat.

Ayelet Hashahar

Ayelet HaShahar ($–$$)
near Kiryat Shmona tel: 06 693 2302
fax: 09 959 7091
Excellent kibbutz guest house offering accommodations and a lively, enjoyable resort atmosphere, with plenty of entertainment and activities.

Ginnosar

Nof Ginnosar Kibbutz Hotel ($$)
tel: 06 670 0300
e-mail: ginosar@netvision.net.il
Delightful, high-quality modern kibbutz hotel with comfortable rooms in several blocks set in beautiful grounds on the banks of the Sea of Galilee. Good restaurant. Well placed for sights. The Museum of the Ancient Boat is located next door.

HaGoshrim

HaGoshrim Kibbutz Hotel ($$)
tel. 06 681 6000
fax: 06 681 6002
www.hagoshrim_hotel.co.il
Good, comfortable, simple rooms in guest accommodation complexes at this prosperous kibbutz, set in pleasant and attractive attractive grounds. Pool and plenty of other facilities. Inner-tubing down the nearby Jordan River is great fun.

Karmiel

Hotel Kalanit ($)
tel: 04 998 3878
You may find newly arrived immigrants lodged in the next room at this simple, but modern and adequate, hotel in the heart of town. Well-placed for Galilee touring, and very inexpensive.

Kinar

Kinar Hotel ($$)
tel: 06 673 8888 fax: 06 673 8811
Attractive, efficient kibbutz hotel with good accommodations. Glorious garden setting on the eastern shore of the Sea of Galilee. Pleasant, spacious public areas and restaurant.

Korazim Junction

Vered Hagalil ($$)
just off Route 90, north of Sea of Galilee
tel: 06 693 5785 fax: 06 693 4964
e-mail: avril@canaan.co.il
A riding center, meaty restaurant and rustic ranch-style (actually very comfortable) complex of cottages and cabins, with swimming pool and peaceful country location.

Rosh Pina

Kibbutz Kfar Hanassi ($$)
near Rosh Pina tel: 06 691 4870
fax: 06 691 4077 e-mail: corrin@canaan.co.il
A few neat, clean, simple guest rooms with kitchenette, plus breakfast in the kibbutz dining room, and Golan views, make for a peaceful break at this easy-going community.

Sea View Hotel ($$)
on Sefat-Rosh Pina highway tel: 06 699 9666
fax: 06 699 6555
The name is earned by a splendid view across the Sea of Galilee. This comfortable little hotel by the road has good fitness equipment and also serves good, mainly vegetarian, meals.

Sefat

Ron ($)
near Metzuda, Sefat tel: 06 697 2590
Decent mid-range hotel with good clean rooms and restaurant, a 10-minute walk from the synagogue quarter and sights.

Howard Johnson's Rimon Inn ($$)
Artists' Quarter tel: 06 699 4666
fax: 06 692 0456
Charming and well placed in an attractive area. One of the best hotels in town.

Tiberias

Several budget hostels ($) and pilgrim hospices can be found around the town. One of the very best is the **Church of Scotland Sea of Galilee Center** ($)
tel: 06 672 3769
e-mail: scottie@rannet.com
A delightful place with air-conditioned rooms and private bath. Not far from the lake.

Galei Kinneret ($$$)
1 Eliezer Kaplan Street tel: 06 792331
The toniest, best, and most civilized place in town, by the lake in a lovely setting.

Ron ($)
12 Ahad Ha'am Street tel: 06 791350
fax: 06 679 1351
This is a pleasant mid-range hotel in a good spot.

Sheraton Moriah Plaza ($$$)
Habanim Street tel: 06 679 2233
fax: 06 679 2320
Big, lavishly equipped modern luxury hotel in the Old City.

JUDAEA AND SAMARIA (THE WEST BANK)

Bethlehem

There are several low-budget hotels and hostels around Manger Square and on Freres Street.

Bethlehem Star ($)
Freres Street tel: 02 743249 fax: 02 741 494
This hotel has comfortable rooms, air-conditioning, roof restaurant, cable TV, and is reasonably priced.

Shepherd Hotel ($$)
Jamal Abed Al-Nasser Street tel: 02 274 0656 fax: 02 274 4888 www.shepherdhotel.com
This comfortable, modern hotel with spacious, well-equipped rooms has a popular "restaurant in the garden". Good value for Bethlehem.

Jericho

Jericho Resort Village ($$)
Qasr Hisham tel: 02 321 1255 fax: 02 322 189
Quality hotel with spacious. well-furnished rooms with cable TV, balconies, pool, good facilities. Good value.

THE SOUTH

Arad

Margoa ($$) *tel: 07 951222*
and the **Nof Arad** ($$) *tel: 07 957056*
are conventional, modern mid-range hotels located close to one another on Moav Street, the road out of town on the eastern side. Both have treatment centers for respiratory conditions.

Dead Sea

Dead Sea Gardens ($$$)
Ein Bokek tel: 07 658 4351 fax: 07 658 4383
Resort and health hotel, with entertainment, sports. Heated indoor pool, filled with water from the Dead Sea.

Kibbutz Ein Gedi ($$)
Ein Gedi tel: 07 659 4222 fax: 07 658 4328
The kibbutz runs a hotel with basic accommodations in simple row-house style blocks scattered around attractive grounds full of flowerbeds. There is a good self-service dining room.

Sheraton Moriah Plaza ($$$)
Neve Zohar tel: 07 659 1591 fax: 07 658 4238
Big, top-flight health-oriented spa hotel on the salty shore in weird, desert location. Full spa in the hotel—pools, mud baths, etc. Lots of facilities, including good restaurants.

Eilat

There are over 60 hotels in Eilat. Most reach a high standard and cater to well-to-do visitors on family vacations. The cream of the selection—the Princess, Dan Eilat, Royal Beach, and Herods—are probably among the best vacation hotels in the world.

In addition to the beach hotels, lower-priced modern, comfortable hotels, popular with Israeli families, can be found in the town center away from the beach. Examples include the huge, all-suite **Club Hotel** ($$), Arava Road *tel: 07 636 1666*; **Etzion** ($$), Hatmarim Avenue *tel: 07 637 4131*; **Mercure Mirage Eilat** ($$), 3 Hativat Hanegev *tel: 07 638 2333*; the fully equipped aparthotel **Nova Hotel** ($$), 6 Hativat Hanegev *tel: 07 638 2444*; **Hotel Pierre** ($), near the bus station *tel: 07 632 6601*; and **Shalom Plaza** ($$), 2 Hatmarim Ave *tel: 07 636 6777.*

Closer to the beach, between the town airport and the lagoon, are popular mid-range quality hotels with pools, restaurants, good facilities, and bargain prices, such as **Americana Inn** ($$) (tel: 07 633 3777); **Moon Valley** ($) (tel: 07 636 6888); and **Palmyra** ($–$$) (tel: 07 636 6000).

Dalia Hotel ($)
North Beach tel: 07 633 4004
Probably the best low-cost hotel, with a good position near the seafront.

Dan Eilat Hotel ($$$)
North Beach tel: 03 636 2222
East of the lagoon. A large, opulent, state-of-the-art hotel with everything and more, including jazz, sport facilities, and a huge pool area, plus lots of facilities for children.

Herods Palace and Herods Vitalis ($$$)
North Shore tel: 07 638 0000 fax: 07 638 0010
At the eastern end of the resort, set back from the shore. Unabashed luxury on an Ancient Roman theme. Several excellent restaurants. The Vitalis is also a magnificent spa hotel, for total self-indulgence in the name of health. All food is organic.

Hilton Queen of Sheba ($$$)
North Beach tel: 07 630 6655 fax: 07 630 6644
Well placed beside lagoon and beach, this luxurious, grandiose hotel claims to be based on the Queen of Sheba's palace.

Kibbutz Eilot Apartments ($$)
Kibbutz Eilot, M P Eilot 88805 tel: 07 635 8816
Two miles north of Eilat on the main road, the kibbutz has a small complex of apartments in attractive grounds surrounded by desert hills. Breakfast is served in the kibbutz members' dining room. There's a children's zoo and play area. An "Israeli folklore evening" every Saturday is popular. A good spot for bird-watchers in spring and fall. Car essential. Handy for the Jordan crossing.

King Solomon's Palace ($$$)
North Beach tel: 07 633 4111
Eilat's refurbished family favorite, a comfortable luxury hotel backing onto the east side of the lagoon. Crowded, informal, and noisy resort atmosphere, with many facilities.

Lagoona Hotel ($$)
North Beach tel: 07 636 6666
Not-quite-so-expensive, all-inclusive family-fun hotel built around a large pool and sunbathing terraces. Masses of facilities, including six cafés and restaurants.

Meridien ($$$)
North Shore tel: 07 638 3333 fax: 07 638 3300
High standard chain offers all-suite beachside luxury a few minutes down the Taba Road. Lots of greenery and polished wood, and excellent facilities.

Neptune ($$$)
North Beach tel: 07 636 9369
This is a popular luxury resort hotel with superb facilities set beside the North Beach promenade.
Orchid Hotel and Resort ($$$)
Coral Beach tel: 07 636 0360
Inspired by Thai architecture and set on a hill overlooking the sea, this attractive chalet complex has footpaths winding through clusters of greenery.
Princess Hotel ($$$)
Taba Beach tel: 07 636 5555
Opulent, top price hotel, set amid desert cliffs just a few paces from the narrow beach. Near the Taba crossing, 5 miles from Eilat. A free shuttle bus operates into town. Huge atrium, marble floors, and an amazing wall of glass almost touching a rocky mountainside.
Reef Hotel ($)
Coral Beach tel: 07 636 4444
fax: 07 636 4488
Unpretentious, attractively equipped sea-facing hotel, popular with Israelis.
Riviera Apartment Hotel ($$)
North Beach tel: 07 630 3666
Isrotel's low-rise apartments provide unpretentiously furnished rentals for two, four, or five people. The complex is arranged around a large pool with children's pool and playground. Ten minutes' walk to the beach. Cafés and a small supermarket in the building.

Royal Beach ($$$)
North Beach tel: 07 636 8888
Sumptuous top-of-the-line hotel near the lagoons. White marble reception area full of light, magnificent atrium with acrobatic sculpture, hallways made of glass with fantastic views. A dozen good restaurants and two large, palm-fringed pools with waterfalls, plus a huge array of other facilities.
Sheraton Moriah Plaza Hotel ($$$)
North Beach tel: 07 636 1111
Large and luxurious hotel, closest to North Beach promenade. Vast range of facilities, with plenty for children, five restaurants, two pools, a nightclub, and regular entertainment.
Sport Club Hotel ($$)
North Beach tel: 07 636 8818
fax: 07 636 8886 e-mail:
cro_asst@isrotel.co.il
Comfortable, quieter-than-average offering all-inclusive hotel accommodations with two pools and many sport facilities.
Youth Hostel ($)
corner of Elot Boulevard and Arava Road
tel: 07 637 0088
An unappealing location, but within easy walking distance of everything (including main bus station). Good, large, modern hostel, with family rooms and an inexpensive dining room.

Mitzpe-Ramon

Ramon Inn ($$)
1 Ein Akev tel: 07 658 8822 fax: 07 658 8151
Unusual modern apartment-hotel in a desert town beside the breathtaking Ramon crater. Rooms are spacious home-away-from-home suites, each with a kitchen/dining room. Excellent value. Bar and restaurant.

RESTAURANTS

Almost all luxury hotels have high-quality restaurants open to the public. For cheap-and-cheerful eating there is little distinction to be made between bars, cafés, and restaurants. They can be found with ease in the center of any city or town.

Price and dining guide:
- budget $ less than $10
- moderate $$ $10–$30
- expensive $$$ more than $30

JERUSALEM

Eucalyptus ($$$)
7 Horkenos Street tel: 02 624 4331
fax: 02 622 2922
One of very few places that describe their cooking as Israeli rather than French, Italian, East European, or Middle Eastern, this restaurant is acclaimed for a new authentic Israeli haute cuisine, making good use of traditional local ingredients prepared with unusual flair.
Fink's ($$$)
2 HaHistadrut Street tel: 02 623 4523
A historic Jerusalem institution, this atmospheric evenings-only bar-restaurant on the corner of King George Street dates back to the 1930s, when British officers frequented the place. It still serves the same classic East European favorites (the goulash is renowned).
Gilly's ($$)
16 Yoel Solomon Street tel: 02 625 5955
This popular place off Nahalat Shiva is usually packed, so arrive early or late if you don't want to wait for a table. Delicious salads are followed by hearty meat dishes, including steaks with sour cream (the ultimate nonkosher combination).
Oceanus ($$$)
7 Rivlin Street, Nahalat Shiva area
tel: 02 624 7501 fax: 02 624 0863
Imaginative fish and shellfish cooking is the specialty at this stylish, well-established restaurant. The carpaccio of fish is especially recommended. The service can be erratic, but the atmosphere is decidedly pleasant.
Pepperonis ($$)
4/6 Rabbi Akiva Street tel: 02 625 7829
An authentic Italian restaurant with a vast selection of antipasti—marinated vegetables, melon with Parma ham, salami platter—followed by a choice from the blackboard. Very popular, and with good reason.
Pie Shop ($$)
Horkenos Street
One of several good moderately priced eateries in this lane, the ever popular Pie Shop specializes in—you guessed it—filling pies, vegetarian or meat, served with salads, and more pies (sweet) for dessert.
Primavera ($$$)
Sheraton Plaza Hotel tel: 02 629 8666
Classic Italian food of a high standard at this hotel

restaurant includes peppers with mozzarella, fish specialties, and tasty desserts. Kosher.

La Rotisserie ($$$)
Notre Dame Guest House, New Gate, Paratroopers Road tel: 02 627 9111
A curious gastronomic find, this extremely good French restaurant is attached to a guest house frequented by pilgrims and owned by the Vatican. Located just outside the walls of the Old City, the building itself is over 100 years old, though the restaurant was only established in 1978. Under vaulted ceilings, enjoy coquilles St. Jacques, Châteaubriand, crêpes suzettes, and a fine selection of imported French wines. Open: dinner only Monday to Friday, lunch and dinner Saturday. Closed: Sunday.

Shemesh ($$)
21 Ben Yehuda Street tel: 02 625 2418
Middle Eastern food in a buzzing spot in central Jerusalem. Salad starters of eggplant, tomato, pickles, hummus, and tahini are followed, if you have room, by hearty grills, kebabs, and shishliks (grilled meats).

Spagettim ($$)
8 Rabbi Akiva Street tel: 02 623 5547
A convivial and inviting spaghetti house in charming old premises. Sit on the terrace and try any of around 50 different pasta sauces.

Strudel—Café Internet ($$)
11 Munbaz Street tel: 02 623 2101
fax: 02 622 1445 e-mail: strudel@inter.net.il
Nosh, shmooze, and surf the net at this enjoyable internet café, something still fairly rare in Israel. The food's pretty good too.

Le Tsriff ($$)
5 Horkenos tel: 02 6242478
Continental food with an Israeli accent and a great range of seafood. Since 1978, its position in the center of town has pulled in Palestinians and Israelis alike, and anyone looking for a diverse environment in which to enjoy their food. Open 364 days a year (closed Yom Kippur).

TEL AVIV

There are thousands of eating places in Tel Aviv, with constant change on the restaurant scene. Most are small and stylish and offer acceptable cooking in a multitude of different styles—but don't be deceived by the rather meaningless "gourmet" tag. In the city center, look around Kikkar Dizengoff and Kikkar Yitzhak Rabin, and along Dizengoff, Ben Yehuda, Allenby, and Yehuda Hamaccabi avenues and their side streets. South of the center are districts noted for their inexpensive characterful local eateries—in Old Jaffa and Jaffa port, the Neve Tzedek quarter, the Yemenite quarter, and the increasingly trendy Shekunat Florentin area near Jaffa. Just stroll and choose. As well as restaurants, typical Tel Aviv eating places include informal falafel bars, juice bars, cake shops and coffee bars, bagel bakeries and ice-cream parlors.

Apropo ($$)
4 Tarsat Boulevard, Kikar Ha'Bima
tel: 03 526 9288
also at 75 Ben Gurion Boulevard
tel: 03 527 3208
and Opera Tower tel: 03 510 6627
Good food, sometimes eccentric, always plentiful, the Apropo menu includes everything from "kosher" Thai shrimps to American waffles, and satisfies all tastes in between. Each of the Apropo restaurants—there are now 10 of them in Tel Aviv—has its own character and appeals to a slightly different clientele: to the theater and concert crowd, to the chic north Tel Avivis, and to tourists and beach babes, respectively.

Aubergine ($$$)
David Intercontinental, 12 Kaufman Street
tel: 03 795 1255 fax: 03 795 1108
Highly regarded young Italian chef Gianluca Re Franscini (not Jewish) surprised a lot of people when in 1999 he made the move to Tel Aviv, a city he has fallen in love with. Installed at this elegant Italianate restaurant within the huge atrium of a top modern hotel, he has been given a free hand to devise a variety of light, fresh, delicious dishes combining Israeli, Provençal, and Italian themes—but everything is kosher and all ingredients sourced locally. Gianluca is interested in what can be done with vegetables (he gathers them himself each morning) and offers some completely vegetarian meals. Beside the restaurant is the hotel's iMac Internet Café.

Birenbaum and Mendelbaum ($$$)
35 Rothschild Boulevard tel: 03 566 4949
Top score to the restaurant that has made traditional East European Jewish food the in thing again. Chopped liver, soused herrings, and *lokshen* soup (chicken broth with noodles) take on a different character when served in this modern restaurant. A great favorite with the local legal eagles, it is an ideal spot to watch Tel Aviv movers and shakers at their ease. Reservations essential.

Cactus ($$)
66 Hayarkon Street tel: 03 510 5969
Enjoy authentic enchiladas, chimichangas, and fajitas at this popular informal Tex-Mex restaurant close to the city center and the beach.

Golden Apple or Tapooah HaZahav ($$$)
40 Karl Netter Street tel: 03 566 0931
The pioneer of haute cuisine in Israel is recognized to be Yisrael Aharoni, though he modestly denies it. Now a TV chef and successful cookbook author, he still owns, runs, and cooks at this elegant downtown French-style restaurant. Try his gazpacho, grilled sea bass with balsamic vinegar and chutney, or herb-rich lamb chops encrusted with eggplant purée. Finish with orange crême brulée. Oriental flavors may creep in too—Aharoni is so fond of Chinese food that he has also opened three Chinese restaurants.

Houmous Ashkara ($)
45 Yirmiyahu Street tel: 03 546 4547
An institution among hummus houses, and useful to remember as it's open 24 hours a day except Shabbat (Friday evening to Saturday evening). It's hummus with everything, from broad beans to pine nuts and, of course, pita, pickles, and salad.

Keren ($$$)
12 Eilat Street, Jaffa tel: 03 518 1358
A beautifully restored American colonial style two-story restaurant, serving arguably the best food in

Tel Aviv. Owner-chef Haim Cohen, inspired to open his own restaurant after a spell at Le Moulin de Mougins restaurant near Cannes, brings together Mediterranean and Middle Eastern cuisines. Flavorful, regional dishes include liver pâté on a bed of artichokes and lentils, and saddle of lamb in gazpacho sauce. It's worthwhile taking the fixed-price business lunch (available on Saturday too) otherwise you could pay triple to eat à la carte. Book ahead.

Mika ($$$)
27 Montefiore tel: 03 528 3255
One of the top names in Israel's haute "world cuisine" brings together, for example, a delicious tuna tartare with tempura goat cheese and salad.

Mul Yam ($$$)
Tel Aviv Port tel: 03 546 9920
One of the new Israeli greats, this excellent seashore restaurant has a Mediterranean focus with seafood specialties such as coquilles St. Jacques with morel mushrooms, or black pasta and *fruits de mer*. Coffee ice cream with espresso sauce makes a good finish.

Shaul's Inn ($$)
11 Elyashiv Street, Yemenite Quarter
tel: 03 517 7619/3303
Two-level restaurant, with two levels of prices, at this extremely popular Yemenite eating house. Set up in the '70s, it's a veteran of the Tel Aviv restaurant world and is now something of a tourist trap, but the food—typically succulent offal meat and sauce served with a selection of Oriental dips and salads—is delicious and authentic, and there's a good atmosphere.

Shipudei Hatikva ($)
37 Ezel Street tel: 03 687 8014
Part of a popular chain, this is a simple restaurant in the less frequented south of Tel Aviv but which the locals know is the place to get outstanding salads, kebabs, shwarma (doner kebab), and falafel. Immediate service, with no frills. If this place is full, fear not, the street is teeming with similar choices—several of them run by the same people.

Spaghettim ($)
18 Yavne Street tel: 03 566 4479
www.spagetim.co.il
Businesslike by day, bohemian by night, this bright, modern restaurant serves no fewer than 50 variations of pasta and sauce—so the customers keep coming back to try the next one on the menu.

Takamaru Sushi Barú ($$$)
10 Ha'Arbaa Street tel: 03 562 1629
Enormous, painted Japanese characters hang against the brick and metal interior of this trendy upwardly mobile spot. Tel Aviv folk have taken to Japanese cuisine with a passion, and no wonder—here is pure, clean-tasting, and authentic food in every conceivable sushi combination, as well as tempura, yakitori, and teriyaki dishes. Kimono-clad Israeli staff guide the novice around the menu. Also at 118 Hayarkon (tel: 03 527 8858).

Tnuva ($$)
34 Ben Gurion Boulevard tel: 03 527 2972
A consistently delicious fish and dairy restaurant that has never been matched by its other branches. Open until the small hours. The daily pasta dish is almost irrelevant when the menu is so huge. From the yogurt and granola breakfast to brochettes of mixed cheeses or trout with almonds, it is all fabulously fresh and generously served. In fact, one portion will often be enough to satisfy two hungry diners.

Yotvata–Kibbutz in the City ($$)
80 Herbert Samuel Boulevard tel: 03 510 4667
Expect to wait in line for a table at this big, bright and cheerful yogurt ice-cream parlor and fish restaurant facing the beach. You may have to remain patient, too, even after you're seated. But when the food does come, portions are vast, quality is high, and the specialty smoothies and fresh fruit shakes are made using milk from the Yotvata Kibbutz dairy in the Negev (everyone in Israel has heard of it). When queues are *very* long, waitresses sometimes come out and give free samples to keep your spirits up!

Zion ($$)
28 Peduyim Street tel: 03 517 8714
In the Yemenite quarter, this much-liked eating place specializes in the classic Jewish Yemenite fare—offal meats, tasty sauces, and a spread of delicious dips and salads. The lavish decor has a touch of the exotic, with Oriental arches, fabrics, and lamps. It's open all day and until late at night.

Haifa

Jacko ($)
12 Hadkalim Street tel: 04 8664 109
This thriving Middle Eastern canteen, in the heart of Haifa's Turkish market, lures diners from Tel Aviv for the evening, such is its reputation. Traditional Middle Eastern *mezze* begin the meal (try the ikra—fish eggs), followed by whatever happens to be fresh that day—shrimp, sea bass, squid, or perhaps sole. Fast service, and friendly to children.

La Chaumière ($$$)
40a Ben Gurion Boulevard tel: 04 8538 563
If you ever feel the desire to eat snails, this is one of the few places you will find them in Israel. The darkly furnished, plant-filled French bistro also serves a mean filet mignon, fine fois gras, and excellent seafood and gratin dishes.

Yotvata in Town ($$)
Bat Galim Promenade, by cable car station
tel: 04 852 6853
A bright and cheerful Kibbutz Yotvata diner by the sea, serving its usual generous portions of salads, fish, and excellent dairy dishes.

Herzliya

Gargantua ($$$)
5 Sadnaot, Industrial Zone, Herzliya Pituach
tel: 09 589722
The robust and omnipresent Leon Elkalai is owner/chef of this popular Bulgarian/Turkish restaurant. The meat dishes are equally robust and flavorful.

GALILEE

Amirim

Misedet Dalia (Dalia's Restaurant) ($)
Amirim tel: 06 698 9349
Light modern dishes skillfully prepared can be

enjoyed at this convivial, relaxed eating place in the vegetarian *moshav* high in the hills near Sefat.

Hananya

Ein Kamonim ($$)
off Route 85 near Hananya tel: 06 698 9680
In a rustic hillside setting with fantastic views, this must be one of the only restaurants in the world where they don't cook. Instead, eat a huge, delicious meal of a multitude of sheep and goat cheeses (*kamonim* means goats) with vegetable salads. The set price also includes as much tasty bread, country wine, and coffee as you want, plus a dessert.

Korazim Junction

Vered Hagalil ($$)
just off Route 90 tel: 06 693 5785
Guests sit at wooden tables for good meat and salads at this amiable ranch-style restaurant in the countryside. The restaurant forms part of a popular riding center, and you can visit the stables before or after your meal.

Rosh Pina

The Baron's Stables ($$)
Old Rosh Pina tel: 06 930666
Tables on a terrace at the top of the town are the setting for this high-quality, elegant meat restaurant with a wide range of menus offering accomplished French-style cooking. One of the restored original settlement buildings, this was once the quarters of Baron Rothschild's horsemen, and it overlooks the Baron's gardens.
Indigo ($$)
Ramat Gan Street tel: 06 693 5333
Appealing tables set outdoors, hold huge portions of delicious vegetarian and fish dishes at this low-key café-restaurant with mellow music.

Sefat

Almost all Sefat's eating places are arranged along central Rehov Yerushalayim (Jerusalem Street). There's a selection of shwarma and falafel diners, bars, and other restaurants. Among the best are **HaMifgash** (tel: 06 692 0510) for meat dishes and **Café Bagdad** (no phone) for meat-free cooking.

Tiberias

Habayit ($$)
Lido Beach tel: 06 679 2564
Step across a bridge over a little stream to enter this delightful Chinese restaurant. Choose between upstairs dining rooms and the terrace.
The Pagoda ($$)
Lido Beach tel: 06 672 5513
Good-quality Thai and Oriental cuisine served beside the lake.

Dan and Upper Galilee

Dag al HaDan ($$)
Kibbutz Hagoshrim tel: 06 6959 008
A charming cabin-style fish restaurant poised right over the pool from which you select your dinner. Trout with nuts and garlic is a specialty.

THE SOUTH

Eilat

Eilat's more expensive beach **hotels** nearly all have at least one restaurant open to the public. In opulent settings, but often with surprisingly incompetent service, these generally reach an acceptable standard of cooking. There are many cheap-and-cheerful eateries in the scruffy **New Tourist Centre** in town.

Au Bistro ($$$)
Eilot Street tel: 07 6374333
Romantics head here for good French food. Secluded, small, clean, and friendly, with seafood and meat specialties.
The Dolphin Reef Pub ($)
Dolphin Reef tel: 07 374293
Tree stumps to sit on, cushioned booths to curl up in, and a menu ranging from simple seafood—such as shrimps in garlic and white wine—to beefier meat meals. It is also perfect for hummus and salads. Open late (except in December and January), with occasional live music—the dolphins apparently love it.
El Gaucho ($$)
Ha'arava Street tel: 07 6331549
The "grill man" is flown in from Argentina especially to perform his wonderful ways with beefsteak. This restaurant gives great helpings, though you could skip the main course and just have a meal of Argentinian starters—such as *empandas* filled with cheese and beef, or spicy sausages. Serving a young and noisy crowd, the waiters act the part in embroidered vests and dashing red sashes.
The Last Refuge ($$$)
Coral Beach tel: 07 6373627).
This is one of the first places a seafood lover should come to. Rustic and comfortable, it is hung with fishing nets and oil lamps and serves top-quality food.
Mandy's Chinese ($$),
Coral Beach tel: 07 6372238
Much loved and long-established Chinese restaurant, right on the beachfront.
Red Sea Star ($$$)
Southern Square (opposite Le Meridien Hotel) tel: 07 634 7777
This amazing restaurant stands in the water at the end of a walkway. First you arrive at a café with great views across the gulf, while on an upper deck there's an informal "pub". Then go down to reach the underwater bar and restaurant, with windows looking straight out onto the magical world beneath the waves (illuminated at night)—it's thought to be the world's largest underwater observatory. Seafood and meat dishes are the specialty (*Open* daily, 10 AM till the early hours).
Tricolore ($$$)
Meridien Hotel tel: 07 638 3333
Rated one of Israels best. An imaginative kosher restaurant that brings together international flavors. The emphasis is on fish, but also with such dishes as goat cheese salad on rösti, and fish and mushroom ravioli in a sushi cone.

Index

Principal references are given in **bold.**

Acknowledgments

The Automobile Association would like to thank El Al Israel Airlines, car rental specialists Holiday Autos, and the Israeli hotel chain Dan Hotels for their help in researching this book.
The Automobile Association would also like to thank the following photographers, libraries, and associations for their assistance in the preparation of this book.
JON ARNOLD PHOTOGRAPHY 11 Judaean Desert, 21 Mt. Hermon, 26 Egyptian tanks, Negev, 28a Sheckels, 60a Jerusalem, Holy Sepulcher, 80 & 81 Herodian Wohl Arch Mus, 83 Ruins of City of David, 90 Jerusalem, Tombs in Kidron Valley, 97a Jerusalem, Mt. Zion Church of Dormition, 99a Jerusalem, Torah Scroll Western Wall, 124 Jaffa harbor, 125b Jaffa window, 128 Tel Aviv old cemetery, 129a Jaffa street name, 130b Tel Aviv Mus of Art, 136a Passover, 136b Burning yeast, 147 Caesarea, 153 Lod Church of St. George, 160 Rosh HaNikra, 172a Golan Heights, Hexagonal Pool, 185 Korazim houses, 197 Sea of Galilee, 205b Zipori Roman theater & fort, 207a Wadi Qelt. Judaean desert, 208 Wadi Qelt. St. George's Monastery, 213a Bethlehem, Church of Nativity, 225a En Avedat Negev, 226 Ibex, 228b Beersheba, Abraham's Well, 229b Bedhouin camp. Sinai Desert, 229c Bedhouin & camel, 237b Coral World, Eilat, 239 Negev Desert of Zin, 242a Masada, 246 & 247 Negev Makhetsch Ramon, 249b Ben-Gurion's house, 251 Timna Nat Park Remains of Temple, 263b Sea of Galilee; **THE BRIDGEMAN ART LIBRARY** 36/7 Victory of Constantine over Maxentius—the Battle of the Milvian Bridge, from the True Cross Cycle (fresco) by Pierro della Francesca (1419/21-92) San Francesco, Arrezo, 36 Baptism of Constantine by Pierre Puget (1620–94) Musée des Beaux Arts, Marseilles/Giraudon; **MARY EVANS PICTURE LIBRARY** 14/15 'Ben-Schemen' colony, 29b Alexander the Great, 30/1 Israelites march, 30 Red Sea re-forms over Pharoah's army, 31 Moses with Ten Commandments, 33 Mattathias kills desecrator of Temple, 37 Hadrian, 39 Saladin watches defile of Christian Captives, 40b Sulieman I, 41b Zionist settlement at Machnajim, 42a Field marshall Viscount Allenby, 43 British peacekeepers, 70b Foundation of the Temple, 122b Shmuel Yosef Agnon, 175 Farmworkers on Kibbutz; **OWEN FRANKEN**: Cover silhouette; **HULTON DEUTSCH COLLECTION LTD.** 22 Begin, Carter & Sadat at Camp David, 27b Clinton, Rabin & Yassar Arafat, 42b Arab brigands, 44b Ben-Gurion, 122c Max Brod, 141a Vladimir Jabotinsky, 210/11 Demonstration, 210 Palestinian demonstrator, 211a Arab prisoners, 211b Gaza Strip barricade, 249a Ben-Gurion; **ISRAEL GOVERNMENT TOURIST OFFICE** 131a Tel Aviv Hexchal Hatarboot, 145b Succot at Wailing Wall, 214a Bethlehem St. Catherine's Chapel; **THE ISRAEL MUSEUM, JERUSALEM** 222b Pottery from Qumran, 223 Prof. Bie Berkraut; **JULIAN LOADER** 8 Children; **MAGNUM PHOTOS** 13 Refugees in Tel Aviv; **THE MANSELL COLLECTION LTD.** 141b Theodor Herzl, 216 Walls of Jericho; **P. MURPHY** 32/3 Citadel Mus, Jerusalem, 82 Biblelands Mus, Jerusalem, 118 Tel Aviv Eretz Israel Mus, 126/7 Diaspora Mus, 170 Capernaum Greek Orthodox Church, 232 Eilat Dolphin Reef Beach, 242b Masada cable car, 250 Timna Nat Park; **NATURE PHOTOGRAPHERS LTD.** 230a Dead Sea Salt Rocks (H. Miles), 244/5 Wild flowers (R. Tidman), 248a White pelican (P. R. Sterry), 248b Raftor Watch Point (R. Tidman); **REX FEATURES LTD.** 23 Israel Government, 123 Amos Oz; **SPECTRUM COLOUR LIBRARY** 137 Man, child & candles, 236b Eilat fish; HUGH SKION/STONE Front cover (top).
All remaining pictures are held in the Association's own library (A.A. PHOTO LIBRARY) and were taken by P. Aithie with the exception of the following pages: 34a was taken by D. Mitidieri, 16/7 was taken by T. Harris, 99b, 148a were taken by C. Lees, 5a, 5c, 9c, 10b, 16, 17a, 20/1, 20, 24, 29a, 34b, 38/9, 42/3, 44a, 46, 50a, 53a, 55b, 59a, 68, 72, 73a, 73b, 75, 78, 84, 85a, 85b, 87, 88a, 88b, 89b, 91b, 94b, 95, 97b, 98, 100a, 100b, 101a, 101b, 104, 106b, 108, 109a, 110, 122a, 229a, 261b, 263a, 267, 271 were taken by A. Souter, 215 wask taken by J. Loader, 74a was taken by W. Voysey.

Contributors

Original copy editor: Christopher Catling
Revision verifier: Andrew Sanger Revision copy editor: Sheila Hawkins and Janet Tabinski